THE TRANSFORMATION OF THE JAPANESE ECONOMY

THE

TRANSFORMATION

OF THE

JAPANESE
ECONOMY

KAZUO SATO
EDITOR

AN EAST GATE BOOK

M.E.Sharpe
Armonk, New York
London, England

An East Gate Book

As will be clear from the source/permissions note at the end of each chapter, most of the
articles in this text were first translated in *Japanese Economic Studies: A Journal of Translations* (recently retitled *The Japanese Economy: Translations and Studies)*. Kazuo Sato has
been the editor of the journal since its inception in 1972. Two previous volumes edited by
Professor Sato, also drawn from the journal, are *Industry and Business in Japan* (1980) and
The Anatomy of Japanese Business (with Yasuo Hoshino, 1984).

Library of Congress Cataloging-in-Publication Data

The transformation of the Japanese economy / edited by Kazuo Satō.
p. cm.
"An East Gate Book"
Includes bibliographical references and index.
ISBN 1-56324-775-5 (hardcover : alk. paper).   ISBN 1-56324-776-3 (pbk : alk. paper)
1. Japan—Economic conditions—1989– . I. Satō, Kazuo, 1927 Jan. 5– .
HC462.95.T73 1999
338.952—dc21   99-32697
CIP

Printed in the United States of America

The paper used in this publication meets the minimum requirements of
American National Standard for Information Sciences
Permanence of Paper for Printed Library Materials,
ANSI Z 39.48-1984.

BM (c)   10   9   8   7   6   5   4   3   2   1
BM (p)   10   9   8   7   6   5   4   3   2   1

Contents

THE

TRANSFORMATION

OF THE

JAPANESE
ECONOMY

Part I

The Japanese Economy in Transition

The sound of the bell of Jetavana echoes the impermanence of all things. The hue of the flowers of the teak-tree declares that they who flourish must be brought low. Yea, the proud ones are but for a moment, like an evening dream in springtime. The mighty are destroyed at the last, they are but as the dust before the wind.

—*Heike Monogatari* [Tales of the Heike]
(c. 1220, author(s) unknown),
as translated by A. L. Sadler
(Rutland, VT: Tuttle, 1972).

1

Japan at a Crossroads

Kazuo Sato

Introduction

The celebrated quote from a Japanese classic, *Heike Monogatari*, laments the impermanence of the mighty. The prosperous is destined to fall. This old Japanese saying is more apt to the present Japan. For four successive years (1992–95), the Japanese economy stagnated with near zero per capita growth.

This is an entirely new experience for Japan since the end of World War II. Even when Japan entered the slow growth period in the mid-1970s, the growth rate has never been so low for such a long time as in the early 1990s. Not only has the production sector been depressed, but the financial sector has also shown signs of unraveling. Banks and nonbanks are now saddled with huge amounts of "nonperforming" or bad loans—an inevitable consequence of overextended bank credit in the bubble period of the late 1980s.

The objective of the following essays is to take stock of economic changes that have culminated in the poor economic state of the early 1990s, and then to conjecture on the direction that the Japanese economy is likely to take from this time forward. As many experts now agree, various indications point to the possibility of a systemic change in the Japanese economy. Whether Japan will be able to cope with it or not will determine the future of Japan.

Historical Evaluation gives a bird's-eye view of the Japanese economy by tracing its historical evolution since the Meiji Restoration (1868). *Japanese-Style Capitalism* considers Japan's contemporary economic system—which we call Japanese-style capitalism. *Recent Changes* gives an extensive review of recent economic changes in Japan, both on the micro and macro levels. *Quo Vadis?* speculates on where the Japanese economy will move from here. *Systemic*

Change and *Concluding Remarks*, respectively, consider the possibility of systemic change and conclude this section.[1]

Note

1. Major statistical sources are abbreviated as follows:

BOJ-*ESA*, Bank of Japan, *Economic Statistics Annual*
EPA-*ARNA*, Economic Planning Agency, *Annual Report on National Accounts*
JSYB, *Japan Statistical Yearbook* (Prime Minister's Office)
ERP, *Economic Report of the President* (United States)
SABUS, *Statistical Abstract of the United States* (Department of Commerce).

Historical Evolution

Chronological Overview

Let us first present a broad overview of the evolution of the Japanese economy since the Meiji Restoration (1868), the start of Japan's take-off. Over more than a century, there were two historical landmarks that signify major transformations in Japan's economic system. The first was the Meiji Restoration, which replaced feudalism with capitalism. The second was Japan's defeat in World War II (1945). This brought Japan's militarism to a forced end, and a new, democratic society and economy were created under American tutelage. With these two landmarks, we divide the entire period into several subperiods, each of which is briefly described below.

1. *1868–1918.* The decentralized *bakuhan* system in the feudal Tokugawa era was replaced by a centralized bureaucratic system in which the central government controlled the entire country. The central government was dominated by those erstwhile radical samurais—the same people who had helped to topple the Tokugawa government. This was the period of autocracy. Although the Constitution was adopted and the National Diet was opened in 1889, the absolute monarchy ruled the country from above. The actual ruling was entrusted to the bureaucracy–military in this period. Following the pattern of Western imperialism, Japan expanded its territory by means of wars.[1]

2. *1918–1931.* The public's demand for political participation started to intensify about the time of the turn of the century. Nonetheless, the autocratic government hung onto power. However, one after another, the leaders of the Meiji Restoration were dying. Finally, in 1918, the autocratic government was no longer able to cope with the political unrest (rice riots), and the reins of the government were handed over to political parties. Prime ministers were elected in the Diet. Parliamentary democracy seemed to be established in Japan. The military assumed a low posture as the demand for disarmament prevailed all over the world. Unfortunately, the national politics were unstable. Prime ministers changed at frequent intervals with eleven cabinets in thirteen years. The 1920s were a decade of economic confusion, and the disturbed economy did not help political stability. The Great Depression ended this subperiod.

3. *1931–1945.* The Great Depression, which first started in the United States, was imported into Japan as the raw silk market bottomed out in New York. The

farm sector was particularly hard hit as farm prices fell precipitously. However, the nonfarm sector was spared as far as employment and production levels were concerned.

The Cabinet in place was a firm believer in classical economics and engineered Japan's return to the gold standard system starting at the beginning of 1930. Anticipating the eventual devaluation of the yen, capital flew out of the country. The resulting contraction of the money supply worsened the deflation.

After the change of the government which occurred in December 1931, Finance Minister Korekiyo Takahashi took the Keynesian policy measures of large-scale deficit spending and the devaluation of the yen. The policy succeeded and the economy was reflated. Unfortunately, once begun, the deficit spending policy could not be stopped because the army—which precipitated the Manchurian Incident in September 1931—demanded the continuation of increased military spending. The military wanted to regain its glory. The army's success escalated into a war with China (July 1937) and finally into the Pacific War (December 1941). After an initial success, the war ended in August 1945 with Japan's unconditional surrender.

Japan's big businesses, *zaibatsu*, strengthened their foothold in the Japanese economy during World War I. In the depressed 1920s, the big businesses diversified into heavy industry. Then, in the 1930s, they prospered when the economy was under the influence of wartime conditions. When Japan expanded during World War II, *zaibatsu* grew as well.

4. *1945–1959.* Japan was occupied by the Allied (U.S.) forces for six years. The U.S. government wanted to remake Japan in its ideal image of a democracy. The Japanese military was disbanded, a new Constitution was adopted, *zaibatsu* families were ordered to give up their holdings of *zaibatsu* firms, *zaibatsu* firms themselves were divided into smaller units, women were given equal rights with men, and workers were encouraged to organize unions. This was the second overhaul of the entire system of Japan. After the devastations of World War II, production was reduced to the minimum and inflation raged.

However, by 1952, when the Occupation ended, production had been restored to the peak prewar level and inflation was under control. The rest of the 1950s signaled a return to normalcy. Economic growth was high, and people started to rebuild their financial wealth. By the end of the 1950s, Japan fully recouped the losses caused by the war. It was generally believed that Japan had reached a turning point and would return to the prewar growth rate of 3 percent.

5. *1960–1974.* The subsequent growth of the economy exceeded everybody's expectations. Throughout the decade of the 1960s, the growth rate, on average, stayed above 10 percent. This rapid growth resulted in a complete transformation of the Japanese economy. Though growth started to slow down in the early 1970s, it stayed relatively high until Japan was finally hit by the first oil shock toward the end of 1973. In 1974, for the first time, the growth rate turned

negative (–1 percent). A feature of this subperiod was a shift from an agrarian economy to an industrial economy, which involved a mass transfer of the farm population to urban areas. A serious bubble in the stock and land markets also occurred in the early 1970s—an indication of financial instability.

6. *1975–1990.* This was a period of slow growth in which the growth rate permanently fell to the level of 5 percent per annum. In the meantime, the inflation rate was steadily falling: 6.9 percent in 1975–79, 3.1 percent in 1980–84, and 1.3 percent in 1985–89.

By the early 1980s the economy was relatively depressed (with a long recession that lasted thirty-six months, February 1980 to February 1983) and the average growth rate was 2.9 percent. However, the economy recovered in the last half of the 1980s. The upswing was the second longest one in the postwar period, lasting fifty-one months from November 1986 to February 1991. This boom was remarkable not because of the high growth rate (5.0 percent), but because of strong asset inflation. The stock market bubble collapsed in December 1989 and the urban land market bubble crumbled sometime later in the fall of 1990.[2]

7. *1991–present.* The Heisei Recession started in February 1991 and ended in October 1993. This second longest postwar recession was also notable because economic growth did not recover after the recession ended. Between 1992 and 1995, the growth rate was below 1 percent (1.0 percent, 0.1 percent, 0.4 percent, and 0.8 percent, respectively). The early 1990s were a very much depressed half decade in both real and financial terms. The stock market as well as the urban land market both continued to be depressed.[3] Banks were saddled with a large number of nonperforming loans. Though the Bank of Japan relaxed monetary policy (the discount rate fell to the all-time low of 0.5 percent in September 1995), and the national government renewed deficit spending in 1993–96, the economy has remained sluggish.

Fifteen-Year Cycles

History may not repeat itself. However, we may still try to make sense out of our review of Japan's historical evolution.

The reader may have noted that the period from 1918 to 1990 is divided into five subperiods, each running, on average, for fourteen to fifteen years. In other words, every decade and a half, the Japanese economy entered into a new phase, distinct from the preceding one.[4]

In the second subperiod during the 1920s, politics turned to parliamentary democracy but the economy was in the "muddles." In the third subperiod during the 1930s, after the Great Depression, the system veered toward militarism and the economy went into a wartime boom. In the fourth subperiod during the 1950s the economy recovered, and in the fifth subperiod during the 1960s it zoomed. In the meantime, Japan modified the made-in-America system imposed on Japan by the Occupation authorities into its own system of Japanese-style capitalism. The modifications started in the 1950s and finished in the 1960s. Slow growth came in the sixth subperiod during the 1980s.

If fifteen-year cycles are the rule, the seventh subperiod of the 1990s must be a new era in which Japan changes its direction. Did the environment change enough in the sixth subperiod to push Japan into a new direction in the seventh? We review recent economic changes in *Recent Changes* below to verify this point. However, before proceeding to this fact-finding job, we will first review what we mean by Japanese-style capitalism.

Notes

1. This subperiod can be further divided into 1868–88, 1889–1905, and 1906–18. The first part of the subperiod was that of nation building. The second starts with the adoption of the Constitution (1889), covers the Sino–Japanese War (1894–95) in the middle, and ends with the Russo–Japanese War (1904–05). The third includes the annexation of Korea (1910) and Japan's participation in World War I (1914–18) which brought a superboom to Japan.

2. The Nikkei Stock Price Average rose from ¥7,041 (August 1982) to ¥38,130 (December 1989). The urban land price index for the six largest cities (1990 = 100) rose from 35.1 in September 1985 to 105.1 in September 1990.

3. The Nikkei Stock Price Average bottomed out at ¥15,039 in June 1995. As of mid-1996, the urban land price index for the six largest cities was still falling, reaching 48.6 in March 1996.

4. Fifteen-year cycles can also be applied to the first subperiod (1868–1918) if we accept its division into three subperiods. It may even be extended to the last part of the Tokugawa era, namely circa 1830–52 and 1853–67. As commonly accepted now, the development of the money economy, which continued throughout the Tokugawa regime, finally reached a level which caused serious systemic instability. The central government's last-ditch effort to balance the budget was the Tempo Reform (1840–44), which failed. This is the first subperiod.

Then, in 1853, the United States sent a naval fleet to Japan to force the country to open its doors to foreign trade, and the central government succumbed to this demand. The result was to upset the domestic economy with high inflation, which turned political sentiments against the central government. The final outcome was that the military insurgency of the rebellious people in the ruling samurai class toppled the central government.

Japanese-Style Capitalism

The Genesis

The reader may wonder why the author has gone back in history to 1868 when he is supposed to be looking at the contemporary economy. The reason for the history is I want to show that—in an essential sense—the command mechanism of Japan's economic system has not changed despite some major changes over the years in the economic system. The Japanese economy is still ruled top down. The ruling class (top) rules the country from above, and the masses (down) obey the orders from above. Though the top has changed a number of times, the basic scheme has not.

In the Tokugawa period (1600–1867), the ruling class was the military (samurai) class.[1] The Tokugawa feudalism collapsed because, although the government was based on an agrarian economy, the economy itself became increasingly monetized with the consequent rise of the merchant class in economic power.

The Meiji Restoration, which followed the Tokugawa regime, however, was not a revolution in the sense of a revolt of the masses. Government leadership was merely handed over from one segment of the samurai class to another. Though the country was centralized and the economy was turned into a capitalist system, the ruling over the country was still conducted from above. On the top, civilians and militarists were interchangeable because they both came from the same roots. Thus, the government of bureaucracy-military continued until the end of World War I. Then parliamentary democracy was the form of government that ruled for a while in the 1920s, but militarism again usurped the top. In the meantime, *zaibatsu* firms came to the fore, and eventually the military-*zaibatsu* coalition led the country into a catastrophic war.

Japan was defeated in the Pacific War, and a new governmental system was introduced in 1945. The postwar reform was an attempt by the Americans to remake Japan in their ideal image by transplanting American institutions. The military was eliminated, *zaibatsu* families were liquidated, big *zaibatsu* firms were broken up, tenant farmers were given the land on which they worked, women were given equal rights, and workers were encouraged to form unions. Japan was supposed to be turned into a democracy by the political participation of the common people.

After the Americans left, these changes were modified to a large extent, even though some were not to be undone (e.g., the loss of wealth by the *zaibatsu* families and the economic independence gained by tenant farmers). However, the split *zaibatsu* firms regrouped themselves into a new form of business groups, called *keiretsu*, without *zaibatsu* families.

Unions did not become American-style trade unions but were organized instead as company unions, with the unionization ratio moving straight downward. Women were given equal rights with men on paper, but the actual elevation of their status in society was very slow. Belatedly, the Equal Employment Opportunity Law (EEOL) was adopted in the mid-1980s to encourage women to enter the labor market. The law was supposed to see that women received equal treatment with men, but women are still underpaid and discriminated against in the workplace.

Modifications during the Postwar Reform gave rise to Japanese-style capitalism, which refers to the basic makeup of the contemporary economic system of Japan, especially its command mechanism. This Japanese-style capitalism is still top down, although the composition of the top has changed because of the postwar reform. During the wartime and the immediate postwar confusion, the national economic management was entrusted to the elite bureaucracy which gained even more political power. Then, the postwar reform eliminated the military and instead placed politicians in Japan's command mechanism.

The Diet, especially the House of Representatives, elects the prime minister who is in charge of national-level policy-making. However, contrary to the original American intention, political power was continually monopolized by the Liberal Democratic Party (LDP) for thirty-eight years from its creation in 1955 to its fall in 1993. Then, the *keiretsu* (the reborn *zaibatsu*) claimed full membership at the top. Thus, the postwar economic growth was carried out by big business. Naturally, these big businesses wanted their clout fully reflected in national economic policy. Therefore, the command mechanism of Japanese-style capitalism became the triad of elite bureaucracy, national politicians, and big business. Japan is still governed by the few.

The three parties of the triad help one another. National politicians depend greatly on contributions by big businesses to support their expensive election campaigns. Big business, in turn, expects to be paid back in the form of special favors. Politicians also depend heavily on the expertise of elite bureaucrats during policy-making. By exercising their power in the enforcement administrative regulations (which abound in Japan), bureaucracy can give favors to big businesses. In their later careers, elite bureaucrats either enter national politics or find employment in big business.

When the three parties are interdependent in this give-and-take of favors, each can increase its own utility. In other words, this is not a zero-sum game but a positive-sum game. The give-and-take among the players also means that the triad is a quasi-permanent arrangement because the exchange of favors goes beyond the short term and the maintenance of the triad is costly. This is why Japanese-style capitalism has continued for so long.[2]

Though the triad itself is a positive-sum game within itself, its trade with the rest of the economy is a zero-sum game; that is, the gains of trade by the triad must come from somebody else's losses.[3] This "somebody else" is the consumers and the small businesses.

Needless to say, each member of the triad is a group of its own members. When we present such a group as an independent entity, we assume that the group has already succeeded in reconciling any conflicts of interest among its members. This, as we shall argue below, is the maximization of the group's collective utility. This exercise in reconciliation requires the establishment of a certain control mechanism within each group. In politics, the dominance of the LDP solved this problem of interest aggregation. Within the bureaucracy, the Ministry of Finance usually plays the leading role because of its budget allocation power, although the Ministry of International Trade and Industry (MITI) wants equal rights from time to time. In the business group, each *keiretsu* group organizes its hierarchical structure and a market-sharing agreement is made among *keiretsu* groups to avoid open competition.

The Principle of Collective Utility Maximization

Let us offer a somewhat more theoretical discussion about the reasons why and how members of the triad participate in the give-and-take game. For this exercise, it is useful to apply the prisoners' dilemma game from game theory.

There are two players in the prisoners' dilemma game. When they do not cooperate, the outcome is a poor solution; when they do cooperate, they both gain; that is, this is a positive-sum game. In reality, payoffs are not single numbers but vary according to the amount of cooperation among the players. Each player decides how much cooperation he will offer and how much he should get back from the other player. Since their interests are at odds with each other, an arrangement must be made through mutual negotiations to settle these conflicts of interest. Needless to say, the settlement depends on how strong each player is relative to the other player.

Given their relative strengths, the settlement mechanisms can be analytically described as the maximization of the two players' collective utility. The application of a standard utility analysis shows that the necessary condition for collective utility maximization is the equality of the marginal rates of substitution in favors given by the two players.

However, there are many combinations of these favors that satisfy the necessary condition. Which combination is chosen is determined by the maximization of the two players' collective utility. In turn, this determination depends on the players' relative power. We must also note that it is costly to settle these conflicts of interest between players. To recoup the cost, the settlement arrangement must be made quasi-permanent; that is, the settlement will last as long as the payoffs are sufficiently beneficial.[4] It will begin to collapse when payoffs are less advantageous (see Appendix I for a more formal analysis).[5]

When there are three players with differing objectives, the game often becomes more complex. However, we can still visualize the game as the maximization of the three players' collective utility. The game can continue quasi-permanently as long as each player remains robust. In a true democracy, the weak link may be thought to be politics because the ruling party can change so often.

Japan solved this problem by placing the LDP in the ruling position semi-permanently. The LDP seemed to be so secure in maintaining its ruling position that it came as a great shock when the LDP lost its majority in the Lower House in the July 1993 general election. A fundamental political reform seemed to be in the offing when the cabinet was formed by a non-LDP coalition. Unfortunately, this hope for reform was short-lived. Within a year, the LDP came back—though it received help from other parties, especially the Japan Socialist Party (JSP).

As we noted, the triad makes its gains by "exploiting" the rest of the economy (i.e., small businesses and consumers). This exploitation can take various forms. For example, it can be disguised as the workings of the free-market mechanisms. In the case of small businesses, the form is the dual structure which is characterized by large, interfirm wage differentials (Sato 1995c). Consumers are exploited via high consumer prices relative to the low prices of producer goods, especially by the prices charged by large firms.

The government has followed a pro-producer (more exactly, a pro–big business) policy rather than a pro-consumer policy. The high price of rice was a symbol of the government's attitude. The differential between domestic prices and foreign prices—a hot issue in Japan for the last several years—concentrates on consumer prices. Amazingly, an outcry by the consumers about inequity has remained muted because groups representing consumer interests are still disorganized. So-called consumer organizations even gave express support to the government's policy of banning rice imports.

The government pacifies consumers by pointing out that the tax burden on individuals is very low in Japan as compared to other developed countries and the income inequality in Japan is the lowest among people of the world. People are told, time and again, that they should feel content because they are given a fair shake. As long as people accept this, the triad can continue on its own way.

Collective Utility and Long-Term Relationships

We have observed that the maximization of collective utility for the triad helps to make it a quasi-permanent relationship. The same observation can be made on the micro level whenever a group is formed. Such groups can be very basic economic units (i.e., the household and the firm). They can also be groups of households (i.e., the community) or groups of firms (as in the *keiretsu* groups). All of them are engaged in maximizing their collective utilities, and they are bound together by long-term economic relationships. Indeed, these long-term economic relationships are a defining characteristic of Japanese-style capitalism. Although the subject has been discussed on numerous occasions, let us consider a few examples below.

The Japanese family places a great deal of value on the education of its children and is willing to sacrifice the interests of individual members for that objective. Adult family members even refrain from divorce so as not to harm the children's welfare. Apparently, the collective utility of the family is more important than the utility of individual members, and this entails durability of the Japanese family.

The Japanese firm, especially the big firm, is another example. Lifetime employment is practiced for its core male employees. An employee, in turn, devotes his whole life to the firm. The collective utility of the firm overrides the individual utility of any single employee. Thus, employees stay in long-term relationships with their employer.

Long-term relationships can also exist at higher levels (e.g., a group of firms). Subcontracting agreements between buying and selling firms are quasi-permanent in Japan (unlike agreements in the United States which are predominantly short-term). This is because, in Japan, both subcontractees and subcontractors are interested in securing long-term profits which can be ensured by maintaining subcontracting agreements on the long-term basis.

Keiretsu is another quasi-permanent relationship among member firms of a *keiretsu* group. Member firms are supposed to benefit from dependence on other member firms. Mutual ties among them are made more permanent by various arrangements, including cross-firm share ownership, interchanges of executives, and a sales-financing network within the *keiretsu* group.

In all these instances, the collective (whether it be the family, the firm, or the *keiretsu*) has its own utility to maximize. The members of a collective must subjugate their individual utilities for the sake of the collective utility. These actions require long-term relationships among the members of the collective. Thus, members stay in the collective because they believe that their short-term losses will be compensated by their long-term gains. Parents put up with the high cost of rearing children because they expect to be compensated for it by the eventual satisfaction of a job well done. Employees stay with the same employer for their "lifetime" because they expect to be rewarded by higher wages in the latter part of their careers. *Keiretsu* firms stay in the same group because they can rely on assistance from the group in times of exigency.

The maximization of collective utility and long-term relationships goes hand-in-hand. If one breaks down, the other also falls.

In Versus Out

When a collective is organized on the long-term basis, the collective is pitted against other collectives. Members of a collective consider themselves to be insiders and discriminate against members of other collectives as outsiders. The in-versus-out distinction is another well-known characteristic of Japanese society. When the distinction is strong, society tends to be fractionalized. Therefore, the staff in a Japanese firm is often divided into factions each vying for the company's presidency. The LDP has been a party of several factions; the party presidency is elected from among these various factions. Sociologist Chie Nakane (1970) called it "vertical society."

However, the in-versus-out distinction is multilevel. Who are viewed as the outsiders depends on from what level the outsiders are being considered. Within a faction, members of other factions are outsiders even though they all belong to the same firm. However, when the members are considered on the *keiretsu* level, all the firms in the *keiretsu* group are insiders, and all other firms are outsiders. Finally, at the national level, all Japanese nationals are insiders and all foreigners are outsiders.

The point here is that the in-versus-out distinction is a natural corollary of the collective that maximizes its joint utility. Thus, it permeates throughout the Japanese society and economy.

Notes

1. This system started in 1165 when the Taira family, a royal descendant, replaced the civilian government of the Fujiwara family (894–1164). Since then, though the ruling family has changed a number of times, the system has remained the same. The Tokugawa rule is notable in that its rule extended over the entire nation. The Tokugawa set up a decentralized command system in which local domains were ruled by individual lords while all lords were under the command of the central government of the shogun.

2. The idea of the triad has been used in the popular press, but has not been given full attention by academicians, as Okumura (1995, chap. 1) observes. See Okumura (1995) for an explicit, qualitative assessment of the triad thesis with many references on the subject. (Okumura has been writing on the subject for the last twenty years.)

3. In the "Japan, Inc." thesis, the government acts as the head office of a joint-stock company and big businesses as its operational departments to pursue the export-or-perish policy. This thesis is said to have been put forth in a U.S.–Japan business conference held in Washington, D.C., in June 1971. At this conference, American business executives criticized Japan's national economic policy. See Kaplan (1972) on this thesis. For the rejection of this thesis by Japanese economists, see Komiya et al. (1988), especially Tsuruta (p. 58) who notes that it is not government intervention but the market mechanism that supported the rapid growth of the 1960s.

4. When the LDP stepped down after the general election of July 1993, the political contributions it received also fell.

5. The "power theory" has been espoused by many economists in the past. In Japan, Yasuma Takata (1885–1972) put forth such a theory fifty years ago (Takata 1947).

Recent Changes

Japanese-style capitalism, which had been brought to fruition in the rapid growth period, started to be eroded in the slow growth period because of various significant economic changes in recent years that, of necessity, have affected Japan's economic institutions. In what follows, our review of these recent changes is divided into microeconomic and macroeconomic changes—though the distinction is rather arbitrary. Recent history is also loosely defined. How far we look into the past varies from case to case.

Microeconomic Changes

The Family System and Demography

The Family Structure

The traditional family structure in Japan was, as is common in Eastern society (Asia and Africa), the three-generation family. That is, the second generation of working age supports the first generation in retirement and nurtures the third generation. By destroying the concept of the *ie* (family), the Postwar Reform was supposed to phase out the three-generation family. Indeed, three-generation families were on a rapid decline between 1955 and 1995, as shown in Table 1 (column 2b). This decline is matched by a rapid increase in single-person households (column 3) while the percentage of nuclear families (column 1) remained stable. However, in both columns (1) and (3), parents who are older (sixty-five and over) increased (columns 1a and 3a). When all sixty-five and over parents are added together, the total number (column 4) fell at first but turned upward after 1975. The year 1975—the beginning of the slow growth period—serves as the turning point for long-term changes of the family structure.

Demographic Changes

Behind the changes in the family structure, there have also been demographic changes. People are living longer and young people are marrying later and having fewer children. The average family size continues to decline, from 5.0 persons in 1955 to 2.9 persons in 1995. The standard family is now two young parents and a child. The birth rate has been declining steadily from 1.5 percent in

Table 1

Family Type, Percent of Total

	(1)	(1a)	(2)	(2a)	(2aa)	(2b)	(2ba)	(3)	(3a)	(3b)	(4)
1955	59.6	—	36.5	2.6	—	33.9	—	3.4	—	—	—
1960	60.2	3.5	34.7	2.5	0.8	32.2	17.2	4.7	1.0	3.7	22.5
1965	62.5	4.2	29.8	2.4	1.0	27.4	15.6	7.9	1.2	6.7	22.0
1970	63.5	4.7	25.4	1.3	0.8	24.1	14.5	10.8	1.4	9.4	21.4
1975	59.5	5.3	20.8	1.5	1.1	19.3	12.4	15.5	1.9	13.6	20.7
1980	60.3	6.5	19.9	1.7	1.3	19.2	12.4	19.8	2.5	17.3	22.7
1985	60.0	7.5	19.0	1.8	1.4	17.2	12.2	20.8	3.1	17.7	24.9
1990	59.6	9.3	17.1	1.9	1.6	15.2	11.4	23.1	4.0	19.1	26.4
1995	59.1	12.0	15.8	2.0	1.7	13.8	10.9	24.8	5.2	19.6	29.9

Source: The Census of Population.

Notes:
(1)   Nuclear family
(1a)   Column (1) with parents 65 and over
(2)   Other relatives family
(2a)   Two-generation family
(2aa) Column (2a) with parents 65 and over
(2b)   Three-generation family (including others)
(2ba) Column (2b) with parents 65 and over
(3)   One-person household
(3a)   Column (3) age 65 and over
(3b)   Column (3) otherwise
(4)   Parents 65 and over, total columns (1a) + (2aa) + (2ba) + (3a)

the early 1970s to 1.0 percent now. The death rate also declined from 0.5 percent to less than 0.3 percent. Consequently, the population growth rate declined from 1.1 percent to 0.7 percent.

The decline in the birth rate is also related to the decline in the reproduction rate for females. Their total fertility rate was about 4 until 1949 and settled to approximately 2 between 1958 and 1975. After 1975 the fertility rate declined toward 1.8. It started to decline again after 1984, passing the level of 1.5 in 1992.

The total fertility rate for females has been declining because females are marrying later or not at all. This is seen in the long-term changes in the marriage ratio (new marriages : population). After it peaked at 1.2 percent in 1947–48 (compensating for the war), it declined to around 0.8 percent between 1952 and 1956. Then it started to rise through the rapid growth period and peaked at 1.04 percent in 1972–73. It declined again to around 0.6 percent after 1984 to the present—this is an all-time low.

The same point is clearly seen in the population distribution (aged fifteen and over) by marital status (Table 2). For both males and females, the married status peaked and the unmarried status bottomed out in 1975–80. Since then the married percentage has been declining, and the unmarried percentage has been rising. More striking are the changes in the proportion of people who are divorced. For both males and females, the divorced rate reached its lowest point in 1965; since then the proportion has been inching up, more or less doubling by 1990.

That people marry later and divorce more often is confirmed by a comparison of 1975 and 1995 (see the lower half of Table 2). The change is most striking in the age range of 25–39. Witness a sharp decline in the proportion of the married, especially in the 25–29 age bracket. People are either marrying later or do not marry at all. The divorced population has also increased over time. For a comparison, we also show changes in the older population in the age range from 60 to 74. The rise in the divorce rate for this age bracket is notable here as well.

Why do women marry later and have fewer children? One powerful reason is found in the increased educational attainments of females (see below). They now prefer to have more time to be single before marrying and bringing up children. This change in attitude among females occurred in the slow growth period.

Modes of Marriages

When we examine Japanese marriages and divorces, we should not overlook the biggest change in this area in postwar Japan—namely, how Japanese people find marriage partners. Until the end of World War II, more than 85 percent of the marriages in Japan were via *miai* (i.e., "interview marriage").[1]

In the prewar years, boys and girls were segregated in primary schools and there were no coeducational secondary schools. As a general rule, women with higher education did not enter the paid labor force. Thus the opposite sexes had no chance for free association. Marriages had to be "arranged," that is to say, some busybody old ladies circulated photographs of prospective candidates with short biographies among acquaintances. If a boy and a girl were both willing, a formal, chaperoned get-together was arranged—hence, the name of *miai* or "see one another." If each party thought the other party was promising, the boy and the girl would consent to a few more dates and then decide whether to continue or discontinue. If they continued, they might eventually reach the goal of marriage.

Thus, though the *miai* was arranged, the final decision rested with the free will of both parties (though often marriages were forced for family reasons). In Japan's prewar social structure, the *miai* was the rule. If young people fell in love and decided to marry—often against the opposition of their families—the marriage was considered a violation of the social protocol. If the family was dominant, the romance often ended in a Romeo-and-Juliet type of tragedy (a popular theme in *kabuki* plays).

Table 2

Marital Status by Sex, Population of Age Fifteen and Above

	Male				Female			
	Unmarried	Married	Widowed	Divorced	Unmarried	Married	Widowed	Divorced
1950	34.3	60.3	4.5	0.85	25.7	56.3	16.1	1.90
1955	35.3	59.7	4.1	0.94	27.0	55.8	15.2	1.98
1960	34.7	60.8	3.5	0.90	26.9	56.8	14.1	2.13
1965	34.5	61.7	3.0	0.76	27.1	57.9	13.1	1.86
1970	32.3	64.2	2.7	0.84	24.9	60.3	12.8	2.03
1975	29.1	67.7	2.6	0.94	21.5	63.7	12.7	2.08
1980	28.5	67.6	2.4	1.22	20.9	64.0	12.4	2.45
1985	29.6	66.2	2.4	1.62	21.7	62.5	12.7	3.20
1990	31.1	63.8	2.4	1.84	23.4	58.4	12.3	3.23
1995	31.8	62.7	2.6	2.23	24.0	58.9	13.0	3.71
Younger Generation, Selected Ages								
1975 25–29	48.5	51.0	0.05	0.42	21.0	77.7	0.21	1.05
30–34	14.3	84.6	0.13	0.93	7.7	89.8	0.64	2.27
35–39	6.1	92.3	0.32	1.27	5.2	90.7	1.53	2.50
1995 25–29	66.4	31.4	0.00	0.78	49.0	48.5	0.08	1.75
30–34	37.3	60.2	0.01	1.69	19.7	75.9	0.30	3.52
35–39	22.6	74.2	0.01	2.41	9.7	84.8	0.62	4.54
Older Generation, Selected Ages								
1975 60–64	1.1	91.8	5.6	1.49	1.9	60.0	35.5	2.87
65–69	0.9	87.4	10.4	1.32	1.8	49.1	46.7	2.30
70–74	1.0	79.8	18.2	0.93	1.5	34.5	62.4	1.62
1995 60–64	2.8	90.1	3.7	2.88	4.3	74.4	16.6	4.24
65–69	2.0	89.3	5.8	2.40	4.3	65.3	25.8	4.86
70–74	1.5	87.2	9.4	1.76	3.5	50.7	42.8	3.61

Source: The Census of Population.

The spread of coeducation and the elevated status of women gave people a strong impetus to repudiate the *miai* system. The *Shussei doko chosa* [Vital Statistics Survey], a sample survey conducted every five years (since 1940) by the Ministry of Welfare, inquires about the mode of marriage for newlyweds and arrives at a fascinating result. *Miai* marriages started at 70 percent in 1940–45 and continued to decline over the years so that by 1992 the level had reached 15.2 percent. "Love" marriages, on the other hand, started at 12.8 percent and rose to 82.8 percent. (These percentages do not equal 100 because there are several percentage points of "no answer.") The two proportions crossed each other between 1965 and 1970. Thus, the late 1960s may be considered a turning point in Japan's marital history.[2]

In the prewar system of *miai* marriages, the *ie* had much to say, especially concerning the marriage of its male heir. The family imposed social constraints on its members concerning marriage. In turn, the divorce rate at that time was low (a little less than 0.07 percent).[3] Has the spread of love marriages changed all this? After all, when people freely choose the person they marry, they can also freely choose to divorce. The divorce rate stayed below 0.08 percent in 1956–66 but started to inch up thereafter. Since 1984 the divorce rate has been 0.15 percent or thereabouts, but it is still less than in the West. The highest divorce rate is in the United States with 45 percent (1993).

However, it would seem that married couples in Japan must be unhappy in their married life as often as couples in the United States. Then why are Japanese couples divorced less often than American couples? There must be some factor at work. One powerful constraint against divorce is the strong propensity by Japanese families toward the maximization of the family's collective utility. We can see it clearly in the Japanese family's response to the education of its children.

Family's Response to the Education of Its Children

In an egalitarian society, the key factor for a person's advancement in society is his or her educational attainments. The Japanese family is eager to support its children in school from kindergarten to college. In the prewar period, the children receiving educational support were limited to boys, who were expected to be the bearers of the family name; now both boys and girls proceed to college. To gain acceptance to the best colleges, however, they have to prepare for highly competitive college entrance examinations. Therefore, the family must provide a good study environment for the children at home.

In addition, the family believes that children ought not to be disturbed in their formative years. At the time the children are preparing for college examinations, their fathers (if they happen to be employees of big businesses) are often transferred to branch offices of the company far away from home. As junior executives, the fathers cannot afford to refuse assignments. Rather than forcing their families to relocate with them, the fathers travel to their new assignments alone.

This is the well-known *tanshin funin* phenomenon (transfers unaccompanied by family). That is to say, the father sacrifices his own utility for the sake of the family's collective utility because providing his children with a good education is considered of paramount importance in the family utility function. Through the sacrifice endured by the father, the family as a whole achieves a higher level of utility.

Needless to say, there are other economic factors involved in this decision. Another important objective in the family utility function is home ownership. Since the family is still paying off its mortgage, the family has to remain behind while the father works elsewhere.

The Target Is Achieved and the Family Dissolves

In recent years, the increase in so-called silver-age divorces has attracted public attention; that is, the number of divorces has been rising among couples in the retirement age. This is clear in Table 2. The proportion of the divorced population among the older generation has been on the increase from 1975 to 1995.

By the time the husband reaches the mandatory retirement age of sixty, the family will have completed its task of raising children and will have paid off its housing loan. The husband may be looking forward to beginning his post-retirement life, but the wife may object to continuing the marriage. She is now relieved of the responsibility of raising children (which rested on her shoulders alone while her husband was at work and away from home), and she hopes for a free life unencumberedered by any further responsibility at home.

Certainly the wife is loath to take care of her husband who, once he is retired, would stay home twenty-four hours a day. She regards the husband as *sodai gomi* ("big gross rubbish"), a term coined by the press a few years ago. Therefore, she asks for a divorce in which she expects to receive a half share of the husband's retirement benefits.

When the family has achieved its long-term target of maximizing its collective utility, the family itself loses its raison d'être. It is at this point that the family disintegrates. The number of silver-age divorces is still small, but the cases are of interest because it points to a possibility of the Japanese-style system unraveling.

The Employment System

Lifetime Employment and Mandatory Retirement

The mandatory retirement age, which was raised from age fifty-five to sixty, was gradually adopted by companies through the 1980s. Now nearly all firms with compulsory retirement set sixty as the mandatory retirement age.[4] However, many male workers want to continue to work beyond the age of sixty. This desire is so strong that the labor force participation ratio (LFPR) of male workers aged sixty-five and over has remained at about 38 percent since the mid-1980s.[5] A person's life expectancy at birth is currently seventy-six years for males and eighty-three years for females, that is, males who reach the age of sixty can expect to live twenty years more and females, twenty-five years more (1992 Abridged Life Table).

The upward adjustment of the mandatory retirement age is critically related to the fate of the lifetime employment system and the state of the social security system. As is well known, lifetime employment has been the employment system of large firms for regular male employees. Employees were hired by companies when they graduated from school, and they stayed with the company through their "lifetime," that is, until their mandatory retirement. Wages usually rose with continued service, or equivalently, with the worker's age—though how much a worker's wage actually increased often depended more on an individual's abilities.

The mandatory retirement age, which is now almost universally set at sixty, was raised from fifty-five in line with the increase in life expectancy.[6] The age of sixty coincides with the age at which social security benefits can begin, albeit at the reduced rate of 80 percent of full benefits receivable at age sixty-five.

The seniority-related or *nenko* wages were feasible because the age structure of the workforce was of a pyramid type. With the main body of the workforce young, large firms could keep the wage cost relatively low even though they paid much higher wages to senior workers, certainly much higher than wages paid by smaller firms.

However, with the aging of the population (see below), the entire wage and retirement structure can no longer be maintained in its present form. There are fewer younger workers and more older workers. The average wage cost is bound to increase if the present age-wage profile is continued. However, the mandatory retirement age of sixty is becoming increasingly unrealistic because there will continue to be more older males in the labor force, and because it is projected that the starting age of social security benefits should now be raised to sixty-five.

The further advance in aging of the Japanese people and the resultant change in the age structure of the population spell the end of the seniority-related wage system and, by the same token, the demise of the lifetime employment system as it is presently constituted. However, older workers expect to live longer, and they must find a way to tide over the five-year gap between the mandatory retirement age and the start of social security benefits. Thus the drive to find paid employment will intensify on the part of older workers—meaning that they have to remain in the labor market. As the supply of younger workers decreases, firms may be more willing than before to hire older workers. Definitely, the employment system must change one way or another.

Table 3

The Spread of College Education (in percent)

(A) Japan: Students advancing to colleges (1–4 years) from senior high schools

	1970	1980	1990	1995
Male	29.2	41.3	35.2	42.9
Female	17.7	33.3	37.4	47.6
Total	23.6	37.4	36.3	45.2

(B) Japan: Higher-education graduates[1] as percent of the population, 15 years and over, and of the labor force

	Population			Labor force
	1970	1980	1990	1990
Male	12.0	17.4	22.1	27.2
Female	5.1	10.2	16.1	21.0
Total	8.4	13.7	19.0	24.7

(C) United States: College educated (1–4 years) as percent of labor force, 25–64 years

	1970	1980	1990	1995[2]
Male	27.9	42.0	47.7	55.2
Female	22.1	36.1	46.4	56.8
Total	25.9	39.6	47.1	56.1

Sources: (A) Ministry of Education, *Mombu tokei yoran* [Handbook of Education Statistics], 1995, pp. 36–37; (B) The Census of Population; (C) *SABUS*, 1995, Table 629 and 1996, Table 618.

[1]Excludes those in attendance.

[2]Definitional changes in 1992. The percentage rose from 1991 (old definition) to 1992 (new definition) as follows: male (47.8% to 51.3%), female (47.4% to 51.9%), and total (47.6% to 51.6%).

Female Labor Force Participation

We have argued that the increased educational attainments by females contributed to later marriages and fewer children. Does this also foster an increased labor force participation by females? We examine this point below.

At the present time, most junior high school graduates proceed to senior high school (males, 95.8 percent; females, 97.6 percent, 1995). The percentage of senior high school graduates proceeding to college (1–4 years) is shown in Table 3 for 1970–95.

After World War II, the number of years for compulsory education was raised to nine (i.e., through junior high school). However, at first, the prewar legacy was strong, and far fewer female students advanced to senior high school, not to mention to college. However, as the economy entered the rapid growth period of the 1960s, the proportion of students attending senior high school rose to nearly 100 percent for both males and females. At that time, females started to advance to college—though still at a rate much lower than males.

However, as Table 3 indicates, the college advancement ratio for males peaked around 1980 and then began to decline through the 1980s. The ratio, however, started rising once again after 1990. In contrast, advancement to college for females continued to increase with no interruption; thus, by the late 1980s, there were more female college students than male students.

However, this point needs one qualification. While most of the male students go to four-year colleges, two-thirds of the female students attend junior colleges. Increasingly now, though, more female students opt for four-year colleges. Also, the female students are no longer confined to their favorite "soft" departments in college such as English literature or home economics. They are increasingly enrolled more in "hard" departments such as science, technology, and medicine. In turn, when female students receive professional training, they endeavor to enter the professional fields for employment.

Female employees used to be discriminated against in the workplace because employers assumed that they would not remain with the company for a career but would quit when they married in their mid-twenties. However, later marriages or no marriages mean that females are now more intent on striving for careers. In 1985, the government finally adopted the Equal Employment Opportunity Law (EEOL) to improve working conditions for female workers. While the law is alleged to have contributed to the advancement of female employment,[7] the depressed economy in the early 1990s has worked against female entrants into the labor market. Although the overall percentage of college graduates finding employment at graduation has decreased, female graduates have been affected more adversely than male graduates.[8] The law is apparently not powerful enough to fight against macroeconomic forces.

Changes in the labor force participation ratio (LFPR) for females are shown in Table 4. We note first that the LFPR for males has been on a downward trend as the result of two effects. First, the increased schooling of young people tended to reduce their availability as a labor supply and, second, the continued withdrawal of older workers from the labor market (until the mid-1980s).

However, we found the LFPR for females was behaving differently. At first, their LFPR declined through 1975. This is a reflection of the continued shrinkage in the agricultural sector since more women participated in this type of work than in urban industries. As agriculture sufficiently shrank, this effect disappeared. Then, as more females became better educated, they started to join the labor market. Hence, their LFPR has been rising.[9]

However, this increase is very modest, and it is small indeed when compared with the increase in college-educated women. A comparison with the United States is instructive. As shown in Table 3, the number of college-educated

Table 4

The Labor Force Participation Ratio (LFPR) by Sex (in percent)

Japan

	LFPR						Labor-force composition	
	1970	1975	1980	1985	1990	1995	1970	1995
Male	81.5	81.4	79.8	78.1	77.2	77.6	60.7	59.5
Female	49.9	45.7	47.6	48.7	50.1	50.0	39.3	40.5
Total	65.4	63.4	63.3	63.0	63.3	63.4	100.0	100.0

United States

	LFPR				Labor-force composition	
	1970	1980	1990	1995	1970	1995
Male	79.7	77.4	76.4	75.0	61.8	54.0
Female	43.3	51.5	57.5	58.9	38.2	46.0
Total	60.4	63.8	66.5	66.6	100.0	100.0

Sources: Japan: Prime Minister's Office, *Labor Force Survey*; United States: *SABUS*, 1996, Table 615.

women has increased in the United States as well. In the United States, however, the increased number of college graduates is matched by a substantial increase in the female LFPR.

The difference between female employment in the United States and Japan is clearly reflected in changes in the labor force composition by sex. In 1970, the labor force in both countries was divided into nearly equal proportions—six males for every four females. A quarter century later, the labor force composition has hardly changed in Japan, but it is now five males for every five females in the United States. This is clear evidence that, in the United States, more of the better educated women enter the labor market. Why not Japanese women?

The question here boils down to the following: Is the failure to increase educated women in the labor supply due to supply-side or demand-side factors? In other words, are Japanese girls attending college only for enjoyment and not for careers, or are Japanese employers unwilling to hire educated women? The answer seems to be the latter as the next subsection indicates.

Part-Time Workers

It is ironic that the enforcement of the EEOL—which was to protect the interests of female workers—coincided with the appearance and then the rapid increase of part-time workers who were predominantly female (81 percent in 1995). In 1986, female part-workers were 24 percent of female regular employees; in 1995, the percentage had increased to 29 percent. This increase means that two-thirds of the rise in female employment from 1986 to 1995 can be accounted for by the increase of part-time workers. These part-time workers are most numerous in wholesale and retail trade and eating establishments, roughly equal in number to female regular employees. Female part-time employees also are found in the service, real estate, and manufacturing sectors.

The reason that employers hire part-time workers is that they are much cheaper to employ and easier to hire and fire. Their average hourly earnings were about ¥800 in 1992 when female regular employees were paid about ¥1500 per hour. In addition, employers do not pay fringe benefits and bonuses to part-time workers. During the late 1980s, female part-time workers increased in number by 11 percent per annum while female regular workers increased by only 3.5 percent per annum. However, in 1993, the number of female part-time workers declined by 9 percent while the number of female regular workers increased by 1.8 percent.

When most of the increase in female employment is part-timers, the increase in the female LFPR is definitely not a matter for rejoicing. Working conditions are becoming worse as female employment grows. This outcome is not what the EEOL is supposed to produce.

Foreign Workers

Japan was closed off from the rest of the world for 215 years (1639–1853) except for intermittent trade with Holland, China, and Korea. Though the country was opened in 1853, foreign immigrants residing in Japan continued to be few in number except for Koreans who migrated to Japan after Korea was annexed in 1910. The limited direct contact with foreigners helped Japan to retain its strong sense of xenophobia, which, in turn, contributed to Japan's "pure blood" policy. Its geographical location and language difficulty also precluded Japan from the flow of migratory foreign workers which expanded in the postwar world.

Thus, the arrival en masse of foreign workers to Japan in the late 1980s was a shock to the Japanese. What happened was that migratory workers from poor Asian countries had been cut off from their usual places of work because of the worldwide economic slowdown. They had to look for work elsewhere and found Japan to be a very promising place. To them, even meager wages for menial jobs seemed to be attractive enough to offset the high transportation costs.

The menial jobs were crying for employees because the well-educated Japanese workers looked askance at such jobs. Most Japanese people refused to accept these jobs unless they were older workers desperate enough to seek them. Thus there was a pent-up demand for low-class jobs, and employers were willing to accept any warm bodies to fill them. The incoming supply of unskilled foreign workers filled this bill nicely. These jobs included, among others, construction hard hats for males, bar hostesses for females, and restaurant attendants for both sexes. That is, these are jobs which Japanese workers regarded as 3K—*kitsui* (tough), *kitanai* (dirty), and *kiken* (risky).

Foreign workers arrive in Japan on a nonwork visa which allows them to stay for only a short time, but they seek employment illegally and overstay. According to the Ministry of Justice, the number of such illegal aliens rose from 28,000 in 1986 to 100,000 in 1989 and then to 299,000 in 1993. The number has been somewhat lower since then because of the depressed job market in Japan.[10]

Though the number of illegal aliens is still 0.5 percent of Japan's labor force, the increase is highly noticeable in pure-blood Japan because foreign workers tend to form their ghettos in large cities such as Tokyo. Many unsavory crimes are attributed to these groups of people. Despite the increased influx of foreign workers, the Japanese government has not changed its tough immigration law. It still permits a long-term visa to be granted only to those who are regarded as highly qualified.

However, the trend for internationalization in the human area seems to be inevitable in this increasingly global world economy. One consequence of increased contact with foreigners is an escalation in the number of international marriages. The latest statistics show that nearly 4 percent of new marriages in Japan are international marriages.[11] The pure-blood policy of Japan is being eroded in a slow but steady manner.

Unions and Shunto

The Occupation policy encouraged workers to organize themselves. The unionization ratio reached 56 percent in 1949—the postwar peak. By 1954, however, the ratio had declined to 35 percent, the level it stayed at until 1970. Then, the ratio started to decline again: 31 percent in 1980 and 25 percent in 1990. The latest information in 1995 shows a level of 23.8 percent. The ratio declined not because union membership fell, but because unions are concentrated in nongrowth industries such as manufacturing. In fact, membership has remained flat, with new workers going into the tertiary sector which is largely nonunionized.

Unions are strong in manufacturing, finance, transportation, public utilities, and government. Large companies are unionized, and base wages are annually determined by collective bargaining in the first quarter of the year before the new business year begins in April. This *Shunto* (Spring Offensive) determines the annual rate of across-the-board wage increases ("baseup"). When union agreements are concluded, nonunion firms follow suit. Though the unionization ratio has been falling, the *Shunto* has been considered an important annual ritual ever since it started in 1955.

However, the depressed economy of the early 1990s put union power in jeopardy. The *Shunto* rate of wage increase is known to fluctuate, with a short time lag, according to prevailing macroeconomic conditions. The next year's wage increases tend to be lower when the economy is in a recession. In recent years, the peak wage increase in the *Shunto* negotiations was 5.9 percent in 1990. From then on the rate of increase continued to fall until it reached 2.8 percent in 1995. The rate was only slightly higher in 1996. Thus, it is widely believed that unions have outlived their usefulness, and that the *Shunto* mode of wage negotiations is outmoded.

The Business System

One member of the triad is big business, which can be identified with the six *keiretsu* groups of Japan.[12] The dominance of the *keiretsu* groups over Japan's business sector is too well known to need any detailed explanation. Our interest here is in determining how the *keiretsu* groups as a whole have adapted themselves to macroeconomic changes in the Japanese economy.

A *keiretsu* group consists of firms which are members of the group's presidents' club. While the number of firms varies from group to group, the average is thirty-two per group. Member firms are divided broadly into banking/insurance and nonfinancial. On average, one group has four financial institutions—one city bank, one trust bank, one life insurance company, and one marine and fire insurance company.[13] Of twenty-eight nonfinancial firms per group, nineteen are manufacturing firms.[14]

Let us first see how the six *keiretsu* groups as a whole divide their activities between their banking and insurance and their nonfinancial activities (see Table 5A). In terms of employment, the *keiretsu* are about 85–90 percent in the nonfinancial sector. However, in terms of total assets, there is a large difference. In 1970, the *keiretsu* divided their business equally between the two fields, but by the early 1990s, the division had changed to three to one. To begin with, the banking and insurance sector is highly capital-intensive and has become even more so over time (Table 5B).

The above is an internal change within the *keiretsu* groups. Next, we will look at how the *keiretsu*'s relative importance has changed within their respective industries (see Table 6). The industry total shown for banking and insurance firms is the sum total of the total assets (book value) of all banks and insurance companies. The industry total shown for nonfinancial firms is the total assets (book value) of all nonfinancial corporations as reported in the Ministry of Finance's *Corporate Enterprise Statistics*.

Table 6 shows that, in the nonfinancial field, *keiretsu*'s share fell from 24 percent in 1970 to 11.2 percent in 1995. In contrast, for banking and insurance, the *keiretsu*'s share rose from around 40 percent in 1970 to above 50 percent in the late 1980s. This result means that the *keiretsu* groups have shifted their resources from nonfinancial to financial far more than respective industries have

Table 5

The Six Keiretsu Groups

(A) Banking and Insurance/as Percent of Group Total

	Employment	Total assets
1970	8.5	49.4
1975	10.2	53.5
1980	11.8	61.1
1985	11.3	70.4
1990	14.3	77.3
1995	15.0	77.1

(B) Total Assets/Employment (¥ mn per person)

	(1) Financial	(2) Nonfinancial	(1)/(2)
1970	13.59	1.84	7.4
1975	35.31	3.44	10.3
1980	62.70	5.19	15.9
1985	122.96	6.57	18.7
1990	227.19	11.10	20.50
1995	213.76	11.20	19.10

Source: Toyo Keizai, *Kigyo keiretsu soran.*

done. This is clearly seen in Table 7, which compares the quinquennial growth rates of total assets (book value) between *keiretsu* and industry totals.

The financial sector has been the rising star of the Japanese economy in the slow growth period. The nonfinancial sector has lost its erstwhile luster as the engine of Japan's economic growth. In response to this macroeconomic change, the *keiretsu* groups have adapted themselves by shifting the center of their business activities from the nonfinancial areas to the financial sphere, namely, from production to services. This adaptation reveals the ability of Japan's big businesses to survive.

This ability to adapt has been demonstrated time and again in Japan's business history. Late in the prewar period—at the time when Japan started to develop heavy industry—it was *zaibatsu* which poured resources into capital-intensive heavy industry. The *keiretsu*, the successor to the *zaibatsu*, rebuilt the production sector of the war-torn Japanese economy. The rapid growth period was the *keiretsu*'s heyday for industrial growth. Now in the slow growth period as financial deepening proceeds at a rapid rate, the *keiretsu* groups are increasingly moving into the financial area.

This, however, does not mean that the *keiretsu* groups have stopped improving themselves in the nonfinancial field. As shown in Table 8, while their market shares

Table 6

Total Assets (Book Value): Keiretsu/Industry (in percent)

	B&I	NFC
1970	41.5	24.0
1975	40.9	20.9
1980	41.9	16.8
1985	53.8	15.6
1990	57.3	14.8
1995	52.40	11.20

Source: Toyo Keizai, *Kigyo Keiretsu Soran.*

Note: Industry totals are: B&I = all banks and insurance, from BOJ, *ESA*, 1996, Tables 13, 30, and 31; NFC = Ministry of Finance, *Hojin kigyo tokei* [Corporate Enterprise Statistics].

Table 7

The Growth Rates of Total Assets (Book Value) (in percent)

	Keiretsu			Industry total		
	T	F	NF	T	F	NF
1970–75	15.3	17.9	12.6	17.3	18.3	16.7
1975–80	8.5	22.0	5.4	9.7	10.5	9.3
1980–85	12.3	16.0	5.6	8.3	10.3	7.1
1985–90	13.3	14.9	9.0	11.6	13.4	10.2
1990–95	−0.8	−0.9	−0.6	0.8	0.5	3.3
1970–90	12.3	14.9	8.1	11.7	13.1	10.8

Source: Table 6.

Note: T: the sum of F and NF, F: banking and insurance, NF: nonfinancial.

have been falling, the *keiretsu*/non-*keiretsu* differentials have been rising in sales per worker and total assets per worker (except in the early 1990s). Roughly speaking, the *keiretsu* firms are four times as productive and capital-intensive as smaller non-*keiretsu* firms. It is these *keiretsu* production firms that compete in the international market.

The Government System

From November 1955 when the Liberal Party and the Democratic Party merged to form the Liberal Democratic Party (LDP) to July 1993 when the LDP lost the majority in the general election of the House of Representatives, the LDP contin-

Table 8

**Shares of the Keiretsu Groups in the
Nonfinancial Corporate Sector** (in percent)

	Sales	Employment	Total assets	*Keiretsu*/All NFCs (multiple)		
	(S)	(N)	(A)	S/N	A/N	S/A
1970	19.3	8.2	24.0	2.7	3.2	0.8
1975	18.2	7.4	20.9	2.8	3.1	0.9
1980	17.1	5.8	16.8	3.4	3.3	1.0
1985	17.6	5.3	15.6	3.8	3.3	1.2
1990	14.8	3.9	14.8	4.3	3.9	1.1
1995	12.6	3.6	11.2	3.5	3.2	1.1

Sources: Toyo Keizai, *Kigyo keiretsu soran*; nonfinancial total from Ministry of Finance, *Hojin kigyo tokei.*

ued to be Japan's ruling party; that is, the LDP ruled Japan for thirty-eight years. Even though there were many other parties—the largest of which was the Japan Socialist Party (JSP)—Japan was a de facto one-party country for a very long period of time. The LDP oversaw Japan's economic recovery and rapid growth, and the economic policy which the LDP pursued was instrumental in promoting that growth.

Though it is a conservative, pro-business party, the LDP is not a single party unified along a well-articulated political ideology. Rather, it is a party of several factions, each of which is led by a powerful leader who has the ability to collect funds from the public, particularly from the business sector. None of these factions claims a majority in the party. Thus, a couple of the factions usually agreed to cooperate in electing one of the competing leaders to the party's presidency, who, in turn, automatically assumes premiership.

This arrangement, which continued for the full thirty-eight-year period, did not lead to political stability. During this time the LDP appointed fifteen presidents-cum-prime ministers. There were only four presidents who served for more than three years (the normal tenure of presidency): Nobusuke Kishi (three years, three months, February 1957–June 1960), Hayato Ikeda (four years, four months, July 1960–October 1964), Eisaku Sato (seven years, eight months, November 1964–June 1972), and Yasuhiro Nakasone (five years, six months, November 1982–October 1987). The first three ruled Japan consecutively through the rapid growth period. In other words, the rapid growth period was also a period of political stability—rare in Japan.[15]

Between Sato and Nakasone, there were five ministers in ten years. The first of them, Kakuei Tanaka (two years, five months July 1972–November 1974) had to resign because he was indicted for his involvement in the Lockheed Scandal. He was later found guilty of having accepted a large bribe, but he died of a long illness before he went to prison.

The presidency did not take a turn for the better after Nakasone. Noboru Takeshita, his successor (one year, seven months November 1987–May 1989) was forced to resign before his tenure was over because of another economic scandal. The last phase of the LDP rule witnessed four prime ministers in less than six years, during which time the LDP was plagued by successive revelations of economic scandals.

Finally, in the July 1993 general election, the LDP lost the majority of the Lower House—not because it became less popular but because a sizeable segment of the party seceded from the party. However, it was the economic scandals that rocked the foundation of the LDP and eventually splintered it.[16]

By its nature, politics is prone to be a dirty business. Diet members face reelection every four years or less, and winning elections is expensive. Politicians must solicit election funds from private sources, especially from big businesses. In turn, the big businesses make large political contributions because they expect to be repaid later with special favors granted by the politicians they support. The more regulated the industrial sector in which a big business is involved, the greater the payback for its political contributions.[17]

Gift giving is a common social practice with a long history in Japan. In the final analysis, all gifts are self-serving. Gifts must be a form of bribes even if they are given strictly on good will. Likewise, it is difficult to distinguish between bona fide political contributions and bribes since, either way, the contributors expect some kind of repayment later. Because of the extensive practice of gift exchanges, the Japanese tend to be insensitive and indifferent to the whole affair. In this general climate, political corruption becomes an everyday affair.

As long as the contributions or gifts remained hidden from the general public, people remained complacent and politicians were safe from public scrutiny. However, this all changed in the late 1980s—the boils burst open and politics was forced to clean its dirty linen.

Then, how clean or how corrupt is Japanese politics at present? Though it covers more than politics, a recent international comparison of forty-one countries by a think tank concerning corruption shows that Japan stands exactly in the middle.[18] Generally speaking, the more economically developed a country is, the less corrupt it tends to be. Thus, most countries above Japan are developed countries and most below Japan are developing countries.

The observed correlation between the stage of economic development and political cleanliness hinges critically on how concentrated political power is in a country. In developing countries in which the masses are illiterate, governance falls in the hands of a few elite who, in turn, are supported by big business and the military. Bureaucracy is strong in these countries; if one wishes to have anything done quickly, one must bribe the proper authorities. As countries develop, they become more democratic because the masses demand political participation. Political power tends to be deconcentrated, and therefore corruption declines.

Japan stands much lower in this scheme of international rankings than it should based on its stage of economic development. Obviously it is still controlled by the few, namely, the triad. It can be said that Japan is economically well developed but politically underdeveloped. An important corollary follows: If Japan wishes to reform itself, it has to begin by cleaning up its politics.

Deregulation

One means by which politicians and bureaucrats exercise their power is administrative regulations, and Japan is alleged to be a country burdened with administrative regulations. This is almost tautological with the top-down nature of Japan's method of governing. Without regulations, the government finds it hard to rule effectively.

However, regulations tend to proliferate. It is in this light that the national government started to reduce the number of regulations. It appointed a succession of Administrative Reform Councils starting in the early 1980s.[19] After its tenure of three years, each council submitted its recommendations to the prime minister. In addition to the official council, Prime Minister Hosokawa (who succeeded the LDP government in August 1993) created a special private commission to prepare a set of recommendations for deregulation.[20]

Needless to say, Japan continued to be regulated heavily by the goverment in the prewar period, but 1940 is singled out as the year that brought government regulations to a higher level. To mobilize resources for wartime, the National Mobilization Law was adopted in 1938. A new economic system was declared in 1940. Noguchi (1955) calls it the 1940 system and argues that it is the 1940 system that has survived into postwar Japan.

Regulations were a vital element of the 1940 system. They made economic ministries powerful during the war. Because of the shortages during the immediate postwar years, the Postwar Reform even strengthened their control power since strict administrative guidance was needed for resource allocation. The food supply had to be controlled by the Ministry of Agriculture, funds had to be supplied by the Bank of Japan, foreign exchanges by the Ministry of Finance, and import restrictions by the MITI, to cite just a few. All these controls needed regulations, and they stayed in place through the rapid growth period because the resource supply was less than the resource demand. Resources had to be rationed by the intervention of the government in the free market mechanism.

This supply-and-demand imbalance disappeared as the economy slid into slow growth. However, regulations survived even though their usefulness was over. Those in power disliked any change in the status quo because that meant the loss of their vested power. Despite their resistance, the market insisted that these regulations be removed for its own sake. The demand for deregulation arose from this market force. How the Japanese government will continue to respond to this demand is yet to be confirmed.[21]

Macroeconomic Changes

The Labor Market

Population Aging

Population aging—a phenomenon common to all countries—is a problem which impacts with inordinate intensity on both the supply and demand sides of the Japanese economy. What makes Japan's case unique is the rapid speed at which its population aged. The Japanese used to die young with a life expectancy not much above forty years in the 1930s. After World War II life expectancy started to rise steadily. By 1994 it was 83.0 years for females and 76.6 years for males—the highest in the world.

The other side of a longer life expectancy is a steadily increasing older population. As a percent of the total population, people aged sixty-five and over rose from 5.7 percent in 1960 to 14.1 percent in 1995. Its future level is given in Table 9 based on the January 1997 Ministry of Welfare's population projection.[22]

The labor force, 44 years and younger, saw its share falling from 1970 on.

Table 9 shows a significant change in the age structure of the labor force. Its median age has been steadily rising over time since 1970, and the trend of the labor force becoming older will continue. As we noted, the emerging age structure will be incompatible with the maintenance of the lifetime employment system as we know it.

However, there are other economy-wide impacts. One is on the household savings rate. The continued increase in population aging means more households which contain retired persons. If one accepts the life-cycle saving hypothesis, retired households dissave to support themselves in retirement. That is, negative savings will increase while positive savings will decrease among these households. The net effect will be a decline in the average household savings rate.

However, the actual record shows that, so far, the decline in the average savings rate has been relatively modest. In fact, the household saving rate remained at 13 percent from 1988 to 1995 (EPA, ARNA, 1997). If anything, the observed decline in the average household savings rate can be explained by the narrowing of the wealth gap, namely, the gap between the target level of accumulation and the actual level of accumulation (Sato 1995d). The target level itself has remained stable thus far in relation to household disposable income.

Further, Japan's older households are not decumulating their assets as the naive version of the life-cycle savings hypothesis claims. It is true that those older households who are at the poverty line because their spendable incomes are mostly from pension benefits do not save. However, about 38 percent of males

Table 9

The Labor Force by Age

Age	1960	1965	1970	1975	1980	1985	1990	1995	2000	2005	2010	2020	U.S. 1995
15–19	10.1	8.2	5.8	3.2	2.6	2.5	2.8	2.2					5.8[1]
20–44	59.1	61.9	63.7	62.7	60.1	57.7	54.8	53.5					63.2
45–54	15.4	15.1	15.8	19.9	21.3	21.8	22.2	22.4	92.0	90.8	89.7	87.3	9.0
55–64	10.4	10.0	10.2	10.5	11.1	13.0	14.6	15.2					9.0
Over 65	5.0	4.8	4.5	4.6	4.9	5.0	5.6	6.7	8.0	9.2	10.3	12.7	2.9
LFPR	69.2	65.7	65.4	63.0	63.3	63.0	63.3	63.4	63.3	62.5	63.2	61.9	66.6
Median age													
Labor force	35.9	35.8	35.5	38.5	39.9	41.3	42.9	43.3					36.6
Population	25.6	27.4	29.0	30.5	32.8	34.1	39.6	39.7					29.2
Over 65/Total pop.	5.7	6.3	7.1	7.9	9.1	10.3	12.1	14.6	17.8	19.6	22.0	26.9	12.7
Females/Labor force	40.7	39.8	39.3	37.9	38.7	39.7	40.6	40.5	41.5	42.2	43.5	44.4	46.0
Growth rate													
Labor force		1.2	1.5	0.6	1.2	1.1	1.4	0.9	0.4	0.0	0.2	−0.4	1.0[2]
Population		1.0	1.3	1.4	1.1	0.7	0.4	0.3	0.2	0.1	0.0	−0.3	1.0[2]

Sources:
Labor force: Prime Minister's Office, *Labor Force Survey;* population: *Census of Population.*
United States: *SABUS,* 1996, Tables 16, 24, 614, and 615.
Projections: Population, due to the Ministry of Welfare (January 1997, medium version); labor force, obtained by population × LFPR, where LFPRs of males, 15–64 and over 65 and females over 65 are assumed to remain unchanged from the 1993 levels and the LFPR of females, 15–64 is assumed to increase by 2.2 percentage points per five years (the trend increment between 1975 and 1993).

Notes:
1. Ages 16–19.
2. 1990–95 (Population is projected to grow at 0.8 percent per annum from 1995 to 2025).

aged sixty-five and over are still in the labor force, and they earn more than they spend. Thus they tend to have a relatively high savings rate. When rich and poor older households are taken together, their average savings rate is quite compara-ble with that of younger households. This means that population aging does not automatically translate into a decline in the household savings rate—provided that a member of the older household continues to work at the present rate.

There is, however, at least one negative factor in this scenario. The increase in the older population will force the national government to cut back on social security and health benefits to older households. The decline in public support must be offset by an increase in private support, either by the older generation themselves out of their accumulated savings or by their children who then have to reduce their own rate of savings. Either way, private saving will be reduced.

The Labor Force Participation Ratio and the Unemployment Ratio

The labor force participation ratio (LFPR) does not remain constant. For male workers aged fifteen to sixty-four the LFPR declined slightly from 85.2 percent in 1975 to 82.8 percent in 1990. For males, sixty-five and over, the LFPR continued to decline until 1985 but it has stayed at 37–38 percent through the present. For female workers aged fifteen to sixty-four the LFPR continued to rise from 49.6 percent in 1975 to 57.0 percent in 1990. For females, sixty-five and over, the LFPR has remained stable at around 15–16 percent since 1975.

As we have already explained, the LFPRs temporarily deviate from their long-term trends when the labor market is depressed, as in the early 1990s. As a result, the unemployment rate does not accurately reflect the state of the labor market. A more reliable indicator of the prevailing condition in the labor market is the ratio of job offers to job applications at the government-run job exchange, which is referred to as the vacancy ratio below.

The vacancy ratio of 1 may be taken as a sort of labor-market equilibrium. The vacancy ratio was above 1 in 1967–74, peaking at 1.76 in 1973. Then the labor market collapsed and it fluctuated around 0.6 between 1975 and 1987. It rose above 1 again in 1988–92, peaking at 1.40 in 1990–91. Since then, the vacancy ratio has remained at slightly over 0.6 (0.67 in 1996).

Working Hours

A significant contribution of the Postwar Reform was a reduction in the number of working hours. In the prewar period, a twelve-hour workday was common. Though the number of hours per day was cut substantially, monthly hours still totaled as high as 200 hours in the early postwar years (Table 10). However, when the slow growth period started, hours declined to around 175 hours per month or 2,100 hours per year.

This yearly total was still very high when compared with other advanced countries. Therefore, a reduction in the number of working hours became a press-

Table 10

Monthly Hours of Work, Regular Workers, and Establishments with Thirty or More Employees

Sector	Total			Nonscheduled		
Year	II + III	II	III	II + III	II	III
1955	194.8	197.1	192.1	16.5	17.3	15.6
1960	202.7	207.6	195.6	21.9	24.7	17.8
1965	192.9	194.6	190.4	16.5	17.5	15.1
1970	187.7	189.9	184.5	17.8	19.6	15.2
1970	186.6	189.9	183.5	16.7	19.6	13.9
1975	172.0	172.7	171.4	10.7	10.4	10.8
1980	175.7	181.1	171.4	13.5	16.0	11.5
1985	175.8	181.8	171.5	14.8	17.6	12.8
1990	171.0	179.9	164.7	15.5	18.7	13.2
1995	159.1	166.3	154.1	12.6	13.7	11.8
	$g(H)$ (in percent)					
1955–60	0.8	1.0	0.4			
1960–65	−1.0	−1.2	−0.5			
1965–70	−0.4	−0.5	−0.6			
1970–75	−1.6	−1.9	−1.4			
1975–80	0.4	1.0	0.0			
1980–85	0.0	0.1	0.0			
1985–90	−0.6	−0.2	−0.8			
1990–95	−1.4	−1.6	−1.3			

Sources: Ministry of Labor, *Monthly Labor Statistics*; industries are weighted by persons engaged, reported in EPA, *ARNA*.

Note: II+III and III are exclusive of services for 1955–70 and inclusive of services for 1970–95.

ing political issue. The 1992 national economic plan, which advocated "Better Quality of Life," proposed a target of 1,800 working hours per year. Unwittingly, the depressed economy of the early 1990s helped the government achieve this goal. Monthly hours fell to 152.7 hours per month or 1,900 hours per year by 1994.

Will the number of working hours rise once again if the Japanese economy is revived? The Labor Standards Law reduced the work week from forty-four hours to forty hours as of April 1994. However, firms with less than 300 workers were exempted from this law until March 1997. As of now, only 37 percent of firms with less than ten workers enforce the forty-hour week, and there is strong resistance to enforcing the law on schedule. Nonetheless, the trend is for less working hours.

Paid Holidays

Another well-known feature in Japan's labor economics is a reluctance of workers to take paid holidays. Workers were authorized to take up to 14.4 days in paid holidays in 1980 and 17.2 days in 1995, but the number of actual days taken was 8.8 days in 1980 and 9.5 days in 1995. Though a few large Japanese firms started to force their employees to take one week off by closing their offices and factories in the summer, apparently Japanese workers are still unwilling to exercise their legal right in this regard.[23]

Technical Change and the Industrial Structure

Needless to say, technical change is the most vital factor in economic growth. A country's productivity is increased in three ways: (a) by technological innovations introduced in individual industries, (b) by increases in capital intensity, and (c) by transfers of resources from low-productivity industries (agriculture) to high-productivity industries (modern manufacturing). All three occur simultaneously in the process of strong economic growth. This is why overall productivity growth was particularly high in the rapid growth period, especially in the late 1960s.

We quantify technical change by the rates of labor productivity growth.[24] Excluding the public sector,[25] private industry is divided into three sectors: primary (I) is agriculture, forestry, and fisheries + mining; secondary (II) is manufacturing + construction + electricity, gas, and water, and tertiary (III) is all the rest. Output (Y) is measured by the GDP produced in each sector in constant prices. Labor is measured by the number of persons engaged in production (N).[26] The growth rate of labor productivity (Y / N) has been measured every five years since 1955 (see Table 11).[27]

Productivity growth was high before 1970. Growth of the overall output was accentuated between 1955 and 1970 because of a massive reallocation of resources from the primary sector to the secondary and tertiary sectors. Productivity growth was low in the early 1980s when the economy was generally depressed. This was the period in which Japan's "hollowization" (*kūdōka*) was frequently discussed. Again, productivity growth declined sharply in the early 1990s, even to negative levels for the secondary sector.[28] It is clear that the demand side and the supply side interact in the growth process. When demand is high, productivity growth is stimulated and resources are transferred from agriculture to industry. When demand is depressed, productivity growth also declines and resource transfers stop.

As the economy develops, the primary sector shrinks and resources are

Table 11

Labor Productivity Growth and the Employment Structure in Private Industry

(A) Labor productivity growth ($g(Y/N)$, in percent)

	Total GDP	Labor productivity growth $g(Y/N)$				United States
	$g(Y)$	Total	I	II	III	$g(Y/N)$
1955–60	9.0	6.2	5.6	5.9	4.9	1.1
1960–65	8.5	6.8	4.6	7.1	4.4	2.2
1965–70	11.8	9.7	1.2	11.1	7.9	1.2
1970–75	4.6	4.3	6.4	3.2	3.4	0.9
1975–80	5.5	4.5	4.0	5.5	4.0	0.6
1980–85	3.0	2.2	3.8	2.3	1.3	1.3
1985–90	5.2	4.1	4.3	4.1	3.3	0.9
1990–94	1.3	0.3	1.1	–0.5	0.6	1.1

(B) The employment structure (in percent)

	Total	I	II	III
1955	100.0	45.0	25.6	29.3
1965	100.0	27.8	36.8	35.6
1975	100.0	17.1	38.6	44.3
1985	100.0	12.1	37.0	50.9
1994	100.0	8.2	37.5	54.3
U.S.				
1970	100.0	6.4	34.4	59.2
1992	100.0	3.7	25.5	70.8

Sources:
(A) Japan: EPA, *ARNA*; United States: *ERP*, February 1996, Table B–2 and B–31.
(B) Japan: EPA, *ARNA*; United States: OECD, *National Accounts*.

poured into the secondary and tertiary sectors. However, at some point in time, manufacturing (secondary) becomes saturated and employment stops growing in that sector. In Japan, this point was reached in 1973. Since that time the employment share for the secondary sector has remained stable. The continued contraction of the primary sector has been matched by a corresponding expansion of the tertiary sector. Japan's Service Revolution is identified with this turnaround. In the following "Quo Vadis" section, we shall examine how Japan's employment structure will change henceforth.

The information in Table 11 reveals an interesting feature: Labor productivity growth fluctuated in the same direction among the sectors with one significant exception—the primary sector from 1965 to 1970. We relate

Table 12

Productivity Growth Regressions

$$g(Y_i / N_i) = d_ig(Y / N) + d_{i0} \text{ (in percent)}$$

i	d_i	d_{i0}	R^2
I	0.57 (0.22)	2.0 (2.2)	0.572
II	1.18 (0.09)	−0.8 (1.2)	0.964
III	0.77 (0.07)	1.1 (0.09)	0.958

Note: Sector I calculation excludes 1965–70.

$g(Y_i / N_i)$ to $g(Y / N)$ with the result reported in Table 12.[29] This table shows a well-known fact: that productivity growth is above average in the secondary sector and below average in the primary and tertiary sectors. The closest relation is between the secondary and the tertiary sectors, as is verified by the following regression:

$$g(Y_3 / N_3) = 0.63 \, g(Y_2 / N_2) + 0.27 \, (\%), \, R^2 = 0.988$$
$$(0.065) \qquad\qquad (0.93)$$

Equation 1

According to equation (1), we have:

$$0.72\% \lesseqgtr g(Y_3 / N_3) \lesseqgtr g(Y_2 / N_2).$$

According to this inequality, productivity growth was higher in the tertiary sector than in the secondary sector during 1990–94. Normally, productivity growth in the tertiary sector is about two-thirds of that in the secondary sector. In every country productivity growth tends to be lower in the tertiary than in the secondary sector. In the case of Japan, there is an additional feature that the productivity level is absolutely lower in the tertiary sector than in the secondary, and the difference between them is very sizable.

This feature becomes apparent when we compare the tradable PPP (purchasing power parity) and the nontradable PPP between Japan and the United States. We may assume that the tradable PPP can be approximated by the exchange rate of ¥110/$ (September 1996).[30] The overall PPP for 1994 was ¥155/$ (private consumption) between Tokyo and New York City (EPA) and ¥177/$ (GDP) between Japan and the United States (OECD).[31] When corrected for price changes, the 1995 PPP was estimated to be ¥150/$ (EPA) and ¥174/$ (OECD). For the former, we note that the cost of living is higher by 12 percent in Tokyo and by

60 percent in New York City relative to the national average.[32] Then the PPP (private consumption) is raised from ¥150/$ to ¥214/$. The overall PPP for 1995 amounts to ¥174/$ (OECD) and ¥214/$ (EPA). The nontradable PPP then is estimated to be ¥181/$ – ¥226/$.[33]

Thus, nontradables are 65 percent to 105 percent more expensive than tradables when Japan is compared with the United States. Nontradables are more expensive in Japan for various reasons such as: (a) services are produced inefficiently by small firms (especially in retail trade); (b) many service prices are publicly regulated (including public utilities, postal and telephone rates, train fares, taxi fares, and so on); (c) markets for services are imperfectly competitive; and (d) results of restricting free entry into the regulated industries. Existing suppliers have less incentives to improve productivity because of the heavy protection. Thus, postal rates are 2.6 times and train fares are 1.7 times higher in Japan than in the United States.[34] Why can't these rates be reduced to the international level?

The Balance-of-Payments

One salient feature of Japan's balance-of-payments is that it has been continuously in a surplus since the mid-1960s except for a few oil shock years. The current-account surplus adds to the net accumulation of foreign assets. Japan has been the largest net creditor to the world since the late 1980s when the United States switched from the world's largest net creditor to the largest net debtor. As foreign assets earn investment income, the balance-of-payments now has a built-in mechanism to remain in a surplus. Even though the Japanese yen has been much stronger since the G5 Plaza Accord of September 1985, a surplus has continued in Japan's balance-of-payments.

The main part of the current-account surplus, however, is the trade surplus of merchandise. Japan has a net deficit in the service trade because Japan depends more on foreign shipping than on domestic shipping. Merchandise trade (f.o.b.) as a percent of the GDP is shown in Table 13 for 1985–95. The trade surplus has been on the positive side for the entire period. There is a rule of thumb that Japan's trade surplus tends to rise in a recession year because exporters engage in an export drive to promote sales overseas. Accordingly, the trade surplus peaked in 1986–87 (1986 was a recession year), and then fell in 1988–90 when the Japanese economy was in a boom. Then, once again, the trade surplus rose from 1991 to the present.

The performance of merchandise exports and imports is also influenced by the export and import prices relative to the domestic prices. The relative prices are also affected by the position of the exchange rate relative to the PPP. The yen–dollar rate has been in a downward trend ever since the September 1985 Plaza Accord. The export price index relative to the domestic price index has also been in a downward trend (particularly in the early 1990s), reflecting the faster rate of technical change in large (exported-oriented) firms than in small

Table 13

Merchandise Trade, 1985–95 (in percent)

	X / Y	M / Y	NX / Y	P_X / P	P_M / P	e (¥/$)
1985	13.0	9.0	4.0	124.6	155.5	238.1
1986	10.3	5.8	4.5	104.4	98.4	163.0
1987	8.7	5.3	4.5	98.1	90.7	144.5
1988	8.9	5.7	3.4	93.8	84.4	128.2
1989	9.3	6.7	2.6	98.3	92.5	138.1
1990	10.2	7.3	2.9	100.0	100.0	144.9
1991	10.2	6.0	4.2	97.1	88.2	134.6
1992	10.0	5.4	4.6	95.5	80.7	136.6
1993	9.3	4.9	4.4	90.2	64.5	111.1
1994	9.3	5.1	4.2	89.1	64.3	102.2
1995	8.5	5.1	3.4	88.5	64.5	94.0

Sources: EPA, *ARNA*; Ministry of Finance, *Foreign Trade Returns.*

Notes:

X: exports (f.o.b.).
M: imports (f.o.b).
Y: GDP.
NX : X – Y.

P_X: export price index.
P_M: import price index.
P: GDP deflator.
e: exchange rate (annual average).

(domestic-oriented) firms. The import price index declined even more because of the reverse oil shock and because of the falling yen–dollar rate. Since the terms of trade became increasingly adverse to imported goods, the trade surplus tended to be sustained. Thus, despite (or because of) the depressed economy in the early 1990s, the trade surplus remained high.

We will next look at changes in the trade composition (see Table 14). Exports fell most conspicuously in the areas of textiles, metal products (iron and steel), and transportation equipment (automobiles). In other words, the traditional export industries have been in a phase-out stage. In contrast, general and electrical machinery both expanded their shares of exports, being Japan's growth industries in recent years.

Turning to the import side, we find that there has been a remarkable increase in the importation of manufactured goods since 1980, especially in the late 1980s. This expansion must be discounted somewhat though because the reverse oil shock made petroleum very cheap, thereby raising the share of manufactured imports.[35] However, individual items on the importation list indicate that manufactured imports are becoming more important over time, especially textile products, machinery (office machinery, semiconductors, electrical parts, automobiles, scientific instruments, etc.) and miscellaneous products.

Table 14

The Composition of Japan's Merchandise Trade (f.o.b.)

Exports

	1980	1985	1990	1995
Total	100.0	100.0	100.0	100.0
Foods	1.2	0.7	0.6	0.5
Textile materials	4.7	3.6	2.5	2.0
Chemicals	5.0	4.4	5.5	6.8
Nonmetal materials	1.4	1.2	1.1	1.2
Metal products	15.8	10.5	6.8	6.4
Iron/steel	11.4	7.7	4.4	4.0
Machinery	60.2	71.8	74.9	74.7
General	13.4	15.8	22.1	24.1
Electrical	13.8	16.9	23.0	25.6
Transport	25.4	28.0	25.0	20.2
Automobiles	17.2	19.6	17.8	12.0
Precision	4.6	4.9	4.8	4.7
Miscellaneous	7.8	7.7	8.5	8.2

Imports

	1980	1985	1990	1995
Total	100.0	100.0	100.0	100.0
Manufactured goods	22.8	31.0	50.3	59.1
Foods	10.4	12.0	13.4	15.2
Textile materials	1.7	1.7	1.1	0.5
Metal materials	8.0	4.8	3.9	2.8
Other crude materials	9.2	7.5	7.1	6.4
Fuels	49.8	43.1	24.2	15.9
Crude petroleum	37.5	26.7	13.5	8.9
Chemicals	4.4	6.2	6.8	7.3
Textile products	2.3	3.0	5.5	7.3
Nonmetallic products	0.8	1.0	2.3	1.9
Metallic minerals	4.6	4.3	6.2	5.0
Machinery/precision	7.6	10.5	18.4	27.4
Miscellaneous	11.4	15.2	26.0	26.5

Source: Ministry of Finance, *Gaikoku boeki gaikyo* [Foreign Trade Returns].

Table 15

Foreign Assets and Liabilities, as a Percent of GDP

	FA	FL	NFA	FDI out	FDI in
1970	9.9	7.6	2.3	0.7	0.5
1975	12.1	10.1	1.5	1.9	0.4
1980	16.1	14.9	1.2	2.0	0.3
1985	34.7	24.4	10.3	2.9	0.3
1990	64.8	53.4	11.4	7.0	0.3
1995	52.4	38.4	14.0	5.7	0.4
U.S. 1995	46.2	56.9	−10.7	7.9	14.1

Sources: Japan: EPA, *ARNA*; United States: *ERP*, February 1996, Table B–105.

Notes:

FA: Foreign assets

FL: Foreign liabilities

NFA: Net foreign assets

FDI: Foreign direct investment

Investment income (another important entry in the current account) has been in a net surplus reflecting Japan's rising net foreign asset balance. Table 15 shows Japan's foreign assets and liabilities as a percent of the GDP between 1970 and 1995. The 1980s were the decade in which Japan made a big splash in the international field. Toward the end of this decade, Japan became the largest net creditor in the world.

Japan's net foreign asset balance rose from a mere 1 percent of the GDP in 1980 to 10 percent by 1985. The latest (1995) was 14 percent. Foreign direct investment going out from Japan increased remarkably in this period, but foreign direct investment into Japan remained minuscule. Japan remained as closed to investment in the 1990s as it was in the 1970s.

Japan provides a good contrast with the United States. Both countries are involved in many foreign transactions, but in foreign direct investment the two countries differ markedly. While Japan is almost totally closed to foreign direct investment, the United States is wide open. That is, the United States continues to be a paradise for foreign investors, while Japan remains as secluded as Shangri-La. It is very difficult to do business with Japan—as many foreign businessmen complain. This is nowhere clearer than in foreign direct investment. If Japan is going to participate in the global world economy, it must open up its domestic market and invite foreign direct investors into the country.

Figure 1

The Foreign Exchange Market

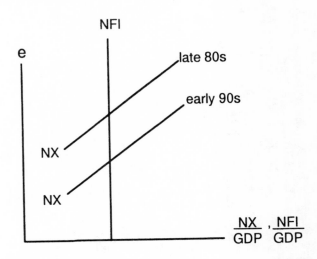

The IS Balance

The most important and the most succinct representation of a macroeconomy is its IS balance, which is represented by:

Domestic   Foreign

$$\underset{(S-I)}{\overset{HH}{}} + \underset{(S-I)}{\overset{BB}{}} + \underset{(S-I)}{\overset{GG}{}} = \underset{(X-M)}{\overset{NX}{}} = NFI$$

Equation (2)

where *HH* is the household sector, *BB* the business (corporate) sector, *GG* the general government, and *NX* net exports. *S* is savings, *I* investment, and *NFI* net foreign investment.[36] Table 16 gives the IS balance for 1985–94 as percent of GDP.

In reading this table, note that the Japanese economy was on a cyclical upswing between November 1986 and February 1991. Thus, the growth rate was relatively high from 1988 to 1990. This business cycle had the most noticeable impact on the IS balance of the business sector. Its investment is sensitive to the business cycle, but its savings is not. The business sector's borrowing from the rest of the economy peaked in 1989–91.

The household sector's IS balance, on the other hand, has been relatively stable. Since the mid-1970s, the national government ran in a deficit. However, its strenuous efforts to maintain a zero-growth budget ceiling finally paid off in the late 1980s. Since 1987 the general government has had a budget surplus,

Table 16

The IS Balance, 1985–95, Percent of GDP

		1985	1986	1987	1988	1989	1990	1991	1992	1993	1994	1995
Households[1]	S	14.9	14.7	13.2	12.4	12.5	11.9	12.5	12.6	13.0	13.2	13.3
	I	5.5	5.4	5.4	4.8	4.5	3.8	5.0	5.7	7.5	7.7	5.6
	S–I	9.4	9.3	7.8	7.6	8.0	8.1	7.5	6.9	5.5	5.5	7.7
Businesses[2]	S	12.0	12.3	13.2	13.2	12.6	12.7	12.6	12.9	13.5	12.7	13.6
	I	17.1	16.5	17.1	19.1	20.9	22.5	21.0	18.5	15.8	13.4	15.4
	S–I	–5.1	–4.2	–3.9	–6.0	–8.3	–9.8	–8.4	–5.6	–2.3	–0.7	–1.8
Government	S	4.8	4.7	6.4	7.6	8.4	8.9	9.0	8.3	6.2	5.4	3.9
	I	5.6	5.6	5.9	6.1	5.9	6.0	6.1	6.9	7.8	7.7	7.6
	S–I	–0.8	–0.9	0.5	1.5	2.5	2.9	2.9	1.4	–1.6	–2.3	–3.7
Domestic	S	31.7	31.7	32.8	33.2	33.5	33.5	34.1	33.8	32.7	31.4	30.6
	I	28.2	27.5	28.4	30.1	31.3	32.3	32.1	30.8	29.7	28.7	28.5
	S–I	3.5	4.2	4.4	3.1	2.2	1.2	2.0	3.0	3.0	2.7	2.1
Foreign	X	14.5	11.4	10.4	10.0	10.6	10.7	10.2	10.0	9.3	9.3	9.4
	M	11.1	7.4	7.2	7.8	9.2	10.0	8.5	7.8	7.0	7.2	7.9
	X–M	3.4	4.0	3.1	2.3	1.4	0.7	1.7	2.2	2.3	2.1	1.5
	NFI[3]	3.6	4.2	3.6	2.7	0.9	1.2	2.1	3.1	3.0	2.7	2.1
	g(Y)	4.4	2.9	4.2	6.2	4.8	5.1	3.8	1.0	0.3	0.6	1.4

Source: EPA, ARNA, 1997.

Notes:
1. Households + nonprofit organizations.
2. Financial institutions + nonfinancial corporations.
3. Domestic (S–I), NX, and NFI differ by statistical discrepancies.

which peaked in 1990–91. Note that this increase in the government surplus was not the result of a countercyclical measure, but it turned out that the government budget surplus nicely complemented the increase in the business sector's funds demand.

Finally, in 1993, the national government realized that it had to take action concerning the depressed economy. The national government started to use deficit spending, which continued into 1996. As a result, the outstanding balance of government debt started to rise from a bottom of 48.1 percent of the GDP in 1991 to nearly 70 percent in 1996. Thus Japan has become one of the most indebted countries as far as government debt is concerned. (At the height in 1987, the ratio was 55.5 percent.) After the fact, the government's fiscal policy turned out to be quite countercyclical.

Since the business sector's and the government sector's IS balances tended to offset each other, fluctuations in the domestic IS balance were minimized. This domestic surplus can be equated with *NX* and *NFI*. How these three values are equated to one another depends, among other factors, on what happens in the foreign exchange market.

For simplicity, suppose for the time being that the domestic surplus flows automatically into the country's *NFI*. In the foreign exchange market, this *NFI* would be equated with the *NX*, a value determined in the international trade market. While both imports and exports of goods and services depend on many factors, the exchange rate is no doubt the most important equilibrating variable under the flexible exchange rate regime.

Using current values, exports respond positively and imports negatively to the yen–dollar exchange rate. The net export curve then is sloped upward in Figure 1. Using the simplified assumption that the domestic surplus is independent of the exchange rate, *NFI* is represented by a vertical line in Figure 1. The exchange rate is determined at the intersection of the *NFI* and the *NX* curves. The reverse oil shock in the 1980s made imports much cheaper than exports. This resulted in a shift to the right of the *NX* curve. As long as the *NFI* curve remains unchanged, the exchange rate must fall. This is what happened in the early 1990s.[37]

The Financial System and the Bubble

Real growth slowed down beginning in the mid-1970s, but financial growth accelerated during the slow growth period, eventually ending in a stock-market and land-market bubble of tremendous magnitude in the late 1980s. The depressed condition of the Japanese economy in the early 1990s may be considered as a recuperation from the bubble's ill effects. Details of the bubble and its collapse are described and analyzed in several of my papers (Sato 1995a, 1995b, 1997a, 1997b), of which the following is a summary.

We begin our story with the two Great Ratios observed in Japan's financial economy over the last four decades. These ratios are F/M and L/M, where F is the economy's total financial asset balance, L the total land value, and M the money balance, all at current values. Both ratios have stayed around their respective long-run levels of 4.0 and 2.0 (Sato 1997).[38] They, however, greatly deviated upward during the two bubbles of the early 1970s and the late 1980s.

The other side of the money balance is bank loans (BL), which are also a part of the financial asset balance and roughly equal to the money balance in size. It may be better to consider $M + BL$ for the denominator. Then, $F/(M + BL)$ and $L/(F + BL)$ tend to converge at the long-run values of 2.0 and 1.0, respectively.

$M + BL$ is connected with the banking sector, so the remainder of F is mostly nonbanking financial assets including government bonds, corporate bonds (though bank debentures are the debt of long-term credit banks), corporate equities, life insurance reserves, trade credits, and so forth. The long-run stability of $F/(M + BL)$ at 2.0 means that the economy somehow divides its financial asset balance in roughly equal proportions between bank and nonbank assets.

To explain why such long-run stability exists in Japan's financial system is beyond the scope of the present writing. Here, let me give an heuristic explanation by taking the household sector as a representative case. Japanese households have continued to save a great deal, a smaller part of which is used to buy real estate and a larger part to acquire financial assets. Households hold 60 percent of their financial assets in the form of money.[39] M/Y continues to rise in the portfolios of households. As long as households divide F between monetary and nonmonetary assets in a stable manner, M/Y and F/Y both steadily rise, leaving F/M relatively stable.

L/M, or equivalently L/F, is also found to be stable in the long run. The value of land is determined mostly by the movement of urban land prices (P_L). As the urban population increased within a small urban area, P_L continued to rise relative to the general price level (P). Thus, L/Y tended to rise over time because of the continuously rising P_L/P which, in turn, was based on the continuing urbanization and growing real income. New purchasers borrow mortgages for both dwellings and land from financial institutions. The increase in P_L then is connected to the increase in the number of mortgages, which are a part of bank loans. The L/M has been stable as a result.

People continue to save and put their savings into bank deposits, postal savings, life insurance, and so on. With the banks creating more deposits, the financial institutions—which receive people's money—make loans and create more financial assets. In this way, F/Y keeps pace with M/Y as both continue to increase. The ongoing financial deepening has resulted in a more rapid expansion of the financial sector than the production sector—a feature which has become more prominent since the Service Revolution began. The *keiretsu* groups have taken advantage of this opportunity and have diversified themselves into the financial sector. Thus, financial deepening has exerted its impact on all aspects of the Japanese economy.

Bubbles are financial deepening run amok. Asset inflation sets in with a violent rush. Stock prices and then land prices shoot up. Consequently, F/M and

L/M depart from their long-run levels in an upward direction. A few years later the bubble collapses, and asset deflation takes over. Then F/M and L/M again converge to their former long-run levels. From the beginning to the end, a bubble lasts for several years. The latest bubble was of inordinate strength. Not only did it go extremely high, but also it finished with a bang. Though stock prices seemed to hit bottom in June 1995, urban land prices were still on the descent in the fall of 1996. (In 1995, their fall was 13.5 percent.)

How does a bubble break out? The stock market may turn bullish as the animal spirits of the investors are revived. However, the potential demand turns real in the stock market only if investors have funds to invest. For those funds, investors must depend on credit—credit supplied by banks. An increase in the credit supply is matched by an equal increase in the money supply.

From the early 1980s on, the Bank of Japan had an easy-money policy in order to stimulate the relatively depressed Japanese economy in this half decade. Accordingly, the money supply ($M2 + CD$) maintained a high rate of expansion. Then, as the economy entered the late 1980s, the money growth rate reached beyond 10 percent for a while, but real GDP growth was around 5 percent and inflation was modest. This, in turn, led to two developments. First, the nominal interest rate started downward from around 1980. The continued decline in the interest rate was one factor in asset inflation. Second, bank credit—which was increasing at a comparable rate with the money supply—poured fuel on the fire starting in the asset markets. In this way, money growth was the principal, if not the initial, cause of the bubble.

What then caused the especially high money growth in the late 1980s? As the money multiplier formula tells us, the starting point of the money supply was the central bank's monetary base. The main part of the monetary base is the currency supply, with the remainder being the required reserves of the member banks. As a percent of the nominal GDP, currency in circulation increased from 7.0 percent in 1985 to 8.9 percent in 1989. In response to the increase in the monetary base, the money supply —in particular the M1′ (the sum of currency, demand deposits, and corporate time deposits)—was increased.

Our quest for the most fundamental cause of a bubble brings us to the central bank's monetary policy—in particular its management of the monetary base. The central bank issues currency (on the debit side of the monetary base), but it cannot simply print bank notes (the common fallacy notwithstanding). The bank must increase the asset side of the monetary base by giving: (a) loans and discounts to member banks (mostly discounts), (b) credit to the government (mostly government bonds), (c) foreign reserve (in the form of foreign exchange certificates issued by the Ministry of Finance), and (d) all the rest. While all four of these items are important in monetary-base management (see Sato 1997b), we highlight here the role of the foreign reserve.

The main target of the central bank's monetary policy is price stability. The rate of domestic inflation is sensitive to changes in import prices, which, in turn, depend on variabilities in the exchange rate. When the yen–dollar exchange rate is falling out of line, the central bank wants to prevent an excessive decline in the exchange rate. With this objective in mind, the central bank intervenes in the foreign exchange market. As it buys up foreign exchanges, the central bank's foreign reserve expands. However, this purchase of foreign exchanges must be financed by new currency, so the amount of currency in circulation is increased.

An increase of the foreign reserve in the monetary base (which can be abrupt), and an increase in currency in circulation relative to the nominal GDP occur at the same time when the yen–dollar exchange rate seems to be declining rapidly. These three events have occurred simultaneously three times since 1970: the early 1970s (1971–72), the late 1980s (1987–89), and the early 1990s (1993–present). This is shown in Table 17.

Recall that the exchange rate began floating in February 1973, but it was revalued a few times after the Nixon Shock of August 1971. In the late 1980s, the yen–dollar rate began a rapid and deep decline in response to the September 1985 G5 Plaza Accord. Once again, in the early 1990s, while the Japanese economy was still depressed, the yen started to be inordinately strong. The yen–dollar rate broke the ¥100/$ barrier in July 1994 and was nearing the ¥80/$ level by April 1995 (¥83.67/$). The central bank repeated its response by increasing its foreign reserve (which continued into the summer of 1996).

In all three cases, the C/Y ratio rose. The two earlier cases gave rise to bubbles. In the early 1990s, there was no bubble as the economy was too depressed to respond.

Financial deepening has continued for a long time in the Japanese economy and is likely to continue as long as the household sector continues to save in the form of money. Banks and postal savings occupy a prominent position in Japan's financial economy with their combined share of financial assets as high as one-half. At the center of the financial system, there is the Bank of Japan. Its monetary policy has played a key role in Japan's macroeconomy because bubbles are attributed to how the central bank has managed the monetary base. However, the bank's seemingly good intentions backfired.

The central bank has to play the role of a tightrope walker. On one side, there is the danger of putting the national economy into a recession if it allows a high value for the yen with its depressing effect on Japan's exports. On the other side, there is a danger of causing asset inflation if the bank attempts to stabilize the yen value. So far, the bank tended to come down on the second side. The financial mess following the latest bubble is the bank's own making.

As the Japanese economy recovers, financial deepening will continue to a higher level. With that, the danger of financial instability will be more intense. This is one systemic risk Japan must face in the future.

Table 17

C / Y, FR / MB, and e

Year	C / Y (%)	FR / MB (%)	e (¥/$)
1969	6.9	24.8	360.0
1970	6.8	28.1	358.1
1971	7.2	67.2	347.9
1972	8.1	77.8	303.2
1973	7.9	28.9	271.7
1974	8.0	27.8	292.1
1975	7.8	25.1	296.8
1976	7.7	29.9	296.6
1977	7.6	38.2	268.5
1978	8.0	34.6	210.4
1979	7.7	16.0	219.1
1980	7.3	23.0	226.8
1981	7.2	22.6	220.5
1982	7.3	19.0	249.3
1983	7.3	19.6	237.5
1994	7.4	19.1	237.6
1985	7.0	19.7	238.1
1986	7.5	20.8	168.0
1987	7.9	33.8	144.5
1988	8.2	29.8	128.0
1989	8.9	19.9	138.1
1990	8.7	15.9	144.9
1991	8.3	8.7	134.6
1992	7.8	7.5	126.6
1993	8.3	10.6	111.1
1994	8.5	14.7	102.3
1995	9.6	21.6	94.0

Sources:
C: Currency in circulation at end of year, BOJ, *ESA*.
FR: Foreign reserve at end of year, BOJ, *ESA*.
MB: Monetary base at end of year, BOJ, *ESA*.
Y: GDP in calendar year, EPA, *ARNA*.
e: ¥/$ exchange rate, annual average, Toyo Keizei, *Keizai tokei nenkan*.

Notes

1. Japanese-English dictionaries invariably translate *miai* marriages as "(an) arranged marriage" or "marriage by arrangement." These translations do not convey the correct meaning of the term.

2. The survey also shows that the average prenuptial period increased from 1.97 years in 1972–73 to 2.97 years in 1992 indicating that people involved in "love" marriages took more time to know each other better, one reason why people now marry later.

3. In the prewar period, divorces were unilaterally from the man's side. The so-called *mikudarihan* (literally, three lines and a half) is a summary letter of divorce the husband gave to the wife ostensibly for such reasons as she had not "adapted to the ways of the family."

4. Of those firms which enforce mandatory retirement, those setting the retirement age at fifty-five and those at sixty were equal at 39.7 percent in 1980. The percentage of the former retirement age continued to fall and the latter continued to rise through the 1980s. By 1993 the proportions were 9.7 percent and 80.0 percent (Ministry of Labor, *Survey on Employment Management*).

5. The LFPR of females aged sixty-five and over is 16 percent. In the United States, the LFPR for males and females sixty-five and over is 16.8 percent and 8.8 percent (1995). In Western Europe, they are much below 10 percent.

6. Mandatory retirement age was set at fifty-five before World War II when life expectancy at birth was barely above forty years.

7. Female workers with ranks of subsection chiefs or higher increased from 2.5 percent of all workers (both male and female) in 1985 to 4.2 percent in 1995 (JETRO, *Nippon, 1997*, p. 124). However, by 1995, female employees in managerial positions were still only 1.0 percent of all female employees as opposed to 11.4 percent in the United States (1993) (ibid., p. 125, based on Ministry of Labor).

8. The percentage of college graduates finding jobs at graduation reached a peak of 81.3 percent in 1991 for both males and females. This rate then started to decline and reached 68.7 percent for males and 63.7 percent for females in 1995. In some cases, those who were not hired for jobs attended graduate schools but most (particularly females) stayed home. Graduates of graduate schools also found it difficult to obtain jobs (in 1995, 67.3 percent for masters and 62.6 percent for doctorates) (*Yomiuri Shimbun*, November 5, 1995).

9. The stagnant economy of the early 1990s depressed the labor demand. Consequently, the LFPR declined from 78.0 percent in 1993 to 77.6 percent in 1995 for males and from 50.7 percent in 1992 to 50.0 percent in 1995 for females. Thus workers who would have entered the labor market were discouraged by the lack of labor demand. Assuming that the decline in the LFPRs was involuntary, I estimate the number of discouraged workers to be 0.19 mn (male) and 0.39 mn (female) in 1995. If they were added to the labor force, the unemployment rate would have risen from 3.10 percent to 3.56 percent (male) and from 3.22 percent to 4.60 percent (female) in 1995. The female LFPR rose from 45.9 percent in 1975 to 50.7 percent in 1992. If this upward trend was extrapolated to 1995, the female LFPR would have been 51.9 percent in 1995. The number of discouraged female workers would then be raised from 0.39 mn to 1.05 mn. Thus the female unemployment rate could be considered to be as high as 6.78 percent in 1995.

10. The number of legal aliens working in industry was 93,775 (December 1994). The breakdown was 61 percent in manufacturing and 20 percent in services (JETRO, *Nippon, 1996*, p. 131).

11. Foreign spouses living in Japan were 0.5 percent of the number of all marriages in Japan in 1994.

12. The six *keiretsu* groups are Mitsui, Mitsubishi, Sumitomo, Fuyo, Sanwa, and Daiichi-Kangin. In terms of total assets, they are roughly equal in size, ranging between 15 percent and 18 percent of the group total. For details, see Fair Trade Commission (FTC), annual reports on the six *keiretsu* groups after 1987.

13. The Sanwa group has only three financial institutions since it lacks marine and fire insurance; the Daiichi-Kangin group has five financial institutions (one city bank, two life insurances, and two marine and fire insurances).

14. Within the *keiretsu* groups, manufacturing as a percent of nonfinancial was total assets (54 percent), sales (38 percent), and employment (82 percent) in 1992 (see FTC 1994).

15. Before this period, from August 1945 to November 1955, there were seven prime ministers, but Shigeru Yoshida, the president of the Liberal Party, served two terms for a total of seven years (one year, May 1946–May 1947; six years, two months, October 1948–December 1954).

After this period, from August 1993 to today, there have been four prime ministers: Morihiro Hosokawa (7 months, August 1993–March 1994), Tsutomu Hata (3 months, April 1994–June 1994), Tomoichi Murayama (one year, seven months, June 1994–December 95), and Ryutaro Hashimoto (January 1996 to the present). When the LDP lost the majority in the July 1993 general election, several political parties (which later merged into the Shinshinto or New Frontier party) formed a coalition government. The first head of this government was Hosokawa, who resigned prematurely when he was threatened with a possible impeachment for his ten-year-old scandal. Hata succeeded him but the arrangement did not last. In June 1994, the LDP talked the JSP and another party into a coalition to take over the cabinet. Murayama, the chairman of the JSP, was put forward for premiership as a compromise although the JSP had lost heavily in the July 1993 general election. The LDP supplied the vice premier. After taking care of the aftereffects of the Great Hanshin Earthquake of January 1995, Murayama expressed political fatigue and resigned in early January 1996. Hashimoto, who was elected to the presidency of the LDP in the same month, assumed premiership.

16. In this, the role played by Shin Kanemaru, vice president of the LDP, is important. He was a powerful, behind-the-scenes manipulator of Japanese politics and aptly called the "don" of the LDP or "the shogun in the dark." He controlled the Takeshita faction, the largest in the LDP. He colluded with major construction firms to help them win public-work projects and concealed a large sum of money received as bribes in his secret bank accounts. His illegal acts were discovered and he was indicted in 1992. His resignation from the LDP was one of the causes of the splintering of the Takeshita faction. Kanemaru died in April 1996 in infamy.

17. One such industry is the parcel delivery service which started to expand rapidly in the 1980s. One of the rising firms in this industry gave bribes to a wide range of politicians including Prime Minister Hosokawa when he was governor of Kumamoto Prefecture ten years ago.

18. Transparency International (Berlin) collected expert opinions about the reputations of individual countries and tabulated them into index numbers (ranging from 0 for corrupt to 10 for honest). Of the forty-one countries in the sample, the least corrupt was New Zealand (9.55). The most corrupt were Indonesia (1.94) and China (2.16). Japan stood exactly in the middle of the list at 20th out of 41 (6.62). The United States was 15th (7.79). Above Japan, most were developed countries, the exceptions being Singapore (3rd, 9.26), Chile (14th, 7.94), and Hong Kong (17th, 7.12). Below Japan, most are developing countries, except for Italy (33, 2.99), Greece (30, 4.04), Spain (26, 4.35), and Portugal (22, 5.56). See *New York Times*, August 20, 1995.

19. From 1981 to 1993, there were four councils: Temporary (March 1981– March

1983), First (June 1983–September 1986), Second (April 1987–April 1990), and Third (October 1990–October 1993).

20. The Commission is called the Economic Reform Study Group and is headed by Gaishi Hiraiwa, the president of Keidanren (Federation of Economic Organizations). The Commission submitted two reports (referred to as the Hiraiwa Reports), one on deregulation (November 1993) and another on economic reform (December 1993). The reports are reprinted in Nakatani and Ohta (1994).

21. Interim reports show that the pace of deregulation has been slow.

22. The September 1992 projection was based on the fertility rate of 1.8. But the rate fell to 1.42 in 1995. The Ministry of Welfare revised its population projection downward based on this lower rate (January 1997). In the new projection, the medium version (on which Table 9 is based) assumes that the fertility rate will stabilize at around 1.4. The population will increase from 125.6 million (1995) to the peak of 127.8 million (2007) and then fall to 120.9 million (2025) and 100.5 million (2050). However, if young females continue to postpone marriage, the fertility rate will go down farther. The low version assumes it to go down to around 1.3. The population will peak at 127.1 million (2004) and then go down to 117.5 million (2025) and 92.3 million (2050). See Toyo Keizai, *Keizai tokei nenkan* (1997), 600–605. The dismal picture of population aging, portrayed in Atoh (1996 for the 1992 projection), applies even more forcibly to the new projection

23. By firm size we have the following for 1995:

Firm size (employment)	Paid holidays	
	Authorized	Actually taken
Total	7.2	9.5
More than 1,000	18.7	1.0
100–999	16.8	8.7
30–99	15.2	7.9

Source: JETRO, *Nippon, 1997*, p. 123, based on Ministry of Labor.

24. As is well known, total-factor-productivity (TFP) growth is measured by the growth rate of T in the aggregate Cobb-Douglas production function.

$$Y = TK^a N^{1-s}$$

where Y is real output, K capital stock, and N labor force. Hence:

$$g(T) = (1-a)g(Y/N) - ag(K/Y).$$

We take labor productivity growth $g(Y/N)$ as a proxy for TFP growth. As

$$g(Y/N) = \frac{1}{1-a}g(T) + \frac{a}{1-a}g(K/Y),$$

$g(Y/N)$ fails to reflect $g(T)$ correctly if a is not constant or if $g(K/Y)$ is not 0. Both were violated in the early 1970s. From 1970 to 1975, K/Y rose from 1.08 to 1.47 for all industry and a (operating surplus / NDP at factor cost) fell from 53 percent to 41 percent.

25. Whether government output is correctly measurable in real terms or not is a methodological issue in national accounting.

26. The labor input ought to be man-hours (NH) rather than the number of persons (N). Table 10 shows that H rose in 1955–60, declined in 1960–75, rose in 1975–80, constant in 1980–85, and declined in 1985–94.

27. The revised national accounts of Japan start at 1955.

28. In terms of man-hours, productivity growth was positive.

29. Since $g(Y_i / N_i)$ aggregates into $g(Y / N)$, we should have:

$$\sum d_i \theta_i \equiv 1, \quad \sum d_{i0} \theta_i \equiv 0$$

where θ_i is the value-added share. In the present case, applying the 1982 values of θ (0.041, 0.429, 0.520), we find the two sums to be 0.941 and 0.0035.

30. It was generally believed (in 1996) that the equilibrium exchange rate was ¥110–120/$.

31. For the former, EPA, *Price Report, 1995*; for the latter, OECD, *National Accounts, 1961–1994* (1996).

32. For Japan, see *JSYB, 1996*, Table 15–11. For the United States, see *SABUS*, 1991, Table 774 (Cost of living index for Nassau-Suffolk, New York, was 159.3 in 1990 relative to nation = 100).

33. The weights for tradables and nontradables are set at 0.1 and 0.9.

34. See EPA, "Survey on Domestic–Foreign Price Differentials," November 1994. The exchange rate was ¥102/$.

35. The average crude oil price fell from $35.5 per barrel in 1980 to $13.8 in 1988 and was $17.2 in 1995 (IMF, *International Financial Statistics Yearbook*, series 001).

36. The IS balance of the general government is equal to the government surplus.

37. Though we have pretended that the domestic surplus and *NX* shift independently of each other, this is an oversimplification as far as oil shocks are concerned. During oil crises imported materials (petroleum) become relatively more expensive than domestic goods. As imported materials are embodied in domestic finished goods, the economy must spend more on imports. This shifts *NX* to the left. On the other hand, domestic consumer goods which embody imported materials are priced higher and domestic consumers must spend more and reduce saving. Thus the domestic surplus is shifted to the left as well. Since the domestic surplus which equals the *NFI* is likely to shift less than the *NX*, *e* is to increase. This is what happened during the two oil crises of 1973–74 and 1979–80.

38. Another Great Ratio is K / Y, where K is the net fixed capital stock. The level of the net fixed capital stock has been relatively stable except for a one-time jump in the early 1960s.

39. Household deposits with deposit money banks are 53 percent of the total deposits and 64 percent of the total time deposits (1995). However, their bank loans are less than 20 percent of all bank loans, 70 percent of which are mortgage loans.

Quo Vadis?

Likely Scenario

Recent economic changes, which we reviewed in the preceding section, all suggest that Japan is now truly at a crossroads. If our thesis of fifteen-year cycles is correct, Japan must already be in a new era. Our question here is which way Japan is now moving. In the following, we examine the quantitative side of the question.

Population Aging

The most prominent feature of Japan from this point forward is the rapid expansion of the older population and the continued decline of the younger population through the year 2010 according to the Ministry of Welfare's projection (see Table 9, page 46).

In Table 9, we have estimated the labor force from the projected population on an assumption that the LFPR will remain unchanged from the 1993 level except for females aged fifteen to sixty-four. For the latter, the LFPR is assumed to increase by 2.2 percentage points every five years following the trend of growth between 1975 and 1993. In view of the stagnant labor-force growth, employers may finally decide to hire more females.

The total working-age population (aged fifteen to sixty-four) started to decline around 1995. However, with the increase in older workers and female workers, the growth of the labor force will turn negative only after 2010. Using our assumptions, the overall LFPR will remain around 62–63 percent.

In figuring the growth of the labor force, we must consider a possible reduction in the working hours (H). Because of the depressed economic condition, total working hours fell from 2,100 hours in the 1980s to 1,900 hours in the mid-1990s. If the forty-hour week is enforced for all firms and if more paid holidays are taken, working hours may eventually fall to the 1992 plan target of 1,800 hours. If this reduction is to be accomplished by the year 2000, $g(H)$ will must be −1 percent per year between 1995–2000.[1]

Changes in the age and sex structure of the labor force and population have supply-side and demand-side effects. On the supply side, older workers are less vigorous if not less efficient. Female workers seem to be employed in less productive ways if the experience of the last decade is a guide. On the demand side, population aging has two discernible effects. First, it will shift personal consumption to more services (see below); second, it will reduce personal saving.

Since there will be more retired people, they will not save as much, especially as social security benefits—their major source of income—are reduced. The decline in their saving, however, will be offset to some extent by an increase in saving by younger households in preparation for their longer retirement. For the time being, the reduction in aggregate saving is more likely to come from the narrowing of the wealth gap (i.e., the gap between the wealth target and actual accumulation [Sato 1995d]).

Sectoral Allocation of the Labor Force

We next project the employment structure in the year 2010. Let us assume that $g(Y/N)$ will be 2.5 percent from 1994 to 2010.[2,3] Then the employment structure in the year 2010 can be projected with the following formula:

$$\left[(N_i/N) \; \frac{2010}{1994} \right] = \left[(Y/N) \; \frac{2010}{1994} \right]^{\eta_i - 1}$$

where η_i is the apparent income elasticity of demand for the output of sector i (Y_i).[4] The past values of η are shown in Table 1 (including the values for the United States). For our projection exercise, we have to modify the past values of η because η cannot remain constant over time.

For the primary sector, we assume that its employment share will fall from 8.2 percent in 1994 to 4.0 percent by 2010 for the following reasons. In every country, agriculture has been shrinking. Table 2 outlines the changes from 1970 to 1992. The G7's experience indicates that the primary sector's employment share is likely to fall as low as 4.0 percent. In the case of Japan, the process of convergence to the minimum may be faster because, by now, nearly 60 percent of the agricultural labor force is sixty years of age and over. As the older generation exits and the younger generation refuses to enter, the agricultural labor force is bound to fall further.[5]

The projected value of sector I's employment share assumes implicitly $\eta_I = $ ™0.77. The (η_2, η_3) must satisfy $\Sigma \eta_i \theta_i = 1$ where θ is the value-added share. From 1965 to 1994, N_2/N remained stable, implying $\eta_2 = 1$. Should η_2 remain at 1 in the projection period, N_2/N must remain at the 1994 level. The increase in N_3/N must be equal to the decrease in N_I/N. The resulting value of η_3 is 1.18. This is case (1) in Table 1. It is the case in which sector II, especially manufacturing, will remain robust at the past level.

However, there are many reasons to believe that η_3 will refuse to go down, including the reason that private consumption will turn more to services as the population ages.[6] Case (2) assumes that η_3 will remain at the same point as the past level in the projection period. As the employment share of sector III continues to expand, the employment share of sector II must contract. In case (2), sector II

Table 1

The Apparent Income Elasticity of Demand by Sector (η) and Projections of the Employment Structure

Japan

Sector	η			Employment structure (%)			
	1965–94	1994–2010			1994	2010	
		(1)	(2)	(3)		(1)	(2)	(3)
I	−0.01	−0.77	−0.77	−0.77	8.2	4.0	4.0	4.0
II	1.01	1.00	0.72	0.24	37.5	37.5	33.5	27.6
III	1.35	1.18	1.35	1.57	54.3	58.5	62.5	68.4
g(Y / N)	5.0	2.5						

United States

Sector	η	Employment structure (%)	
	1970–92	1970	1992
I	−0.55	6.4	3.7
II	0.06	34.4	25.5
III	1.57	59.2	70.8
g(Y / N)	1.6		

Sources: United States: OECD, *National Accounts*, 1992; Japan: EPA, *ARNA*.

will contract but the reason will not be the economy's "hollowing-out" or dein-dustrialization. If manufacturing loses international competitiveness and relo-cates overseas, the economy will lose sector II in an accelerated manner—a situation which corresponds to the historical experience of the United States.[7] Thus, in case (3), we assume that η_3 takes the historical U.S. value.

The employment structure in 2010 is projected for these three alternative cases.[8] In my judgment, case (1) is too optimistic a scenario. Case (2) is more plausible, but we cannot rule out the possibility of case (3) if Japan follows the path of deindustrialization demonstrated in the United States.[9]

The Balance of Trade

Changes in the industrial structure and the trade structure are inseparable. One significant change in the balance-of-merchandise trade has been the steady increase in the importation of manufactured goods. Its share of total

Table 2

Agriculture[1]/ Private industry: G7, 1970–92 (in percent)

	Employment		GDP (current prices)	
	1970	1992	1970	1992
Japan	21.2	9.2	6.3	2.3
United States	5.5	3.1	3.1	1.9
Canada	—	4.7	5.2	3.0
France	15.8	7.0	7.8	3.5
Germany	9.9	3.9	3.8	1.4
Italy	21.2	11.3	9.1	3.7
United Kingdom	—	2.7[2]	3.2	2.1

Source: OECD, *National Accounts*, 1992.

Notes:
1. Agriculture, foresty, and fisheries.
2. 1991.

merchandise imports has risen significantly from the early 1980s to today. It was 22.8 percent in 1980, 31.0 percent in 1985, 50.3 percent in 1990, and 59.1 percent in 1996.

Despite this remarkable growth, it is still far below the level achieved by the other G7 countries, that is, their level is between 70 percent and 90 percent (Table 3). The high ratio in the other countries reflects the fact that their manufactured trade is mainly intra-industry, while in Japan inter-industry trade still dominates (Sato 1995e). Japan's ratio will reach levels equivalent to the other G7 countries when its manufactured trade shifts to intra-industry trade.

However, given Japan's industrial structure, this shift will occur only if the Japanese economy becomes "hollowized." Then, for manufactured goods, exports will fall and imports will rise. This was the path taken by the United States. Thus, our case (3) in the preceding subsection is likely to be accompanied by a substantial decline in the ratio between net exports and GDP.[10]

The IS Balance

Now we combine our observations in the form of the IS balance. For the household sector, we anticipate that S/Y will eventually decline because of the increase in the dependency ratio for older people. I/Y will also decline because there will be fewer people in younger households who will want to build new

Table 3

Imports of Manufactured Goods/Total Merchandise Imports (in percent)

Country	Year	Percentage
Japan	1995	59.1
United States	1993	82.7
Canada	1994	87.4
France	1991	79.1
Germany	1992	77.9
Italy	1991	72.5
United Kingdom	1994	82.0

Source: JETRO, *Nippon,* 1996, p. 71.

houses. However, the decline in S/Y will be larger than the decline in I/Y so that $(S-I)/Y$ will fall.

For the business sector, we expect that slower growth will result in reductions in both S/Y and I/Y. As a consequence, $(S-I)/Y$—which is negative—will be closer to zero.

For the government sector, based on the traditional way the Japanese government works, the national government will eventually succeed in balancing the budget once growth recovers. Then, $(S-I)/Y$ will be zero.

Altogether, the domestic surplus—the sum of the three $(S-I)/Y$—will be much reduced. The domestic surplus will turn into the country's net foreign investment (*NFI*).

If our prediction in the preceding subsection is correct, NX/Y will be reduced toward zero if not negative. In the external account, NX and NFI must be equated. Since both will be reduced, the exchange rate will be at the equilibrium rate (determined by the PPP of exportables). At what level $NX/Y = NFI/Y$ will equilibrate depends on how far deindustrialization proceeds. If there is no deindustrialization, as shown in Table 1, case (2), it may settle down, at say, 1 percent. However, if deindustrialization does take place, as shown in Table 1, case (3), it may turn negative.

Conventional Views in Japan

Our probable scenario can now be compared against the models that Japanese forecasters believe will likely be part of Japan's future. We divide our review into medium-term and long-term projections.

Medium-Term Projections Through the Year 2000

We will begin our analysis of medium-term projections for the late 1990s by examining the government economic plans. Let us see how national plans

Table 4

Growth Targets of National Economic Plans, 1970–95

Prime minister	Plan date	Plan period	Duration (years)	g(Y) (in percent) Target	Actual
Sato	May 1970	1970–1975	6	10.60	5.1
Tanaka	February 1973	1973–1977	5	9.40	3.5
Miki	May 1976	1976–1980	5	6.40	4.5
Ohira	October 1979	1979–1985	7	5.70	3.9
Nakasone	August 1983	1983–1990	8	4.00	4.5
Takeshita	May 1988	1988–1992	5	3.75	4.0
Miyazawa	June 1992	1992–1996	5	3.50	1.3*
Murayama	December 1995	1996–2000	5	1.75–3.00	—

Sources: EPA, *Keizai yoran*, 1997.

performed in 1970–95 with regard to target growth rates (see Table 4).

As is well known, the national plans were ambitious in the 1960s through the mid-1970s. In the 1980s, the plan target and actual performance did not differ very much. However, the 1992 plan ended miserably. Consequently, in the latest plan, the plan makers set up two targets—if structural reforms are to be implemented successfully, $g(Y)$ will be 3 percent; if not, 1.75 percent. The plan makers may now be free from criticisms of failure, but can this be called a plan? Besides, if $g(NH)$ is –0.6 percent (that is, $g(N) = 0.4$ percent, $g(H) = -1.0$ percent), $g(Y/NH)$ has to be 3.6 percent with the higher target. This may be too high a target unless growth is very vigorous.

In Table 5, we assemble a few of the latest medium-term projections developed by private forecasting agencies. The $g(Y)$ ranges between 1.3 percent and 3.0 percent, with 2.5 percent roughly the median of $g(Y)$. As the assumption is made that the $g(N)$ is around 0.5 percent, then the $g(Y/N)$ is about 2.0 percent. For NX/GDP, most forecasters assume that it will fall from 2 percent to 1 percent during the late nineties. Imports are projected to grow faster than exports. Overall, private forecasters are less ambitious than the government's plan.[11]

Long-Term Projections Through the Year 2010

The apparent income elasticities of demand, implicit in the NIER projections, are given in Table 6 along with their historical values in the last ten years. Roughly

Table 5

Medium-Term Projections, Mainly 1995–2000 (in percent)

Predictor[1]	$g(Y)$[2]	$g(N)$	$g(X)$	$g(M)$	NX/GDP[3]
JCER					
1994–1999	2.2	0.63	3.3	5.6	2.7 → 1.5
1995–2000	2.8	—	3.7	6.0	2.1 → 1.0
Sumitomo					
1995–2001	3.0	0.46	4.6	6.1	2.1 → 0.5
Tokai Bank					
1994–2000	1.7	—	4.1	5.4	—
Daiichi-Kangin					
1995–2000	2.4	—	6.6	10.7	1.8 → 1.0
Hokkaido Electric					
1995–2000	1.3	—	3.9	0.5	0.7 → 4.0
Japan Energy					
1994–2005	2.5	—	2.5	2.5	0.3 → 0.3

Sources: Toyo Keizai, *Keizai tokei nenkan*, 1995, pp. 30–33; 1996, pp. 34–38.

Notes:
1. Predictors (date of release):
   JCER: Japan Center for Economic Research (2/28/95 and 1996).
   Sumitomo: Sumitomo Life Insurance Institute (2/26/96).
   Tokai Bank: Tokai Bank (12/94).
   Daiichi-Kangin: Daiichi-Kangin Bank Institute (12/95).
   Hokkaido Electric: Hokkaido Electric Power Institute (12/05/95).
   Japan Energy: Japan Energy Economy Institute (12/08/95).
2. *Y:* GDP in constant prices.
   N: Persons engaged in production.
   X: Exports of goods and services.
   M: Imports of goods and services.
   NX/GDP: Net exports/GDP.
3. The initial value → the end value, monotonically changed over the period.

speaking, the assumed elasticities are close to the historical values observed in the late 1980s, and the employment projections seem to correspond to the ones between cases (1) and (2) of Table 1.

Two forecasting agencies, the Japan Center for Economic Research (JCER) and the National Institute of Economic Research (NIER), have both given long-term projections for the industrial/employment structure through the year 2010. They are summarized in Table 7. For the output structure, both projections report that the status quo will remain basically unchanged. For the employment structure, the NIER projections are such that sector I will decline slightly and sector III will increase slightly.

Table 6

Apparent Income Elasticity of Demand: Historical and Projected

	Historical		Projected		
Sector	1984–1989	1989–1994	1994–2000	2000–2005	2005–2010
I	0.18	−2.75	0.44	0.38	0.42
II	0.88	1.03	0.94	0.71	0.69
Manufacturing	0.83	0.41	0.82	0.82	0.82
Construction	1.02	1.64	1.00	0.35	0.29
Electric, etc.	0.89	1.58	—	—	—
III	1.27	1.63	1.13	1.18	1.17

Sources: Historical: Computed from EPA, *ARNA*. Projected: Derived from NIER (see Table 7).

Note: The elasticity (η_i) is computed by:

$$\eta_i - 1 = g(N_i / N) / g(Y / N).$$

The long-term projections which are available make it clear that Japanese forecasters believe in the continuation of the status quo with few changes in any of the years through 2010. Manufacturing industries, especially general machinery and electronics (the current leading industries), will continue to be robust and will be providing for Japan's merchandise exports. This may be so, but as we have observed, we cannot wholly rule out the possibility of Japan's deindustrialization, as shown in the figures for case (3) of Table 1.

Notes

1. We assume that there will be no change in Japan's tough immigration policy—at least in the near future.

2. This growth rate is within the range assumed by most long-term projections (Table 7 (1) and (2) below).

3. The Industrial Structure Council of the MITI made public its super-long-term projection up to year 2025 (9/18/1996). It assumes $g(Y)$ to be 3.1% (1995–2000), 1.9–2.4% (2000–2010), and 0.8–1.7% (2010–2025). If $g(N)$ is 0.4%, 0.1%, and -0.4%, respectively (Table 9), the higher estimate of $g(Y/N)$ is 2.0–2.5%.

4. Case (3) is derived from the sector output demand function:

$$Y_i / N = A_i(Y / N)^{\eta_i} (P_i / P)^{-\varepsilon}, \ i = 1, 2, 3$$

(3a)

Table 7

**Long-Term Projections of the
Industrial/Employment Structure** (in percent)

(1) NIER

Sector	Output (Y)			
	1994	2000	2005	2010
I	2.2	1.8	1.6	1.4
II	33.5	34.8	34.2	33.3
Manufacturing	26.2	27.2	27.4	28.3
Construction	7.3	7.6	6.3	5.0
III	64.3	63.4	63.4	65.3
Total	100.0	100.0	100.0	100.0
$g(Y)$		2.7	2.6	2.4

Sector	Employment (N)			
	1994	2000	2005	2010
I	5.8	5.3	4.9	4.5
II	30.7	30.0	28.9	27.7
Manufacturing	23.2	22.5	21.9	21.4
Construction	7.5	7.6	7.0	6.3
III	63.5	64.7	66.2	67.8
Total	100.0	100.0	100.0	100.0
LFPR	61.4	60.7	60.4	59.7
$g(N)$		0.3	0.08	−0.4

Sector	$g(Y/N)$		
	1994–2000	2000–2005	2005–2010
I	0.3	1.5	2.0
II	3.4	2.9	3.2
Manufacturing	3.6	3.5	3.8
Construction	3.0	0.4	0.5
III	1.8	2.4	2.6
Total	2.4	2.5	2.8

Table 7 (continued)

	Sector	(2) JCER Output (Y) 1990	2000	2010
I		2.2	2.0	1.8
II		43.5	44.1	44.0
	Manufacturing	34.2	33.9	33.6
	Light	15.9	14.8	13.6
	Heavy	18.3	19.1	20.0
	Construction	9.3	10.2	10.4
III		54.3	53.9	54.2
Total		100.0	100.0	100.0
$g(Y)$		2.3	3.3	

Sources:
(1) NIER: National Institute of Economic Research, *Choki keizai yosoku* [Long-Term Economic Projections], March 1996, as quoted in Toyo Keizai, *Keizai tokei nenkan*, 1996, p. 36.
(2) JCER: Japan Center for Economic Research, "2010-Nen: Nihon Kabushiki Kaisha no Kessansho" [Year 2010: The Income Statement of Japan, Inc.], February 1994, as quoted in Toyo Keizai, ibid., 1994, p. 30.

Notes:
NIER: Sector I is agriculture, forestry, and fisheries, sector II is manufacturing (total) and construction, and sector III consists of environment, distribution, information, leisure, and living.

JCER: Sector I is the primary industries, sector II is manufacturing and construction (light is basic materials industry—iron and steel, chemicals, cement, and paper-pulp; heavy is processing and assembly industry—consumer electric machinery, electronics, and automobiles), and sector III is living-related, services, and others.

Notes *(continued)*

where:
Y_i=the real GDP for sector i
Y=the real GDP for private industry
N =employment in private industry,
P_i =GDP deflator for sector i
P =GDP deflator for private industry
η_i =true income elasticity of demand for the output of sector i
ε =price elasticity of demand for the output of sector i
(common to all sectors)
There is an identity $\Sigma\eta_i\theta_i \equiv 1$ where $\theta_i = P_iY_i / PY$. It must be noted that η_i does not remain constant as the income level changes.
By transforming (3a), we obtain:

$$N_i / N = A_i (Y/N)^{\eta_i - 1} (P_i / P)^{-\epsilon} \left(\frac{Y_i / N_i}{Y/N} \right)^{-1}.$$

(3b)

Suppose that prices are set in proportion to the average wage cost, i.e.:

$$P_i = m_i W_i N_i / Y_{i,} \quad P = mWN/Y$$

(3c)

where W is the money wage rates and m is the markup ratio. Then:

$$P_i / P = \left(\frac{m_i W_i}{mW} \right) \left(\frac{N_i / Y_i}{N / Y} \right).$$

(3d)

Since the money wage rates are likely to change at similar rates across sectors, we can assume that $m_i W_i / mW$ will be constant over time. Then the last two terms of (3b) is in proportion to $(P_i / P)^{1-\epsilon}$.
Similarly, let:

$$P_i / P = D_i (Y/N)^{d_i - 1}, \quad \Sigma d_i \theta_i \equiv 1$$

(3e)

(neglecting the autonomous shift to which D_i is subject). Then, we find that:

apparent η_i in (3) = true η_i in (3b) + $(1 - \epsilon) (d_i - 1)$.

(4)

5. In the agricultural labor force, farmers aged sixty and over increased as follows: 27 percent (1970), 32 percent (1975), 36 percent (1980), 43 percent (1985), 51 percent (1990), 59 percent (1994), (*JSYB*, 1996, Table 6–5). In 1994, 64 percent of the younger farmers were female. This corresponds to the fact that full-time farms are now very few in number (16.1 percent in 1994) and part-time farms mainly working outside agriculture are the main type (70.0 percent in 1994). For farmers' children, those who remain on farms after graduating from school are few (falling from 3.2 percent in 1975 to 1.3 percent in 1994).

6. See Appendix II.

7. Our sector-output demand equation (3a) is incomplete because it ignores the effects of foreign trade. When deindustrialization takes place, it apparently lowers η_2 and raises η_3. This is why apparent levels of η are so different between the United States and Japan.

8. When we project N_i / N, we implicitly project Y_i / Y and P_i / P as well. As we observed, Y/N is a composite sum of Y_i / N_i, and Y_i / N_i is a function of Y/N. In the projection period, I is nearly negligible and Y/N can be considered as a weighted sum of Y_2 / N_2 and Y_3 / N_3. Employing equation (1) and using the value-added shares of 1994, we derive $g(Y_2 / N2) = 3.0$ percent and $g(Y_3 / N_3) = 2.1$ percent for a weighted sum of $g(Y/N)$ = 2.5 percent. Assuming that $g(P_3 / P_2) = g(Y_2 / N_2) - g(Y_3 / N_3) = 0.9$ percent, we can project Y_i / Y and P_i / P.

9. It is unrealistic to assume that $g(Y/N)$ remains unchanged in these three cases. As deindustrialization proceeds, as in case (3), $g(Y_2 / N_2)$ will be lower and, if the past relation (1) continues to hold, $g(Y_3 / N_3)$ will also decline. Then, $g(Y/N)$ has to be lower. We neglect this important point in Table 1 in the section.

Baumol et al. (1989) propose the convergence hypothesis, that is, that productivity growth of late-coming countries will eventually converge at the rate of productivity growth in the United States, which has been around 1 percent (see Table 11 in the previous section). Sectoral data show that labor productivity growth in the United States was 1.1 percent (overall), 0.7 percent (sector I), 1.8 percent (sector II), and 0.6 percent (sector III) between 1970–85 (OECD, *National Accounts*).

10. Japanese factories which relocate overseas export their products to the home market. This "boomerang" effect has already begun, though not yet to the extent of the United States.

11. For the LFPR, Sumitomo assumes that it will fall from 63.5 percent in 1995 to 63.0 percent in 2000. For the unemployment rate, Sumitomo assumes 3.2 percent → 3.4 percent, Hokkaido Electric 3.6 percent → 6.0 percent, JCER 2.9 percent → 2.4 percent (1994 Report) and 3.2 percent → 2.1 percent (1996 Report). For *H*, Daiichi-Kangin assumes the number of hours worked will declime from 1,899 hours in 1995 to 1,856 hours in 2001.

Systemic Change

The Need for a Systemic Change

The previous section considers the Japanese economy in the next decade and a half in purely quantitative terms. However, as we discussed in section entitled "Japanese-Style Capitalism," there have been many profound economic changes in Japan. Along with population aging, later marriages, and fewer children, the family system is in the process of transformation and the lifetime employment system is on the verge of demise. When the principle of collective utility maximization—which we argued is the guiding principle of Japanese-style capitalism—is finally eroded, can the system itself remain intact?

When parts of an economic system change, the system itself must adapt to these changes by altering other parts of the system as well. This process of piecemeal adjustments may be able to maintain the system, but there is a limit to this sort of partial adaptation. When individual changes go beyond certain thresholds, the system can no longer cope with them and may self-destruct in a manner which is similar to the disintegration of Soviet communism. What about Japanese-style capitalism? Will the triad be able to continue its rule over the Japanese economy?

If Japan is to remain viable in the new era, there must be a systemic change as fundamental and momentous as the 1868 Meiji Restoration and the 1945 postwar reform. However, the current change must come from internal sources and in peaceful conditions. This will certainly be very difficult to achieve.

There is a consensus in Japan that Japan needs a large change if Japan is to survive in the new environment. Much has been written lately on Japan's needs for reform and restructuring (e.g., Noguchi 1993; Kosai 1995). Nonetheless, they do not advocate any large-scale systemic change, despite people's increasing "distrust in the establishment which bears responsibility for national policy" (Kosai, p. 3). The government's decision to enforce deregulation in recent years is its attempt at piecemeal adjustments of the economic system.

In a recent speech, Yoshio Suzuki (1996), chief counselor of the Nomura Research Institute, argues that Japan's top-down system must and will change and that this systemic change is comparable to the 1868 and 1945 reforms. Despite these assertions, Suzuki seems to believe that this systemic change will come about without much friction.[1]

In his many writings on Japan's corporate capitalism (e.g., 1994, 1995),

Okumura discusses the possible demise of the triad. According to him, this outcome will happen because the big-business system will disintegrate. He thought that the mass production undertaken by Japan's big businesses is now at a dead end, and controlling a multitude of affiliated firms in *keiretsu* groups is becoming difficult. The collapse of the stock prices in the early 1990s would force big businesses to dispose of their holdings of the equities of other firms. Big businesses will be on the decline.

Unfortunately for Okumura, the *keiretsu* groups seem to have adapted to the new environment (as we already noted) by shifting the center of their business activities from production to finance. Statistics do not show that interlocking share ownership has declined.[2] While households continue to be successfully excluded from corporate management, it is difficult to imagine that big businesses will disintegrate.

The Present Economic Structure Against a Spontaneous Systemic Change

To change an economic system in a peaceful manner, by its own nature, is almost impossible. Those who have vested interests in the current system will adamantly oppose any threat to the status quo. In the case of Japan, the triad which has ruled Japan for so long has a vital stake in keeping Japanese-style capitalism in its present form as long as possible. Though circumstances have been changing, the triad is still intact.

In politics, though national politics is still in a state of flux, the LDP has once again returned to power and seems to be in a fairly secure position. Elite bureaucracy is still robust and strong despite recurring disclosures of scandals. The *keiretsu* groups have successfully diversified into the financial sector which is currently Japan's growth sector.

As long as households continue to save in the form of money, banking and insurances will continue to grow faster than the nominal GDP, and the *keiretsu* groups will grow even faster. Since big businesses have found a way to exclude individuals from share ownership, Japanese-style capitalism is not "of the people, by the people, and for the people," but "of the triad, by the triad, and for the triad." Under these conditions, a large systemic change is only a remote possibility.

Why are the masses content when power is monopolized by the triad? The answer is found in the high degree of equality for the distributions of both income and wealth among individuals. An important contribution of the Postwar Reform was to make the size distribution of income among households highly equal. The Gini coefficient fell from 0.55 or so (1940) to around 0.35 (1962–1990) (Minami 1996).

Japanese households have a strong penchant for home ownership, with the

Table 1

Income and Wealth Inequality,[1] Japan and the United States

	top Y[2] median W (multiple)	top W[2] median Y (multiple)	Shares of highest income class (percent)		
			Number	Y	W
Japan 1995	3.4	2.5[3]	6.1	17.2	11.7[3]
United States 1992	4.0	10.9	7.3	25.0[4]	43.9

Sources: Japan: Prime Minister's Office, *Family Saving Survey*, 1995, all households; United States: *SABUS*, 1995, Table 757.

Notes:

1. The highest income class is households with income above ¥15 mn (Japan) and $0.1 mn (U.S.).
2. The average of the highest income class; Y = income, W = net worth.
3. Financial.
4. Crude estimate.

level being around 60 percent (59.5 percent in 1993, *Housing Survey*)—nearly as high as U.S. home ownership (64.7 percent in 1993, *SABUS* 1995, Table 1225). After dwellings and land, Japanese households keep financial savings mostly in the form of monetary assets (65.4 percent in 1970, 66.9 percent in 1980, 55.2 percent in 1990, and 62.9 percent in 1995, EPA, *ARNA*). U.S. households keep only 15 percent of financial assets in the form of money (*SABUS* 1996, Table 770.) Because financial assets are mostly of the fixed-price type, they do not appreciate with inflation. Consequently, the financial-asset distribution is even more equal than the income distribution. By contrast, the United States has highly unequal income and wealth distributions among households. Table 1 compares these distributions in the United States and Japan.

The high degree of distributional equity leads Japanese households to believe that they are all middle-class. The government's public opinion survey never fails to demonstrate this consensus. The latest one is reported in Table 2. This situation has led some Japanese social scientists to argue that Japan has been in the "era of the new middle class" (e.g., Murakami 1984). Obviously, when people consider themselves to be middle-class, they are reasonably content with the status quo and find no reason to rock the boat. Politically, they have become increasingly conservative—as their voting records reveal. This is why the LDP has recaptured its ruling position.

However, distributional equity, of which Japan is so proud, is close to an

Table 2

Self-Perception of Class Status by Japanese Households, July 1996
(in percent)

Upper class	0.4
Middle class	91.2
Upper	10.8
Middle	57.4
Lower	23.0
Lower class	5.2
Don't know	3.1

Source: Jetro, *Nippon 1997*, 146.

illusion when we look at the household sector within the private domestic economy. Table 3 shows the asset distribution among individual sectors of the private domestic economy in 1995. For the household sector, the most important assets (in descending order) are land, money, life insurance equities[3] and dwellings. These account for more than 90 percent of the household asset balance.

None of these assets empower households to participate in corporate management. For that objective, households must own corporate bonds and corporate equities. Households own only 2 percent of industrial bonds[4] and 26 percent of corporate equities (1995). This means that large corporations are their own masters and their executives can run them as they wish with almost no intervention from the outside. This is Japanese-style capitalism par excellence.

Under these circumstances, the triad will be able to keep its firm grip over Japan, provided that households continue to be content with their "exploitation"—and there is no evidence to the contrary. Nonetheless, as financial deepening continues, the economy will exhibit signs of internal contradictions.

If the monetary authorities of Japan do not change their traditional response to the internal-external balance, the mismanaged monetary policy will give rise to another round of a bubble. The next bubble will be far worse than the last one, and when it collapses, it will transmit shock waves throughout the entire economy. This is the systemic risk that Japan has to face. Then, a systemic change will be forced on Japan—but the cost might be as enormous as the Great Depression of the 1930s.

Table 3
The Asset Distribution by Sector, Private Economy, 1995, percent

	Private economy, total = 100				Total assets = 100				
	FIS	NFCs	NPOs	HHS	All	FIS	NFCs	NPOs	HHS
Total assets	30.3	28.4	1.5	40.0	100.0	100.0	100.0	100.0	100.0
Net fixed assets	2.5	63.0	4.1	30.5	13.1	1.1	29.0	36.8	10.0
Inventory	—	88.4	—	11.6	1.2	—	3.8	—	0.4
Land	3.0	29.0	1.0	67.0	26.8	2.7	27.4	18.6	44.9
Financial assets	49.5	19.2	1.1	30.1	58.9	96.2	39.8	44.6	44.4
Money	0.4	22.2	3.0	74.5	14.5	0.2	11.3	29.9	27.0
Bonds	85.4	4.3	0.9	9.4	7.7	21.8	1.2	4.9	1.8
Corporate equities	37.6	36.5	0.1	25.8	7.1	8.8	9.1	0.4	4.6
Life insurance	—	—	—	100.0	4.0	—	—	—	10.1
Bank loans	99.1	—	0.9	—	11.4	37.2	—	—	—
Trade credits	51.6	48.2	0.2	—	8.9	15.2	15.1	7.3	—
Others	76.6	16.6	0.2	6.5	5.2	13.1	3.0	1.4	0.8

Source: EPA, ARNA, 1997.
FIS, financial institutions
NFCs, nonfinancial corporations
NPOs, nonprofit organizations
HHS, households

Notes

1. Suzuki believes that cross-firm share ownership and the main banking system will continue in a modified form.

2. Corporate equity ownership was as follows:

	1989/03	1996/03
Financial institutions	37.6	40.2
Nonfinancial corporations	35.8	35.0
Households	26.7	24.9

Source: BOJ, *ESA*, 1996; Table 92.

3. Though insurance policyholders are "shareholders" of life insurance companies, the overall operation of life insurance companies is at the discretion of management.

4. Of long-term bonds, households own 7.9 percent of government bonds (central, local, and public corporations), 2.3 percent of industrial bonds, and 11.5 percent of bank debentures (as of March 1996, EPA, *ARNA*).

Concluding Remarks

The postwar reform was intended to democratize Japan, but it failed to change Japan's top-down system. The triad of national politics, elite bureaucracy, and big business has become too well entrenched. However, many circumstances are changing and will continue to change, including population aging, growth slow-down, deindustrialization, the breakup of the three-generation family, the demise of the lifetime employment system, and so on.

When parts of a whole system are changed, the system itself must be modified significantly for its own survival. Can Japanese-style capitalism remain intact under changing conditions? At the moment, the triad seems to be as powerful as ever. The LDP has regained its control of the government, elite bureaucracy remains strong despite recurring scandals, and the *keiretsu* groups have successfully diversified into the financial field.

Japan will be increasingly financialized. With the primary sector on the verge of disappearance, the tertiary sector will continue its expansion. The secondary sector is likely to be finally shrinking. The pace of its contraction will be accelerated if Japan loses international competitiveness in manufacturing with Japanese factories relocating overseas in search of cheaper production costs. With increased imports by manufacturers, Japan's trade balance will move from a surplus to a deficit. At the same time, population aging with reduce household savings, resulting in a decline in the domestic surplus.

All this means that the Japanese economy will find itself in a new era. Yet the ruling mechanism of the economy will remain unchanged. A highly financialized economy must face the possibility of systemic risk such as a bubble of even greater magnitude than the last one. In the final analysis, there is no denying that Japan's economic future is uncertain. This is why Japan is now at a crossroads.

Appendix I

Collective Utility Maximization

This appendix presents a formal (heuristic) model of two players. Each player has a fixed endowment $\bar{Z}_i$ ($i = 1, 2$) which he can consume by himself, but he can increase his utility if he can get a favor Z_j from the other player ($i \neq j$). However, the other player wants to receive something back in the form of a favor Z_i. The i-th player gives a part of his endowment for Z_i. Obviously, each player is in a trade-off position with respect to (Z_1, Z_2).

Since "favors" are nonmarketable goods, there is no open market that determines the exchange rate between the two favors. However, the optimization principle asserts that the marginal rate of substitution (MRS) between the two favors—which each player calculates within his own utility function—must be equated between the two players if the exchange is to be "fair."

The trouble is that there is an infinite number of mixes for the position (Z_1, Z_2) which satisfies the optimization condition. If there is an open market, the matter is settled simply by the market. With no open market, bilateral negotiations ensue. The outcome of the negotiations greatly depends on the relative "power" of the two players.

This much is common sense. However, as a good economist, we must make it look more unintelligible. This is the principle of collective utility maximization.

Let each player's utility function be represented by:

$$\begin{cases} U_1 = U_1(\bar{Z}_1 - Z_1, \ Z_2), \ U_{11}, \ U_{12} > 0, \\ U_2 = U_2(\bar{Z}_1 - Z_2, \ Z_1), U_{21}, \ U_{22} > 0. \end{cases}$$

Needless to say, we assume that all the values for Z are quantifiable. The utility functions satisfy the usual convexity property.

Each player wants to maximize his utility. Player 1 wants to have $Z_1 = 0$ and Z_2 as high as possible. Likewise, player 2 wants to have $Z_2 = 0$ and Z_1 as high as possible. Clearly this is impossible to achieve. It, however, is obvious to the players that they each can improve their respective utilities if they agree about give-and-take.

The question is how much to give and how much to take. The players must negotiate. This negotiation is embodied in the collective utility function of the two players:

$$U = F(U_1, U_2), \ F_1, \ F_2 > 0.$$

Collectively, the players want to maximize U. The instruments are (Z_1, Z_2). The first-order condition is given by:

$$U_{11} = fU_{22},$$
$$U_{12} = fU_{21}.$$

where $f = F_2 / F_1$. The condition can be rewritten in the form of:

$$MRS \ (dZ_2 / dZ_1) = U_{11} / U_{12} = U_{22} / U_{21}.$$

As we noted, the collective utility maximization requires that the *MRS* be equated between the two players. The *MRS* is nothing but the shadow price (in relative terms). However, there are an infinite number of combinations for (Z_1, Z_2) which meet this condition. One combination must be chosen by the two players. This is where the collective utility function enters the picture. The choice depends on the size of f, which is the *MRS* within the collective utility function. Thus f depends on the relative power of the two players.[1]

Up to this point we have worked with the assumption that there is an internal solution. There may not be $f = 0$ or ∞, that is, if $F_1 = 0$ or $F_2 = 0$. In this case, there is no mutually satisfactory solution. This is the case if one player is willing and the other is not. Then, we have $(Z_1, Z_2) = 0$. Considering the heavy cost of transactions, this outcome must hold when F_1 or F_2 are sufficiently close to 0 (in relation to cost). When the LDP ceased to be the ruling party, political contributions to the LDP by big businesses fell considerably for an obvious reason.

Although, so far, we have limited ourselves to a two-player game, we can extend it to a three-player game. The only difference is that the formal analysis becomes more cumbersome because now there are six favors instead of two. However, the principle is unchanged.

In real situations, "favors" are more qualitative than quantitative. Surely, for politicians, favors are political contributions which can be counted in monetary terms. However, the return which the businesses receive, for example, might be an exemption from a regulation. Needless to say, that may be translated into money terms. For bureaucrats, they give favors to businesses and expect to be repaid by their future appointments with businesses. That again can be stated in pecuniary terms. However, the time dimensions involved in such exchanges may differ from one player to another. The simple, one-period utility analysis is given merely for an illustration.

Note

1. Let us give some concrete form to the utility function. Let the form of *CES* be:

Figure A–1

The Values of MRD for a Given $Z_1 > 0$

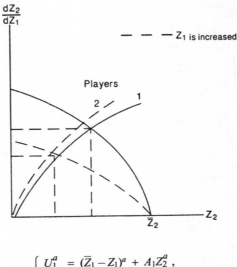

$$\begin{cases} U_1^a = (\bar{Z}_1 - Z_1)^a + A_1 Z_2^a , \\ U_2^a = (\bar{Z}_2 - Z_2)^a + A_2 Z_1^a , \\ U^b = U_1^b + B U_2^b \end{cases}$$

where $a < 1$, $b < 1$, and A and B are non-negative. The *MRS* is derived as follows:

$$\frac{dZ_2}{dZ_1} = \begin{cases} \dfrac{1}{A_1}\left(\dfrac{\bar{Z}_1 - Z_1}{Z_2}\right)^{a-1} & \text{for Player 1,} \\[3mm] A_2\left(\dfrac{Z_1}{\bar{Z}_2 - Z_2}\right)^{a-1} & \text{for Player 2.} \end{cases}$$

The *MRS* is illustrated in Figure A–1. One Z_2 corresponds to one Z_1 when the marginal rates of substitution are equated.

The trade-off locus of (Z_1, Z_2) is illustrated in Figure A–2. It is represented by:

$$\left(\frac{\bar{Z}_1}{Z_1} - 1\right)\left(\frac{\bar{Z}_2}{Z_2} - 1\right) = (A_1 A_2)^{1/(a-1)}.$$

The locus moves inward as $(A_1 A_2)$ is reduced. In the limit, for $A_1 A_2 = 0$, the locus coincides with the two axes. It is obvious that the optimal point in this case is the origin (i.e., the no-trade point). Thus, the size of $(A_1 A_2)$ represents the willingness by the two players to give and take. As we move down the locus, dZ_2 / dZ_1 or the relative shadow

Figure A–2

The Locus of (Z_1, Z_2) When the Values of *MRS* Are Equated

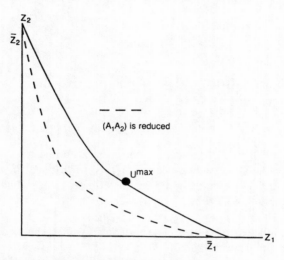

price of favors changes from ∞ to 0. Which point on the locus will be chosen depends on the collective utility function. Note that $U_1 = 0$ at $(\bar{Z}_1, 0)$, and $U_2 = 0$ at $(0, \bar{Z}_2)$. Then, the value of U will be maximized at some internal point. The location of this point depends on the size of B, making B the indicator of the relative power of the two players. When player 2 dominates player 1, the value of B is higher, and the U^{max} point shifts more to the right on the locus. The value of dZ_2 / dZ_1 then declines.

Appendix II

Private Consumption and Income Elasticities of Demand

In our projection exercise of the employment structure, the size of the apparent income elasticities of demand, especially η_3, is of critical importance. Will population aging shift sectoral demands more to services? If so, η_3 ought to be as high as the value assumed for case (3) of Table 1 in the "Quo Vadis?" section.

We can formulate a better estimate by looking at the makeup of personal consumption available in the *Family Income and Expenditure Survey*. This survey gives cross-sectional data classified by the age of the head of the household. Personal consumption is 60 percent of final demand (GDP) so that the head of the household's apparent income elasticities of demand ought to be a good guide to the sectoral elasticities.

Model

Suppose that we divide total personal consumption (C) according to our three-sector classification. Then, the per-household consumption demand function is:

$$C_i = A_i C^{\eta_i} (P_i / P)^{-\varepsilon}, \ i = 1, 2, 3.$$

We then have:

$$P_i C_i / PC = A_i C^{\eta_i - 1}(P_i / P)^{1 - \varepsilon}.$$

With cross-section data, we disregard the relative-price term. With time-series data, assume that:

$$P_i / P = B_i C^{d_i},$$

then,

$$P_i C_i / PC = (A_i B_i^{1 - \varepsilon}) C^{\eta_i - 1 + d_i(1 - \varepsilon)}.$$

These are our estimating equations.

Data

Accepting the classificatory scheme of the *Family Income and Expenditure Survey*, we have sector I (foods), sector II (nonfood goods including housing services), and sector III (services). The information in Table A–1 presents statistics showing the time-series data (1955–1995) and the cross-section data (1995).

Time-Series Elasticities

The apparent income elasticities of demand are estimated as shown in Table A–2. Note that the 1975–95 values are closer to our Case (3) of Table 1 in the "Quo Vadis?" section.

Cross-Section Elasticities

The cross-section data of Table A–1, Part B reveals that sector I is more or less stable through all the age ranges, sector II falls. Sector III rises until the age of 50–54 while income roughly doubles. The apparent income elasticities of demand before age 50–54 are roughly $\eta_1 = 1.0$, $\eta_2 = 0.05$, and $\eta_3 = 1.6$.

Above age 50–54, the sectoral shares are stable while income declines as a person becomes older. This means that the income effect and the age effect cancel out each other when a person is older. From this it follows that, with income fixed, the aging of the population will push the share of sector II downward and the share of sector III upward. Then, in time-series data, this factor will keep η_3 high and η_2 low. Therefore, case (3) of Table 1 in the "Quo Vadis?" section becomes more likely.

Table A–1

**Composition of Worker Household
Consumption Expenditure** (in percent)

(A) Time-series Data

| | Sector | | | |
Year	I	II	III	C
1955	44.5	20.5	35.0	39.4
1965	36.2	25.8	48.0	53.9
1975	30.0	24.0	46.0	84.6
1985	25.7	21.8	52.5	93.2

(B) Cross-section Data, 1995

| | Sector | | | |
Household head age	I	II	III	C
24 and under	23.6	34.3	42.1	63.0
25–29	20.1	30.4	49.5	75.3
30–34	21.5	27.2	51.3	82.1
35–39	23.7	23.7	52.6	90.3
40–44	24.6	21.7	53.7	102.0
45–49	22.3	19.9	57.8	116.7
50–54	21.2	19.3	59.5	115.1
55–59	22.1	21.9	56.0	100.7
60–64	23.0	21.8	55.2	93.8
65 and over	23.5	17.8	58.7	87.8

Source: Prime Minister's Office, *Family Income and Expenditure Survey.*

Notes:
Sectors:
   I: Foods.
   II: Housing, light-heat-water, furniture and household equipment, and clothing and footwear.
   III: insurance and medical care, transportation and communications, education, culture and entertainment, and others.
   C: Consumption expenditure per household in 1990 prices (GDP deflator for household consumption).

Table A–2

**Apparent Income Elasticities of Demand,
Personal Consumption, and Time-Series**

	1955–75	1975–95
η_1	0.48	−0.70
η_2	1.21	0.48
η_3	1.36	2.11

Source: Table A–1, Part A.

References

Atoh, Makoto. 1996. "Fewer Children, More Seniors," *Japan Echo* 23:10–16.

Baumol, William J., Sue Anne Batey Blackman, and Edward Wolff. 1989. *Productivity and American Leadership: The Long View*. Cambridge, MA: MIT Press.

Fair Trade Commission (FTC). 1994. *Nihon no rokudai kigyo shudan no jittai* [The State of Japan's Six Keiretsu Groups]. Tokyo: Toyo Keizai Shimposha.

Kaplan, Eugene. 1972. *Japan: The Government-Business Relationship: A Guide to American Businessmen*. Washington, DC: Department of Commerce.

Komiya, Ryutaro, Masahiro Okuno, and Kotaro Suzumura, eds. 1988. *Industrial Policy of Japan*. Tokyo: Academic Press.

Kosai, Yutaka, ed. 1995. *21-seiki eno keizai seisaku* [Economic Policy for the 21st Century]. Tokyo: Nihon Keizai Shimbunsha.

Minami, Ryoshin. 1996. *Nihon no keizai hatten to shotoku bumpai* [Economic Development of Japan and Income Distribution]. Hitotsubashi University Economic Research Monograph No. 45. Tokyo: Iwanami Shoten.

Murakami, Yasusuke. 1984. *Shin chukan taishu no jidai* [The Era of the New Middle Masses]. Tokyo: Chuo Koronsha.

Nakane, Chie. 1970. *Japanese Society*. Berkeley: University of California Press.

Nakatani, Iwao and Hiroko Ohta. 1994. *Keizai kaikaku no vision* [Vision of Economic Reform]. Tokyo: Toyo Keizai Shimposha.

Noguchi, Yukio. 1993. *Nihon keizai kaikaku no kozu* [The Blueprint for Reforms of the Japanese Economy]. Tokyo: Toyo Keizai Shimposha.

Noguchi, Yukio. 1995. *1940-nen taisei, saraba 'senji keizai'* (The 1940 System, Adieu 'War Economy'). Tokyo: Toyo Keizai Shimposha.

Okumura, Hiroshi. 1994. *Nihon kabushiki kaisha daikaizo keikaku* [The Plan for a Big Reform of Japan, Inc.]. Tokyo: Tokuma Shoten.

———. 1995. *Hojin shihonshugi no ummei, kabushiki kaisha no "shi niitaru yamai"* [The Fate of Corporate Capitalism: Corporations on the Way to Death]. Tokyo: Toyo Keizai Shimposha.

Sato, Kazuo. 1995a. "Bubbles in Japan's Urban Land Market: An Analysis." *Journal of Asian Economics* 6 (Summer): 153–76.

———. 1995b. "Bubbles in Japan's Stock Market: A Macroeconomic Analysis." *Japanese Economic Studies* 23 (July–August): 33–58.

———. 1995c. "Dual Structure and Japan's Macroeconomy." *Japanese Economic Studies* 23 (July-August): 3–31.

———. 1995d. "The Target Wealth Hypothesis and Japan's Household Saving" (in Japanese). *Nihon Keizai Kenkyu* No. 30 (December): 25–50.

———. 1995e. "Economic Growth, Foreign Trade, and Trade Policy in Japan." *World Economy* 18 (March): 193–217.

———. 1997a. "Economic Development and Financial Deepening: The Case of Japan." *Journal of Asian Pacific Economy*, 2 (March) 1–27.

————. 1997b. "The Monetary System, Monetary Policy, and Macroeconomics of Japan." Mimeo.

Suzuki, Yoshio. 1996. "The Japanese Economy at a Historical Crossroad." Keynote speech to the Conference on the Japanese Economy, Marquarie University, Sydney, August 22.

Takata, Yasuma. 1947. *Keizai no seiryoku riron* [The Power Theory of Economy]. Tokyo: Jitsugyo no Nihonsha.

This chapter originally appeared in *Japanese Economic Studies* 24, No. 4 (July–August 1996).

2

The Japanese Economy in the 1990s

Kazuo Sato

1. Introduction

The 1990s have proved to be Japan's economically least successful decade over the last half century. Japan's economic system, which was reestablished after World War II, achieved remarkable success. Nevertheless, the same system has proved to be incapable of coping with the new environment of the 1990s. Why has this new situation emerged in this decade? What is the significance of the 1990s in Japan's modern economic history? After discussing this issue (Section 2), we describe major economic events in the decade (Section 3), connect them to the several parts of this book (Section 4), and indicate the need for a new economic system (Section 5).

2. Japan's Systemic Changes

Japan's economic system underwent two major reforms over the last century and a half. The first was the Meiji Restoration of 1868 under which the Japanese economy shifted from Tokugawa feudalism to Meiji capitalism. The second was the defeat in World War II in 1945, which modernized Japan. In each of these, Japan's old system had to be overhauled because it was no longer compatible with the new environment that confronted the country. The 1990s are thought to be the third occasion when such an overhaul is needed.

The first reform took place because Tokugawa feudalism, which kept the Japanese economy secluded from the rest of the world, was no longer able to resist the foreign pressure that forced Japan to open itself to international commerce. The Meiji Restoration introduced capitalism into Japan, but it was characterized by the top-down rule of absolute monarchy. Militarism remained dominant and eventually brought Japan to the catastrophe of World War II.

The second reform was forced on to Japan by the U.S. occupation authorities, who wanted to remake Japan into the American ideal. The reform covered all aspects of Japanese life. But after Japan regained independence, a new system which may be dubbed Japanese-style capitalism emerged. This system is a mixture of the postwar reform and a number of institutions inherited from the prewar system. It was highly regulated from the top. The system functioned well in support of rapid growth of the 1950s and the 1960s.

Even in the slow growth period starting in the mid-1970s, the system performed comparatively well until the economic bubble of the late 1980s. When the bubble collapsed, the general consensus in Japan, both private and public, was optimistic, i.e., the Japanese economy would resume its satisfactory growth after usual cyclical adjustments. But this has proved to be wishful thinking. The Heisei Recession continued for nearly three years (1991/02–1993/10), and the subsequent recovery was anemic. The Japanese economy went into another recession in 1997/03. In 1998, the growth rate went down to –2.8 percent, and in 1999 IQ the unemployment ratio went up to 4.8 percent, both records for the last four decades (Table 1). Japan which was the leader in growth among the G7 in the slow growth period (1975–89) fell to the bottom of the G7 in the last seven years (1992–98). Apparently, the 1990s have not been a mere cyclical down swing of the Japanese economy but a time of more permanent changes—changes in the environment that are momentous enough to require an overhaul of Japan's economic system once again.

There are a number of such changes, but we may single out two here. One is the continued aging of the population. People not only live longer but also women marry late and have fewer children over their lifetime. Consequently, population growth is expected to turn negative by the year 2007. The working-age population (ages 15–64) has already started to decrease. Such demographic changes require multifaceted changes in Japan's economic system in the twenty-first century.

Another momentous change is the absolute contraction of manufacturing. The Service Revolution dates back to 1973 in Japan, but unlike in the United States and Western Europe, manufacturing employment continued to grow at a rate comparable to total employment. But this process ended in 1992. From 1992 to 1998, manufacturing employment decreased by 11 percent. Correspondingly, Japan's macroeconomic structure has to undergo a fundamental change.

One may consider the ultra-slow growth of the 1990s as an indication that Japan's postwar economic system is no longer compatible with the new environment which it now faces. Then, Japan's economic system must be transformed once again. The economic doldrums of the 1990s may be the birth pains of the new system.

The Japanese Economy in the 1990s

Let us take a closer look at the Japanese economy in the 1990s. As Table 1 clearly reveals, even in the slow growth period (1975–89), Japan's growth rate

Table 1

Macroeconomic Variables (percent except for V)

	G(Y)	g(P)	U.R.	V	g(L)	g(Pop)	g(working age)
(A) Quinquennial averages							
1955–59	8.0	3.4	2.2	.30	2.1	1.0	1.9
1960–64	10.7	6.2	1.4	.70	2.0	1.0	2.2
1965–69	10.3	5.3	1.2	.96	2.0	1.1	1.5
1970–74	6.0	10.3	1.3	1.33	0.9	1.5	1.0
1975–79	4.4	5.9	2.1	.62	0.7	1.0	0.8
1980–84	3.5	2.7	2.4	.66	0.7	0.7	0.9
1985–89	4.5	1.1	2.6	.86	0.8	0.5	0.8
1990–94	2.2	1.5	2.5	1.06	1.0	0.3	0.3
1995–98	1.3	−0.4	3.5	.65	0.3	0.2	−0.07
(B) The 1990s							
1990	5.0	2.4	2.1	1.40	1.67	0.39	
1991	3.8	2.7	2.1	1.40	1.98	0.35	
1992	1.0	1.8	2.2	1.08	1.06	0.33	
1993	0.3	0.6	2.5	.76	0.39	0.25	
1994	0.6	0.2	2.9	.64	0.13	0.22	
1995	1.5	−0.7	3.2	.63	0.16	0.43	
1996	5.1	−1.5	3.4	.70	0.46	0.23	
1997	1.4	0.1	3.4	.72	1.09	0.47	
1998	−2.8	0.3	4.1	.53	−.61	0.32	

Notations and sources:

g(y)	the growth rate of real GDP,	PA, *Annual Report on*
g(P)	the growth rate of the GDP deflator	*National Accounts*
U.R.	the unemployment ratio	
V	the ratio of job openings to job applications	Ministry of Labor
g(L)	the growth rate of the employed	EPA, op. cit.
g(Pop)	the growth rate of population	Prime Minister's Office,
g(working age)	the growth rate of the working-age population (age 15–64)	*Census of Population*

was around 4 percent, the highest among the G7. But in the 1990s, the growth rate fell abruptly. Excluding the initial two years (1990 and 1992), the average growth rate over the seven-year period 1992–98 was 1.1 percent, the lowest among the G7. In particular, the 1990s had two recessions. The first one, 1991/02–1993/10, ran thirty-two months, the second longest postwar recession. During this recession, the growth rate was low but was never negative. The second recession, 1997/03– is still going on, and the growth rate has been consecutively negative from 1997 IVQ. In 1998, the growth rate was as low as –2.8 percent, the first negative since the oil-shock recession of 1974 (–0.6 percent).

With the exception of the 1970s, inflation has never been a serious problem in Japan, once the postwar hyperinflation was brought under control. In the 1980s, inflation became increasingly lower. From 1993 on, inflation has been nearly absent and there was even deflation in 1995 and 1996—the phenomenon of "price destruction."

Behind the low inflation, there are changes in the labor-market tightness. This is measured by the ratio of job openings to job applications (V in Table 1). When the ratio is one, the labor demand and the labor supply are roughly in balance. In terms of this measure, the labor market was extremely tight in the early 1970s, an important reason why this half decade was highly inflationary. With the advent of slow growth in the mid-1970s, the labor market went slack. The next time the ratio exceeded one was the bubble period of the late 1980s (from 1988 on), spilling over into the 1990s. From 1993, the ratio again fell much below 1 and went below 0.50 from 1998 IIIQ on. The weak labor market is behind the phenomenon of extremely low inflation in recent years.

In Japan, the unemployment ratio is relatively insensitive to business cycles and, from the mid-1970s on, fluctuated between 2.0 percent and 3.0 percent over a business cycle. But in the 1990s, the unemployment ratio stopped falling even when the economy recovered. It was 2.0 percent in 1990 IVQ, rose to 2.6 percent in 1993 IVQ when the recession was over, continued to rise through the subsequent recovery to 3.3 percent in 1997 IQ, and rose further to 4.8 percent at the end of 1999 IQ. Apparently, the labor market has been in a chronically depressed state for the last six years.

Finally, let us examine how population and employment behaved. The population growth was around 1.0 percent until the late 1970s. Since then, it has been falling steadily, principally because women are marrying increasingly later and the total fertility rate fell below 2 after 1975 and went below 1.50 from 1993 on.

The Japanese population used to be young, and the population age structure was of a typical pyramid type. Hence, in most of the rapid-growth period, the working-age population grew faster than the total population. But as population aging continued, the two population growth rates have been changing *pari passu*. By 1995, the working-age population reached a peak and started to decline. The total population is expected to peak by 2007 and then start falling. Roughly speaking, total employment has grown at a rate comparable to the working-age population. But in the 1990s, the former maintained a higher growth than the latter, because in 1990–93 the labor demand was temporarily very strong.

We next turn to the composition of national accounts in the 1990s. The ultra-slow growth in the 1990s can be attributed principally to the fall of investment. The inducement to invest was very subdued because of the joint operation of weak demand-size and supply-side factors. Growth, however, remained positive because of the strength of private consumption which kept on growing albeit at a low rate (actually, growth of per capita consumption was higher in Japan than in the United States at this time). It is also remarkable that the household saving rate, which had been falling from the mid-1970s, stopped falling at the level of 13.0 percent in 1987–97 (15.4 percent in 1998).

Let us turn to the role of fiscal policy in the 1990s. It is remarkable that, through the 1990s, government consumption was a relatively stable proportion of GDP, government investment kept on rising as a proportion of GDP, and tax revenue kept on falling as a percent of GDP. In other words, seen as a trend, fiscal policy has been very active. The problem was its timing.

The national government budget went into a large deficit in 1975 and remained so for quite some time. The national government tried hard to balance the budget and eventually succeeded. The government budget turned to a surplus in 1988 and remained so until 1992. In its peak of 1990–91, the surplus was as high as 3.5 percent of GDP. Deficit spending was resumed from 1993 on. In 1996, real GDP growth went up to as high as 5.1 percent. The Hashimoto Cabinet mistook this as a sign of Japan's full recovery and decided to straighten out the national budget. Government investment expenditure was cut down for FY1997 and raised the consumption tax from 3 percent to 5 percent as of April 1, 1997. These measures coincided with the onset of the latest recession, poor timing indeed.

Likewise, monetary policy has also been a miserable failure. In the early 1980s, the Japanese economy was thought to be relatively depressed (the longest recession of thirty-six months, 1980/02–1983/02). The Bank of Japan repeatedly cut the discount rate. In the late 1980s, money-supply growth was above 10 percent. This relaxation of monetary policy was instrumental in causing the economic bubble in the late 1980s. The result was runaway asset inflation in both the stock market and the real estate market. The Bank of Japan, belatedly deciding to control the asset-market bubble in the late 1989, raised the discount rate from 2.50 percent to 6.00 percent in five installments. The stock-market bubble burst in December 1989 and the real estate-market bubble likewise burst a year or so later. But monetary policy at the time was a schizophrenic mixture of high interest and high money growth. The economy went into a recession from 1991/02 on, and the Bank of Japan started to cut the discount rate from 1991/07 on. With several cuts, the discount rate was lowered to 0.50 percent in 1995/09. But this monetary policy was again a schizophrenic package of low interest and low money growth. It is hard to see how such an irrational monetary policy could really be effective.

When stabilization policy did not perform its stabilization function in a proper manner, it is no wonder that the Japanese economy sank deeper and deeper into the economic doldrums, the most prominent of which was the worsening financial crisis. In the postwar economy of Japan, households maintained a high saving rate and kept most financial assets in the form of money. Consequently, monetary assets grew much faster than nominal GDP. The other side of money is bank loans. For banks to increase bank loans faster than nominal GDP, banks must lend increasingly more to new borrowers—including smaller firms, large firms' subsidiaries like housing loan companies, and real estate speculators. While the bubble continued, borrowers seemed to be getting richer. But when the bubble collapsed, a large number of loans became "nonperforming." Banks tried to hide this from the public, but the depressed state of the Japanese economy dragged on, and it became increasingly difficult to continue to do so. Finally, by 1995, the bankruptcy of housing loan companies had to be announced, and the Ministry of Finance was forced to make public the extent of nonperforming loans. Not only small, less efficient financial institutions, but also very large ones started to go under. How to clean up this financial mess has been an urgent task imposed on the monetary authorities.

Recent Changes in the Japanese Economy

The seven parts in this book cover various aspects of Japan's economic system. This section gives a brief overview of these parts supplemented with descriptions of relevant changes in recent years which are not covered by the essays assembled in this volume.

The Japanese economy in transition. Essay 1 (Sato) delineates the Japanese economic system in flux. Fundamental changes in the underlying factors are making the prevailing economic system incompatible with reality, and the system itself has to be significantly modified. It discusses the future course the Japanese economy may take. More recent changes that have taken place in the Japanese economy, especially in the late 1990s, do not change the observations made in Essay 1.

The economic system. When we argue that the contemporary economic system is no longer able to cope with the new environment, it is important to understand how that system came into being to begin with and how that system could perform so well within the existing environment. Essay 3 (Okuno-Fujiwara) undertakes this task. It attributes the genesis of the postwar system to the wartime economic planning, circa 1940, which imposed economic regulations on the Japanese economy. though the postwar reform and subsequent changes transformed the Japanese economy tremendously, the wartime legacy survived, in particular because of the strategic complementarity among various institutions and practices, e.g., the Japanese-style employment system and the severely restricted authority of shareholders. The question now is how the Japanese-style interlocking shareownership will fare when lifetime employment—the hallmark of the Japanese-style employment system—is about to go out of existence.

The business system. In Japan's corporate capitalism, major corporations own one another. Essay 4 (Okumura) explains how this situation came about—especially in the development of "stable" shareownership. Corporations in a business group own stocks of other corporations in the same group, so as to prevent takeover attempts. On the one hand, this reduced publicly traded corporate shares, with resulting skyrocketing stock prices. On the other hand, "stable" shareholders are interested in control, not in dividends. Hence, dividends were kept low in Japanese corporations. The situation could not go on forever. When the contradictions became unbearable, the stock market collapsed, placing Japan's corporate capitalism in peril. In Japan's corporate capitalism, financial institutions—city banks, life insurance companies, and the like—are the most important shareholders. It is these financial institutions that suffered most in the mid-1990s. The peril of corporate capitalism is real and threatens the very existence of Japan's economic system.

In Japan's business system, large business groups maintained an important place in the production sector, especially manufacturing. Most prominent is the subcontracting arrangements whereby major manufacturing firms of a group control many small subcontracting firms. How these subcontracting arrangements worked is described and analyzed in Essay 5 (Yaginuma). In this connection, it is important to note that manufacturing employment has been in the process of absolute contraction since 1992. Both the smallest and the largest firms are disappearing faster. large firms are disappearing because they have been shifting their base of operations overseas. This means that the subcontracting system itself is in the process of change.

The employment system. How does Japan's employment system differ from that of the United States? This question is examined in Essay 6 (Koike). Koike finds it in the slow promotion in large Japanese firms and the quick promotion in the U.S. firms. He explains why this difference has arisen and how it affects various aspects of the employment system.

As is well know, the most significant characteristic of Japan's employment system has been lifetime employment. However, lifetime employment in the true sense of the term is limited to regular white-collar male employees of large firms, no more than 10 percent of the nonagricultural labor force. Nonetheless, whether under lifetime employment or not, labor mobility has been limited to regular male employees. An important change that has taken place in the 1990s is a significant erosion of the lifetime employment system. Large firms have been shifting from the seniority-related (*nenko*) wage system to the annual wage system in which the worker's annual pay is determined by his/her work performance. A recent rise in unemployment also means that workers can no longer be guaranteed employment security. The traditional trust between the employer and the employee is now on the way out.

Japan's labor market is segmented not only by firm size but more importantly by gender. While labor mobility is much lower among male workers in Japan as compared with the United States, labor mobility of female workers is as high in Japan as in the United States. This fact is reflected in the persistence of large male-female wage differentials in Japan. this phenomenon is analyzed in Essay 7 (Ozawa).

The Equal Employment Opportunity Law (EEOL) was enforced in 1986 in

Japan. The law is intended to eliminate sex discrimination in employment. But what actually happened over the past dozen years has been a sharp increase in female part-time employment. In fact, one half of the increase in female nonagricultural employment from 1985 to 1996 was attributed to part-timers (total female nonagricultural employment increased from 15.4 million to 20.7 million and female part-time workers from 2.06 million to 4.45 million). Likewise, the recruitment ratio of new female college graduates caught up with that of male graduates in the late 1980s when the labor demand was strong, but it has been lagging behind the male ratio in the 1990s. Though the EEOL has been revised to toughen its enforcement, its positive effect is yet to be seen.

The financial system. The postwar hyperinflation wiped out financial assets, especially wartime bonds. Inflation was brought under control from 1952 on, and households maintained a rising saving rate to make up for lost wealth. Households continued to accumulate financial wealth even when the Japanese economy went into slow growth, keeping most of their financial wealth in the form of money and life insurance equity. Correspondingly, financial institutions which accept households' deposits expanded loans to the private sector and purchased government bonds and corporate bonds and stocks. This Japanese-style financial deepening continued under the growth slowdown and led to the economic bubble of the late 1980s as the monetary authorities relaxed monetary policy. Asset inflation was accelerated in both the stock market and the real estate market. Eventually, it collapsed in the early 1990s. This sequence of events is examined quantitatively in Essay 8 (Sato).

When households accumulated money and life insurance equity at a rate faster than their incomes grew, banks and life insurance companies had more financial withdrawals than they ever had. It also coincided with the deregulation of the banking system. This background of the economic bubble of the late 1980s is described in Essay 9 (Tsuda). Essay 10 (Sato) analyzes the macroeconomic mechanism of the stock market bubble by applying the standard decomposition based on the fundamental equation of the stock price. The financial mess that resulted from the collapse of the economic bubble has turned out to have been far more serious than anticipated at the time and worsened further from 1995 on. To restructure and reinforce Japan's financial system is the essential prerequisite for the revival of Japan's economic growth.

The international system. We date Japan's Service Revolution at 1973 in the sense that the secondary sector stopped expanding its employment share in the labor force in that year. For the next two decades until 1992, this share remained stable (manufacturing employment of private-industry employment was 29 percent in 1973 and 27 percent in 1992). Then, from 1992 on, manufacturing employment started to contract absolutely. This contraction of manufacturing has been the fastest among the smallest manufacturing establishments, obviously because they are being phased out, and followed by the largest establishments, which are apparently being relocated overseas, in East Asia in particular. This is the so-called one-set or full-set principle whereby large business groups attempt to cover a full set of domestic industry to enforce their industrial control. Essay 11 (Seki) analyzes this process.

Essay 12 (Sato) reviews how Japan's foreign trade performed in 1951–1992. There are a number of peculiarly Japanese features of Japan's commodity exports, commodity imports, and foreign direct investment. This essay covers most of them up to the early 1990s. However, a remaining question is how these features are to change as postindustrialization has finally come to Japan. As Japanese industry is relocating overseas, will Japan's balance of trade finally go into a chronic deficit as the U.S. economy has been doing for so long? Will Japan eventually slip from its current position of No. 1 net creditor nation to the rest of the world? Future developments in this field have much to do with the on-going transformation of the Japanese economy.

The government system. In the G7, along with Italy and France, Japan is one of the most highly regulated economies. This means that politics and the elite bureaucracy are endowed with strong power over the private sector. Unfortunately, power corrupts. Economic scandals involving prominent politicians and elite bureaucrats have been uncovered in rapid succession from the late 1980s on. To scale down their power, it becomes essential to remove cumbersome and unnecessary regulations. Thus, deregulation has been a challenge to the Japanese government in the 1990s.

Essay 13 (Muramatsu) describes how Japan's governance system came into being and how it performed. In this connection, it is useful to note that the national government has announced its intention to consolidate itself into a fewer ministries with a sizable reduction in government employment.

As we noted, Japan's post-World War II system owed much to wartime economic planning. That and the postwar economic dislocation increased the power of the elite bureaucracy. Noguchi calls it the 1940 system. In Essay 14 (Noguchi), he explains why it is now necessary to overcome the 1940 system and to create a new system. We may remind ourselves that such a systemic transformation requires all-round reforms, not only political reforms but also economic and social reforms.

A New System Needed

Though Japan's economic system has undergone fundamental changes from Tokugawa feudalism through prewar (1868–1945) capitalism to postwar (1945–) capitalism, one thing has remained unchanged. The Japanese economy is ruled from the top down. The post-World War II reform was intended to change Japan's top-down system to the American bottom-up system, but it failed. The system that emerged was Japanese-style corporate capitalism ruled by the triad of elite bureaucracy-national politics-big business. This corporate capitalism was made possible because corporations were mostly owned by corporations. Households put most of their wealth in housing and monetary assets. They kept financial wealth in the form of bank deposits, postal savings, and life insurance equities. In other words, they delegated corporate control to financial institutions and major nonfinancial corporations which controlled the corporate sector *via* their interlocking stock ownership. It is this system that finally ended up in the economic doldrums of the 1990s. Hence, it is this system that has now to be restructured. This is easy to say but very difficult to achieve as this restructuring must be undertaken voluntarily in a comprehensive and simultaneous fashion. The two previous overhauls of Japan's economic system were much easier to achieve because Japan had no choice other than to undertake them. The future of Japan depends now most crucially on whether it can undertake another overhaul of its system without external coercion. Among others, this overhaul requires Japan to reshape its corporate capitalism from its present form. Unless the general public participates in running the corporate sector, Japan's economic system cannot shift from the top-down to the bottom-up. How Japan will be able to adjust to the new reality of the twenty-first century is to be determined by the success or failure in this shift. A new system is urgently needed.

Part II

The Economic System

3

The Economic System of Contemporary Japan: Its Structure and the Possibility of Change[1]

Masahiro Okuno-Fujiwara

1. Introduction

The economic system of contemporary Japan is often referred to as the "Japanese-style" system. This is because, whether consciously or unconsciously, many people consider the economic system in Japan to be different from that in Western Europe and, in particular, from that in the United States. Specifically, the following phenomena, considered characteristic of the Japanese-style system, are seldom observed in other countries:

- Long-term fixed employment, a seniority-based wage system, and internal promotion in the labor-management relationship
- The dominance of indirect financing and the "main bank" system in the financial market
- The subcontracting and corporate affiliates (*keiretsu*) in the interfirm relationship
- The limited power of stockholders within a corporation, the interfirm stockholding which supports it, and a board of directors whose dominant majority is composed of executives who advanced through the ranks
- The prevalence of administrative guidance in the government–business relationship, and
- The unique position of trade associations that are supported by former bureaucrats.

In the past, the "uniqueness of the Japan" argument stressed the distinctive features of the Japanese economic system, which differed from other countries in various aspects and is often regarded by mainstream economists as heresy. The Marxist economists said the economic system and its mechanisms progressed historically, meaning that much of the Japanese system was nothing more than a manifestation of the "backwardness" of the Japanese economy.

From this standpoint, it follows that the elimination of obsolete structures is an indispensable step in modernizing the Japanese economy. At the same time, neoclassical economists in the mainstream of modern economics maintained that its theoretical framework is implicitly governed by the Anglo-Saxon economic system. They maintained that the Japanese system, which differed from traditional economics, is idiosyncratic and wrong.

In contrast to these progressive historical views, which is the basis for traditional economics, recent developments in economics gave credibility to numerous proposals for analyzing differing economic systems. This new economics, which utilized multidimensional and contemporaneous methods of analyzation, avoided the preconceptions of the earlier economics. This new area of research is termed the "comparative institutional analysis."[2]

Today the world as a whole is exposed to rapid changes in terms of the economic system as well as in terms of political and diplomatic structures. Multidimensional possibilities are sought regarding the future of the earth and humankind. Therefore, it is very important to compare and objectively analyze the Japanese economy in this new manner relative to the systems of other countries—particularly those of the West.

The principal objective of this chapter is to explain—from the standpoint of such a comparative economic system analysis—the two points that are considered important in examining the Japanese economic system. First, most of the systems and mechanisms that are stable in a given society are not established by necessity. This is because different systems and mechanisms can exist with stability in societies that are physically identical. The kind of system that emerges and is maintained with stability in a given society often depends on an accident of history (path dependence). Second, the kind of economic mechanism that emerges in a society depends greatly on what other mechanisms exist in it. Various economic mechanisms or systems that are present in a given society do not exist independently of each other; they exist as a stable economic whole only because they complement and support each other.

In other chapters in this book, we examined the historical process which produced the economic system of modern Japan. The following is a brief summary of that discussion. The major elements composing the economic system in contemporary Japan were created to support the "controlled economy" in order to implement the "planned economy." This was designed to mobilize the full national resources needed in the wartime economy during the period from the Sino-Japanese War through World War II. Needless to say, in the postwar period, the wartime Japanese economic system changed on the surface. It lost its original form through the process of transformation—the democratization imposed by the occupation forces, rapid economic growth, and globalization. Nevertheless, as we discussed in detail in another chapter, the wartime economic system, which was forcibly introduced by the full national mobilization system, intensively governs the essence of the economic system of contemporary Japan.

What prompted us to be interested in this historical process is the realization of the issues that should be addressed to reform the economic system of contemporary Japan and what we need to be aware of in transferring the Japanese economic system to other countries as a developmental strategy. The heightening of trade friction with Western countries and the rapidly progressing globalization demand a change in the Japanese economic system which lacks both transparency and international currency. At the same time, the transplantation of the Japanese system is a focus of interest as a strategy to be used by the former Soviet Union, the Eastern European countries, and the developing nations—countries were excluded from the growth of Japan and the NIEs (Newly Industrialized Economies)—for transforming themselves into market economies.

The second objective of this chapter is to emphasize the circumstance that is the basis of our analysis in this book. Various elements which compose the economic system of modern Japan retain strong mutual complementarity. If each of these different elements had been introduced by itself, independent of others, they would not have taken root as stable institutions or conventional practices, and the economic system of modern Japan might not have been born.

The modern Japanese economic system that emerged may be greatly dependent on the emergency, system-wide transformation imposed during the war period. In this chapter, we would like to use economic theory (particularly the analysis of comparative economic systems) to examine such a possibility, along with the character of the modern system and its composing elements.

2. The Game of Cooperation and Historical Coincidence

Throughout this book we have examined various institutional characteristics of the Japanese economy—in concrete terms, various mechanisms and conventional practices. As is apparent from the labor-management practices in Japan, the economic mechanisms and practices that exist in a free society such as Japan are not necessarily born or maintained by the force of law or governmental authority. Rather, despite the absence or presence of any legal sanctions in choosing other mechanisms or practices, they are formed as an institution because it is advantageous to the persons involved to maintain such mechanisms. The issue is what is the incentive for those involved to maintain these mechanisms and practices. Let us examine this with a concept widely known in game theory—the "game of cooperation."

Let us consider a situation in which a person (Individual A) is about to climb a staircase and another (Individual B) is about to descend. Unlike driving an automobile, the side of a staircase one uses is determined by each individual. Assuming that there are only two choices—using the right side (Strategy $s = 0$) or using on the left side (Strategy $s = 1$), the social situation that occurs on this staircase is any of the four cases shown in Figure 1.

Of these four cases, the upper left block indicates the situation in which both

Figure 1

Example of the Game of Cooperation

A \ B	Left Side Traffic (s = 1)	Right Side Traffic (s = 0)
Left Side Traffic (s = 1)	+1 / +1	0 / 0
Right Side Traffic (s = 0)	0 / 0	+1 / +1

A and B take their respective left side. The two figures in this box (+1, +1) show that each individual gains the +1 "merit" (game payoff) since both can move smoothly without bumping into each other. In contrast, the lower left box in Figure 1 is the case in which A climbs on his right side while B descends on his left side. Therefore, A and B bump into each other on the staircase, at worst hurt themselves or at the very least waste time. As a result, the payoff gained by each is 0. The upper right box in Figure 1 shows a similar situation.

If A and B pass each other many times on the stairs, eventually the situation will adjust itself to that shown by the upper left box (both on left side) or that shown by the lower right box (both on right side).

Let us restate this situation from a technical viewpoint. From A's standpoint, depending on whether A expects B to choose the left side or right side, the most advantageous way for A to use the staircase (strategy) varies. If B is anticipated to choose the left side, it is preferable for A to choose the left side and receive the game payoff of +1, rather than the right side and receive the game payoff of 0.

This is referred to as the optimal response of A, that is, moving on the left side in response to B's choice of the left side. Similarly, A's optimal response to B's choice of the right side is to use the right side. Since the expectation and the reality would eventually match after repeatedly passing each other, the condition adjusts itself so that both persons choose the optimal response—the Nash equilibrium. In the game of cooperation, both the upper left box and the lower right box stand for the Nash equilibrium.[3]

The game of cooperation can be played by more than two people. In fact, during rush hour, left-side traffic is customary on staircases in some train stations while right-side traffic is customary in others. This can also be explained by using Figure 1. In place of the individual B choosing either left side or right side, suppose that all the individuals descending the stairs choose either the left side or the right side. More generally, we can think of a proportion p $(0 \leq p \leq 1)$ representing the persons descending the stairs who choose the left side and a proportion $1 - p$ representing persons who choose the right side. If the individuals who climb the staircase choose the left side, they would bump into the proportion $(1 - p)$ of the people who are descending the stairs while they avoid bumping into the proportion p of these people. Therefore, the game payoff to the individuals who climb the stairs on the left side is:

$$p \times (+1) + (1-p) \times 0 = p.$$

At the same time, the game payoff to the individuals who climb on the right side is:
$$p \times 0 + (1-p) \times (+1) = 1-p.$$

Clearly, if p is smaller than one-half, the right-side traffic is the optimal response, while if it is larger than one-half, the left-side traffic is the optimal response. Letting the probability s of choosing the left side be the probability of choosing the optimal strategy, then the optimal response can be expressed as:

$$s^*(p) = \begin{cases} 0 & p < \frac{1}{2} \\ \text{Any value between 0 and 1} & p = \frac{1}{2} \\ 1 & p > \frac{1}{2} \end{cases}$$

This fact is shown on Figure 2 as the optimal response curve where the horizontal axis is p and the vertical axis is s. Since the game is symmetrical between the individuals who climb up and those who go down, if the proportion of those who climb up on the left side is p, the optimal response of the individuals who go down is completely identical.

If $p < 1/2$, and $s^*(p) = 0$, then the right side is the optimal response. The individuals who might have chosen the left side would now choose the right side, and the value of p declines (as shown by the arrow in Figure 2). If, in the end, $p = 0$, it implies that everyone used the right side (which is advantageous) and a stable stationary state of the Nash equilibrium A is reached. In contrast, if $p > 1/2$, the right side (which is disadvantageous) declines, and the Nash equilibrium B in which $p = 1$ (that is, everyone uses the left side) is reached in the end. Thus, the Nash equilibrium is shown as the intersection between the optimal response curve and the line drawn at a 45° angle from the horizontal.[4] When the slope of the optimal response curve is less than the slope of the 45° line, it is a stable Nash equilibrium. There are three (two of which are stable) Nash equilibriums in the game of cooperation; thus, this game has multiple equilibriums.

Figure 2

Proportion of Individuals Who Choose the Left Side (*p*)

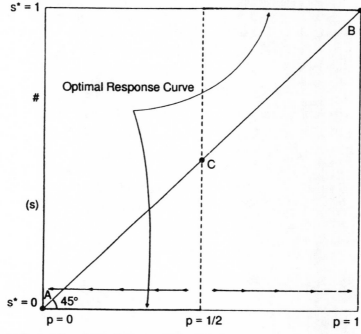

(**#** Probability of Choosing the Right-Side Traffic)

Thus, even when an individual has a free choice, whether it is advantageous to oneself depends on the choice made by others in society. As a result, there are train stations in which it has become a custom (that is, equilibrated) for all passengers to take the right side (the right-side traffic) and there are other train stations in which the left-side has become customary.

In this instance, which side is chosen by people in a society or a station is determined not by exogenous factors, such as the physical environment or legal control, but by which side is previously chosen by the majority—an endogenous factor. In other words, it is determined by historical coincidence or past policy intervention. When, as in this case, there is a rational explanation showing why different mechanisms in physically identical societies become stable equilibriums, the fact that one mechanism is formed in one society and a different mechanism is established in the other does not imply that the first society is more developed than the second. The differences in the mechanism and institution are due to historical coincidence and past policy interventions; that is, it is merely the past historical path governing the present (path dependence).[5]

3. Strategic Complementarity and the Japanese-Style, Labor-Management Relationship

Let us consider the Japanese economic system in concrete terms. One area in which the unique character of the Japanese economic system is especially prominent is the labor-management relationship. Even though the Japanese-style, labor-management relationship—which has the unique features of lifetime employment, seniority-based pay, a bonus system, and internal promotions—is showing signs of changing, it is still viewed as the foundation of Japanese-style management. . . . Using statistical data, workers in Japan, particularly male, full-time employees, have a strong tendency to stay at the same firm on a long-term, continuous basis (the so-called lifetime employee) and possess low labor mobility. Further, while seniority-based wages exist in any country, a worker's pay in Japan is particularly responsive to the number of years of service as compared to other countries. The Japanese bonus system—in which improvement in the firm's performance is rebated to employees—scarcely exists in other countries. In addition, reflecting long-term employment, the senior-ranked positions in a firm are filled through internal promotion.

. . . Such Japanese-style labor-management relationships created a mechanism in which fluctuation in the firm's performance is translated into fluctuation in the employees' pay (through the bonus system) within the system of long-term, stable employment at the same firm. The internal promotion system is also a mechanism in which benefits are redistributed among employees because the number of senior-ranked positions and promotion possibilities expand with the growth of the firm and its scale of operation.

This Japanese-style labor-management relationship has contributed to the competitiveness and efficient production of Japanese businesses in several ways. First, the seniority-based pay and retirement pension systems are essentially a deferred reward for labor. They serve the role of "ransom" in that the employee has to forfeit them if he or she resigns before the mandatory retirement date. They also give the employee an incentive to remain at the same firm. For this reason, the employee is motivated to make a large contribution to the firm (such as working diligently or making suggestions to improve the product quality) in order to reduce the chance of being fired.

Second, workers are employed at the same firm for a long period of time. Since improvement in the firm's performance means profits are redistributed among the existing employees (through salaries and promotion), employees look at the firm as a place of investment. As a result, workers are motivated to improve their skills (i.e., skill formation). In particular, they have an incentive to improve the firm-specific skills that are usable only within the firm and not transferable to other firms.

Third, through the redistribution of the firm's profits among employees, the worker's objective is homogenized to a single objective: improvement of the firm's business performance. As a result, conflict of interest within the firm is reduced. At the same time, the dissemination of information within the firm and cooperation among the employees are promoted.

We need to emphasize here that the institution and practice of lifetime employment, seniority-based pay, and internal promotions (these will be referred to collectively as "Japanese-style labor-management practice") possess "strategic complementarity." This refers to reciprocal behavior whereby the more other firms adopt these practices, the more pressure is put on each individual firm to adopt these practices.[6] Such strategic complementarity contains multiple equilibriums (examined above in the game of cooperation) and has the possibility of internally realizing the labor-management practices that vary among different countries. This point can easily be understood from Figure 3. One axis plots the non-Japanese-style, labor-management practice (the fluid employment, merit-pay-based wages, and promotions and raises through external employment opportunities) opposite the second axis of the internal, Japan-style, labor-management practice.

The horizontal axis of Figure 3 represents the average extent (p) of the Japanese-style, labor-management practice among all firms in the society. Thus, the value of p declines with the movement of the line to the left which stands for the prevalence of the non-Japanese-style, labor-management practice in society. Conversely, the degree of the presence of Japanese-style practice increases with the movement of the line to the right. On the vertical axis, the movement upward means the desirable labor-management practice for the individual firm (and the individual employee) changes from the non-Japanese-style ($s = 0$) to the Japanese-style ($s = 1$).[7] The very fact that the optimal response curve $s^*(p)$ for each firm (and each employee) is upward and to the right indicates that Japanese-style, labor-management practice fulfills the definition of strategic complementarity.[8]

Taking into consideration the lifetime employment and seniority-based pay systems, the more society as a whole engages in the usual Japanese-style, labor-management practice (the larger the value of p), the less mobile is the labor market and the greater is the role of retirement pensions and seniority-based pay. This is because, in the event of dismissal, the possibility of reemployment at another firm is much smaller and, even if rehired by another firm, earnings are reduced drastically since the employee has to accumulate seniority from scratch. If a worker leaves the firm and chooses employment outside the company (the external option), the worker would be at quite a disadvantage compared with the internal option because of lifetime employment and seniority-based pay. In this case, to remain with the firm that utilizes the Japanese-style, labor-management practice (that is, to choose $s = 1$) is the employee's optimal response.

In contrast, if the society as a whole employs non-Japanese-style labor-management practice (that is, it is close to $p = 0$), it is easy to find employment

Figure 3

Average Degree in Society of the Japanese-Style Labor-Management Practice (p)

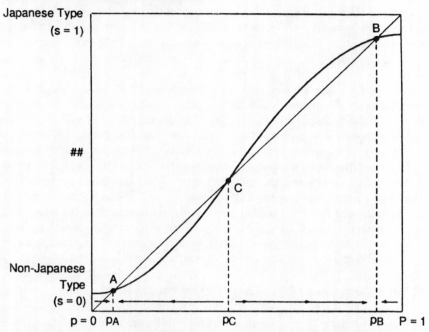

(## Degree of the Optimal Labor-Management Practice of the Japanese Style)

opportunities in other firms. Since salary does not depend on seniority, earnings would not change very much. If the labor market is characterized by labor mobility and uses the non-Japanese-style, there is a value for the external option. Moreover, if the worker chooses a firm that retains the Japanese-style practice, there is a possibility that the full amount of the "ransom" such as the retirement pension would not be paid in the end since there is no guarantee of employment through the retirement age. Therefore, if the labor market is of non-Japanese-style $(p = 0)$, the employee's optimal response is to choose a non-Japanese-style firm $(s = 0)$.

The more pervasiveness the ideas of lifetime employment and seniority-based pay is in the society, the more vulnerable is the firm's reputation among prospective job applicants if it is quick to lay off its workers in the event of business downturns or to reduce the wages of older workers. Therefore, there is a strong incentive on the part of the firm to maintain the level of employment. Thus, the lifetime employment system also has strategic complementarity from the standpoint of a firm's own incentives.

In other words, lifetime employment and seniority-related pay exist as stable employment practices for the very reason that they are widely accepted in the society. In contrast, if the firms that adopt these practices are few, there would be a tendency for employees to move among firms, and the firm would not have to be concerned about its reputation among prospective employees. In other words, the society in which such practices as lifetime employment or seniority-based pay is not present—in concrete terms, a non-Japanese-style labor practice in which employment is fluid and merit pay is widely practiced—is also stable and rational.

The Japanese-style labor-management relationship with such strategic complementarity can generate two different stable equilibriums—the situation in which it is widely present in the society (Equilibrium B in Figure 3) and the situation in which it is present but only as an exception (Equilibrium A in Figure 3). This diagram illustrates that the labor-management relationship in contemporary Japan is different than that in other countries. However, this difference is not due to physical factors (such as people's taste or the size of land). Instead, it means that contemporary Japan has adjusted to an equilibrium different from other countries or from the prewar Japan because of historical circumstances, cultural factors, or mere coincidence. Moreover, since it was created by such factors, the Japanese-style, labor-management relationship is maintained as a stable social custom or institution merely because it pervades the entire society.

4. Mutual Complementarity of Japan's Economic System

The idea of strategic complementarity is applicable to more than one individual institution or practice. Mutual complementarity—strategic complementarity among various institutions and practices that comprise an economic system—is also an important element in understanding the stability of an economic system as a whole.

For example, the Japanese-style labor-management relationship, which we examined in the preceding section, is not always consistent with the interest of the stockholders who want short-term profits. In this environment, the stockholders may find it preferable to lay off employees to increase earnings when the business environment slumps. In addition, if the management of affiliate companies which employs long-term workers is unsatisfactory, the firm may prefer to sell these affiliate companies or declare them bankrupt to ensure long-term and stable employment for the firm as a whole. Stockholders are permitted by law to take action such as dismissing the current management executives or using techniques such as a hostile buyout. Therefore, it is difficult to maintain the Japanese-style labor-management relationship without some restraint on the power of stockholders.

In reality, there are mechanisms to control the power of stockholders in Japan, such as the interfirm stockholding and the rule against having external directors.

Figure 4

Average Extent in Society of the Japanese-Style Labor-Management Practice

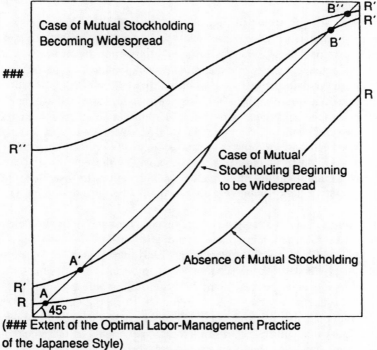

(**###** Extent of the Optimal Labor-Management Practice
of the Japanese Style)

Through stockholding among the corporations which belong to the former Zaibatsu group or among members of a corporate group, through stockholding by financial institutions in the form of bank affiliates (*keiretsu*), and through mutual stockholding among the firms that do business with each other, the ratio of the "secure stockholders" is quite high among the public corporations. Few hostile buyouts have occurred since the period of rapid economic growth. In other words, the mechanisms of mutual stockholding and boards of directors (which are composed solely of internal directors) have played the role of reinforcing the stability of the Japanese-style, labor-management practice.

Let us explain this from a technical viewpoint using the diagram we examined above. Similar to Figure 3, the horizontal axis of Figure 4 is the proportion (*p*) of the firms that have adopted the Japanese-style, labor-management practice and the vertical axis stands for the degree of optimal, labor-management practice in individual firms. The optimal response of an individual firm does not necessarily depend on the proportion of firms that adopt the Japanese-style practice in the society as a whole. For example, as pointed out earlier, the more mutual stockholding there is in the entire society, the more advantageous it is to the Japanese-style, labor-management practice which is in a mutually complementary relationship with it. As a result, compared with the situation which has no mutual stockholding, the optimal response curve shifts upward when mutual stockholding is prevalent.[9]

For this reason, as shown in Figure 4, when mutual stockholding does not exist and the optimal response curve is $R-R$, the equilibrium that is attained in the society can only be A, which is centered around non-Japanese-style, labor-management practice. However, when mutual stockholding becomes more widespread, the optimal response curve would shift to $R'-R'$, and, added to the non-Japanese-style equilibrium A', the Japanese-style, labor-management practice may be formed as a stable equilibrium B'. Furthermore, if the mutual complementarity between the two becomes sufficiently great and the mutual stockholding becomes widespread in the society, the optimal response curve turns to $R''-R''$. At this point, it is conceivable for the equilibrium centered around non-Japanese-style, labor-management practices to disappear and for the Japanese-style, labor-management practice to be the only stable equilibrium B''.[10]

Thus, even if there is strategic complementarity among individual elements which make up the economic system in modern Japan, it does not necessarily mean that it leads to a stable mechanism. Only when each of the mutually complementary elements in the economic system become a widespread mechanism in the society does the stability of the system as a whole emerges.

However, it is not very easy to sustain mutual stockholding. In the so-called bubble boom in the late 1980s, the ratio of secure stockholders declined with the advent of equity financing. Thus, if firms want to perpetuate mutual stockholding and at the same time they want to procure funds through stock issues, they have to keep buying each other's newly issued stock—even at the risk of jeopardizing their own funds. One reason that mutual stockholding was possible in Japan was because the fund supply (in a macro sense) was carried out, not in the form of direct financing such as stocks and corporate bonds, but through indirect methods such as bank loans.

. . . Before 1935 most corporate funding was obtained through the issuance of stocks and bonds. However, during and after the war bank lending became the main channel for the supply of funds in modern Japan through a system of indirect financing. The democratization and reduction in the size of stockholding through an event, such as the dissolution of *zaibatsu*, gave birth to the fund circulation structure in Japan that is oriented toward indirect finance. Subsequently, the rapid growth of mutual stockholding caused a drastic restriction in the voice of the stockholders and assured the voice of employees and affiliate firms (stakeholders) who made a commitment to the firm through their long-term investment in it.

Nevertheless, a moral liability could arise if the voice of the firm's stakeholders (employees and affiliated firms) is permitted with no restraint. In fact, when the labor movement grew during the 1950s, production activities were interrupted and investments declined in many firms. To promote efficiently the activities of businesses, mechanisms to control moral liability are necessary.

The main mechanism for carrying out this role in postwar Japan is the "mainbank system," (as mentioned in Chapter 3 of this book). In this system, the main bank represents all the parties concerned in monitoring the management and financial conditions of an individual firm. It can be expressed as as a system in which other banks that have loans outstanding with the firm are saved the expense of monitoring. If the main bank fails to monitor the firm, it is possible for the firm's management condition to decline. In such a case, the main bank has to bear the major expense (relative to other banks involved) of rescuing the firm.[11]

Thus, the main bank has a more than normal incentive to monitor the financial condition of the firms to which they made loans. Other lending banks know that their own risks are small even if they curtail their monitoring activities. In other words, the indirect finance system in Japan permits, through the main-bank system, an individual firm to borrow from various banks in order to avert any disadvantage in business transactions. It also reduces an individual bank's risk because several banks share the risk of lending money to a given firm, while it enables banks to undertake monitoring activities at a low social cost.

Thus, in comparison with the stockholders' power over management and the hostile buyouts stressed by the neoclassical economics, the safeguard against any moral liability within the firm functions through the monitoring activities of the main bank. Furthermore, because of its reputation as the main bank and its concomitant rescuing responsibility at the time of a management crisis, the main bank is compelled to commit itself to the firm's long-term stability and growth. In this sense, the postwar fund procurement system (characterized mainly by indirect financing) and the main-bank system can be thought of as a mutually complementary relationship with lifetime employment and seniority systems. In turn, this system generates an incentive for employees to commit themselves to the firm's long-term investment.

A similar relationship exists in the production affiliation (subcontracting or *keiretsu*) between parts producers and assemblers in the manufacturing industries such as automobiles and home appliances. For example, if production affiliates (*keiretsu*) make a few producers responsible for parts supply, the competition produces cost reduction and enhances quality. As a result, the manufacturers are able to obtain better parts at lower prices.

At the same time, by making the parts manufacturers responsible for the parts supply until the next model change, a favorable climate is created because parts producers invest capital in facilities to build the needed parts. Further, by returning a part of the profits earned from the cost reduction to the parts producers, the industry creates an incentive for parts producers to reduce costs. The production affiliates (*keiretsu*) also contribute to employment stability in the manufacturing industry because, if business slacks, it switches to internal production while reducing the supply of the parts producers.

As discussed above, through a variety of mechanisms between labor and management and between individual firms, the economic system of the modern Japan has generated incentives for long-term commitments from stakeholders such as employees, corporate executives, main banks, and affiliate firms. Through the resulting trust relationship, the system created efficient business activities by promoting cooperation and harmony among the stakeholders.

However, such a system develops hand in hand with rigid and immobile economic transactions, as typically observed in the employment of workers. Therefore, once an immobile transaction collapses, it is difficult to find a replacement partner for transactions. In particular, the collapse of a firm or an industry creates lost employment opportunities for a large number of workers and lost business opportunities for firms. This has the potential to create a crisis in the entire economic system.

The government-business relationship covers the systemic risk that is inherent in the Japanese economic system. Since each industry is overseen (that is, protected and nurtured) by a single administrative agency, a long-term relationship (or collusion) develops between existing businesses and the overseeing government agency. In particular, guidance provided by the government administration in Japan is frequently conducted through trade organizations. It is said that the overseeing government agency has input into every decision a firm makes.

This industrial policy, using the "protective convoy method," was evident during the reconstruction period, the period of high economic growth, as well as in the banking administration of the Ministry of Finance. The concern of government administrators is to maintain order and stability in the industry by controlling excess competition and preventing drastic changes within the industry they oversee, especially the destruction of existing major firms. In addition, in the event existing major corporations are confronted with a crisis, these government administrators strive to stabilize employment and business transactions with buyouts, mergers of related firms, or direct administrative intervention.

This system functions only because the give-and-take relationship creates an environment in which private business can expect government assistance in times of crisis. The firms follow the administrative guidance and, in return, the overseeing government agency receives the benefit of guaranteed jobs for retiring bureaucrats (the golden parachute) at the firms and trade organizations under its supervision. . . . Such a relationship itself is a system that was established after the war as a carryover of the wartime, economic-control system.

The economic system in Japan as a whole is extremely resilient and stable, being the product of mutual complementarity among the individual elements (such as lifetime employment, seniority-based pay, mutual stockholding, and the government-private sector relationship that makes use of government administrative guidance). It is reasonable to assume that the economic system of modern Japan formed because the various mechanisms that comprise this economic system were forced on the government during the war.

5. Conclusion: The Possibility of a System Reformation and the System Inertia

In this chapter, using the concepts of strategic complementarity and mutual complementarity, we examined the economic system of modern Japan from a theoretical standpoint. Another implication of such a theoretical assessment is that the origin of the contemporary Japanese economic system (which is the theme of the entire book) is closely related to the system change which occurred during the war period. In other words, if we are to understand an economic mechanism or economic system that is established within a society as a "state of stable equilibrium," we must appreciate the inertia within the economic system itself that tends to perpetuate the system, as well as the unified coordinating behavior necessary for the society as a whole to change it.

For example, take the case illustrated in Figure 3. Assume that the system established in a society is a non-Japanese-style labor-management relationship and the current state is at point A. Thus, in this society, the average number of labor-management relationships that are Japanese-style or the proportion of firms that adopt the Japanese-style, labor-management relationship is only p_A. As the arrow in the diagram indicates, this equilibrium A is locally stable, and the society sustains the inertia to maintain A.

For this reason, even if some firms return to the Japanese-style labor-management relationship, it remains advantageous to use a non-Japanese-style relationship unless their proportion exceeds p_C. In time, the Japanese-style relationship would vanish, thus returning the society to equilibrium A.

In order for the Japanese-style, labor-management relationship to take root, it is necessary that the proportion of the firms exceeding p_C adopt the Japanese-style, labor-management relationship all at once. If a proportion of the firms larger than p_C adopts the Japanese-style labor-management relationship all at once, it becomes more advantageous for the firms that had not adopted it to switch to the Japanese-style labor-management relationship. Therefore, in time the equilibrium B is realized. Thus, in order to move from one equilibrium to another, it is necessary that the whole society simultaneously adopt a new institution or mechanism.

Also, as illustrated in Figure 4, an effort to change only one of the components of a system (such as the labor-management relationship) is often not possible by itself. When various components are mutually complementary, the inertia to return to the original system cannot be overcome without changing these elements at the same time and for the society as a whole. Japan's experience during the period between the 1930s and the 1940s indicates that such an inertia could have been overcome by the forced introduction into the entire society of an artificial system as a result of the abnormality during war.

Viewed in this manner, it must be evident that it is not easy to reform the business society of modern Japan, to transplant the Japanese-style system overseas, or to reform the economic system of the former socialist countries. In order to carry out these changes intentionally, the ideal situation is to have the following preconditions. First, to change one economic system into another economic system, it is necessary to examine whether the new system under consideration possesses a desirable property as a future system. Second, even if the new system is a desirable system, it is essential to assess in advance the various mechanisms that comprise it, to examine the property of these components such as their strategic complementarity and their mutual complementarity among the incentives and mechanisms, and to examine beforehand whether the system is stable overall. Third, assuming that the new system is both desirable and stable, it is crucial to clarify the unified effort necessary to the entire society (both to overcome the inertia inherent in the existing system and to realize the new system), and to make a commitment to create the needed incentives.

We cannot necessarily assume that the operations carried out in wartime Japan . . . fulfilled these three conditions. The debate that persists in Japan today focuses only on individual mechanisms and neglects the consistency and inertia within the system as a whole. However, in comparison with this debate, it is certain that, added to a unique condition of wartime, our argument was presented with systematic analysis and action.

Notes

1. This article is the concluding chapter of the above book [see note, p. 96] whose objective is "to make it clear that the economic system of contemporary Japan is such that many of its constituent elements were deliberately created during the period from the wartime of the 1930s to the defeat in World War II, superseding the Anglo-Saxon classical market economic system" (p. ii). The book is volume 6 of the *Contemporary Economic Study Series* and consists of the following nine chapters:

(1) The Economic System of Contemporary Japan and Its Historical Origin (Okazaki and Okuno)

(2) The Financial System and Regulation (Ueda)

(3) The Main Bank System (Teranishi)

(4) The Enterprise System (Okazaki)

(5) "Japanese-Style" Labor-Management Relationship (Odaka)

(6) Functions of Trade Associations (Yonekura)

(7) "Japanese-Style" Taxation and Public Finance (Kanno)

(8) The Food Control System and Agricultural Cooperatives (Kawagoe)

(9) The Economic System of Contemporary Japan: Its Structure and the Possibility of Change (Okuno)

2. For example, see Aoki (1988, 1992). However, the main objective of the re-

search in these papers is a comparison of a planned economy with a market economy in their economic system.

3. Readers who are looking for a technical discussion of game theory and the Nash equilibrium should see, for example, Okuno and Suzumura (1988), Chapter 26.

4. If $p = \frac{1}{2}$, both the right-side traffic and the left-side traffic are the optimal response and there is no reason for p to change. Therefore, such a state C is also a Nash equilibrium. However, if the value of p deviates even slightly from one-half, p changes according to the direction of the arrow. This means that the Nash equilibrium is not stable.

5. For multiple equilibriums and path dependence, see Cooper and John (1988) and Romer (1986). Also, see Ito, Kiyono, Okuno and Suzumura (1988), Chapter 6, for a study of Japan's industrial policy from this point of view.

6. For details of strategic complementarity see Bulow, Geanakoplos, and Klemperer (1985) and Okuno and Suzumura (1988), Chapter 28.

7. It is not necessarily possible to define continuously the degree of desirable labor-management practice from $s = 0$ to $s = 1$. However, the concept of strategic complementarity can easily be expanded to a noncontinuous and discrete strategy. See Milgrom, Qian, and Roberts (1991).

8. As made clear in this diagram, the presence of strategic complementarity (the fact that the response curve is upward and to the right) is a necessary condition but not a sufficient condition. This is because, for example, there is only one equilibrium if the response curve is upward and to the right, but its slope is less than the slope of the line at a 45° angle.

9. Here, for the sake of clarity, we differentiate between strategic complementarity and mutual complementarity, but they are basically the same concept. See Bulow, Geanakoplos, and Klemperer (1985) as well as Okuno and Suzumura (1988), Chapter 28.

10. If mutual stockholding and labor-management practice are mutually dependent, it is obviously conceivable that an opposite effect may occur. That is, as the Japanese labor-management practice becomes more and more widespread, the advantage of mutual stockholding increases.

11. Another point of discussion pertains to the reason why the main bank rescues a firm whose business performance has declined. We will argue that the main bank engages in a rescue when a decline in the bank's reputation exceeds the cost of rescue.

References

Aoki, Masahiko. 1988. *Information, Incentives, and Bargaining in the Japanese Economy*. Cambridge: Cambridge University Press.

———. 1992. "Japanese Businesses as a System: An Overview of English Language References and Research Issues" (in Japanese). *The Economic Studies Quarterly* 43 (5).

Bulow, J., J. Geanakoplos, and P. Klemperer. 1985. "Multimarket Oligopoly: Strategic Substitutes and Complements." *The Journal of Political Economy* 93:488–511.

Cooper, R., and A. John. 1988. "Coordinating Coordination Failures in Keynesian Models." *Quarterly Journal of Economics* 103:441–64.

Ito, Motoshige, Kazuharu Kiyono, Masahiro Okuno, and Kotaro Suzumura. 1988. *Sangyo Seisaku no Keizai Bunseki* [An Economic Analysis of Industrial Policy]. Tokyo: The Tokyo University Press.

Milgrom, P., Y. Qian, and J. Roberts. 1991. "Complementarities, Momentum, and the Evolution of Modern Manufacturing." *The American Economic Review* 81:85–88.

Okuno, Masahiro, and Kotaro Suzumura. 1988. *Micro Keizaigaku II* [Micro Economics]. Tokyo: Iwanami Shoten.

Romer, P. 1986. "Increasing Returns and Long-Run Growth." *Journal of Political Economy* 94 (5): 1002–37.

Masahiro Okuno-Fujiwara is professor of economics, University of Tokyo.

Source/Permission: "Gendai Nihon no Keizai System: Sono Kozo to Henkaku no Kanosei." Chapter 9 of book *Gendai Nihon Keizai System no Genryu* [The Origin of the Economic System of Japan], edited by Tetsuji Okazaki and Masahiro Okuno-Fujiwara. Tokyo: Nihon Kezai Shimbunsa, 1993. (Translation originally appeared in *Japanese Economic Studies* 22, Nos. 5 and 6 [September/October-November/December 1994].) Translated with permission by Jane Kurokawa.

Part III

The Business System

4

Japan's Corporate Capitalism in Peril

Hiroshi Okumura

I. Principles of corporate capitalism

Capitalism without capitalists

Yataro Iwasaki (1834–1885), who founded the Mitsubishi Co. about 120 years ago and then later built the Mitsubishi *zaibatsu* around it, openly and without apology proclaimed, "The Mitsubishi Company is nominally a corporation, but it is in fact entirely a private enterprise of the Iwasaki family in which all decisions are made by and all profits belong to the president, myself."

Following Yataro, first his younger brother Yanosuke, then his son Hisaya, and then Yanosuke's son Koyata succeeded in turn to the leadership of the Mitsubishi zaibatsu as stocks of first the Mitsubishi Heavy Industries and then the other companies formed under the "umbrella" of the zaibatsu were publicly offered, but in the prewar period the zaibatsu itself continued to belong to the Iwasaki family. Not only Mitsubishi but also Mitsui and Sumitomo, and even Yasuda, Furukawa, and other smaller zaibatsu, were controlled by a family that owned the stock of and directed the various companies of the group. These families were wealthy capitalists.

Prewar Japan was a capitalist society controlled in this way by capitalist families, a society of antagonism and confrontation between capital and labor. Of course, in prewar Japan the Left identified these capitalist families, together with the Emperor system and the military, as the enemy and called for their overthrow. But, as seen in the May 15 (1932) Incident and the February 26 (1936) Incident, the Right and some of the younger commissioned officers of the military also attacked the zaibatsu monopoly on wealth. They assassinated Takuma Dan (1858–1932), general manager of the Mitsui zaibatsu, and others.

After the war, the zaibatsu were broken up by the American Occupation authorities. The stock holdings of the zaibatsu families were expropriated and the

Table 1

Principal Stockholders of Mitsubishi Heavy Industries (March 1991)

	Stock ownership (percent)
Mitsubishi Trust Bank	7.03
Mitsubishi Bank	3.60
Meiji Life Insurance	3.08
Tokio Marine & Fire Insurance	2.08
Sumitomo Trust Bank	2.01
Nippon Life Insurance	1.99
Mitsubishi Corporation	1.58
Toyo Trust Bank	1.55
Sumitomo Life Insurance	1.36
Mitsui Trust Bank	1.34
Subtotal	25.67

families were directed to discontinue participation in the management of the various companies. So, in the cluster of companies now called the Mitsubishi Group there is no company in which the Iwasaki family is a principal stockholder, and the Mitsui and Sumitomo groups are the same.

Examining the principal stockholders of Mitsubishi Heavy Industries, we see that before the war its principal stockholder was the Mitsubishi parent company, and the principal stockholder of the parent company was the Iwasaki family. Today, however, the principal stockholders of Mitsubishi Heavy Industries are all banks, insurance companies, and business corporations, most of them members of the Mitsubishi Group.

As can be seen in Table 1, the principal stockholders of Mitsubishi Heavy Industries are corporations; there are no longer any individual persons in the group. This is true not only of Mitsubishi Heavy Industries but also of almost all of the larger corporations of Japan today. This phenomenon is called "capitalism without capitalists," but, of course, a more accurate label would be "capitalism without individual capitalists."

At present, there are over 1 million corporations in Japan, but of that number there are no more than 2,000 whose stocks are offered publicly and traded on securities exchanges. Most of those companies whose stock is not publicly offered are small- and medium-sized firms, and most of these are family companies. Individual capitalists exist in these companies, of course; they manage them. But, although these companies are organized as corporations in fact they are really individual or family enterprises.

In contrast, most of Japan's large firms, corporations with capitalization of ¥1 billion or more, are companies without individual capitalists, as described above. These companies own more than 40 percent of all the corporate assets of Japan. Of course, there are large companies whose stock is publicly offered in which individuals or families are principal stockholders, but these comprise less than 10 percent of companies whose stocks are listed on securities exchanges.

Japan is dominated by corporate capitalism today because almost all of the principal stockholders of the larger firms are corporations. Corporate capitalism is characterized by features other than just this form of stock ownership, but Japan is today dominated by corporate capitalism, in contrast to the individual capitalist or family capitalism of prewar Japan and of contemporary Europe and America, because of this ownership structure.

The way in which Japan differs from America

And, what about the principal shareholders of large American corporations? The Ford and DuPont families, for example, have always been principal stockholders of the Ford Motor and DuPont Corporations, and to this extent America is an example of capitalism with individual capitalists. Although the Rockefeller family's rate of stock ownership in Exxon and Mobil and others of the old Standard Oil group and in Chase Manhattan Bank and so forth is declining, they are still principal stockholders of these companies.

But, the noteworthy thing about America is the way in which institutional investors have risen to prominence side by side with these individual capitalists. In America, institutional investors include pension funds, investment trusts, life insurance companies, foundations, and so forth. The trust departments of banks, which are entrusted with the management of the assets of pension funds and individual trusts, may also be considered institutional investors. At present, bank trust departments own a notably high percentage of American stocks.

Of these institutional investors, pension funds, for example, are entrusted with the management of the assets of the actual owners (beneficiaries) of the fund, the pension fund participants (company employees). Those responsible for managing these assets, fund managers, must constantly endeavor to maximize the return to the beneficiaries. If a fund manager in a bank trust department were to manage funds to benefit his or her own bank, that would be considered a violation of law and the manager could be punished, in addition to being dismissed as manager by the customer.

Therefore, when stock prices rise institutional investors sell, and they sell quickly in response to attempts to corner stocks such as takeover bids. Institutional investors move quickly to make continuous short-term use of stocks, and as a result corporate managers are forced to manage from a short-term perspective. This phenomenon has been criticized as ruining American corporate management.

In the United States and United Kingdom, these kinds of institutional investors have come to predominate among principal shareholders, but institutional investors own shares of stock as agents of individual pension fund participants and investment trust investors, not as their own assets.

In contrast, in Japan the corporations such as banks and industrial enterprises that are principal shareholders of large companies own stocks as their own assets, a situation decisively different from that in the United States and United Kingdom. As will be noted below, corporate ownership of stocks is also permitted in America, but stock ownership by commercial banks is prohibited and the rate of stock ownership by commercial corporations is lower than in Japan. American antitrust laws are strict, and so corporations cannot freely hold shares of other corporations, as in Japan.

In recent years, stock ownership by institutional investors has increased in Japan, but even together the stock holdings of investment trusts, pension funds, special money-in-trust (*tokkin*), fund trusts, and so forth still constitute a small percent of overall stock ownership. As will be explained below, Japanese life insurance companies cannot be categorized with true institutional investors.

Institutional investors are related to individual stock owners as agents, but Japanese corporations own stocks as corporate assets and so individual ownership is completely absent. This is ownership "of the corporation, by the corporation, and for the corporation." This is the distinctive characteristic of corporate capitalism.

Persons die, but corporations never die

A corporation is an entity endowed by law with the status of a person, but, of course, it has no body, no brain, and no will of its own. While human beings are fated to die, a corporation can live on forever, as long as it is not dissolved. A joint stock company is, of course, a corporation that theoretically can continue to exist forever. In Japan, there actually are companies that have continued in existence for over 100 years, and in Europe there are many companies even older.

Companies directed by individual capitalists are necessarily influenced by the vagaries of mere mortals. And, mortals must die, so questions of inheritance and succession are unavoidable. If an heir is willing to succeed to leadership, then all is well. But, if not then stock holdings must be disposed of in some way.

Even giant American corporations such as Getty Oil, which was owned principally by the Getty family, must be sold off when there is a dispute over succession among the heirs or when a successor able to manage the company cannot be found among the heirs. Getty Oil was acquired by Mobil Oil in 1984.

It has also happened in Japan, as in the case of Akai Electric, that when a company founder dies suddenly and a successor cannot be found in the family the shareholdings must be disposed of and the company is absorbed by a large firm (in this case Mitsubishi Electric).

Sometimes, even when a successor can be found heirs pursuing their own interests demand an increase in dividends even when the company is not making a profit. And, sometimes, for example, in the Recruit case, an owner/founder will sell his holdings to another company (Daiei) to suit himself.

The immortal corporation is free from the whimsies and circumstances of individuals. And, when a corporation becomes a stockholder in another company that company is then also freed from the predicaments and fancies of individual human beings. It then becomes possible to manage these companies with a long-term perspective. When freed from the arbitrariness of the individual, the management of a company can then be based upon rational calculation.

In contrast, when institutional investors are principal stockholders, as in America, the situation is different. For example, in the case of pension funds participants desire to maximize pension benefit amounts, so investments are made in pursuit of short-term profits. Especially in the case of America, company pensions are usually fixed-amount benefits, and when the return on investments is insufficient the company must make up the balance. Therefore, companies constantly pressure the fund managers who invest their pension fund assets to maximize return on investment. And, fund managers are remunerated on an incentive basis, in proportion to their success, so they invest with short-term returns in mind.

As a result, American institutional investors are mobile, undependable investors while Japan's corporate stockholders are, in contrast, permanent, settled shareholders, owners with long-term, fixed commitments. Because the shares of Japanese joint stock companies are held by established, enduring corporations with steady, reliable interests, these companies can be managed with a long-term perspective. Because there are no individual investors to demand an increase in dividends even when profits are low, profits are as much as possible not distributed as dividends but are instead retained within the company.

Many economists assert that in Japan there are no stockholders, so corporate directors, free from stockholder influence, can manage their companies with a long-term perspective. But, these economists are mistaken; Japan's joint stock companies are not without shareholders, but their principal shareholders are predominantly corporations. They are without individuals as principal shareholders, but corporate shareholders are in existence, and it is the existence of these corporate shareholders, and, as will be described below, the way in which corporations hold each other's stocks, that are the special characteristics of Japanese companies that make it possible for them to operate with a long-term perspective that transcends individual arbitrariness.

Pursuit of long-term returns

Capitalism based upon individual capitalists, of which prewar Japan was an example and in which category the institutional ownership of the United States and United Kingdom may also be included, cannot avoid instability caused by the capriciousness of the individual person and the inevitability of death. In contrast, corporate capitalism is immune from the problem of death, unimpeded by individual arbitrariness, and free to solely pursue profit. Companies in a corporate capitalist system can be managed on a purely rational basis and with a long-term perspective. This has been the strength of the Japanese economy since the end of the period of rapid economic growth, particularly after the "oil crisis" of 1973. This is the secret of the success of Japanese companies.

The basic principle of corporate capitalism is company loyalty. Executives and employees are devoted to the company and work zealously for its success. Of course, when they do so the company's profits increase, but in the west this kind of company loyalty is rarely obtained. There, the tradition of individualism is powerful, and as long as individualism continues to be a strong force corporate loyalty will be weak.

However, Japan is the only country in the world that has succeeded on the basis of an ideology of company loyalty and in which corporate capitalism is firmly established, and therein lies an important and fundamental problem. No matter how strong corporate capitalism becomes, it can never completely do without the natural individual human being. Capitalist systems and socialist systems and all other systems are, after all, creations of human beings. Both the nation state and the corporation originate as the creations of human beings.

Thoroughgoing statism eventually provokes individuals to react to overthrow it; this is the lesson of Nazi Germany and Japanese militarism. Soviet state socialism met the same fate. In the same way, if corporate capitalism becomes absolute its excesses will be evident and it too will be overthrown by individuals.

At present, the contradictions of Japanese corporate capitalism are exposed, and individuals are retaliating against it. The structure of corporate capitalism is showing cracks; it is beginning to break apart.

II. Corporatization of stock ownership

Stock ownership in Japan

Table 2 shows changes over time in the ownership of Japan's listed, publicly held companies. Herein, ownership by financial institutions (other than investment trusts) and business corporations is referred to as "corporate ownership." We can see that in 1991 corporate ownership reached 66.0 percent and individual ownership was a mere 23.2 percent.

The decline of the rate of ownership by individuals from the almost 70 percent level at which it stood soon after the war is conspicuous. In contrast, in the increase of the rate of corporate ownership from a mere 15.5 percent to nearly 70 percent we can see just how rapid the advance of corporate stock ownership was in Japan during this period. From these figures, we can see that the decline in the rate of stock ownership by individuals and the increase in the rate of corporate ownership occurred simultaneously, but it was the increase in corporate ownership that caused the decrease in the rate of individual ownership, not vice versa.

Taking a look at the specifics of corporate ownership, we can see that the rate

Table 2

Stock Ownership by Corporations and Individuals
(All Listed Companies, percent)

Year	Financial institutions (except investment trusts)	Business corporations	Individuals
1949	9.9	5.6	69.1
1950	12.6	11.0	61.3
1955	19.5	13.2	53.1
1960	23.1	17.8	46.3
1965	23.4	18.4	44.8
1970	30.9	23.1	39.9
1975	34.5	26.3	33.5
1980	37.3	26.0	29.2
1985	40.9	24.8	25.2
1991	41.5	24.5	23.2

Source: Association of National Stock Exchanges, *Kabushihi Bumpui Jokyo Chosa* (Survey of Stock Ownership Distribution).

of stock ownership by corporations reached 66 percent in 1991, but actually this figure includes the holdings of some institutional investors as well. The holdings of investment trusts are excluded from this figure, but still included therein are the holdings of institutional investors such as special money-in-trust, fund trusts, pension funds, and so forth. These institutional investors' holdings are included in the figures for trust banks and insurance companies and the rate is unknown. But, it is estimated that, even including the holdings of investment trusts, the rate of stock ownership by institutional investors does not exceed 10 percent.

And, although the rate of stock ownership by life insurance companies has reached 13.2 percent, Japan's life insurance companies cannot be said to be true institutional investors because gains from increases in stock values are retained as "latent earnings" (*fukumieki*) and not passed on to policyholders. Also, most insurance companies have fixed portfolios, just as do other corporations. So, while in America life insurance companies are considered institutional investors, in Japan life insurance companies maintain a pretense of being institutional investors but are actually more similar to corporate shareholders.

In America, the Securities Exchange Commission (SEC) published statistics on stock ownership through 1980, but the surveys were discontinued as a budget reduction measure by the Reagan administration and current figures are unknown. But, extrapolating from the FRB's "Flow of Funds," in 1990 institutional investors owned 56.4 percent of the total market value of all stocks issued. The extent of corporate ownership of stocks is not revealed in these statistics, but, of course, corporate stock ownership exists even in America.

According to SEC statistics, in 1980 business corporations owned 15.2 percent of all stocks. However, in the SEC statistics business corporation ownership of each other's stock is considered to cancel out, and so the amount is netted out of the total amount of stock issued. Here, we can catch a glimpse of the American way of thinking. But, calculated the Japanese way the figure is 15.2 percent, a low figure compared to the rate of stock ownership of business corporations in Japan.

The point at which America and Japan are fundamentally different is the absence of stock ownership by commercial banks in America. This is because such ownership is prohibited by American banking laws. As institutional investors, American commercial banks hold shares of stock in trust accounts but as bank corporations they own no shares on their own.

Under the provisions of the Antimonopoly Act, Japan's banks are allowed to freely hold up to 5 percent of the stock issued by other companies. This limit on stock ownership by banks was set at 5 percent in the Antimonopoly Act of 1947, loosened to 10 percent when the act was amended for the second time in 1953, and then tightened again to 5 percent in 1977, when the act was amended for the third time.

Stock ownership by business corporations was completely prohibited by the original 1947 Antimonopoly Act, but the prohibition was loosened when the act was amended for the first time in 1949 and then again in 1953, and thereafter it was abandoned in actual practice. If this provision of the Antimonopoly Act had not been relaxed, the corporatization of stock ownership could never have progressed as it did.

This corporatization of stock ownership is not something that has always been characteristic of Japan. Before the war, of course, and for some time afterward, stock ownership by individuals predominated. And, if the Antimonopoly Act had not been amended corporatization would never have progressed as far as it has. So, generally speaking it can be said to have been caused primarily by features of the system. It is certainly not something inherently or traditionally Japanese.

Permanent stockholder systems

The principal cause of the progressive corporatization of stock ownership in postwar Japan was that this was the means devised by Japanese companies to prevent takeovers. The Occupation authorities dissolved the zaibatsu, and shares owned by the zaibatsu parent companies and the zaibatsu families were dispersed. Subsequently, there were instances in which speculators cornered stocks, for example, the Yowa Real Estate (later the Mitsubishi Estate Co.) case and Hideki Yokoi's buyup of the stock of Shirokiya (later Tokyu Department Store Co.).

In principle, once stocks have been publicly issued there is no way to avoid the danger of their being cornered by someone. And, once a company's shares have been bought up the management of the company can be taken over. This is something that cannot be avoided because a joint stock company is based upon the principle of the rule of a majority of the stock. Thus it is that buyouts and takeover bids are openly conducted, everyday business events in the United States and United Kingdom and there are rules governing the way in which they are performed.

However, in Japan while on the one hand stocks were issued publicly on the other an attempt was made to prevent takeovers. Any such attempt would likely be at odds with the tenets of joint stock corporations, but in this case the result was Japan's unique system of permanent stockholding. In the previously mentioned case of Yowa Real Estate, for example, after it was taken over a company of the Mitsubishi Group acquired its shares and became its permanent stockholder. And, to prevent any further takeovers the Mitsubishi company maneuvered to lock up the shares of this company by persuading the bank and the other corporations of the Mitsubishi Group to hold its stock.

In 1964, Japan joined the OECD and agreed to liberalize its capital transactions. But, if Japan's capital transactions had truly been liberalized foreign capital would have been able to buy up the shares of Japanese companies. Fearing takeovers by foreign capital, Japanese companies led by Toyota Motors moved in concert to create permanent stockholder systems.

In this system, a company's permanent stockholders are practically all corporations belonging to the same *keiretsu,* or group of companies, or are corporations with which the company regularly does business as a customer or supplier. From the latter half of the 1960s through the 1970s, the corporatization of stock ownership increased rapidly because of the adoption of these permanent stockholder systems as a way to deal with the liberalization of capital transactions. And, because of this corporatization of stock ownership the number of shares circulating in the market declined and the price of shares rose as the supply and demand relationship became more easily controlled.

And, at that same time Japanese companies' method of raising capital was changing from the allotment of new shares issued at face or par value to shareholders to public offerings at market value. Public offerings at market value became prevalent soon after the first such offering, of Nippon Gakki (now Yamaha) in 1969. With public offerings at market value, when stock prices rose that much more capital became available to the company, so means were sought to raise stock prices. When it became evident that stock prices had risen because of the permanent stockholder system adopted in response to capital market liberalization, then companies further employed the permanent stockholder system to raise stock prices for public offerings at market value. In retrospect, it is nothing but a Columbus' egg, but the idea seems to have been the brainchild of one Hiroshi Okaniwa, managing director of the Sanko Steamship Company. He called it "high stock price management."

However, the establishment of a permanent stockholder system to raise stock prices just prior to the issuance of new shares could be considered stock manipulation, a violation of the Securities and Exchange Act. In 1972, Kyodo Shiryo

(Feedgrain) Co. actually was cited for so doing. So, thereafter companies began to secure their permanent stockholder systems as a routine, continuous business practice. To engage in this practice just prior to a stock issue was considered a violation of the law, while doing so as a continuous procedure was not.

The creation by a company of a permanent stockholder system constitutes interference by an issuing company with the price of its own stock, so it certainly is a kind of stock manipulation. And, while in theory shareholders select the directors of a joint stock company, a permanent stockholder system is a means for an issuing company to select its shareholders, so it is also a violation of the principle of "shareholder democracy." In these ways, a permanent stockholder system is something fundamentally at odds with the basic principles of the joint stock company and so no such practice exists in Europe or America. If ever attempted there, it would be subjected to shareholder lawsuit. However, in Japan this violation of the basic principles of the joint stock company is effected on a large scale, openly in the full light of day, and with the backing of the government.

Excess issues: Plummeting stock prices

This practice of creating permanent stockholder systems to raise capital by issuing stocks at market value became prevalent in the 1970s, but in the 1980s companies devised even more clever methods to raise capital—the issuing of convertible bonds and warrant obligations. Convertible bonds are corporate debentures convertible under specified conditions to equity shares. Warrant obligations are corporate debentures carrying the right to take deli of shares of new stock issues under specified conditions. In both cases, investors profit when stock prices rise.

Along with new issues of equity shares, convertible bonds and warrant obligations are both means by which companies can procure funds and so are referred to collectively as "equity financing," but both are means by which a stock-issuing company can profit from increases in the price of its stock; to take advantage of equity financing, companies create permanent stockholding systems and seek to raise stock prices.

However, equity financing and permanent stockholder systems are fundamentally in conflict with each other. The use of equity financing increases the number of outstanding shares of stock, or potential shares of stock (unconverted convertible bonds and warrant obligations whose rights to deli of shares of new stock issues have not yet been exercised). These new shares are supposed to be absorbed by the permanent stockholder system, so as the use of equity financing increased the permanent stockholder system exerted itself more and more and the interaction between equity financing and the permanent stockholder system became a kind of vicious circle.

Throughout the 1980s, these two fundamentally contradictory systems of equity financing and permanent stockholding proceeded as though they could coexist forever. Japan's stock market prices rose as if there were no ceiling, and individuals became drunk on the seeming alchemy or legerdemain of the contrivance of ever-rising stock prices.

The collapse began in January 1990. The permanent stockholder systems had been unable to keep pace with the enormous expansion of equity financing in the latter half of the 1980s and stock prices plummeted. From the ceiling of ¥38,915 reached by the Tosho Nikkei Index of Stock Prices on December 29, 1989, stocks began to fall on the opening day of trading in 1990 and after one temporary reco continued to decline still further until even the ¥15,000 level was broken through in August 1992, a decline in value of over 60 percent from the 1989 peak and far greater than that of the "Financial Panic" of 1965.

In the midst of this declining market, in summer 1991 the events of the "securities scandal" occurred. The investing public exploded in anger against the major securities firms, and Japan's securities firms, beginning with Nomura Securities, faced their most dangerous predicament of the postwar period. Investors among the general public and the securities firms were not the only ones to feel the effects of the stock market crash. Banks and business corporations also received a heavy blow. The 1965 panic also dealt a heavy blow to individual investors and the securities firms, but its influence on banks and business corporations was slight because at that time the corporatization of stock ownership had not yet advanced far and neither banks nor business corporations owned large numbers of stocks. Beginning in 1990, on the other hand, banks and business corporations were dealt an enormous blow.

Corporations such as banks and business companies can list the value of assets such as land and stocks on their balance sheets at either the original (acquisition) cost or at the lower of the acquisition cost and the current market value, but the value of land and stocks has increased so much that generally the original cost method is used. When the value of stocks rises, the difference between current market value and original acquisition cost is retained within the company as latent earnings and nowhere shown on the company's balance sheet. These latent earnings are a kind of concealed asset, but when the company loses money in its principal line of business these latent earnings are coughed up to cover this loss.

In 1988, the Bank for International Settlements announced that to promote sound bank management it would require banks to achieve a minimum ratio of net worth to total capital of 8 percent by March 1993, but Japan's banks were far from being able to meet that standard. To comply, Japanese banks requested permission to include as much as 45 percent of the latent earnings of their shareholdings in the calculation of their equity capital in the belief that thereby they would barely be able to meet the new requirement. But, when stock prices plummeted even that became difficult to accomplish and they were forced to move quickly to use other methods, such as restricting loans.

Both banks and business corporations were managed in a way dependent upon their concealed assets, these latent earnings. As a result, during the 1980s the management of banks and companies became highly speculative and slipshod, leading to the black market loans that were revealed in the 1990s, but it was the stock market crash that in one blow forced this festering pus to the surface. A series of companies failed at stock speculations and suffered heavy losses, and there were many large companies that covered "latent losses" by making use of reserves and special funds.

The equity financing and permanent stockholder systems of the 1980s compelled Japan's corporate capitalism to become speculative and led company directors into unmanageable predicaments. And, then in the 1990s the stock market crash caused cracks to appear in the structure of Japan's corporate capitalism itself. But, it was corporate capitalism's violation of basic principles of the joint stock company that invited this result. The contradictions inherent in Japan's corporate capitalism finally came to the surface.

III. Irrationality of reciprocal ownership

Japan's unique way of doing things

One unique characteristic of the Japanese business corporation is the high percentage of its outstanding common stocks that are owned by other corporations, but an even more noteworthy feature is the way in which Japanese corporations own each other's stock. Corporate stock ownership can be a one-way relationship between two companies or it can be reciprocal. The latter can be said to be unique to Japan. There are a few cases of reciprocal ownership in Germany also, but there is no other country in which reciprocal ownership is as extensive as it is in Japan.

The simplest form of reciprocal ownership is seen when company A and company B own shares of each other's stock. An example of this is Mitsubishi Heavy Industries, which owns 3.02 percent of the outstanding shares of Mitsubishi Bank while Mitsubishi Bank owns 3.62 percent of stocks of Mitsubishi Heavy Industries. This kind of simple reciprocal ownership is widespread.

When many simple reciprocal ownership relationships are superimposed, more complicated patterns of reciprocal ownership are formed. These can be called circular or matrix forms of reciprocal ownership. Taking another example from the Mitsubishi Group, Mitsubishi Heavy Industries has reciprocal ownership relationships not just with Mitsubishi Bank but also with the Mitsubishi Corp., Tokio Marine & Fire Insurance Co., Mitsubishi Chemical Industries, and other corporate members of the Mitsubishi Group. But, Mitsubishi Bank also has reciprocal ownership relationships with Mitsubishi Corp., Tokio Marine & Fire Insurance Company, Mitsubishi Chemical Industries, and so forth. These relationships, when diagrammed, form a matrix; no matter which direction you go in when tracing ownership, you circle round and round the group—there is no ultimate owner. If you were to construct a table of such ownership with companies owning shares of other companies on the horizontal axis and companies owned in part by other companies on the vertical axis almost every resulting square would be filled in (except for those in the diagonal line representing a company's ownership of its own stock, which is illegal in Japan).

This kind of matrix form of reciprocal ownership can be seen in its classic form in the Mitsubishi, Mitsui, Sumitomo, and other such groups of companies. In contrast, independent companies also have reciprocal relationships with other companies, but these other companies have no such relationships with each other. This pattern can be called a radial form of reciprocal ownership.

Reciprocal ownership patterns of this kind existed before the war. For example, the Mitsubishi parent company, Mitsubishi Bank, Mitsubishi Electric, and Mitsubishi Chemical had reciprocal ownership relationships but the rate of ownership by the Mitsubishi parent company of the other corporations in the zaibatsu was far higher than any of the other reciprocal relationships, and this radial form was the primary ownership structure. In the 1930s, public offerings of zaibatsu shares were made as a reform gesture, and to prevent the acquisition of these shares by outsiders reciprocal ownership was partially developed but the number of shares involved was not large.

Reciprocal ownership developed extensively only after the war, after the zaibatsu had been disbanded. The Occupation authorities ordered disbanding of the zaibatsu; the stock-holding parent companies were dissolved and the shareholdings of the zaibatsu families were confiscated. The various companies that had formerly been associated under the zaibatsu umbrella then dispersed, but after the Antimonopoly Act was amended for the second time in 1953 reciprocal ownership began to advance and the old zaibatsu were reconstituted as company groups.

Reciprocal ownership was adopted to prevent outside takeovers and facilitate the reunification of the old zaibatsu, but in response to the reactivation of the old zaibatsu the Fuyo, Dai-Ichi, Sanwa, and other groups also began to promote reciprocal ownership within their circles. And, independent companies also established radial-type reciprocal ownership relationships with the banks and other business corporations with which they had dealings.

Reciprocal ownership was, of course, widely pursued at the peak of the equity financing period, during the 1980s, but as the use of equity financing expanded the permanent shareholder systems were not able to keep pace, and as a result the rate of reciprocal ownership decreased. In the Mitsubishi Group, for example, the rate of ownership of companies by other firms in the group declined from 36.94 percent in 1985 to 35.45 percent in 1989, and this same tendency was seen in other groups as well.

Violations of the principles of joint stock companies

When company A increases its capitalization by ¥100 million and company B pays up this amount and then increases its capitalization by an equal amount that is paid up in turn by company A, the capitalization of each company has been increased by ¥100 million each without even ¥1 of real investment. If this is done repeatedly, there is no limit to the extent to which capitalization can be puffed up, but in reality no investment has been made at all. Reciprocal ownership relationships between business corporations have an irrationality of this kind.

One of the basic principles of the joint stock corporation is full capitalization, the requirement that a company must hold assets corresponding to the amount of capitalization. When this is not the case, parties dealing with the company and thinking that the company is secure because it has a capitalization of such and such an amount have been deceived. Companies' reciprocal ownership relationships are a violation of the principle of full capitalization and are contrary to the principles of the joint stock company.

Assume, for example, that company B owns 51 percent of the outstanding shares of company A and vice versa. Mr. "a," chief executive of company A, can control company B and the chief executive of company B, Mr. "b," can likewise control company A. Neither Mr. a nor Mr. b own any shares of stock on their own account, but as agents of companies A and B they direct each other's firms. In contrast, parties who have made real investments in subscribing to 49 percent of the stock of the two companies are unable to control these companies despite having actually invested. This is an irrationality.

For this reason, reciprocal ownership is considered a violation of the principles of joint stock companies and is strictly limited in western Europe. In Korea, the Fair Trade Practices Act of 1986 prohibited reciprocal ownership within zaibatsu. In Japan, however, despite the fact that reciprocal ownership existed to an extent unseen in any other country, no attempt to regulate it was ever made until 1981, when amendments to the commercial code were to have regulated reciprocal stock ownership in the following way.

In cases in which a company A owned 25 percent or more of the stock of a company B, even if company B owned shares of company A stock it would be prohibited from exercising its voting rights in general stockholders meetings. This provision does not regulate reciprocal stock ownership itself in any way; it merely restricts the exercise of voting rights. In actual practice, there were few violations of this new provision of the commercial code and the regulation had no practical effect. It seems clear that it was a law designed from the start to be inapplicable to any actual cases. One more provision stipulated that if a company A owned more than 50 percent of the stock of a company B then company B was prohibited from owning any shares of company A stock. But, rather than being a restriction on reciprocal stock ownership, this provision actually strengthened the provision prohibiting company ownership of its own stock because it prevented subsidiaries from owning stock in their parent companies.

Reciprocal ownership became widespread in Japan because of this noninterference of the law, but the practice was still contrary to the principles of joint stock companies and basically irrational. This kind of irrationality could not continue forever; sooner or later, these contradictions would manifest themselves.

Fears of a breakup of reciprocal ownership

As noted above, the rate of reciprocal ownership within company groups began to decline as a result of the widespread use of equity financing in the 1980s, but this was because the reciprocal partners of the permanent shareholder systems did not keep up with the capitalization increases, not because companies sold their holdings of each others' stocks. It was because the denominator (the number of shares issued) increased while the numerator (the number of shares held by the reciprocal partners of the permanent shareholder system) did not increase as much that the rate of reciprocal ownership declined. This was not an actively promoted, intended result but rather an unintended, passively unavoided one.

But, during the stock market crash of the 1990s the situation changed. Prior to that time, with stock prices high, when holdings of other companies' stocks produced latent earnings, corporate shareholders found these holdings rewarding. However, when stock prices plummeted and those latent earnings disappeared those holdings lost their appeal. As prices fell, companies began to quickly dispose of their stocks to realize at least some profit while it was still possible or avoid potential losses from further declines.

Reciprocal shareholding was most advanced in the area of bank stocks; most banks engaged in reciprocal shareholding with their principal corporate customers. And, these companies put their bank stocks up for sale when necessary to save their own skins. As a result, bank stock prices plummeted in 1992 and there was a cry of alarm that the "breakup of reciprocal ownership" had begun as banks whose stocks were being sold off sold their holdings of these companies in return.

But, the breakup of reciprocal ownership was actually not as thoroughgoing as believed because with stock prices plummeting few buyers could be found and stocks could not be sold off when offered. And, when sellers sell in volume it causes stock prices to decline even more precipitously, so sellers in such a condition are unable to dispose of their holdings.

So, while there actually was no widespread breakdown in the system of reciprocal shareholding the fear that such an event could occur became prevalent in the market. It is this fear that continues to pressure stock prices, and it is a fear not without foundation.

As noted above, reciprocal stockholding is an irrationality that is contrary to the basic principles of joint stock companies, and investors harbor the well-founded fear that this irrationality cannot last forever.

When companies practice reciprocal stock ownership, not only is capital not really procured but those stocks owned are actually a waste of capital. Suppose you were a financial officer of a firm considering disposing of reciprocal stock holdings to put funds to work in investment in plants and equipment. It would not do to have the company bought up and taken over as a result; that is why the reciprocal shareholding was necessary in the first place. But, still in that case you would want to be able to dispose of unnecessary shares.

Reciprocal stockholding has also been an object of criticism from foreign countries. This subject has been taken up since 1989 at the United States–Japan Structural Impediment Initiative Talk, and there reciprocal stock ownership has been criticized as an impediment to American acquisition of Japanese companies and an infringement of stockholders' rights.

In response to this criticism from abroad and also domestic fears of a break-down of the reciprocal stockholding system, Japan's leading financial circles have begun to advocate either authorization of the creation of holding companies or a relaxation of the prohibition on a company's ownership of its own stock. The first of these suggestions would require amendment of Article IX of the Antimonopoly Act and the second would require amendment of Article 210 of the Commercial Code, but the interesting thing to note is that Japan's leading financial circles have already become aware of their inability to continue to support the reciprocal stockholding system.

Of course, this system is so well entrenched that it cannot be unraveled in a short period of time, but it cannot be denied now that in the long run this system will be difficult to sustain. And, the foundation of Japan's corporate capitalism is thereby being undermined.

IV. Vanishing dividends

Yield-based investing

The joint stock corporation began with creation of the Dutch East India Company in 1602. Funds invested by capitalists were used in business activities and the profits from those ventures were returned as dividends to the investors; this became the basic idea of the corporation. Investors contributed funds to receive dividends, and so the most important consideration in the management of joint stock companies was the requirement of dividends.

However, in Japan's stock market today there are virtually no investors who invest to receive dividends. Even with stock prices as low as they are today, the average yield on stocks listed on the Tokyo Stock Exchange is about 1 percent. "Yield" is the ratio of the annual dividend to the current price of a stock, and a yield of 1 percent is insignificant. So, investors buy and sell stocks not to receive dividends but solely to realize gains from rising stock prices, but this is not investment; this is speculation.

However, it has not always been so; it has only been since the 1970s that this was true in Japan. Before then, the criterion for stock investments was yield and dividends were an important consideration. Of course, stocks have always been an object of speculation and there have always been speculators looking for gains from rising prices, but before the 1970s most general investors invested on the basis of dividend yields.

If, for example, a company's annual dividend is ¥5 per share and its stock price is ¥100 per share, then the yield is 5 percent. If the yield on government bonds is 7 percent, then an investor will sell this stock and buy bonds. And, conversely, if the stock price declined and the yield increased then an investor would sell bonds and buy the stock. This is yield-based arbitrage. In Japan, yield arbitrage of stocks had been in practice until about 1970.

Government bonds and corporate debentures are issued with fixed-interest-rate yields while stock dividend rates are not fixed. When companies' profits increase, it is possible that dividends will increase, and when there is such an expectation there will be a move to buy stocks and stock prices will increase.

About 1955, the idea of "growth stocks" was imported from the United States to Japan and there was a growth stock "boom" in Japan. The belief was that with corporate growth came increased profits and dividends, and that is true of growth stocks. Because Japan's economy was at that same time entering a period of rapid growth, this growth stock idea became popular. With the anticipation of future dividend increases, current low yields became affordable. Stock prices rose because of the expectation of higher yields on stocks in the future.

As a result, during the growth stock era of the 1950s and 1960s the average yield of Japan's common stocks fell below the interest rate on bank time deposits; at the time, this was called the "yield revolution." Prior to that time, indefinite and uncertain stock dividend yields usually were higher than fixed interest rates on deposit accounts; the yield revolution reversed that relationship. However, this could still be explained in terms of the yield criterion: Even though stock yields based upon current dividends were low, anticipated yields were high based upon expected higher future dividends. This was called the yield revolution but the investment criterion was still yield. The only difference was the calculation of yield based upon future dividend expectations instead of current dividends.

Why not increase dividends?

However, in the 1970s the situation changed. With the 1973 oil crisis as the turning point, Japan's economy shifted from an era of rapid economic growth to an era of slow economic growth, corporate growth rates declined, and the premise of growth stocks was destroyed. Despite that, after a temporary decline in 1974 stock prices continued to rise and yields dropped lower and lower. And, while the phrase "growth stocks" disappeared from use the concept of dividend yield also vanished from the market. During the 1980s, the average stock yield sank through the 1 percent level and by the end of 1989 had declined to 0.4 percent, close to zero.

And, how did this happen? Why did such a contrary phenomenon occur despite the destruction of the basis for growth stocks as Japan's economy entered a period of slower economic growth?

The secret to this phenomenon was the above-mentioned corporatization of stock ownership. Individual investors invest in stocks to obtain dividends or speculate in stocks to realize capital gains when stock prices rise. But, corporate stock investments have a different motive. Japanese corporations form groups of companies, or keiretsu, with ties to each other. The evidence of these ties is stock ownership, and the permanent stockholder system is also a manifestation of these ties.

Corporations that become permanent stockholders of other companies establish bonds with these companies and hold these shares not to obtain dividends but to strengthen these intercompany ties. Stocks are said to have a double nature, with both revenue and control features. The first of these is the right to dividends and the second is the power to direct the management of the company. Generally speaking, corporations own other companies' stock to obtain control, not to claim dividends, so they ignore yields when acquiring shares. In Japan, institution buying has been carried out without regard to yields while stock prices rose.

Further, although these corporations hold each others' shares no company makes demands on other companies for dividend increases because if one company did so its reciprocal shareholding partners would also do so and the result would be completely nonsensical. In this way, when corporations become a company's principal stockholders, and when corporations become reciprocal stockholders, there is no one left to call for dividend increases and no company raises dividends in the absence of a request from principal shareholders.

Here, there is a significant difference between corporate and institutional stockholders. As noted above, in the United States there are many companies whose principal shareholders are institutional investors. Pension funds, for example, must provide pension benefits to retirees, and dividends are necessary to provide these benefits. So, as principal stockholders pension funds demand dividend increases from corporate directors and threaten to dump their shares if no increase is provided. If institutional investors sell off a stock, its price will decline, and so to avoid difficulties the company increases its dividend.

It is often said that Japanese corporations are managed without regard to stockholders and that shareholders' rights are thereby infringed, but this is true only for individual shareholders, not for corporate stockholders. If a principal corporate shareholder were to demand increased dividends, company managers would be forced to comply. And, principal stockholders often interfere with and meddle in corporate management in Japan, so Japanese companies are certainly aware that they have stockholders. The relevant point is that corporate stockholders do not demand dividend increases.

Low payout ratios

It has traditionally been the policy of Japanese companies to declare a dividend of 10 or 15 percent of face value. Most companies have sustained this fixed dividend rate for long periods of time, so it is called the *antei haitou* (consecutive dividend). The face or par value of one share of stock for most companies is ¥50 (although there are some exceptions, such as electric power companies, with the face value of are ¥500, and NTT, with a par value per share of ¥50,000), so the standard stock dividend for most companies has been either ¥5 or ¥7.5 per share, and most Japanese company dividends have been within that range.

At the time when increases in capitalization were effected by new shares issued at face value, a dividend rate of 10 or 15 percent of face value was reasonable, but when new shares came to be issued at market value that rate became meaningless. Despite this, Japanese companies continue to declare dividends based upon par or face value because principal corporate shareholders do not demand dividend increases. As a result, there are many cases in which a company having increased its capitalization by issuing new shares at, for example, a market value of ¥1,000 declares a stock dividend of only ¥5 per share (10 percent of face value), yielding investors who bought in at ¥1,000 a yield of a mere 0.5 percent.

Stock yields declined during the 1970s after companies changed to issuing new shares at market value but yields declined because principal corporate stockholders did not demand dividend increases, not because of the new policy of issuing shares at market value. If principal corporate shareholders had demanded higher dividend rates corresponding to market prices or if they had demanded that new stock not be issued at market prices if dividends could not be raised, yields would never have declined so drastically. Even if individual shareholders were to make such demands, nothing would ever happen unless principal corporate shareholders joined them.

A payout ratio is the percentage of a company's after-tax profits that it disburses as dividends. The average payout ratio of all listed companies declined drastically from 59.31 percent in 1975 to 27.64 percent in 1989. The payout radio rose somewhat, to 30.3 percent in 1990, but this was because profits decreased rather than because dividends were increased. Looking at some of the average payout ratios in other nations for this same time—the United States, 54 percent; the United Kingdom, 66 percent; Germany, 50 percent—we see just how low the Japanese payout ratio actually is.

Examining these low Japanese company payout ratios in detail, we discover further that the more profit a company makes the less its payout ratio. For example, according to a 1991 publication of the Association of National Stock Exchanges of Japan [*Haito Jokyo Chosa* (Survey of Dividends)] there are companies such as Nintendo (7.43 percent) and Fuji Photo Film (7.65 percent) with payout ratios less than 10 percent. And, many of Japan's most profitable companies such as Toyota Motors (16.1 percent), Nomura Securities (13.4 percent), and Matsushita Electric (17.1 percent) have payout ratios of between 10 and 20 percent.

Low payout ratios indicate high rates of retained earnings, a situation favorable for companies, and this is true not just for Japanese companies but for companies in the United States and United Kingdom as well—nothing is better for companies than a low payout ratio. But, principal shareholders do not accept that. And, in Europe and America the idea that the role of a joint stock company is to distribute profits as dividends to shareholders is a generally accepted one, so when profits increase a dividend increase is unavoidable. Japan's corporate capitalism is based upon an ideology of concern for what is good for the company, and this is revealed in the prevalence of low payout ratios. This is, of course, a situation favorable to companies but not to individual investors. While stock prices are rising, individual investors speculate for capital gains, but when stock prices decline they desert the market.

Japanese stock prices plummeted beginning in 1990, an event said to be a repeat of the Financial Panic of 1965, when Yamaichi Securities and Ooi Securities (now Wako Securities) folded and investors and securities firms both were dealt a heavy blow. But, comparing the situation at that time to the current situation, the average yield on stocks at that time exceeded 6 percent, a figure higher than interest rates on 1-year bank time deposits. And, of course, the payout ratio was higher then as well.

In the Financial Panic of 1965, stock prices plunged so stock yields increased. As a result, individual investors began buying stocks again on a yield basis and stock prices eventually recovered. However, in 1990 the decline in stock prices was far greater than that of the Financial Panic but still, even after this sharp decline in prices, average yields are around 1 percent and individual investors have not returned to the market.

In response, the Finance Ministry and securities firms have repeatedly called for listed companies to increase their payout ratios, but few companies have responded to these appeals.

As yields approach zero and dividends vanish, an end to the structure of corporate capitalism appears imminent. But, this trend escaped notice as long as stock prices were rising and no one worried about such things as dividends. In addition, there were scholars who claimed that low payout ratios were a sign of the strength of the Japanese company.

But, with stock prices declining the structure's contradictions have suddenly become evident. Of course, increased dividends are necessary to entice individual and also institutional investors back into the market, but companies cannot easily increase their dividends. And, even if they were able to do so for a time, at current stock price levels even a payout ratio of 100 percent would not suffice to activate yield-based buying. Dividends have decreased to a level from which they cannot be restored. Japanese companies have reached an extremity that can only be called a crisis of corporate capitalism.

In this way, a characteristic that was once considered a strength of Japan's corporate capitalism has in the 1990s completely and suddenly reversed its effect and revealed its hidden contradictions.

Hiroshi Okumura is professor of economics, Ryukoku University, Kyoto.

Source/Permission: "Kiki no Hojin Shihonshugi." Chapter 1 of Hiroshi Okumura, *Kaisha Hon'i Shugi wa Kuzureruka* [Will Japan's Corporate Capitalism Collapse?]. Tokyo: Iwanami Shoten, 1992. (Translation originally appeared in *Japanese Economic Studies* 21, No. 4 [Summer 1993].) Translated with permission by Mark Riddle.

5

The Keiretsu Issue:
A Theoretical Approach

Hisashi Yaginuma

1. Introduction

There have been voices heard pointing out the importance of transactions among firms within an industry as a source of the international competitiveness of Japanese firms in recent years. At the same time, the issue of such a business transaction system, in particular its exclusivity, has come to be discussed internationally in the form of the "*keiretsu* issue." In concrete terms, industries such as automobiles and electric machinery are the subject of this debate. Here, we would like to view the keiretsu issue from the standpoint of economic theory and examine its effectiveness and problems.

The expression of "keiretsu" generally covers "financial keiretsu," "production keiretsu," and "marketing keiretsu." "Financial keiretsu" pertains to business transactions among firms within a group centered around a financial institution. "Production keiretsu" pertains to business dealings between the assembly maker and the suppliers who supply parts to it. Further, the "marketing keiretsu" indicates the relationship between the manufacturer and the distributors and is considered to be included in the "production keiretsu" and "financial keiretsu." We would like to clarify at the outset that the discussion to follow will be on the issue of "production keiretsu" and that it excludes the issue of the "marketing keiretsu."

2. The Actual State of Keiretsu Business Transactions

The structure of interfirm business dealings

As the premise proceeding the discussion, it is necessary to clarify what in reality is the structure of keiretsu business dealings.

Subcontracting and keiretsu

When the issue of business transactions among firms in an industry is discussed, the expression "subcontracting" is often used.

The concept of subcontracting is defined in *Kogyo Jittai Kihon Chosa* (The Basic Survey of the State of Manufacturing) by the Small and Medium Enterprise Agency as follows:

"Subcontracting refers to

(1) the cases of manufacturing products, parts, accessories, and raw materials to be used in the product of the parent firm; or, (2) the manufacturing or repairing of the equipment, machinery or tools used by the parent firm for its production, under contract with the parent firm (a firm with a larger capital or with a larger number of employees). However, in case the product of the firms in question that is being marketed is purchased by other firms through the normal distribution channel, the concept of subcontracting is not applicable—and, in order for the concept of subcontracting to be applicable, the action of the parent firm placing the order directly with the firm under question and, at that time, designating the specification, product quality, performance, form and design is necessary." (From *Dai 5–kai Kogyo Jittai Kihon Chosa Hokokusho* [The Fifth Report on the Basic Survey of the State of Manufacturing], February 1979.)

In this definition, the fundamental condition is that the firm receives an order directly from a firm that is larger in size, that other firms cannot purchase the subcontractor's products through the distribution channel, and that the specification and the product quality are determined by the parent firm.

The first point implies that medium and small size firms that engage in various resin fabrications by purchasing the raw material from large-scale material producers, such as in the petrochemical industry, do not fall in the category of subcontractors while, as in the machinery industry, the case of large firms engaged in parts assembly fall in subcontracting.

The second point means that the product the parent firm procures would not get in the general distribution channel. On the one hand, one can think of the instance in which, even though technically and physically it may be possible to put it in the distribution channel, the parent firm would not approve it for strategic reasons; and, on the other hand, it is conceivable that the applied use in the products of other firms may be difficult for technical reasons due to the parent firm's unique specifications and design. The former instance implies that the firm under question complies with the strategy of the parent firm; but, it does not necessarily mean that this firm accepts the will of the parent firm while viewing it unreasonable. It is quite conceivable that it is a behavior resulting from a rational reasoning. The latter point is related to the issue of the standardization of parts and others, and one can interpret it as that the firm under question is not in a position of developing the products and conducting business on its own. Thus, it is being carried out as a part of the strategy of the parent firm, as an "assembly maker," in dealing with the users.

On the third point that the product quality and specifications are designated by the parent firm, the typical image that is created must be the case of so-called "blueprint lending producer"(Asanuma 1989); but, in the normal business dealings among firms, often the users set conditions, at the time of order, regarding various designs and specifications. One can say that it is the result of the purchasing firms possessing the detailed information or knowledge about the products or projects.

In the past, there has been a convincing image of subcontracting as the "economically weak," specializing in the contract work and with little technological ability, that are likely not to benefit from the business upturns and be the first to be cut during the downturns at the whim of the parent firm. However, the definition in the above cited survey by the Small and Medium Enterprise Agency is not necessarily limited by such an image. In fact, when the activities of many medium and small firms are observed, there are many examples in which such a past image is not applicable today. Viewed in this manner, while the subcontractor may be under a condition where it must meet the parent firm's unique specifications and would not market its products to other firms through the distribution channel, it seems reasonable to capture it simply as "a firm from which to outsource," as viewed from the standpoint of the parent firm (as emphasized by Tadao Kiyonari and Masahiko Aoki). While it is indeed true that there are phenomena such as the demand for "cost down" and the reverting of the return from its own development to the parent firm in the form of price reduction, as we will discuss later, they should be interpreted as pertaining to the distribution in the situation of bilateral monopoly in the parts market under question.

In this manner, the expression "subcontracting" is understood as the concept that pertains to the goods transaction that is integral to the flow of the production process from parts to final products; and, as a result, the image of the corporate group that is positioned under the assembly maker or, in other words, the picture of a pyramid structure with the assembly maker at the top becomes clear.

Next, let us consider the "keiretsu." Keiretsu as a concept is also not necessarily clear. Taking literally the meaning of the word itself, it is the things that are lined up systematically or in the ordered ranking. The question lies in what sense the "systematic lining-up" is made or the "ordered ranking" is formed. When the expression "keiretsu" is used in connection with business transactions among firms, it is often used to denote the personal, capital, and business ties. Normally, the personal ties are often advanced with the ties in the capital aspect as the premise; and, it is expressed by the terms such as the affiliated subsidiaries (*kankei kogaisha*), the affiliated firms (*kankei gaisha*), and subsidiaries (*kogaisha*).

In addition to this type of relationship among the firms, the expression "keiretsu" also includes the case in which the interfirm relationship has become very close through business transactions. Based only on these definitions, the relative sizes appear not to matter in designating the keiretsu hierarchical relationship; but, interestingly enough, in reality there is an asymmetry that, when Firm A is a keiretsu firm of Firm B, one would never say that Firm B is a keiretsu firm of Firm A. In fact, with respect to the financial keiretsu, a firm that belongs to a group of corporations that are tied in interlocking stock holding in terms of capital and personal connection is said to belong to a "financial keiretsu" designated by the name of the financial institution of the largest size that is in the center of the group. In addition, in the machinery industry, the keiretsu firms that supply parts to the assembly maker are referred to with this assembly maker's keiretsu name and not the other way around. Thus, one can say that, as in the case of subcontracting, keiretsu also means a corporate group that is contained in a pyramid structure with a certain large-scale corporation at the top.

This fact clearly indicates that when the concept of keiretsu is applied to industries in the machinery field it applies to the firms that supply various parts and materials to large corporations for assembling. This, indeed, implies exactly the same substance as subcontracting and shows clearly that keiretsu and subcontracting are conceptually very similar. However, there are cases in which the firms with close financial and personal ties are included in keiretsu; so, to be precise, it may be possible to think that keiretsu becomes subcontracting upon exclusion of the personal and financial connections.

This fact does not deny that there are financial and personal relationships in the part where there is a commonality in the two concepts. The most important core concept is the presence of a close relationship with a certain large corporation through business dealings.

Thus, while they are not completely identical, we can see that keiretsu and subcontracting are very similar concepts. In the following sections, we will not differentiate them and proceed with our discussion.

An overview of the subcontracting firms

According to the survey of the Small and Medium Enterprise Agency that was cited earlier, the number of the subcontracting medium and small firms in the manufacturing industry in 1986 was 380,000. The number was 300,000 in 1966, and 370,000 in 1976; thus, the number of these firms grew 27 percent (at an annual rate of 1.2 percent) during the past 20 years. For the past 10 years, this number leveled off; and, at least in terms of the number of firms, subcontracting has not grown.

Table 1 shows the proportion of subcontracting firms in all medium and small firms. According to this table, for manufacturing as a whole, the proportion was 53 percent in 1966 and 56 percent in 1986; hence, the increase was very little. While this proportion rose rapidly in the exceptional circumstance such as in 1976 just after the first oil crisis and in 1981 after the second oil crisis, it has hardly changed; and,

Table 1

Change in the Proportion of Subcontracting Medium and Small Firms

	1966	1976	(%) 1986	Change 1966–86
Manufacturing Total	53	61	56	3
Food	17	15	8	− 9
Textile Manufacturing	80	85	80	0
Clothing and Other Textiles	74	84	79	5
Wood and Wood Products	35	43	22	−13
Furniture and Furnishings	46	41	39	− 7
Pulp and Paper	51	45	41	−10
Publishing and Printing	46	51	42	− 4
Chemical Manufacturing	40	37	22	−18
Petroleum and Coal Products	30	27	18	−12
Plastics	—	—	69	—
Rubber Products	62	61	65	3
Leather and Leather Products	60	63	65	5
Ceramic, Stone, and Clay Products	34	29	35	1
Steel	66	70	52	−14
Nonferrous Metal Products	67	69	62	− 5
Metal Products	66	75	71	5
General Machinery	71	83	75	4
Electric Machinery	81	82	79	− 2
Transport Machinery	67	86	80	13
Precision Machinery	72	72	70	− 2
Other Manufacturing	—	56	43	—

Source: Small and Medium Enterprise Agency, *Kogyo Jittai Kihon Chosa* (The Basic Survey of the State of Manufacturing).

its stability is noticeable. One would think that the rapid rise in the post-oil crisis period reflects the fact that many firms were compelled to engage in subcontracting, under the contracting economic activities, in order to secure work.

However, such changes are quite diverse when viewed by type of business. The following lists the businesses in which the proportion has risen during the past 20 years and those for which the proportion has declined.

—Businesses where the proportion rose: clothing; other textiles; rubber products; leather and leather products; ceramic, stone, and clay; metal products; general machinery; transport machinery.

—Businesses where the proportion declined: food; wood and wood products; furniture and furnishings; pulp and paper; printing and publishing; chemical manufacturing; petroleum and coal products; steel; nonferrous metal products; electric machinery; precision machinery.

—Business where the proportion did not change: textile manufacturing.

Table 2

The Subcontracting Dependency in Major Industries (1986)

Shipment	% Base
Automobiles, Parts	28
Shipbuilding	37
Home Appliance, Electronics Parts	29
Precision Machinery	34

Source: Tadao Kiyonari, *Chusho Kigyo Tokuhon* (A Textbook on Medium and Small Businesses).

The above figures are the weight of subcontracting in terms of the number of firms. As the weight in terms of real economic activities, Table 2 presents the shares of total shipment; the proportion is between 28 percent and 37 percent in the major industries where the dependency on subcontracting is high.

Next, let us examine the number of parent firms that are the main clients of the subcontracting firms. For manufacturing as a whole, the number of parent firms per subcontracting firm was three in 1976, four in 1981, and five in 1986; thus, the number is steadily increasing. While, on the one hand, the fact that there are five parent firms on the average means that there are subcontracting firms with one parent firm. On the other hand, it means that there are firms with more than ten parent firms. Thus, we can discern the situation that the number of parent firms is considerably diffused. It is clear in terms of industry types also that the number of parent firms is increasing in all industries. As of 1986, the industries in which the number of parent firms is large are publishing and printing (twelve parent firms per subcontracting firm), metal products (ten parent firms), steel (nine parent firms), and pulp and paper (eight parent firms); and, the machinery type industries have some-what fewer parent firms per subcontracting firm with six parent firms per subcontracting firm (Figure 1).

Let us classify the business relationship between the subcontracting and parent firms in terms of the number of parent firms and the proportion of subcontracting firms (*Chusho Kigyo Hakusho* [The Small and Medium Business White Paper], 1991):

(a) The exclusive subcontracting type: One parent firm and the proportion of subcontracting more than 90 percent.

(b) The semi-exclusive subcontracting type: two to five parent firms and the proportion of subcontracting more than 90 percent. Or, one parent firm and the proportion of subcontracting less than 90 percent.

(c) The semi-diffused business type: two to five parent firms and the subcontracting proportion less than 90 percent. Or, more than six parent firms and the proportion of subcontracting more than 70 percent.

Figure 1

Changes in the Number of Parent Firms Per Subcontracting Firm

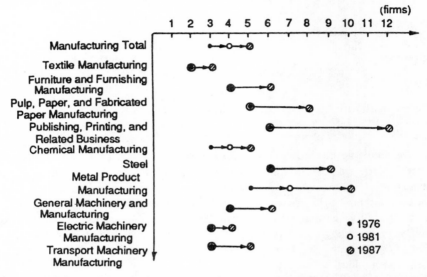

Source: Ministry of International Trade and Industry, Small and Medium Enterprise Agency, *Kogyo Jittai Kihon Chosa* (Basic Survey of the State of Manufacturing), 1976, 1981, and 1987. *Chusho Kigyo Hakusho* (The Medium and Small Business White Paper) (1989).

(d) The diffused business type: More than six parent firms and the proportion of subcontracting less than 70 percent.

Examining changes in these four subcontracting types during the three-year period between 1987 and 1990, we can see that the proportion of firms in the exclusive type declined rapidly; those in the semi-exclusive type declined somewhat; and the proportion of subcontracting firms of the semi-diffused business type and diffused business type increased quite rapidly (Figure 2). This trend suggests that the firms of the (a) type that belong to one parent firm are gradually expanding the range of their business clients thus reducing the proportion of subcontracting and are shifting to the (c) and (d) types with an intensified independence. We can say that this fact has a significant implication in understanding the actual situation in discussing the keiretsu issue.

The structure by firm size and international comparison

As stated earlier, in Japan, the businesses in which the weight of the subcontracting transactions and keiretsu transactions is high are machinery industries (i.e., general machinery, electric machinery, transport machinery, and precision ma-

Figure 2

Distribution of Subcontracting Medium and Small Firms by Type of Subcontracting

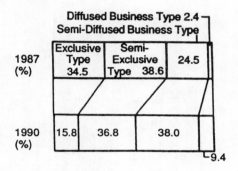

Source: Ministry of International Trade and Industry, Small and Medium Enterprise Agency, *Kogyo Jittai Kihon Chosa* (The Basic Survey of the State of Manufacturing), 1987. Small and Medium Enterprise Agency, *Seizogyo Bungyo Kozo Jittai Chosa* (Survey of the State of Division of Labor in Manufacturing) (December 1990). *Chusho Kigyo Hakusho* (The Medium and Small Business White Paper) (1991).

chinery) and textile industry. At the same time, we have learned that, in the capital-intensive production material manufacturing-type industries such as ceramics, stone and clay, and food and chemical industries, the weight is relatively low.

The fact that the weight of subcontracting or keiretsu transactions is high means that the intermediate goods purchased from subcontractors or keiretsu firms is large. In other words, it would seem that the larger the firm size and closer to the final product supply firms, the greater the amount of intermediate input. In Japan, such a pattern is clearly observed in the transport machinery and textile product industries; and we can discern the presence of the tendency that the ratio of intermediate input rises at a rate greater than the increase in the size of firm and the dependency on subcontracting and keiretsu transactions intensifies (Figure 3).

We can interpret this as a reflection of the acceleration of structural division of labor due to the growth of firm sizes. However, regarding electric machinery, we can see a tendency for the ratio of intermediate input not to change and to stabilize after a certain size (fifty to ninety-nine employees) is reached even though the firm size may grow. This indicates that the growth of firm size and the utilization of subcontracting and keiretsu level have a relative relationship.

With respect to the capital intensive material type industries, there are some differences in the pattern by type of business, but the commonly observed tendency is that, while the ratio of intermediate input is seen to rise up to a certain

Figure 3

A U.S.-Japan Comparison of the Intermediate Input Ratio by Firm Size (1977)

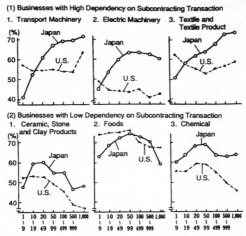

Note:

$$\frac{\text{Intermediate}}{\text{Input Ratio}} = \frac{\text{Intermediate Input}}{\text{Shipment}} \times 100 = \frac{(\text{Shipment} - \text{Value Added})}{\text{Shipment}} \times 100$$

Source: Japan-Ministry of International Trade and Industry, *Kogyo Tokeihyo* (Census of Manufacturers) (1977). U.S., *Census of Manufacturers* (1977).

firm size, it falls above that size (Figure 2). This is related to the pattern that the ratio of intermediate input declines as the firm size grows because large firms in these industries adapt the mode in which they produce materials themselves based on economies of scale. Because, in such industries, basically, large firms do not use the production process of assembling many parts, one would be hard-pressed to regard the pattern by size of the ratio of intermediate input as subcontracting or keiretsu transactions as in the case of the fabrication-type industries. However, the presence of what one could regard as keiretsu transaction is suggested in the sense that, in these industries, mid-size firms often play the role of fabricating the materials to be used by the industries in question as down-stream firms.

Now, let us compare the proportion of the amount of intermediate goods in total shipment in these industries in Japan and the United States using Figure 3.

It is clear that Japan and the United States are alike in the ratio of intermediate input by firm size in the capital-intensive material type industries. In every industry, the ratio of intermediate input of a certain size of firms is declining. However, with the exception of food, we notice that in both the chemical industry and the ceramics, stone, and clay industry, the ratio of intermediate input is lower in almost all sizes in the United States. While one may say the United States produces more high-value-added goods than Japan, this can indicate a situation in which the structure of interfirm transactions is such that firms produce internally even production materials.

Next, let us have a comparison in the machinery and textile industries that are highly dependent on subcontracting. Here, there is a clear difference between Japan and the United States. While, in the United States, the ratio of intermediate input hardly rises with the growth in firm size, in Japan there is a clear tendency for it to rise.

In addition, the gap between the two countries in the ratio of intermediate input tends to widen with the increase in firm size. This phenomenon, which is commonly observed in the transport machinery, electric machinery, textile and textile products industries, suggests that the industries in the United States internally produce the parts, raw materials, and other materials to be used in assembly.

However, what should be noted in the case of the United States is the high ratio of intermediate input in the firms of meager size. Here, in almost all cases, the ratio is higher than in Japan. Considering that large and medium firms in the United States show the internal transaction orientation type pattern, there is a possibility that meager-size firms have developed a mutual network. It is interesting that the mode of interfirm transactions is different among medium and large firms.

The structure of intra-industry division of
labor and international comparison

Let us examine the concrete structure of intra-industry division of labor from the relationship between parent firms and subcontracting firms. As discussed earlier, the subcontracting firms in Japan have what one might call the "system of division of labor in the production process" through the business relationship with parent firms. We will briefly explain now in what form the system of the division of labor is implemented by citing several examples in Figure 4.

In the textile industry normally, the manufacturer-owned trading firms, synthetic fiber manufacturers, apparel producers, and general trading firms are the parent firms. In the case of the synthetic fiber textiles, in addition to the commercial functions of raw materials procurement and marketing, the parent firms characteristically participate in the designing, planning, and capital procurement.

In the case of home electric appliances, there is a pattern of parts producers, who supply parts to the general home electric appliance manufacturers that carry out the final assembly, and, under them there are subcontracting firms. Because parts are relatively standardized, the relationship between the parent firm and parts producers is loose.

In the case of automobiles, the business relationship is even more multilayered; and, what may be called a pyramid-type structure of the division of labor is formed. The interfirm link with the just-in-time (*teiji*) and the exact quantity (*teiryo*) supply method is relatively strong.

Figure 4

Characteristics of the Subcontracting Division of Labor and Conceptual Diagram

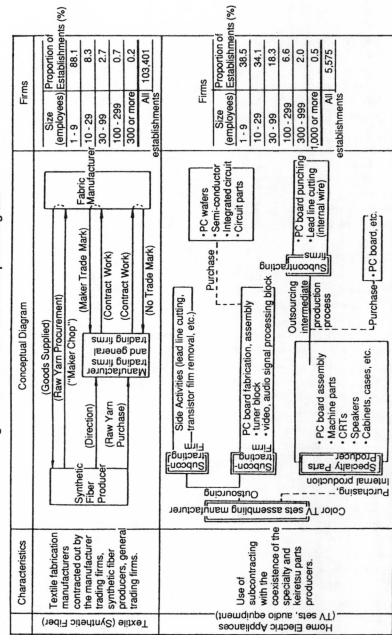

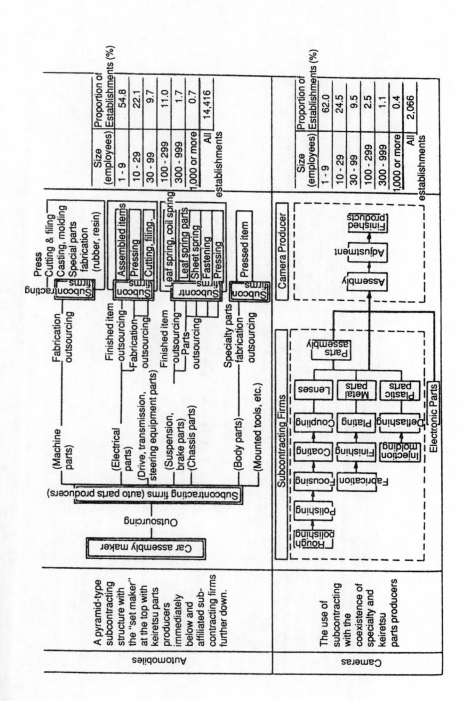

148

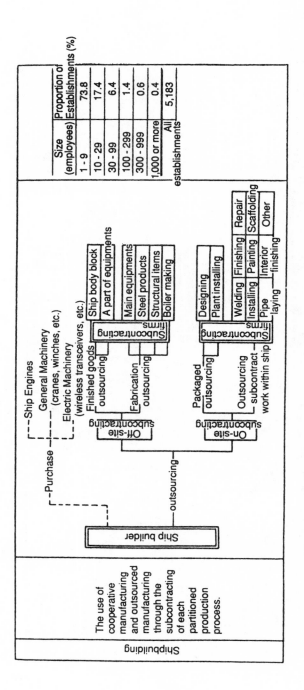

Size (employees)	Proportion of Establishments (%)
1 - 9	73.8
10 - 29	17.4
30 - 99	6.4
100 - 299	1.4
300 - 999	0.6
1,000 or more	0.4
All establishments	5,183

Note: The industry classification numbers (Census of Manufacturers) are as follows:
Textile (20)
Home Appliances (3543, 3544)
Automobiles (361)
Cameras (3752)
Shipbuilding (364)

Source: The Subcontracting Business Research Association (1986).

With respect to cameras, the prevalent mode is for the subcontracting firms to be responsible for metal parts, plastic parts, and lenses and the electronic parts are purchased. In particular, in recent years, there has been an increase in unit orders; and, the cases in which the subcontracting firms engage in a certain amount of assembly are increasing.

The division of labor in shipbuilding is comprised of the off-site subcontracting, in which the shell and equipments are produced off-site, and on-site subcontracting where production process is pursued on-site; the interfirm link is comparatively strong.

Let us compare this kind of structure of the division of labor among different countries. Figure 5 pertains to color television sets.

The comparison is among three countries—Japan, Korea, and the United States; and, in spite of the fact that the basic production process is identical, clearly the structure of the division of labor is different among them. In the case of Japan, mechanical parts depend on the external procurement, and the manufacturing of structural parts and the insertion process of various parts are let to external subcontractors. In contrast, in the United States, the production of almost all parts and assembly process are internalized thus using the approach that is the exact opposite of that in Japan. In Korea, both mechanical parts and structural parts are purchased from external sources, and other parts are produced internally—except that, in the case of goods to meet domestic demand, structural parts depend on external sources. Thus, the structure of the division of labor is extremely divergent between Japan and the United States, and Korea falls between the two.

Next, let us examine the automobile industry. Let us, at the outset, examine the number of firms with which the automobile assembly makers conduct business. The information used here is somewhat dated; but, according to the 1978 *Chusho Kigyo Hakusho* (The Small and Medium Business White Paper), a final product manufacturer of a certain automobile has under it 36,000 so-called subcontracting firms. Table 3 presents these subcontracting firms classified as primary subcontractors, secondary subcontractors, and tertiary subcontractors.

Using these data, we can gain a picture that numerous firms are hierarchically clustered under an automobile producer. The reason why there is a hierarchy of primary, secondary, and tertiary subcontractors is that there is in the background a technologically multilayered structure in production in which final products are created by assembling major semifinished products, these semifinished products are created by assembling individual parts and, further, individual parts are the result of fabricating and assembling even finer parts and materials.

The present situation is that, based on such a hierarchical structure of subcontracting, the suppliers in each layer are positioned as subcontractors, diagrammed as comprising a pyramid-type structure with the assembly maker at the top.

However, to be noted here is the economies of specializing parts for which these subcontracting firms use specific materials or specific production pro-

Figure 5

International Comparison of Color TV Set Production

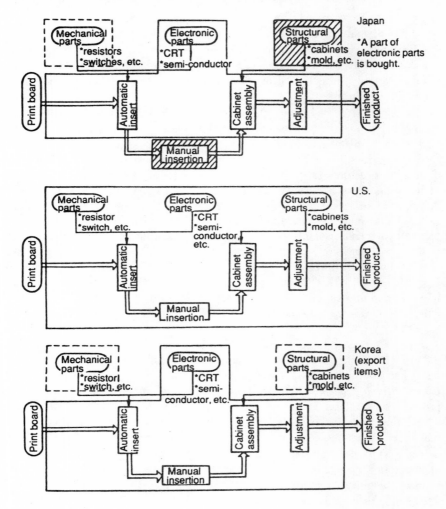

Note:

1. ☐ is mainly internally produced.
2. ▨ is mainly subcontracted.
3.   is mainly purchased.
4. ⇒ is the flow of production process.
5. → is the flow of parts.

Source: Small and Medium Enterprise Agency, *The Medium and Small Business White Paper* (1984).

Table 3

A Certain Automobile Manufacturer's Business Client Firms

Primary Subcontracting Firms	168 firms
Secondary Subcontracting Firms	4,700 (5,437)
Tertiary Subcontracting Firms	31,600 (41,703)
Total	36,468 (47,308)

Note: The figures within parentheses indicate the numbers in case duplicate transactions are counted.
Source: The Medium and Small Business White Paper (1978).

Table 4

The Sales Situation of Parts Producers by Keiretsu

	Toyota	Nissan	Others
Toyota Group	O	—	O
Nissan Group	(O)	O	O
Independent	O	O	O
Other Group	—	—	O

Note: (O) for Toyota indicates the planned action beginning 1993.
Source: Itami et al. (1988), and *Nippon Keizai Shinbun.*

cesses. The fundamental economic basis that enables the continued existence of subcontracting as subcontracting seems to be that scale economies, different from those attained by the assembly maker, or economies of the division of labor (one could call it the economies of network) can exist (Japan Regional Development Corporation 1978).

The flexibility of keiretsu business dealings

As seen above, we might say that the structure of the intra-industry division of labor is comparatively well-developed in Japan as compared to other countries. The image formed by extracting the essence of this structure can be said to be the pyramid-type structure with a certain parent firm at the top. However, in terms of actual business dealings among firms, it does not seem that such a diagram necessarily explains the reality accurately.

Each of the parts producers (the primary subcontractors in   terms of the above-mentioned diagram) that are the suppliers to the automobile assembly makers are, as is well-known, is classified into a keiretsu group such as the Toyota Group, Nissan Group, independents, and other automobile manufacturer groups. Table 4 shows whom parts producers in each keiretsu group supply their products.

With Toyota and Nissan, we can say that up to now there have not been business transactions that go beyond the keiretsus. Nevertheless, Toyota has a plan to purchase sensors from Hitachi, which is in the Nissan group, beginning 1993; and finished car makers other than Toyota and Nissan do not particularly insist on purchasing parts from their own keiretsu groups. This describes the situation at the primary contractor level; so, it follows that, once we go down to the secondary and tertiary levels, a larger number of transactions that transcend keiretsu would be observed. Thus, it is questionable how strong the existence of keiretsu business dealings is.

In the United States, the ratio of internal production is high (Figure 6), and the primary subcontracting level in Japan would be vertically integrated in the activities of the assembly makers.

GM produces parts at ten firms, which are its 100 percent subsidiaries, and is itself the parts manufacturer with the largest share (more than 20 percent). Therefore, the parts producers in the United States are comparable to the secondary and tertiary subcontractors in Japan; and, it would seem natural that they are not grouped in the form of keiretsu as in Japan.

Further, the automobile assembly makers in Japan generally form an organization, called the "cooperative association," with the parts producers, and develop business dealings for production and development while constantly ensuring good communication. Here also, we see participation in the cooperative associations of other firms, transcending keiretsu (Table 5). Sakamoto and Shimotani (1987) point out that this movement is particularly noticeable in the electrical equipment (*densohin*) related industries.

The existence of such business transactions that transcend keiretsu can also be discerned easily from the statistical fact, which was already pointed out, of the increase in the number of parent firms in the subcontracting firms, and it supports the widespread existence of this phenomenon. In addition, while, in the past, "other firms" referred, for example, to the assembly makers in the same automobile industry, the business clients of the parts producers beyond keiretsu no longer are limited to the automobile assembly makers. For example, transactions between automobile parts producers and computer makers, medical equipment makers, and others are in reality taking place. Furthermore, what is important is that such business dealings with the firms in other types of business are being conducted, as in the case of keiretsu transactions, continuously over a long time. Therefore, interfirm business dealings are carried out with much greater flexibility than generally imagined, and, moreover, transactions have long-term continuity.

The inverse pyramid structure

What the preceding discussion implies is the existence of, beside the pyramid-type structure with the assembly maker at the top, the pyramid-type structure viewed from the standpoint of parts producers that portrays the supplying to

Figure 6

Comparison of the Internal and External Production Between Firm A in Japan and Firm B in the United States

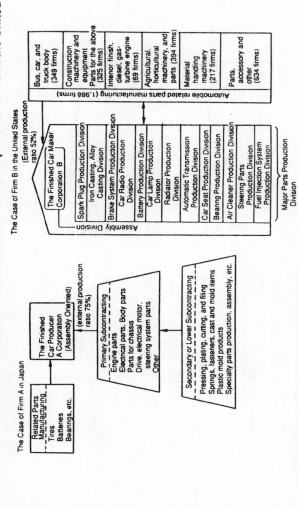

Note: 1. External Production Ratio = $\dfrac{\text{Purchase Cost} + \text{Outsourcing Cost}^*}{\text{Aggregate Production Cost}} \times 100$
(*subcontracting and fabrication)

2. Among the primary subcontracting firms, the number of parent firms per subcontracting firm is not necessarily one.

Source: A survey contracted by Small and Medium Enterprise Agency, ''A Survey on the Role of Medium and Small Firms in the System of the Division of Labor in Production,'' (Contractor: Chusho Kigyo Kenkyu Center) (The Small and Medium Enterprise Research Center) (January 1980).

Table 5

Participation of Toyota Group Firms in Other Parts Producer Cooperative Associations (1970–85)

Cooperative Association	Nissan Takarakai		Nissan Hinpokai		Mitsubishi Kashiwakai		Matsuda Yokokai		Isuzu Kyowakai		Fujiju Kyoryoku-kai		Suzuki Kyoryoku Kyodo Kumiai		Honda Major Suppliers		Grand Total	
	70	85	70	85	70	85	70	85	70	85	70	85	70	85	70	85	70	85
Number of Member Firms	112	105	43	58	337	337	87	178	216	281	147	230	82	97	—	287	1,025*	1,286*
Aishin Seiki					O	O				O					—	O	1	3
Aichi Seiko								O		O							0	2
Kanto Jiko																	0	0
Toyota Jishoku																	0	0
Toyota Gosei					O	O		O	O	O					—	O	2	4
Toyota Koki																	0	0
Toyota Boshoku																	0	0
Toyota Shatai												O					0	1
Toyota Tsusho																	0	0
Nihon Denso					O	O		O	O						O	O	3	3
Sub-total	0	0	0	0	3	3	0	3	2	3	0	1	0	0	1	3	6	13
Aisan Kogyo					△	O		O		O							1	3
Aishin Warner						O				O							0	2
Aishin Keikinzoku																	0	0
Arakawa Shatai										O							0	2
Kyatara Kogyo																	0	0
Gifu Shatai																	0	0
Keisan Denki					△	O		O				O					0	0
Kyoho Seisakusho																	0	0

Kyowa Leather													1	3
Koito Seisakusho	△	△	△					—					0	0
Koyo Seiko	△	O	△	O	O	O	O	—		O			0	1
Jeco			△	O	O	O		—		O			2	6
Central Automobile							O	O					3	6
Taiho Kogyo			O	O									0	5
Takaoka Kogyo													0	0
Takashimaya Nippatsu Kogyo													3	3
Chuo Seiki	△	O	O		O	O		△		O			0	0
Chuo Hatsujo			△	O									0	0
Tsuda Kogyo													1	1
Tokai Rika Denki			O	O	O	△	O			O			3	4
Toyota Kako													0	0
Toyota Tekko					O								1	5
Toyotomi Kiko													0	0
Fujitsu Ten													0	0
Hosei Brake														
Horie Kinzoku Kogyo													0	0
Yutaka Seimitsu Kogyo													0	0
Sub-total	0	3	7	10	0	9	1	7	2	6	0	6	2	15
Grand Total	0	3	10	13	0	12	3	10	2	7	0	9	3	21

Note: * excluding Honda; — not available; △ not a member of the Toyota group at the time.
Source: The Automobile Parts Manufacturers Association (Jidosha buhin Kogyokai), ed., Nihon no Jijidobuhin Kogyo (Japan's Automobile Parts Manufacturing) (1971 and 1986 editions).

Table 6

The Supply Relationship Regarding Major Engine Related Parts

	Toyota	Nissan	Honda
Piston	Aishin Seiki Art Kinzoku Kogyo	Atsugi Jidosha Buhin Art Kinzoku Kogyo	Honda Kinzoku Gijutsu
Cam Shaft	Internally made Tokyo Tanzosho Toyota Koki	Internally made Nippon Piston Ring	Internally made Riken Chuzo
Carburetor	Aissan Kogyo Nihon Kikaki Seisakusho	Hitachi Seisakusho Nihon Kikaki Seisakusho Mikuni Kogyo	Keihin Kikaki Keihin Seiki Seisakusho

Source: Itami et al. (1988).

multiple assembly makers or the supplying to firms in different types of business. Professor Tadao Kiyonari of Hosei University describes this situation as the "inverse pyramid structure." As we have pointed out earlier, the reason why so many subcontracting firms engage in the production of component parts for assembly is the technological condition in which, for each component part or production process, there is a unique level of the economies of scale for the assembly maker and parts producers as well as for the parts producers in each hierarchical level. The fact that such a phenomenon is observed has an important significance in clarifying that the past image of parts producers being completely subservient to the assembly maker is erroneous.

In other words, it means that parts producers themselves possess a considerable technological capability and conduct their business on their own. In fact, among the automobile engine parts producers listed in Table 6, Art Kinzoku Kogyo (Art Metal Manufacturing), Tokyo Tanzosho (Tokyo Foundry), Nippon Piston Ring, Riken Tanzo (Riken Foundry), and Mikuni Corporation are independents; and the fact that these powerful independent producers exist itself supports what we have just stated. In addition, historically also, in many cases the automobile assembly makers have instructed parts producers to avoid relying on the assembly maker for receiving orders, raising funds and personnel (Miwa 1990); as a consequence, there are many parts producers that have come to retain independent capability.

The substance of keiretsu business transactions

Next, we will systematize the substance of the keiretsu transactions in concrete terms; and, as a typical case, we would like to take the automobile industry for which there is an abundance of case studies.

Table 7

Distribution of Parts Suppliers — Toyota and Honda

	Toyota	Honda		Toyota	Honda
1 firm	22	34	5 firms	4	1
2 firms	31	40	6 firms	1	0
3 firms	15	14	7 firms	1	0
4 firms	6	3	Total	80 parts	92 parts

Source: Itami et al. (1988).

The lack of marketed goods and standardized items

In the case of the automobile industry, parts supplied by parts producers have unique specifications, and hardly any of these parts are sold in the market (Asanuma 1989). This means not only that different automobile makers order parts with different specifications and, accordingly, the repairs and maintenance can be performed only by the keiretsu dealers but also that, even within the same automobile manufacturer, can be differ- ent parts if the type of car is different. This fact can be interpreted as reflecting the product differentiation competition among the assembly makers.

Competition among the few firms (the visible hand)

We can next point out that the number of suppliers that supply parts to assembly makers is extremely small, as we can infer from Table 1. Let us examine the distribution of supplying firms by type of part using Table 7, which covers Toyota and Honda. A remarkable characteristic found in this table is that, for both firms, the number of parts supplying firms is about one to three and there are scarcely any cases of more than that many firms supplying parts. This fact would generate the situation in which the supplying firms can easily obtain among themselves the information regarding their technological capability, product prices, and others. Under such a circumstance, the parts producers are obliged to compete by keeping vigil on each other's movement (Miwa 1990).

Such competition is referred to as the "visible hand" (Itami et al. 1988), and it is not limited to the major parts producers and among themselves. It takes place also among the suppliers that supply finer parts to these parts producers. Obviously, this applies also to the interfirm relationship at the level even below these suppliers. This competition among the few firms exists universally at each layer in the hierarchy.

Continuous supply

The firm that supplies parts usually continues its business relationship with the assembly maker for four to five years. This period coincides, in the case of the automobile industry, roughly with the period until the model change is made; any change in the supplying firm is done at the time of model change (Asanuma 1989). So that the ease of supplier change at the time of model change is attained, the assembly maker normally lets the parts producer supply many different kinds of parts.

In addition, the business dealings that last a long time involve unexpected events such as changes in demand. In order to deal with such an event, the volume of transactions is stabilized, thus functioning as a mechanism to avert mutual risk.

Cost control

The assembly maker strives to learn the parts producer's production cost. The acquisition of this information is important in checking the appropriateness of the price in the business transaction.

In regard to the cost reduction due to the technological development originated in the parts producer side, while initially the profit is attributed to the parts producer as the technology developer, in the succeeding years the benefit is reflected in the price reduction thus making it possible to spread the benefit to the assembly makers as well as to the final consumers.

The design

Frequently, in carrying out new development the parts producers participate with the assembly makers from the design stage. Through sharing the information in this form, it is possible to construct a highly consistent and efficient production system (Itami et al. 1988).

The system of parts producer evaluation

Assembly makers have some kind of system to evaluate business dealings with the parts producers. As we have stated earlier, the business dealings are carried out on a continuous basis; so, the assembly makers assess the parts producers in this continuity. The results of the assessment with such a long-term nature take the form of changes in the volume of purchase at the time of model changes (Asanuma 1989).

Definition of keiretsu transactions

Based on the real state of keiretsu as described above, let us redefine the keiretsu transactions.

As we have discussed so far, the structure of division of labor within an industry has conventionally been given the pyramid-type structure. This represents the position of capturing the market structure as the "buyer monopoly" (*monopsonist*) by the parent firm. In contrast, the presence of the inverse pyramid structure whereby the parts producer itself retains other clients than the assembly maker suggests that the position of parts producer is quite strong; and, such presence of various business dealings by parts producers that transcend keiretsu indicates the situation that includes the element, not only of the monopsony by the parent firm, but also the "seller monopoly" by the parts producer. The existence of parts producers with independence clearly shows the presence of such a possibility. In reality, when we consider the relationship between the primary subcontracting firm and the assembly maker, it is more appropriate to interpret this as representing business transactions between the two parties in the form of "bilateral monopoly" than to see it as one of the two forms being present.

When there is bilateral monopoly, both sides have complete knowledge of the information regarding each other's demand and supply; and, the distribution of profit is determined by the political process or in the game-like situation between the two.

With respect to the return on the technological development by the parts producers themselves, such a return belongs to the parts producers as the founder's gain for a while but upon the introduction of the technological development tends to revert to the assembly maker after a while in the form of the reduction in the parts prices. This phenomenon can be considered as the issue of profit sharing under the condition of bilateral monopoly rather than of the monopsony. Thus, one can interpret that, in the case of the parts producer with technological capability, it is in a position close to being mutually equal with the firm with which it is engaged in keiretsu transactions. In addition, there is a characteristic that, in case it has more than one business client, it maintains a long-term business relationship with each of them.

Based on these considerations, expressed in economic terms, keiretsu transactions can be defined as "the relatively independent parts producer having long-term continuous business dealings with specific assembly makers by forming a bilateral monopolistic market." In the discussion to follow, we will proceed with the understanding of keiretsu in this manner.

3. The Economies of Keiretsu Business Dealings

Rationality

In recent years, many people are viewing affirmatively the rationality of keiretsu, in other words, the rationality of "long-term continuous business dealings." This can be drawn from the state of keiretsu transactions that we have so far clarified.

High opportunity cost

We must, at the outset, point out the high opportunity cost of stopping the business dealings. For the firms that are engaged in continuous business dealings, for both the sellers and buyers, the cost of stopping the business dealings is prohibitively high. On the assembly maker's side, it is obvious that the stoppage of the continuous transaction would prevent them from producing the finished cars. There would be a situation where the fixed production facilities, on which investments had been made, cannot operate fully because of such stoppage. Of course, the burden of keeping the employees whom the firm cannot release is great. Further, it is possible that a criticism may arise that the assembly maker is forcing the parts producers into hardship; as a result, it must pay the cost in the form of a tarnished reputation. All of these have a character of the "sunk cost" that cannot be recovered with the stoppage of business dealings.

In addition, when we consider the situation after the business dealings are stopped, the firm has to find a new source of parts supply. It is not very easy to determine whether a parts producer is suitable as the partner in continuing business dealings. It is necessary to take time in making a decision by collecting various information such as the views of the executives of the firm, technological capability, etc. Such search costs would also raise the opportunity cost.

Another factor that needs to be added in our discussion is the size of dynamic opportunity cost. As we have pointed out, the parts producer carries out new technology development jointly with the assembly maker. Technological progress is not carried out only by the assembly maker. Rather, the decision as to what parts are to respond to the new technology relies to a large extent on the information and know-how accumulated on the parts producer side. The stoppage of continuous business dealings would mean a loss of the source of technological progress in such a form.

At the same time, on the parts producer side, the opportunity cost involved in the stoppage of continuing business dealings is large. Aside, naturally, from the loss of sales, recovery of investment on capital equipment installed to meet the needs of the assembly maker, and the loss of various production know-how would become difficult and the sunk cost results. Nevertheless, the production lines and production know-how which have been installed for a certain assembly maker may, to some extent, be applied to the needs of other makers or other industries, and not all would be sunk cost. Further, the search cost involved in finding new business clients suitable to the parts producer's technological capability and field would be expected to be high. If the technological innovations in the industrial world depend greatly on the joint operations such as that shown in the design-in, the parts producer must anticipate a serious cost of losing the opportunity for new technological innovations.

In order to avoid these kinds of situations, firms conduct repetitive transactions through a long-term business dealing (the "repetitive game" in the game theory) and behave in such a way as to realize the merit of cooperation.

Averting the information asymmetry

For the assembly maker, the acquisition of information regarding the parts producer has an important meaning. When the information regarding the production cost and production system of the parts producer is not available to the assembly maker (the asymmetry of information), in extreme cases, the parts producer could cite an unreasonably high production cost to the assembly maker, demand a business at high prices and reduce the quality of the parts thus reaping the profit from the difference. Such a relationship, referred to as a "principal-agent relationship," indicates a problem in case there is asymmetry of information between the parties involved. If the assembly maker, who does not possess the information, sets the price at the transaction, there is an incentive on the part of the parts producer to cut corners and produce low quality parts. Consequently, parts which are traded may be only those of low quality. This is the "lemon issue" of which G. Akerlof speaks.[1] In such a case, the assembly maker needs to take a measure to induce the parts producer to supply correct information or to take a measure to obtain the true information on its own.

As for the assembly maker, it is natural to try to minimize the negative effect of the asymmetry of information by learning accurately the parts producer's production system and production cost in order to avert such a situation. To that end, it is necessary for the assembly maker to take care that the business dealings proceed smoothly by having frequent contacts with the parts producer and to obtain and exchange various information or, while preventing the parts producer's concealment of information, to put into effect the assessment and disciplinary system, such as stopping the business dealings and reducing the purchases, to be used in the event the damage is incurred due to the parts producer's information concealment. These correspond to what is known as the "trigger strategy" in the game theory.

Through the acquisition of such information, it becomes easy for the assembly maker to grasp the technological capability and management ability of the parts producer, and it is possible to judge, without any additional cost, with which parts producer it should enter in joint developments. In particular, with respect to the way to improve the parts, it is possible to expect an active participation of the parts producer and, thus, to proceed with the total development efficiently.

For the parts producer, there is a merit in constantly exchanging information with the assembly maker. Above all, long-term business dealings are maintained by having its own technological capability and management ability recognized. Of course, if the parts producer fails to maintain its effort, there is a good possibility of reduced business from the system of multiple purchases; thus, the parts producer is obliged to make best effort in an aggressive manner. At the same time, it is true that, by doing it, the recovery from the plants and production facilities and the production know-how that are installed to meet the needs of the assembly maker becomes assured.

In addition, there is a merit in that new technological development is made easy through the information exchange and joint ownership. For the parts producer, there is a merit of being able to commit itself in the assembly maker's technology development from the outset in the form of the design-in. There is also a merit in that, with the joint ownership of information at the beginning stage, the points to be improved on the parts involved can be pointed out early on and, in some cases, they can be linked to its own technology development.

Contestability

As we stated earlier, the assembly maker limits the number of supplying firms of specific parts only to a selected few. This fact implies that the parts producer has to continue its business with the assembly maker while being fully aware of the specific rivals. In addition, the number of the items a parts producer supplies is quite large. Therefore, it means that, if the performance of a given parts producer deteriorates, there is a good possibility of the assembly maker switching to another parts producer. In particular, with the presence of an evaluation system of the parts producers, of the assessment of performance over a relatively long period of time such as four to five years, which is a production cycle of an automobile, and of special incentives including an increased purchase are afforded to the high performance firms, it is inescapable that the competition among the parts producers be very intensive.

While not exactly the same, the competition in which the firms supplying similar goods compete in performance is referred to as the "yardstick competition"[2]: and, typically it is observed in the railroad industry. One can say the competition among parts producers retains the similar character.

This is entirely different from the condition of perfect competition in the conventional economics and is quite close to the world of the "contestability" theory, which is drawing attention in recent years as the competition among the few (Itami et al. 1988). The contestability theory maintains that, even if there is a monopolistic firm in a market, the monopolistic behavior (in pricing, etc.) is prevented by the presence of a "potential competitor" that has the equal power in terms, for example, of the technological capability. With respect to the case with which we are now discussing, there are competitors actually rather than potentially; so, it is reasonable to think that it is a world in which the competitive pressure is even greater than the world of the contestability theory.

When the number of firms participating in the market is small, the occurrence of the adverse effect of oligopoly can be pointed out. In the oligopolistic market, it is possible for the firms to collude to maximize the total return among themselves. However, in the case under question, if the parts producers were to collude, such an attempt is very likely to fail because of the assembly maker's many years of business dealings with them and its acquisition of information. On the basis of the above considerations, one would judge that the possibility is high that a market far more competitive than an oligopolistic market is being formed.

Stability

We have so far discussed in what sense the mechanism of keiretsu business dealings as a long-term continuous business dealing is economically rational. It must be clear from these discussions that, once a firm joins the system of long-term continuous business dealing, its participation has continuity from the standpoint of economic rationality. The next issue is stability. The mode of economic transaction is not necessarily limited to long-term continuous business dealings that are discussed here. Then, the questions that occur to us are: "Why does a shift to another mode of business transaction not occur?" and "Are there reasons for a shift not to take place?"

On this point, O. E. Williamson and J. R. Commons who are institutionalist economists and H. Leibenstein have expressed interesting ideas.

In the following, let us briefly summarize their respective arguments.[3]

O. E. Williamson's argument

Williamson classifies business transactions in the economy into "spot transactions," "continuous transactions," and "internal transactions" and discussed the stability of the mode of business dealings. As the "controlling mechanism" unique to each mode of transaction, the price mechanism for the spot transactions, the rules for the continuous transactions, and the hierarchy for the internal transactions are positioned. One can regard the "continuous transactions," spoken here, as a concept roughly similar to keiretsu transactions; and, they can be considered about the same as the idea that is expressed as "intermediate organization" and "network organization."

According to Williamson, economic transactions ultimately shift toward the mode of the spot transaction or the internal transaction and continuous transactions are not stable. The continuous transaction, the third mode, which is neither market transaction nor internal transaction is defined as the transaction that is regulated by the third "rule" that is neither the price nor the organizational authority.

Regarding the point as to why the continuous transaction appears on the scene to start with, his view is that it is because specialized physical and human investment is necessary for the transaction. Further, he maintains that, as the need for the specialized facilities for a specific firm and the human investment to be proficient in specialized know-how grows, the merit of internalizing such business transactions grows.

Because the continuous transaction arose originally out of this kind of background, the price mechanism or the organizational authority cannot be used for its regulation. Here, such a role is borne by the rules that may be mechanically and automatically applied among the parties involved. Williamson's view is that, otherwise, opportunistic behaviors are apt to be provoked. Thus, by constraining the parties involved through the application of such rigid rules thus controlling the opportunistic behavior, the merit arises of not having to go through complex calculations needed for regulation.

However, this rule is, by its original intent, rigid and cannot respond flexibly to the changes in environment, hence the limitation of the continuous transaction. When this constraint grows, there would be a shift toward a different mode of transaction. Two directions can be envisioned of which one is the road toward the spot transaction and another is the road to the integration.

On the one hand, the shift to the spot transaction means that the price in the market replaces the rules as the controlling mechanism; and, in order for that to take place, the goods and services that are traded must be standardized and specialized investment must become unnecessary. On the other hand, integration means the abandonment of the autonomy of the rules and the orientation toward a large organization with much discretion without being constrained by the rules. The condition for integration to be a rational choice is the intensification of the need for specialized investment.

Thus, according to Williamson's views, a paradoxical outcome is produced whereby, while the effort is made to realize the transactions that could not be realized through spot transactions in the form of the continuous transaction, its rigidity leads to the polarization of the transaction forms into the spot transaction and the internal transaction. However, this conclusion is not appropriate to the conditions in Japan today. The long-term continuous transactions we are discussing are indeed "long-term"; and, this form is not shifting toward either the internal transaction or the spot transaction. In order to get a clue to understanding this point, let us next examine Commons's views.

J. R. Commons's argument

Commons captured the corporate organization as an organized body for the sake of the "going concern" and viewed the business dealings of the firm also as continuously maintained as a going concern. Therefore, in the transactions among firms, it is indispensable that the expectation for the future of the parties involved be regulated based on some kind of rule. The rules that can function continuously under such a circumstance have to be based on unwritten rules or custom. In other words, in order for such rules to be maintained, there must always be an expectation that the transactions themselves are conducted fairly and appropriately.

Unlike Williamson's views, the thesis of Commons is very interesting in that it clarifies the universality of the long-term continuous business dealings and it clearly points out the basic conditions for them to continuously be carried out in the long-run. Commons himself does not touch upon the question of whether the continuous transaction is stable or not. He maintains that, as long as the expectation of fairness and appropriateness exists, the mode of transaction retains its endurance.

H. Leibenstein's Theory

Leibenstein captures the corporate organization as a human organization with feelings and will, and he considers that the efficiency of the corporate organization depends on the effort level of the composing individuals. However, various individuals in the firm would fail to expend their maximum effort continuously, and, as a consequence, the "X-inefficiency" emerges. The reason why the X-inefficiency occurs is as follows: Within the internal organization of a firm, camaraderie and group rule take precedence, and competitive pressure among individuals, as in markets, would not operate directly. As a result, individual effort would remain at a lower level than maximum.

The view of Leibenstein points out that inefficiency emerges in the organization of a corporation; and, relating to the issue we are discussing, it must be sufficient to say that the internalization of an organization or integration has the possibility of not bringing about the enhancement of efficiency.

The Stability of the Continuous Transaction Mode

With the understanding of the above theories, let us sort out different arguments regarding the modes of transaction that are of interest. In the market transaction, since the price is the embodiment of all information about the good, obviously the product must be standardized; and, further, it has to be possible to purchase it at the same market price. Since there are always firms that supply the standardized products and parts, there is entirely no problem of supply uncertainty to the firms that purchase them even if they rely on spot transactions without a continuous business contract.

However, as we have pointed out, most of the automobile parts are not sold in the market. Therefore, while there may potentially be firms that can be suppliers, in reality the number of the firms from which the products and parts can be purchased is limited. For this reason, the possibility of market transactions taking place is bound to be small. This fact is considered to be the major factor that prevents the long-term continuous transaction from shifting toward the spot transaction.

In order to shift to the market transaction, the standardization of parts is necessary; and, it has to wait wherein the need for standardization is sought by the assembly maker because a distinctive specification is costly or the technological capability of the parts producer improves to the extent that it can decide, on its own, the standardized product specification. In addition, the transition to the market transaction brings about an increase in the number of the client firms. Even if the parts are standardized, a stable supply cannot be expected unless the production system of the parts producer is known to be consistent with the assembly maker's system or any problems in the management condition of the parts producer are known beforehand. In this regard, the shift to the market transaction can overtax the management ability of the assembly maker.

Thus, we can see that, in the shift from the continuous transaction to the spot transaction, there is a formidable barrier in terms of the standardization and management ability.

Then, what about the shift from the continuous transaction to the internal transaction? The fact that there is an inevitability in the shift to the internal transaction in response to the increase in the specialized investment is exactly as Williamson has pointed out. With the shift to the internal transaction, it becomes easy to collect information on the parts production. Also, depending on the approach, the formation of trust can become easy. However, at the same time, the organizational internalizing implies the invitation to the problem of X-inefficiency that almost inevitably arises. The fact that IBM is trying to revitalize the organization through the disintegration of corporate structure concisely shows that the shift to the internalizing of organization is likely to bring about such a serious problem. Furthermore, in addition to the individual behavior within an organization that is discussed by Williamson, it is quite possible that the economies of scale and the economies of specialization of manufacturing process in the parts production would be lost.

Thus, here also, one should conclude that there is a significant limit to the shift from the continuous transaction to the organizational internalizing and integration.

In the preceding discussion, we have confirmed that there are sufficient reasons why the long-term continuous business dealings need not shift to other forms of business dealings and can continue in their present form.

4. Keiretsu Transactions and New Entry

Continuous Business Dealings and the Trust as a Good

As stated earlier, Commons points out that against the background of the firm's business transaction becoming continuous, there is the concept of fairness and appropriateness toward business dealings. In other words, this means there is the trust relationship behind any business dealing. Alfred Marshall called this the "good will." So, let us briefly discuss the concept of trust.

K. J. Arrow (1974) regards this trust as an economic good and notes the special role played by this "trust good" (trust, loyalty) by defining it as the good that is difficult to purchase but acquisition of which enhances the efficiency of various systems. This points out that the relationship of mutual trust is an important factor in the smooth transaction; and, in particular, it is easily imagined that such judgment is in the background of any lasting long-term continuous business dealing.

Let us examine another aspect. When long-term transactions are carried out, it is difficult to clearly state the contents of the contract terms. This is because it is impossible to predict beforehand what is going to happen. In this case, the business relationship has to be based on the obligations that are not specified in a substantive form. The contracts that do not state what is to be performed would function effectively only when founded on trust.

Further, the issue is how to gain the trust itself. In the case of business dealings among firms, unique installations and skills may be sought in the transaction. Also, there may be cases in which unique organizational, systemic, and personal ties are necessary. In order to secure the trust, it is important to commit something unique in such transactions. This means that the determination be shown in a concrete manner.

Accordingly, the knowledge of what is unique in the transactions is extremely important information.

Continuous business dealings and the entry possibility

The trust good and exclusivity

As we have stated, by making the trust as its foundation, the long-term continuous business transaction is maintained in a stable manner and comes to be lasting. But, for the very same reason, this system embraces a serious weakness that is its exclusivity. Needless to say, it is the organizational internalizing that contains most intensive exclusivity. It is true that the continuous business dealing is not as exclusive as the internalized organization; but, compared with the spot transaction, it has to be exclusive. Trust is, in concrete terms, a relationship that is formed between two people. Therefore, it is not very easy to penetrate the network of trust relationship that has already been built by somebody else.

In order to gain trust, it is necessary to build a friendly relationship by exchanging information, and it would not be gained without incurring a high cost in terms of time. Furthermore, even after the firms come to know each other well through the exchange of information, there is a possibility that it would not necessarily lead to the formation of long-term continuous business dealings. In this sense also, it is reasonable to say that the firm that seeks new entry must gain the trust commodity bearing a considerable risk burden.

This fact is clearly received by the new entrant as exclusivity. However, unlike the intentional exclusivity, this is the issue that arises almost always in the case of the operation of the system that depends on people. The exclusivity that excludes the new entrant intentionally must obviously be denounced. However, with respect to the unintentional exclusivity, one must say that there is a sufficiently rational support to its existence.

The conditions for increasing the entry possibility

The response to the existence of unintentional exclusivity must be done from the standpoint of how to reduce its undesirable effect. Concretely, it would be to identify the minimum conditions for gaining the trust. For example, they may be establishing a short testing period, presenting necessary materials needed for determining the management conditions and technological capability, and so forth.

Also, if the business dealings do not result even then, it would be necessary to explain convincingly why the efforts have been unsuccessful. By doing so, the conditions for entry should gradually become clear and the obstacles would be identified.

What needs to be considered next is the process by which to establish the trust relationship. In order to build the trust relationship, the exchange of information must be promoted. In order to promote the exchange of information, it is necessary for two parties to try to make some form of contact. The question would be with whom and in what form the contact should be made.

Let us look at several actual examples. Approaching the procurement section of a firm is not necessarily the best choice of the window through which to win new business when we consider that it is the window through which normal business transactions take place after the procurement decisions had already been made. Rather, most cases are those in which the assessment of the firms, which seek new business, is made through frequent contacts with the engineers at research centers and production sites that lead to the start of business dealings. Thus, it would be very desirable if there is a system by which the firms seeking new business can be referred to appropriate persons in charge. It would seem that such a system has a great merit not only to the foreign firms seeking entry but also to the domestic firms that are trying new entry.

In the above discussion, we have considered from the viewpoint mainly of the method to build a trust relationship and the strengthening of the system; but, another important subject of discussion is the standardization of parts. To be sure, the actual parts in the automobile industry are mostly not standardized; but, with the recent trend in the goods distribution and rise in production and development costs, there is some movement toward reevaluating the situation.

Also, the enhancement of the technological capability of the parts producers is a great hope for the future as a condition to ease the transition from the nonstandardized parts of the type led by the assembly maker to the standardized parts. As stated earlier, the improvement in the technological capability of the parts producer, which retains a considerable number of parent firms, suggests that such a direction of change is completely realistic.

5. Conclusion

When it is assessed at the present point in time and apart from its historical development, the "keiretsu business dealing" is a phenomenon of bilateral monopoly in a specific market and, as a mode of transaction, can be defined as the long-term continuous business dealing. Such a mode of business dealings has the economic rationality and stability as well as endurance based on the asymmetry of information, the dynamic profit as represented by the technological innovation, the standardization issue, and the efficiency involved in the internalized organization.

At the same time, we have pointed out that the same argument can invite the exclusivity of the system. The issue is how to eliminate the undesirable effects of unintentional exclusivity; we have argued that the method to build the trust relationship and the standardization of parts are important tasks.

Finally, we must mention that these methods must be resolved in a precisely rational form. This is because, if they are realized through a compulsory means, it would not mean that the problems are solved in a real sense.

Notes

1. "The lemon issue" is the following: G. Akerlof focused on the used car ("lemon") market in the United States and pointed out that, under the condition of "asymmetry of information," where the sellers of used cars have information on car quality and the buyers do not, only those cars that are inferior in quality are supplied to the market so that the market itself would not hold.

2. When there are a few firms that are regional monopolies, they are always compared with other firms in terms of various performances such as price (fee) level and service quality. As a result, the firm that engages in monopolistic business in a certain region behaves efficiently under pressure similar to the "competitive mechanism." This is called the yardstick competition.

3. Based on Miyamoto (1991), which gives relevant references.

References

Arrow, K.J. *The Limits of Organization*. New York: Norton, 1974.
Asanuma, Banri. "The Relationship between Producers and Suppliers in Japan," (in Japanese). In *Nihon no Chusho Kigyo* (Small Business in Japan) edited by M. Tsuchiya and Y. Miwa. Tokyo: University of Tokyo Press, 1989.
Itami, Takayuki, Tadao Kagono, Takao Kobayashi, Kiyonori Sakakibara, and Motoshige Ito. *Kyoso to Kakushin—Jidosha Sangyo no Kigyo Seicho* (Competition and Innovation—The Corporate Growth in the Automobile Industry). Tokyo: Toyo Keizai Shimposha, 1988.
Japan Regional Development Corporation (Chiiki Shinko Seibi Kodan). *Oota-ku niokeru Kogyo Ritchi no Tenkai* (The Development of Plan Location in the Oota Ward). September 1978.
Miwa, Yoshiro. *Nihon no Kigyo to Sangyo Soshiki* (Firms and Industrial Organization in Japan). Tokyo: University of Tokyo Press, 1990.

Miyamoto, Mitsuharu. *Kigyo to Soshiki no Keizaigaku* (The Economics of Firms and Organization). Tokyo: Shinseisha, 1991.

Sakamoto, Kazuichi and Masahiro Shimotani, eds. *Gendai Nihon no Kigyo Group* (Enterprise Groups in Contemporary Japan). Tokyo: Toyo Keizai Shimposha, 1987.

Subcontracting Firm Research Association (Shitauke Kigyo Kenkyukai), ed. *Kokusaika no Naka no Shitauke Kigyo* (Subcontracting Firms in the Midst of the Internationalization Trend). Tokyo: Tsusho Sangyo Chosakai, 1986.

Hisashi Yaginuma is professor of business administration, Hosei University, Tokyo.

Source/Permission: "Keiretsu Mondai no Ririnteki Approach." In *Gendai no Keiretsu* [Contemporary Keiretsu], edited by Tadao Kiyonari and KoichiShimokawa. Tokyo: Nihon Kezai Hyonron Sha, 1992. (Translation originally appeared in *Japanese Economic Studies* 21, No. 3 [Spring 1993].) Translated with permission by Mamoru Ishikawa.

Part IV

The Employment System

6

White-Collar Workers in Japan and the United States: Which Are More Ability Oriented?

Kazuo Koike

1. The Findings

Comparison of Workers' Careers

Although there is much that needs to wait for future research because of the present lack of data, let us summarize the results of the examination so far. To begin with, diversity in the United States draws our attention. It seems that, instead of a convergence into a single approach, coexistence and competition among various approaches seem to be present. This is reflected in the "vertical classification" of white-collar workers' careers. They belong to the "rapid promotion approach," in contrast with present-day Japan. However, among the approaches, the mainstream is the one that selects a considerable number of upper- and middle-manager candidates at a relatively late time of three to five years after initial hire. These approaches are different from those in France, Britain, and Japan with regard to the selection of high-grade public servants, in which only a limited number of executive candidates are designated through a tough examination at the point of new hire. However, there are also approaches that screen to some degree at the time of new hire through academic credentials such as the MBA degree. The current use of these approaches may be expected to grow. There are still many approaches in which the performance of the worker is tracked after hire. But what will happen in the future?

In comparison with Japan, the approach in the United States is a sharp contrast to the slow-promotion approach in large corporations in Japan. These Japanese businesses wait for a later date to conduct a final decision, or the selection of the future executive candidates. Although we lack sufficient data, it seems that the selection of future executive candidates occurs probably about fifteen years after employees are hired, when they attain the position of a section chief in the corporate headquarters. However, this does not mean that the United States as a whole is completely different from Japan as a whole. In Japan as well, the medium- and small-sized firms have rapid promotion. They examine the performance on the job, but the period of observation is short. This is expected because, unless good workers are given desirable positions, medium- and small-sized firms get raided by other companies for their talents. Furthermore, in Kasumigaseki (the national government office district in Tokyo) in Japan, as we stated earlier, a far smaller number of employees than in American corporations are identified by test at entry. These employees are similar to candidates for high positions in the central governments in France and Britain, which can be called the true "super-express group," and this is a common approach to rapid promotion. Thus, it is erroneous to regard slow promotion as inherent in the Japanese corporate culture. Slow promotion is applicable merely to the large corporations in today's private sector. Even in these large corporations in the private sector, the situation was different before the war. Although there have been no definitive studies, prewar companies probably used the rapid promotion approach with the former imperial university graduates as the elite class.

Therefore, between rapid promotion and slow promotion in today's large corporations in Japan, which will dominate in the future? Which approach is more efficient? To analyze these issues, it is necessary to assess their economic outcomes. Based on such an assessment, we would like to speculate on the future.

Diversity is also observed in the "horizontal classification" of the worker's career. From the start, we need to observe by differentiating the "super-express group" from the "non–super-express group" in the vertical classification of workers' careers. In addition, in the "super-express group," we can see that there are "multiple-specialization types" who experience more than one area, "main-specialization and subspecialization types," who attain mainly one area of specialization but also experience an additional area of specialization for three to five years, and the "single-specialization types," who concentrate in one area of specialty. However, the workers of the last type are very few; the "multiple-specialty" type and the "main specialty" and "subspecialty" types seem to predominate. These three types are also present among the "non–super-express group," and the main one is probably the third type.

When we compare this diversity with the college-educated white-collar workers in Japan today, it is clear that one can hardly make a sweeping generalization that the workers in Japan are generalists and the workers in the United States are specialists. Perhaps, the breadth of career for upper- and middle-management positions in large corporations in Japan is, for most workers, less than that for workers in the "super-express group" in the United States. At the same time, the majority of college-graduate white-collar workers in Japan are, perhaps to the extent that they are of the "single-specialization type," similar to workers of the "non–super-express type" in the United States. However, we could not find out about the crucial issue from the standpoint of skill formation, which is the substance of the "single-specialization type"—that is, whether it is the "broadly defined specialization" type, which experiences numerous subareas or the "narrowly defined specialization" type, which remains in one subarea of specialty. If the United States is characterized as the "narrowly defined specialization" type, in contrast to the preponderance of "broadly defined specialists," with a wide range among the college-graduate white-collar workers in large corporations in Japan (Koike 1991a,b), it appears that there is a notable gap in terms of technical abilities and skills. Analysis of this point must await future studies. At this time, we will assume that there are differences within the "single-specialization" type in our assessment of its economic outcomes and conclusions and, on that basis, speculate on future policies.

Mechanisms of Compensation

There is considerable commonality in broad terms between white-collar workers in Japan and those in the United States, in the mechanism of compensation. Both countries recognize the three pillars of job qualification pay, periodic raise, and performance evaluation. In the United State, payments are not based on individual products but on merit and grade. For the same work salaries rise by about fifty percent; this rise is due to the periodic raise accompanied by performance evaluation. The difference from the Japanese approach is often said to be the seniority system versus an ability-oriented approach, but this is entirely off-mark.

At a glance, the difference may lie in the number of job qualifications. If the number of required job qualifications is large, in substance it is close to job pay (*shigotokyu*) and would not create a powerful incentive to improve work ability. The approach in the United States is also diverse in this respect; although there are a considerable number of firms in which the number of required job qualifications is nearly as large as in that of firms in Japan, there are many firms in which the number is twice or three times as large as in Japan. However, in operation, three or four job grade levels are treated as a subgroup, and a worker doing the same job can be promoted among three or four grade levels within the same job qualification. Thus, the difference from Japan is not as important as it may seem.

The difference from Japan appears to be with respect to finer points. Whereas the amount of service after which the promotion levels off seems to be five to ten years in the United States, it is probably much larger in Japan, although there are no substantiating statistics. In addition, in many cases the upper and lower limits of the salary for each job qualification is not explicitly stated. But it is dangerous to decide that this is an idiosyncracy of the Japanese approach. As far as I am aware, the upper and lower limits of college graduates' salaries in large corporations in Sweden are not explicitly stated.

The most importance difference between Japan and the United States is the gap between white-collar and blue-collar workers. In large corporations in Japan, there is commonality between these workers in broad terms. Both groups have job qualification pay, periodic raises, and performance evaluations. In contrast, although in the United States these three pillars exist among white-collar workers, none is present among blue-collar workers. Except for a few cases, they are not observed. Therefore, if one were to name the main characteristic of the Japanese approach, we must say that it is the "white collarization" of Japanese blue-collar workers.

The same applies to employment adjustments. According to the commonly held past notion, Japan is characterized by lifetime employment whereas layoffs characterized other countries. However, in reality, in the case of white-collar workers, especially college graduates, "voluntary separation" or "early retirement" (*kibo taishoku*), which is descriptive of the approach in Japan, is prevalent. Compared with layoffs of blue-collar union workers in the United States, in reverse order of years of service (last come, first out), at least in form the volunteers who are willing to be separated are sought. Of course, inducements are necessary. This is a procedure in which as much as possible is done before resorting to layoffs. With respect to a reduction in work hours, in the case of the college-graduate white-collar workers, a furlough every Friday or a cut in salary is implemented. The core of inducements is, of course, monetary pay, and it includes an increase in pension, early start of payment, and payment of severance allowance. Clearly, these measures are focused on older workers. Even if the payment of pension were made to start early, it could not start for the workers younger than fifty years of age, and the amount of severance allowance would be in proportion to the number of years of service. When the number of workers who "voluntarily" agree to leave falls short of the target number, "shoulder tapping" takes place. Such a tactic is common between the United States and large corporations and medium and small firms in Japan. Japan and the United States are also similar in that these workers are not rehired even when the firm's business condition recovers.

However, just as in compensation, this similarity is strictly among the white-collar workers of the two countries; with respect to blue-collar workers, there is a large gap between Japan and the United States even in large corporations. In large Japanese corporations, the approach to laying off blue-collar workers is no different from the one involving white-collar workers that we discussed earlier: it is "early retirement."

The situation for blue-collar workers in the United States is entirely different: it is a practice in which layoffs are established in reverse order of the years of service and rehire.

White Collarization

From a synthesis of this discussion we can derive a relevant theme. The characteristic of the Japanese approach is neither a seniority curve nor internal promotion; it is the "white collarization of blue-collar workers" in large corporations as well as in medium and small firms.[1] As far as white-collar workers are concerned, although there are some differences, the broad characteristics—for example, the three pillars of compensation, internal promotion, and the voluntary retirement in separation—are common between the United States and Japan. At the same time, the blue-collar workers in the United States, Britain, and Germany possess none of these fundamental properties even in large corporations. Their compensations are by jobs, and periodic raises, job qualification pay, and performance evaluation exist only as exceptions. Employment is surprisingly long-term; however, promotions are rare, and unless the workers are promoted to the position of foreman, compensation levels off at a relatively early stage in the worker's career.

The "white collarization of blue-collar workers" can be observed in some blue-collar workers in Britain and Germany. It is especially noticeable in the practice of worker separation, and it appears that early retirement is becoming widespread among blue-collar workers in large corporations with labor unions in Britain and Germany. Performance evaluation was also seen to some extent among the blue-collar workers in Britain through the 1970s.[2] In the United States, where this tendency is least prominent, not only wages for jobs but also pay for skills and pay for knowledge, which are kinds of job qualification pay, have emerged. Nonetheless, the rate of increase in wages associated with skills and knowledge is limited; on a case-by-case basis, the qualification or wage rate rises only during the first four to five years at most. After that, a long period of leveling off begins. In such a situation, it is difficult to promote the enhancement of skills over a long time.

Thus, what does the white collarization of the blue-collar workers in Japan mean? What would be its economic outcome? Why did it emerge? Future policies can be designed based on the analysis of these points.

2. Rapid and Slow Promotion

Long-run Competition

At the outset, we will assess the effect on the economy of the differences in American and Japanese white-collar workers. The hypothesis that we wish to argue here is summarized in the statement that long-run competition exists in a broader scope in Japan than in the United States. What is this long-run competition? Let us begin with an explanation of "long-run." The long run in economics refers to the period during which capital, or in concrete terms, the number of machines, is increased and in particular, the quality of the machinery is improved. It obviously takes time to install new machinery or improve its quality. At the same time, the short run refers to the period during which the amount of capital is fixed; the number or the quality of the machinery does not change.

Today's economics and, in reality, its representative textbooks focus on short-run competition and analyze how such competition develops. They touch on the long run only as an expression; scarcely any analysis is conducted. This must be because, although the use of mathematics in today's economics has been spectacular, it is difficult to treat long-run competition mathematically. As a consequence, the development of short-run analysis must have become mainstream. Once we leave economics and observe the ordinary reality of the economy, inter-firm competition means the introduction of more efficient machines to compete by lowering cost. Long-run competition refers to something that is very commonplace.

When we apply this concept of long-run competition to human resources, its importance becomes distinctly clear.[3] To start with, the increase or improvement of capital is nothing more than the enhancement of skills and technical ability. Skills and technical ability do not improve instantaneously; they take time. The workers whose skills and technical ability improve by taking a certain amount of time move up to positions to be accorded commensurately more desirable treatment. This is long-run competition. If we delve into another fundamental condition for the formation of competition, the precariousness of short-run competition will become more clear.

This condition is one of homogeneous goods; it is an obvious condition for the formation of competition, and it is an unspoken premise that is not given special mention. It seems self-evident that no competition in the real sense would exist unless the merchandise were homogeneous. However, when we apply this reasoning to human resources and examine it in the light of actual experience, it turns out to be a rather curious hypotheses. Here, the quality of goods means a certain skill, and this idea implies that it is determined at the time of transaction—in other words, at the time the employee joins the company. It is an unrealistic postulate that the firms purchase a ready-made skill and, further, that this skill undergoes no improvement in the subsequent job experience of the worker.

Let us pursue this postulate further. Competition means the emergence of the difference between superior and inferior workers and accordingly of the differing compensations. Short-run competition implies the emergence of a compensation gap in response to the difference in the short-term achievement. However, the compensation would not be very attractive in the short run. Because of the assumption of homogeneity (the assumption that skills would not improve), promotion to higher positions would not occur even if the worker made an extra effort on the job. The only reward would be an increase in earnings through the efficiency wage (*noritsukyu*) or the piecework wage (*dekidakakyu*); although this may seem sufficient at a glance, there is no chance for a larger compensation based on promotion. Other than this, one might say that compensation is the small probability of layoff and continued employment. At the same time, when the outcome of work is not favorable, earnings would be reduced in terms of the piecework wage, and the continued employment becomes less certain.

"Long-run competition" switches this postulate to a natural assumption that skills improve through experience. It is a postulate that skills are enhanced through work experience and related skills are learned that enable the worker to perform tasks of increased difficulty. Thus, it disposes of the assumption of the homogeneity of quality. In other words, long-run competition refers to the mechanism by which competition is carried out, with the achievement in the long-run during which skills can be enhanced. The workers with good achievement are promoted to higher positions whereas those with less desirable achievement experience slow promotion or are demoted to the lower positions or, in extreme cases, are fired.

Long-run competition takes place in a realm in which the possibility exists of enhancing skills in the long run and, moreover, in which such enhancement is necessary. In the areas where neither possibility nor necessity exists, short-run competition rules. Therefore, in any organization in any country, both long-run and short-run competition coexist. However, competition is a social institution; once it is established, it takes time to change. For this reason, depending on the country and time, the relative importance of each varies. Even in areas in which long-run competition is more suitable, short-run competition may take place depending on the country, and vice versa. Let us note what happens when the relative weight of each varies. If long-run competition is widespread in areas in which there is a possibility that skills improve in the long run and skill enhancement is necessary, there is a strong incentive to improve skills and technical abilities. At least, there would be an increase in the workers who are prompted to enhance their skill levels.

Difference between the Theories of Internal Labor Market and Transaction Cost

We will now explain the substance of such thought compared with a conventional argument. Usually, the promotion method associated with long-term employment and within the firm is presented as the theory of the internal labor market. Its most standard argument is given in the work by Doeringer and Piore (1971). Their argument identifies knowledge of the idiosyncrasies of the machine and the personalities of co-workers as a factor in internalization. Even the identical machines from the same producer have idiosyncrasies depending on the machine, and the efficiency of the work can vary greatly depending on whether the worker is aware of them. Similarly, the theory argues that efficiency is raised by knowing the personalities of co-workers. This is true, but these reasons are too general. The idiosyncrasies of the machine or the personalities of co-workers exist in any workplace, so the internal labor market should be formed anywhere. However, in reality, in either the United States or Japan the areas in which an internal labor market exists fully are centered on large corporations; it is closer to the truth to say that its emergence is traced to the post–World War I period. The standard theory of internal labor market is hard-pressed to explain this point. My argument emphasizes that it is an area in which the skills remaining within the firm are enhanced in the long-run. This is the difference.

We can say almost the same thing about the transaction cost theory. It is often said that it is the saving of transaction costs that forms the organization of a firm.[4] Of course, such an argument is true—but is it entirely? The argument postulates the imperfection of information. It is premised on a kind of information imperfection in the sense that whether a person is a good worker cannot be well determined unless the firm lets him or her actually work for a certain period of time. It argues that, compared with the danger of hiring a worker with imperfect information, promoting a worker after actually observing his or her work is based on far more accurate information and, as a result, minimizes the loss involved in the transaction. This in itself is a reasonable argument, but perhaps not all of it. There seems to be an assumption of goods homogeneity here as well. However, what I would like to stress is that, when a worker remains in the same firm for a long period of time, his or her skills improve, and if improved skills are needed, the benefit to the organization far exceeds the mere cost saving.

When we premise our argument on the analytic framework of long-run competition, what kind of "vertical" promotion would most effectively promote long-run competition? To answer this question is our task here. In the observations thus far, we have identified roughly two or, to be somewhat more accurate, three approaches. Two roughly classified points are "rapid promotion" and "slow promotion"; the three involve, in addition to "slow promotion," two approaches separating "rapid promotion" into one that selects the workers for a rapid promotion track as soon as they are hired and one that selects them after their performance during the first three to five years in the company. We would like to analyze which of these three approaches fosters long-run competition. The conclusion that this author wishes to present is that the slow promotion approach stimulates long-run competition to an extent perhaps more than would the other two. I would like to explain why I hold this view.

Slow Promotion Approach

For long-run competition to form, it is imperative to decide on what duration and pace should be allowed for the enhancement of skills and technical abilities, and how to assess the degree of their improvement. Generally speaking, it is important to define what competition is and what the workers are competing for—that is, the elements of competition and the measured result of competition. Without these two, no competition is formed. The way one runs differs according to whether it is a 100-meter dash or 10,000-meter race. Unless what the competitors are competing for is clear, a competition would not be formed. Furthermore, competition would not be formed unless it is clear who wins in a 100-meter dash. If the outcome is decided upon by the subjective judgment of the referee, it would become important to curry favor with the referee and the event would not contribute to the improvement of running speed.

Let us apply this idea to the human resource market. First, the arena of skills and technological ability enhancement is the observation of performance for a certain continuous length of time rather than an instantaneous or onetime outcome. It would be unacceptable if the result of measured performance were too divergent from reality. Let us do a more concrete analysis starting with the former.

The period of time necessary for the enhancement of skills and technological abilities must be thought of as two categories—namely, the case that pertains to one single job and the case in which the worker moves from one job to other related jobs. Of course, there must be a number of jobs that can be learned only within a few weeks and for which no skill enhancement is necessary. However, in this study we are focusing on the analysis of college-graduate white-collar workers. They must acquire a high degree of skills and technological ability. In such a case, a period of two to three years would be necessary. To carry out a given set of work, perhaps a shorter duration may be sufficient. In jobs with a high degree of sophistication, however, there must be many elements of work that go beyond given or standard elements but are difficult to standardize, such as the response to the disposition of problems and abnormal events and the response to changes. It seems that the level of skills and technical ability pertains to the extent to which the workers cope with the elements that do not lend themselves easily to standardization. Even with respect to blue-collar jobs in production sites, such responses to nonstandard and unusual events are a crucial aspect of skills among the regular workers in large corporations. Among the college-graduate white-collar workers, it should be even more important.

In addition, there is a shift to different but related jobs. Let us take the example of a personnel management area. Suppose a worker who has been in charge of wage payments for three years moves to the employee welfare and health area, then to the training areas, and finally to a position in charge of labor union negotiation. In negotiating with the labor union, his or her past experience must be beneficial to his or her new work. Discussion in the negotiation with the labor union obviously would include the issues of wages, employee welfare, and health and training. Thus, these experiences must enhance the technical ability of negotiating with the labor union. With this logic, experience in any area would be useful, as all areas in which the employees of the firm work, including production control, sales, and other parts of the firm, are the subject of discussion in negotiating with the labor union. However, to be in charge of production control means having to be proficient in the way production control works, to carry out tasks at a high level. However, past experience in personnel management would not be as beneficial in forming technical ability in production control. If a worker were to be moved from personnel management to production control, it would be very costly because he or she would have to start learning the skill from the beginning. In comparison, within the area of personnel management, the knowledge and experience of wage payments is quite useful for proficiency in the know-how of employee welfare and health. Moreover, without knowledge of wage payments, one could not understand the issue of employee welfare and health. We can say the same thing about training. If a worker moves to different work, the cost of acquiring a new technical ability is minimal; rather, one can expect a multiplicative effect.

Taking this discussion into consideration, let us assume that a worker experiences four different areas of work with three years for each. To complete this cycle will take twelve years. If a final selection were to be made at the end of the third year, there would be neither a sufficient arena for enhancing technical ability nor time for enough observation. Unless the slow promotion approach were taken, for many workers there would be no place to enhance skills and technical abilities or enough time for the employer to observe it in detail. In this sense, it appears that the slow promotion approach has the effect of giving many workers an incentive for the enhancement of technical ability.

Using More Than One Performance Appraiser

Another issue pertains to the mechanism of measuring and assessing the degree of enhancement of technical abilities and skills. If the work is completely standardized, the improvement of skills can be measured by the output. However, such a condition no longer exists in today's production sites in large corporations. Coping with unusual problems and responding to changes are crucial. Furthermore, the object of concern here is college-graduate white-collar workers; it is not easy to measure in quantitative terms. The arguments often stressed with reverence in economics and business textbooks in the United States that the goal should be clearly identified in quantitative terms and performance should be evaluated according to the degree of its achievement—so-called management by objectives. In Japan as well some people propagate this idea as if it were the golden rule. However, if the parts that cannot be standardized are critical, how can we show the goal with clear-cut numbers? In the end, we can only depend on the assessment of the immediate superiors who are thoroughly knowledgeable about the characteristics and contents of the work and are able to assess accurately the degree of improvement in skills and technical abilities of workers and of the immediate superiors who work side by side with their subordinates and know their performance. I have visited work sites—in particular, white-collar ones—in various countries; in each country, performance evaluation hinges on the assessment of immediate superiors.

Herein lies an eternal question. Even if the immediate superior is capable of assessing, and even if he or she is knowledgeable about the substance of the work and understands the degree of improvement in technical abilities, subjectivity and arbitrariness cannot be avoided. Earlier, we stated that the crucial point is that the substance of skills and technical abilities cannot be standardized. If this is true, imprecision in determining the degree of their enhancement cannot be avoided. It is difficult to completely eliminate subjectivity and arbitrariness. It is different from deciding who has won in a 100-meter dash. At times, depending on the referee there must be a difference in opinion as to who was first. If arbitrariness predominated in decision making, competition would degenerate so that the competitors were obsequious to the referee and, as a consequence, competition to enhance skills and technical abilities would not form. Then, what can be done?

The simplest approach would be to increase the number of referees. Gymnastics and figure-skating competitions, which rely on the judgment of referees, provide a number of referees. Thus, the judgment of referees whose arbitrariness is especially prominent is excluded, and the arbitrariness would be minimized. However, unlike gymnastics and figure skating, in actual practice it is almost impossible in corporations to increase the number of referees at any time. Suppose the section chief were the referee and the assessments of the chiefs of the adjacent sections were added. Then, there would be three referees at any one given time. However, the amount of information the chiefs of adjacent sections possess is far inferior to that of the immediate superior. Even if the assessment were done by three section chiefs, there would obviously be differences in the weight of their assessments, which means that it is not really equivalent to increasing the number of referees.

Taking this situation into consideration, the approach of increasing the number of referees would actually mean moving the workers among various sections and making them work under several section chiefs. This is exactly the same as providing the arena of and time for skills and enhancement of technical ability that we observed earlier. Thus, for the same reason, the superior function of the slow promotion approach is clear.[5]

At the risk of being repetitive, let us explain these points in the context of the rapid promotion approach. In the approach in which selection for future promotions is made at the time of new hire, the place and time for enhancing skills and technical abilities would not, of course, be given except to a very few "leader" candidates. A large majority of workers would subsequently advance slightly; whereas there may be improvements in skills and technical abilities within this limit, the degree of such promotion would be very small.

In contrast, the method by which one can observe the performance of workers during the first three to five years after new employment is far more advantageous compared with the method by which one can make a decision at the beginning. Although it is as short as three to five years, a period of observation is allowed for the enhancement of skills and technical abilities. However, it is too short. Assuming that the period of engaging in one type of job is three years, the number of immediate superiors would be one or two. In such a case, there would be the possibility that the selection would be made while the arbitrariness of performance assessment was still pronounced. In concrete terms, this means that whether the superior, who happens to be the first the worker has, thinks highly of the worker is the determining factor in the worker's future career. Thus, to increase the number of performance appraisers, it is desirable to shorten the time period for which the worker is assigned to each job. For example, if the time is from one to one and a half years, the number of performance appraisers would be three to four. However, during such a short period of time is it really possible to observe an improvement in skills and technical abilities and, in particular, an improvement in the skills to deal with problems and unusual situations? When we think in this manner, it is easy to understand the advantage of slow promotion.

Grooming Workers for Upper Managerial Positions

No approach is perfect. The problem with the slow promotion approach lies in the formation of leaders. To nurture leaders in a large organization, it is important to have the workers accumulate experience in the main areas of the organization. This means that, even if an employee were not to become a specialist in the field, he or she should experience a few years in each main area. This process takes a long time; to implement it, the workers must be selected early. Of course, it does not imply that there is no long-run competition in the rapid selection approach. Even the workers in the "super-express" group who were selected early are not guaranteed subsequent promotions. At each stage, competition and selection are rigorous; in that sense, long-run competition is extant. However, such long-run competition takes place only among the chosen few, and there is isolation from competition with other large groups of workers.

The problem is that it is difficult to achieve a formation of leaders and, at the same time, enhanced skills and technical abilities for the majority of workers. Almost by definition, the slow promotion approach is unable to implement an early selection of leaders; at the same time, under the approach of selection at the workers' entry to the firm, a large majority of workers are discouraged and it is unreasonable to demand that they achieve a high level of skills and technical capabilities. The two approaches are in a so-called trade-off relationship: if one is chosen, the other cannot be chosen. Thus, the remaining choice is to pick only one or the other.

If we hazard comparing the two, within a certain premise one can predict the superiority of the slow promotion approach. This premise is to imagine the world of Frank H. Knight, the founder of the economics of uncertainty. According to Knight, the economic world is frequented by unpredictable events and it cannot be expected that even a capable leader would have sufficient advance knowledge about these unpredictable events and make an effective plan. In addition, he argued that the problems that emerge from such uncertainty are not limited to the level of a corporate headquarters with an effect on the corporate organization as a whole, but they arise constantly in individual work sites. If this is true, then the disposition of such a problem is not limited to the operation of corporate head-quarters, but must take place at the grassroots level. This means that the ability to dispose of the problem at the grassroots level greatly influences the efficiency of the organization as a whole. Thus, the enhancement of skill and technical ability at the grassroots level is crucial. In a classic book (Knight 1971), written in the early 1920s, Knight criticized socialism and argued for the superiority of the market economy; his ideas were supported by an international comparison of work sites during the 1980s (Koike and Inoki 1987). If we are to follow this idea, the slow promotion approach would be highly valued. Of course, it is deficient in terms of nurturing prospective leaders, and there is an advantage to adopting this approach while being aware of this problem.

However, there is a particular point about which one should be aware: the advantage in the United States of observing a worker's performance during the first three to five years. It is positioned between the truly rapid promotion approach, which is determined as soon as the worker enters the firm, and the truly slow promotion approach, whereby performance is observed for ten to fifteen years after the worker enters the firm. In this approach, considerable time can be spent on the formation of leaders; at the same time, work performance can be observed. It is doubtful whether this way of evaluating performance is sufficient and whether an improvement in skills and technical abilities can be assessed amply. However, it has the advantage of being able to take into consideration some parts of the two mutually exclusive elements. In addition, the "super-express group" selected here is not composed of only a few workers, as in the case of the senior public servants in Japan, Britain, and Germany, and rigorous competition within the "super-express group" continues. The degree of this competition cannot be underestimated. In the United States, however, this approach is being overwhelmed by one of early selection. Therefore, one cannot say that its advantage is being fully used in the United States.

3. The Broad, Single Area Type

Examples

There is a complexity regarding the breadth of career that cannot be grasped easily. The commonly held notion that the United States is characterized by "specialists" and that Japan is characterized by "generalists" does not even come close to reality. At the outset, one must note the distinction between the "super-express" and "non–super-express" groups and, based on it, diversity in the United States. Diversity is present in both the "super-express" and the "non–super-express" groups. Within the "super-express group," in the United States generally the proportion of workers who experience more than one field seems far larger than that among college-graduate workers in Japan. We have already examined its conclusion, the advantage in the formation of leaders. The breadth of the "non–super-express" group, which is composed of a larger number of other workers, is notable. Because grassroot skills and technical levels are important, we can recognize a greater tendency in the United States than in Japan toward breadth, as indicated by diversity and the "multiple field type"; however, the mainstream still appears to be the "single field type." The issue is whether the field within this single field type is narrow or broad—in other words, whether the worker experiences many subfields within a single field or only one or two subfields. Unfortunately, we have not been able to find any documentary material on this issue. From the few interviews we conducted, we found cases indicating that college graduates in Japan are slightly broader in their scope. We cannot generalize this finding with confidence, and we must add many more research studies on this issue. Here, as an inference from the limited materials available, we will hypothesize that there are more "somewhat broader single field" workers among college-graduate white-collar workers in Japan than in the United States. Based on this, we will analyze the economic outcome.

We have already discussed the advantages of the broad single field type (Koike 1991a). Because of their importance, we describe them here at the risk of being repetitive. To make inferences on this point, it is necessary at the outset to clarify what a single field is. Otherwise, one could not pursue its reasons. However, if we only discuss the definition, there is a danger that the discussion will end up being only abstract and will not contribute to true understanding. Misunderstandings would be minimized if we were to cite examples in many industries, and this would be a valuable basis for making inferences. Unfortunately, we were not able to observe satisfactorily the substance of this type in the United States, nor have we been able to find any past studies. Therefore, we will discuss such cases in large corporations in today's Japan.

Taking, for example, the architectural engineer, one field would refer to one of four following areas: "construction" (*shiko*), or the building of structures, "designing" (*isho sekkei*), "structural engineering" (*kozo*), and "fixtures" (*setsubi*), which is in charge of internal fixtures. Once a worker enters a field, he or she is unlikely to move to another field except for some extraordinary reason. To be broad means, to take for an example the area of construction (*shiko*), to be responsible for the construction of various types of structures such as condominiums, manufacturing plants, stores, office buildings, schools, and hospitals. In the construction of public works, aside from building dams and tunnels, it means to gain experience in construction of roads, harbors, railways, residential lands, and so forth. Construction of dams and tunnels requires unique technical skills, so it tends to be a specialized area.

In major general trading firms, each of the merchandise groups, such as steel, chemicals, food, and energy, comprises a field; within each, the breadth of the field refers to experiences with different kinds of merchandise, duty stations, and business modes within each merchandise group. The field of steel means dealing in different merchandise such as scrap metal and steel plates, being stationed in domestic as well as overseas branches, and experiencing different business modes of import, export, and third-country trading. In concrete terms, it refers to moving from the importing to the exporting function of steel plates and, furthermore, to being in charge of third-country scrap-metal trading (Nakamura 1991).

In a department store, each merchandise group, such as men's clothing, ladies' clothing, and furniture, constitutes a field. In the men's clothing field, for example, the breadth of the field refers to moving around and experiencing all subfields within it: formal wear such as suits and coats, the shirt group, and men's sundry goods such as ties; furthermore, it means moving to the buyer's duty and being in charge of merchandise planning (Koike 1991b). The move from retail sales to buying is clearly seen among workers in the "super-express" group at Macy's in the United States.

In the wholesale food business, one field specializes in domestic sales. The breadth of the field means being in charge of various markets in different regions by shifting every three to five years. With such a move, business clients change and the merchandise varies. Depending on the region, the customers and merchandise of retail stores, which are business clients, vary, and sometimes hotels and supermarkets become clients. In this manner, the worker accumulates diverse experience (Koike 1991b). In the career of sales personnel in a processed food producer in the United States, which we have examined earlier, a similar example is seen. Among college-graduate white-collar workers, those who specialize in domestic sales seem to be the "non–super-express" group, and they shift from one region to another every two to three years. Their geographic moves are more frequent than those of their Japanese counterparts.

Let us look at the example of a large manufacturer in Japan. This seems to reflect a general tendency. The fields are divided into domestic sales, overseas sales, general management, personnel management, accounting, information systems, materials (purchasing), public information, international operations, legal affairs, advertising, distribution, services, product development, research, designing, production engineering, and production control (Nakamura 1991). The subfields within each of these fields are, for example in personnel management, education and training, labor management in charge of negotiations with the labor union, welfare and health, and payments; in accounting, they are general accounting, cost control, budget control, and funds.

Diversity and Response to Changes

The reason for specializing within one field can easily be inferred. In the "non–super-express group," workers are the backbone of actual operations. The organization would not work unless they had the skills and technical ability to carry out these operations. It would be difficult to acquire these technical abilities unless the workers had many years of experience in a field. The needed technical skills would not be realized if the workers moved frequently among completely different fields. There are three probable reasons for accumulating broad experience within each field: response to diversity, response to changes, and the multiplicative effect.

The responses to diversity are recognizable in some cases and difficult to recognize in others. Recognizable cases are, for example, where the work at the point of time important to the worker's career requires handling various different tasks; one of the most easily understandable examples is in a general trading firm. Much of the staff of a general trading firm experiences overseas duty. The overseas offices have fewer workers than the domestic offices, so each worker has to handle many different types of merchandise. For example, although a worker's specialty may remain in the field of steel, within it there is an increase in diversity.

However, there are far more instances of subtle responses to diversity than of recognizable ones. They are fundamental and are the diversities that arise from the individual property of the items with which the worker must deal. Let us look at wholesale operations in the sales department. The skill most demanded in the wholesale is the ability to provide consulting services to retailers. It is to take into consideration the business territories of individual retail stores and recommend the type of goods to stock. Each business territory of retail stores has a unique characteristic, and it is not desirable to standardize all of them and reduce the sales strategy to a simple manual. If such an approach were forced on these retailers, it would be a simplification and an insufficient response. Veterans in sales say that there is no substitute for experiencing diverse retail stores to acquire the know-how to deal with unique traits of each.

Let us take the example of architectural construction from the field of engineers. Even limiting the type to condominiums, each building is different from others. Although the building may be the same, the land may differ. Even if the land is identical, the soil may be different, in which case the actual procedures and substance of construction would differ. Veteran architectural engineers say that there is no other way than to accumulate diverse experience to acquire the skills to cope with this diversity.

Among the responses to changes, the easiest to observe are those to the fluctuation in demand. There are changes that are in response to the business condition; there are long-run structural changes. With respect to the latter, which is the more difficult of the two, let us take the example of civil engineering construction, which is relatively easy to understand. In the past, this area was dominated by railroad and harbor construction, but gradually the weight of road construction and residential land development increased. If the worker's career were fixed in each subfield, a situation would arise such that there would be a shortage of labor in one area and an excess of workers in another. As a consequence, the cost that would be paid by the firm and engineers would be excessive. Even if we consider workers' mobility among firms, the problem would remain.

Furthermore, there are changes in technology and products. Technology often changes to completely new types, and it is frequently said that it cannot be coped with by seasoned technicians. However, in many cases the changes, even if technological, use conventional principles and theories. If this is true, conventional specialized abilities can be fully used. It is necessary only to conduct additional training and studies. Although partially new capabilities are required, in most cases there is continuity with past capabilities. In such a case, the ability to be versatile is a good base of dealing with new technological changes. Of course, it is a different story when it comes to technological changes that require completely new principles and theories. But such changes do not occur very often, and even when they do, they do not seem to overwhelm the existing technologies as a whole.

Multiplicative Effects

Multiplicative effects are the multiplicative interaction among the related subfields. This refers to the fact that experience in a certain subfield contributes greatly to work performance ability in others. Let us cite an example. In case of the retail sales over the counter, the main component of a department store business such as sales in the men's clothing department, the worker moves from retail sales to buying after an experience of about ten years. Of course, the buyer purchases men's clothing. In the buying function, the worker not only carries out buying but also takes charge of merchandise development. He or she would plan promising merchandise, look for and contract with appropriate designers, and arrange for the production of goods by subcontracting with suitable clothing manufacturers. To perform such a function, the worker specializes in a narrow range of merchandise and is responsible for the nationwide procurement of this merchandise. Such a worker switches to other merchandise after a certain period of time. The experience of handling several related kinds of merchandise enables the worker to be knowledgeable about clothing manufacturers, designers, and wholesalers; as a result, not only is the worker's ability to bargain with them enhanced, but also the knowledge needed for realizing ideas, such as which clothing manufacturer to go to for a specific task, is obviously increased.

More often than not, the buyer returns to work at the sales counter. At Macy's in the United States, which we examined earlier, the buyer frequently shifts between buying and store sales. For buying to be successful, on the one hand, the worker must thoroughly know the needs of consumers. The experience of sales work is its most important and direct route. On the other hand, to increase store sales, it is desirable to have merchandise that meets the needs of consumers. To place an order for goods as a part of a concrete merchandising plan incorporating such needs, it is beneficial to have experience in buying. The worker can convey needs to the buyers on the basis of his or her acquaintance with clothing manufacturers and designers. This is an example of the multiplicative effect.

Although one may be likely to think that the multiplicative effect exists only in exceptional cases, in reality such an effect can be pervasive. The example of personnel management work, which we discussed earlier, is indeed an instance in which this effect takes place. We have noted that the subfields of personnel management are labor management, which is negotiation with labor unions, payment, which is responsible for wages and salaries, employee welfare and health, and education and training. In negotiation with a labor union, wages, employee welfare and health, and education and training are obviously main items of negotiation. Thus, experience in these subfields would greatly enhance the ability to negotiate with a labor union; it is no more than a multiplicative effect. It is indeed because of this fact that such a career has emerged in both the United States and Japan.

In general, if such a multiplicative effect cannot be expected, it would be meaningless to prepare for a long career within the firm. It is simpler to hire specialists or temporary workers from the outside. Once the approach of developing a career within the firm is adopted, it is advantageous to try to form a career for the worker from which the multiplicative effect could be expected. At the same time, if specialists were hired from the outside, multiplicative effects would no longer be expected.

There are two reasons why such broad experience would not go beyond one field or, at least, why the worker's main specialization would be established. One is the problem of the cost of acquiring skills and technical ability. To develop the ability to perform in different fields, the worker has to start from scratch as long as the work is different, and the cost incurred would be extremely high. For example, let us consider the ability to perform the work of negotiating with a labor union. Assume that the issue to be negotiated is the number of work hours in the sales operation. If the negotiating worker were knowledgeable about the actual sales operation, clearly his or her negotiating ability would be boosted. Despite this, the reason why sales operations, production, and manufacturing are not included in the worker's career plan must be that the cost incurred in the acquisition of skills to give the worker enough experience to be useful would be far greater than the benefit. Furthermore, in different fields, the fundamental principles and theories are often completely different. Knowledge of personnel management and knowledge required in research and development are drastically different. How useful is experience in personnel management in the enhancement of the ability to perform research and development? Multiplicative effects cannot be expected. Of course, it is a different story if the worker, who is experienced in personnel management, is responsible for personnel in the research and development sector.

In the previous discussion, we discussed the benefit of the broad single field type. The narrow single field type would not be able to use the benefits we have identified. However, it is not clear as to which type college graduates in the United States belong. On the basis of a few examples, we may infer that, in the "non–super-express group," more are of the narrow single field type than in

Japan. If this is true, the benefit that we have previously identified is correspondingly less. Also, the argument we have developed is not limited to the single field type, but can be applied to the "main specialization" and "sub–main specialization" types.

4. Competence Pay (*Shikaku Kyu*)

Pay by Work Is Undesirable

The ability to perform work, in which the multiplicative effect in response to changes and diversity can be expected, would not be formed by itself. There are workers who work diligently without being compensated; for such an effort to be lasting, however, commensurate remuneration is indispensable. Needless to say, the core of reward is the promotion and salary. As a combination of these two, pay by qualification is important. For that reason, pay for qualification exists in Japan as well as in the United States. We must explain why this is so important.

As we stated earlier, in Japan ability-oriented compensation and competence-based compensation are commonly misunderstood as pay by work. However, if payment is made by work, important skills and technical abilities cannot be developed. Suppose that workers A and B are in the same work site and, whereas A has had experience with different types of work in the same section as well as in other sections in the same department, B does not have such experience. In such a circumstance, pay by work would result in the same salary for A and B. However, based on our observations thus far, let us posit that broad experience within the range of related fields is important to produce a multiplicative effect and helps develop the ability to work in response to changes and diversity. Whereas A has this ability, B does not. Naturally, efficiency would be very different between the two workers. However, if the treatments accorded the two did not vary, how could the firm expect A and younger workers to endeavor to acquire broad skills? If the salary were determined on the basis of work, it would be difficult to develop a truly high degree of work ability.

Let us digress somewhat to briefly touch upon efficiency pay, which is often used in western countries as a measure to stimulate the enhancement of work ability. Its rationale is that, with respect to the same work, high work ability results in increased efficiency and wage earnings; thus, efficiency pay makes sense. The argument for it also maintains that, in the case of white-collar workers, whereas it is difficult to apply the same principle because of the lack of output measure, efficiency pay is still implementable if an appropriate proxy index can be found, and that this is indeed what makes management by objectives. However, first, under the efficiency pay system, workers would not have an incentive to broaden their experience. This is because by moving only to the adjacent work site, for example, their output decreases and, concomitantly, wage earnings fall. In such a case, the firm could not strive to realize the multiplicative effect in response to changes and diversity based on broad experience. Second, as we have noted, management by objectives is not always a wise policy. Changes, diversity, and multiplicative effects do not manifest themselves in the short run. Rather than moving from buying to sales, it would be more efficient in the short run for a worker to stick to sales. In such a case, for the long run, is it really possible to define an accurate target figure? Also, in reality, the problem is that salaries and promotions are determined by the degree of achievement of imprecise target figures. Depending on the target figure, the achievement could be 105 percent, 110 percent, or, at other times, 103 percent. As long as salary and promotion are determined on the basis of these differences, valid decisions are impossible to make unless the target figures are precisely defined. It is easier to advocate management by objectives than to implement it.

Range of Pay and the Number of Qualification Levels

In the end, even if workers engage in the same type of work, there is no alternative but to have differences in compensation according to the rate of improvement in their work ability, and there is need for a range of salaries. Obviously, without an approach in which salaries increase when workers move up to higher levels of work, there would be no stimulus to enhance work ability. Qualification pay (*shikaku kyu*) meets these conditions.

Here we have the issue of determining the range of salary grade or the number of qualification levels. If there are too many, they approach work pay infinitesimally; in such a case, as was seen earlier, there would be difficulty in stimulating an incentive to enhance the work ability that occurs when workers engage in the same type of work. In contrast, when the number is too small—for example, three or four—the gap between actual work ability and the qualification level would become too great; as a result, this type of compensation system would not be an effective stimulating measure of work ability enhancement. If we maintain the earlier assumption that the period of improvement in work ability while the worker is engaged in one type of work is two to three years, and the length of this worker's service is about thirty years, we may imagine the number of ten to fifteen to be a benchmark. For a corporation as a whole, the number of levels of competence would be much greater because of the multiplicity of types of worker careers, such as blue-collar, clerical, research, and door-to-door sales.

As we have seen earlier, in both Japan and the United States the actual number is close to this. There seems to be, in the United States, a considerable number of corporations in which the number of the qualification levels is far greater; but when we examine their operations, we find that the number is actually about one third—not too different from that of large corporations in Japan.

The formation of such a high level of work ability takes time. For this reason, the firm would want the worker to accumulate many years of experience within the organization. Of course, even if workers switched organizations, the formation of the worker's career would take place. However, this route is more costly than when it occurs within a firm. We will not repeat the discussion on this point as we have expanded on it elsewhere (Koike and Inoki 1987, chapter 1, p. 14.) To promote the long-term retention of the worker, the system of periodic raise is obviously necessary. This point is common for Japan and the United States, and it is therefore not necessary to discuss it here.

Periodic raises come with performance evaluations. This is true in both the United States and Japan. The degree of improvement in work ability cannot be expressed simply in quantitative terms. Judgment of the increase or decrease in the ability to respond to changes and diversity is difficult unless it is done by experts. Thus, it has to be done only by such experts. To be an expert means to be a person who is knowledgeable about the work and about the necessary skills, and such a person must have worked in the area in question and thoroughly know the work behavior of the employee to be evaluated. Chances are that such an evaluation is the responsibility of the immediate superior.

These points are common among all white-collar workers in the United States as well as in Japan. Therefore, in either country the mechanism to promote the formation of a high level of work ability is in place as far as the aspect of compensation is concerned. Accordingly, the formation of work ability depends on the establishment of the worker's career and the creation of a method of selection. In this regard, there are fine differences between the two countries. Let us examine them.

Competence Pay (Shikakukyu) in Japan

Unlike in the career issue, the problem regarding compensation exists mainly in Japan. This problem is that the upper and lower limits for each level of qualification within the salary scale are not always clearly identified. In general terms, this means that the degree by which the salaries can be expressed explicitly in a table format tends to be low. Such a situation was tolerable when there were few college-graduate businessmen; but when, as today, they are the core of the front-line operations and their number has increased, it is necessary to identify as clearly as possible the relation between enhancement of their work ability and rewards. When their number was small, information could be conveyed without explicit communication and the firm could easily be aware of the growth in work ability of each individual worker. Thus, in such a situation the firm could stimulate an enhancement of work ability with attention to fine details more effectively than relying on impersonal salary tables or rules. However, once the number of workers rises drastically, the function of stimulating work-ability enhancement becomes ineffectual without resorting to formal rules. But competence pay (*shikaku kyu*) comes with both performance evaluations and periodic raises, and not all of them can be explicitly defined. Nevertheless, the upper and lower limits for each level of competence can be explicitly spelled out. This type of explicit description is not done extensively in Japan.

Partly because there are many non-union workers, the mechanism of white-collar salaries in Japan is often unclear to outsiders. We will analyze it with a tentative classification into various types.

First, there is "the salary schedule" type (*kyuyo hyo gata*); its typical example is public employees. It is also prevalent among government-related organizations, such as public corporations, and among giant organizations such as NTT. In this type of salary mechanism, not only are the upper and lower limits of salaries by each qualification level clearly spelled out, but annual amounts of raise are also explicitly stated as step pay (*gobo*). Except for the fact that, in Japan, it takes longer for salaries to level off, its fundamental structure is no different from the salary scale of federal employees in the United States. There is no issue of explicitly stated salaries here. However, this type would not spread among college-graduate white-collar workers in the private sector. The essential character- istics of compensation and assessment associated with the enhancement of work ability are not sufficiently incorporated in this type. Therefore, when workers are at the same qualification level, performance evaluation cannot be included in the annual periodic raise. This is because annual raises are clearly identified as step raises (*goho*). At most, what can be done to incorporate performance evaluation is to award the worker with a two-step raise (*2-goho*) or to disallow the raise. The exercise of performance evaluation thus becomes an exception. The only remaining use of performance evaluation is at a promotion to a higher level. The presence of performance evaluation is reflected in the speed of promotion to higher levels. In the final analysis, it is difficult for a "salary schedule" type to be established among college-graduate white-collar workers in private-sector corporations. For this reason, although we cannot be definitive because of a lack of reliable statistics, this type is applicable only to a small part of white-collar workers centered on government-related sectors.

Second, the majority of the large corporations must belong to the "core pay (*honkyu*) and job function pay (*shokunokyu*)" type. In the salary schedule type discussed previously, the basic part of the salary is strictly base pay (*kihonkyu*). In the "core pay and job function pay" type, which is referred to in different ways by firms, the basic part is separated into "core pay (*kihonkyu*)" and "job function pay (*shokunokyu*)." Job function pay is no more than salary that is determined by qualification level (*shikaku tokyu*). In some instances, upper and lower limits are clearly stated, but in other instances there are no ranges or only a single wage rate, with no upper and lower limits stated with respect to the base pay portion. The core pay (*honkyu*) rises, even in the absence of wage raise, according to the annual periodic raise. The performance evaluation is present in this process, and often it is not clearly stated. Thus, whereas there are upper and lower limits in the portion that is the job function pay within each qualification level, for base pay (*kihonkyu*) as a whole including core pay (*honkyu*), its relation to qualification levels is diluted. In reality, the qualification level is taken into consideration in the periodic raise of core pay (*honkyu*), and the amount of raise is large for those workers with high competence levels, whereas the amount is small for those with low competence levels. For union members, to some extent it is explicitly stated in the pay scale table according to an agreement as the result of annual wage negotiations, but for non-union members it is not explicitly stated in such a way that outsiders can easily comprehend. In such a situation, the stimulation of work-ability enhancement becomes ineffectual.

It is dangerous directly to characterize such a tendency as indicating the underdeveloped nature of Japan's system or its uniqueness. To the extent that this author has been able to observe, salaries of college-graduate white-collar workers in large corporations in Sweden are not spelled out in a pay schedule and are difficult to understand. As long as performance evaluation is an essential element, there remains some unavoidable degree of difficulty in understanding. However, even when the performance evaluation is sufficiently included, the upper and lower limits of compensation by qualification level can be clearly identified. In concrete terms, it is clearly to establish in some form the relation between core pay (*honkyu*) and level of competence.

Recommendation to Use the Work Schedule

We are also obliged to point out a common issue existing in both Japan and the United States: It is the need to identify the degree of work-ability enhancement somewhat more clearly. In actual practice it is difficult to identify clearly all manners in which the enhancement of work ability manifests itself when it applies to a high level of technical ability and skills. Therefore, we propose at least somewhat more extensive identification of such an enhancement. In concrete terms, we recommend the use of work schedules. In blue-collar work sites in large corporations in Japan this is already being done. Although there is no way to know the exact extent of the spread of their use because there are no statistics, we suspect that their use is widespread. For production workers, the following two kinds, or the one schedule that combines the two, are created and often posted on the bulletin board at the work site.

On one side of such a table the names of workers at the work site are listed. More often than not, the size of the work site is about twenty workers. At the top of the table, the areas of responsibility for each worker are identified. Each individual's experience is entered. For example, Mr. Abe is entered as having experience in areas 1, 2, and 3, whereas Mr. Ito is entered as having experience in areas 1 and 2. Skill levels for production workers are also entered. The entries are such that, according to this schedule, "*c*" identifies the level at which the worker has just acquired the skill, "*b*" signifies the level of skill at which the employee can carry out the task independently, and "*a*" identifies the level at which the worker can be an instructor. Similarly, the tasks involving problem

Table 1

Work Schedule 1

Worker	Work Station 1	Work Station 2	Work Station 3
Abe	a	a	b
Ito	b	b	—
Ube	a	c	c
Eto	c	c	—
Odaka	b	a	a

Table 2

Work Schedule 2

	Response to Emergencies		Response to Change
Worker	Type 1	Type 2	Type 1
Abe	a	b	b
Ito	b	c	c
Ube	b	b	c
Eto	—	—	—
Odaka	b	a	b

Notes:
a: High enough skills to be able to teach others.
b: Sufficient ability to work independently.
c: Completed training.

solutions and responses to change are noted here. To post such a schedule at the work site means that a worker's work performance can be subject to the assessment of his peers. Foremen and assistant foremen redraw this schedule every three or six months. In the case of complex and high-level work, a certain arbitrariness cannot be avoided in the judgment involved. It would be useful to check it. Whether an employee has experience working in a given area is clear-cut, and there is little chance of confusion regarding its determination. This schedule presents in table format the breadth and depth of skill and makes the degree of skill enhancement clear. Although performance evaluation does not entirely hinge on this schedule, an evaluation that is drastically at variance with the result shown on this schedule would be very difficult. Thus, the relation between work ability and rewards is made as clear as possible.

The preceding pertains to blue-collar workers. Our proposal is to see whether such work schedules can be applied to white-collar workers. I have never seen a work schedule for white-collar workers. This is probably because it is difficult to create one. First, the range of tasks within which white-collar workers move is broad. Even a single territory is large, and, moreover, at times the tasks move about beyond one territory. Second, even if it were possible to create a work schedule, the factors to be considered in evaluating performance in the case of highly complex work would be numerous, including leadership and the ability to deal with people outside the firm.

With respect to the first type of difficulty, as a start even just information regarding whether the worker possesses experience in different types of work in a section other than his or her own and experience in different sections in the same department other than his or her own would suffice. Speaking in general terms, information regarding experience in the work site in the small area to which the worker belongs and in other subareas would be useful. For example, if the worker currently belonged to the labor management section, experience in different areas of responsibility within the labor management section would be recorded. In addition, whether the worker had experience working in the welfare and health, payment, personnel, or education and training sections would be recorded. Regarding the second type of difficulty, if the evaluation were limited to the first fifteen years after the worker was hired, it would perhaps be eliminated to a large extent. For the workers above the middle management position level, factors other than work experience would play a large role; but before the worker reached that level, the relative weight of work experience would be expected to be large.

This recommendation is generally applicable to Japan as well as to the United States. However, if a firm uses the rapid promotion approach, the effectiveness of this recommendation would be less than when the slow promotion approach were taken. Because in the slow promotion approach many workers are committed for fifteen years, the acceleration of work ability is applicable to many of them. However, in the rapid promotion approach it would be applied only to the "non–super-express group"; therefore, some type of supplementing stimulus would be required in the form of compensations and promotions.

The preceding has been a comparison of white-collar worker salaries for Japan and the United States. When we extend our attention to blue-collar workers, a crucial fact arises. The previously discussed characteristics of competence pay (*shikaku kyu*), periodic raises, and performance evaluation are all common among blue-collar workers in large corporations in Japan. Of course, a similar tendency can be seen in the employment adjustment: the white-collarization of the blue-collar workers in large corporations in Japan. Next, we would like to analyze its economic implications.

5. The White Collarization of Blue-collar Workers

Intellectual Proficiencies

In terms of remuneration and employment adjustment, blue-collar workers in large corporations in Japan are accorded treatment similar to that of white-collar workers in the United States and, perhaps, also in Western Europe. What result would it bring in economic terms? Above all, what kind of work ability such treatment nurtures is critical, and we have expanded on this point in detail elsewhere (Koike and Inoki 1987, chapter 1). Here, we will explain its substance briefly.

In production work sites in large corporations in modern Japan, truly superior skills and intellectual proficiency are formed. An explanation of such intellectual proficiencies will enable us to grasp the economic consequence of white collarization. Intellectual proficiency is the knowlege of how to deal with changes and unusual situations. At a glance, it seems that such knowledge would not require a skill. Let us imagine a work site of repetitive mass production. After observing two to three hours, it becomes evident that surprisingly many changes and unusual situations recur. By changes we mean those in the product mix, personnel composition, and the production method. A change in product mix means that many different kinds of product flow on a given assembly line and the mixture of these products changes within one day or within a month. Such changes are obvious because, when the diversity of consumer demand is premised, it is impossible to provide an assembly line for each kind of product. Variation in the type of product is often small because the products are assembled on the same assembly line. When the variation is somewhat greater, machine tools and jigs are changed. This is called "switching over" (*dantorikae*). If it is done by skillful workers, it is carried out swiftly and, moreover, defective products will be minimized. The skill to perform this switching (*dandori*) is an element in intellectual proficiency.

Changes in personnel composition involve, among others, a reassignment of workers brought about by absenteeism. In any country there are absentee workers. Unless their work were carried out by others, the production line would stop. The larger the number of workers who can handle the work in any assignment at the work site, the less the cost incurred by absenteeism. Thus, the skill to perform at any post is important. When there are many new hires and unexperienced workers, the ability to instruct these workers at any assigned post is a valuable skill.

Changes in production methods imply, in the example of automobiles, model changes every few years with accompanying changes in the allocation of machines, the process of production, machine tools, and jigs. New machine tools and jigs are, of course, designed by engineers. However, engineers are not versatile in every area, and when production actually starts with a new production line, there will be unsatisfactory parts. Such a problem can be easily detected by veteran workers who actually are engaged in production. Efficiency in production varies greatly depending on whether there are such veteran workers who can point out problems. This is the substance of a crucial skill.

Of more importance than the response to changes is one to unusual situations. An unusual situation that can be detected easily is the emergence of defective products. The response to it is, according to common sense, composed of three procedures. First, defective products must be identified quickly and removed. Otherwise the production process to follow will be wasted and it will become difficult to detect defective parts. Second, the recurrence of defects must be prevented. The core of this process is the detection of the cause of defects. If the detective ability is weak, the machine will continue producing defective products. In comparison, if the detective ability is superior, causes will be corrected and defects cease. The effect on efficiency is indeed great, so such a skill is very valuable. Its substance is knowledge of the structure of machineries, the structure of the product, and the mechanism of production. Because something is wrong with the machine, defects will emerge. With knowledge of the structure of the machine, prevention of the emergence of defects cannot be expected. If we were to exaggerate, such knowledge is close to the know-how possessed by engineers. In this sense, we call it intellectual proficiency. Third, with knowledge of the structure of the machinery, the machine operator can fix simple troubles with the machine. The discovery of defects, the ability to detect their causes, knowledge of the structure of the machine, and the ability to fix the trouble with the machine constitute intellectual proficiencies. For the machine operator to possess part of the work ability of the maintenance specialist and part of the work ability of the quality control specialist is an intellectual proficiency.

The World of Uncertainty

High levels of intellectual proficiency are indeed valuable, especially under the condition of uncertainty. Uncertainty refers to a situation whereby unpredictable problems occur frequently and the response measures to them cannot easily be standardized. They are posited to occur not only at the headquarters level of the firm but also often at the work site. This was the idea of Frank H. Knight, the originator of the economics of uncertainty. If uncertainty occurs frequently at the grassroots level, it will be difficult to anticipate perfectly in advance the problems that may occur, to derive perfectly the response measures, and to standardize an optimal response and put it into a manual. Even if these actions were possible, it would be time consuming, and in the meantime, machinery, products, and production methods would change. In such a circumstance, whether workers at the work site possess intellectual proficiencies makes a drastic difference in efficiency.

To bring about the formation of such superior intellectual proficiencies, the firm must pay commensurate remuneration. The most central approach to such a formation is OJT in a broad sense. For OJT to be successful, the retention of workers is necessary. Aside from the period just after the worker is hired, it is desirable that he or she stay with the firm more than two or three years. As an incentive, periodic raises are indispensable. Also, skill in problem disposition can only be evaluated by people who are adept at assessment; thus, in the final analysis, such an evaluation would be the responsibility of the superior. Above all, piecemeal wages would not be compatible with the objective of creating intellectual proficiency. Even with respect to the same type of work, the know-how of problem solving differs between workers with broad experience and those without. The determination of wages by work would be inequitable. For the same work, salaries must be made different by the level of skill in problem solving. In other words, the most desirable pay is the competence pay (*shikakukyu*). If an employee is engaged in work at a high level of skill, the firm should obviously pay a correspondingly high salary. Thus, this is indeed pay for competence (*shikakukyu*). Of course, not all work requires intellectual proficiency. However, these skills are required in many different types of work. The work sites in large corporations in Japan expanded such intellectual proficiencies among blue-collar workers more extensively than those in the United States and realized an important outcome.

6. How Has the Difference Come About?

The Basis of the Slow Promotion Approach

How has such an important difference come about between the United States and Japan? Let us discuss this point.

The fundamental reason is the white-collarization of blue-collar workers. We should pursue the reasons for its origin, but there are a number of differences between white-collar workers in Japan and those in the United States.

There is a difference in the vertical characteristics of careers in the two countries. How has the difference between rapid promotion in the United States and slow promotion in large corporations in Japan emerged? It would be asking too much to seek the cause in the "culture" or customs of Japan. Although we have not been given opportunities to conduct careful empirical studies, we would not be in error if we conclude that large corporations in prewar Japan adopted a rapid promotion approach focusing on an elite group who were graduates of former Imperial universities. It seems that perhaps two reasons explain the slow promotion approach in the period after the Second World War. First, Japan was a late-developing nation among advanced countries. Second, the defeat in the Second World War had much to do with it. In general, in any country the educational gap narrows over time, but the speed of this narrowing can be considered greater among the late-developing countries. The reason is that, although not yet clearly supported by empirical evidence, the late-developing countries can take advantage of the experiences of more advanced countries and purposely expand the higher-level educational institutions. In Japan also, the enormous educational gap during the Meiji Era (1868–1912) was rapidly closed. Furthermore, the shock of defeat in the Second World War was great. Because Japan expended its full resources in fighting the war, its defeat destroyed the social mechanism that was created before the war. As a result, a principle of equality came to permeate the society.

We think that, because of these two reasons, the slow promotion approach spread among large corporations after the war. Because it was not widespread before the war, this change cannot be interpreted as solely due to the Japanese culture. Even today, the national government uses the rapid promotion approach and the selecting of future executives immediately upon hire. Middle- and small-size firms appear to be using a relatively rapid promotion approach as a result of their concern about being raided by other firms for good workers.

With respect to the breadth of careers, there have not been sufficient research and studies. Therefore, we need to wait to pursue its explanation until the gap becomes evident.

With respect to competence pay (*shikakukyu*) and employment adjustments, there is little reason to bother analyzing them as the gap between white-collar workers in Japan and those in the United States is small.

Basis of White Collarization

The most important issue must be to explain why blue-collar workers in large corporations in Japan are undergoing white collarization. There have been few empirical studies on this issue, so I am obliged to present my own hypothesis. It stresses the "late- comer theory" applicable to the late-developing country among advanced nations. Late developedness is not a sufficient explanation. If it were, the greater the degree of late developedness the greater the chance of the country's being ahead. I emphasize that this argument is applicable only to the situation of Japan's being among advanced countries and that the internal development state of Japan happened to have reached a considerably high level just at a time of important transition in the stage of industrial development in advanced countries. However, within such a large flow of events, there are fine substages, and I think that they helped spread white collarization. Let us explain it next.

We have elsewhere explained the industrial development stages of advanced countries and internal development in Japan (Koike 1977, chapter 7; also, for an earlier reference, Koike 1961). There is nothing that need be added, so let us briefly describe them here. In a general sense, industrial development in advanced countries is divided into two stages. The period before the First World War is regarded as the first stage and the period afterward is regarded as the second stage. Depending on the stage, the principal industry, main machinery, production method, and labor use methods vary. One of the principal industries in the first stage was textiles, and its main machinery was the mule. With the method of labor use centered on male skilled workers, England developed it on an unprecedented scale. In the second stage, within the same textile industry the machinery changed to the ring, and the use of female workers became the core. For the English textile industry to shift to the use of the ring, the mule and the method of its use that had grown to an unprecedented scale had to be discarded. The cost involved in the transition was enormous, thus forcing a delay in the shift.

At the same time in Japan, of course, the mule was used in the first stage. As is widely known, its start was tardy in the feudal clans such as the Shimazu Clan and at the early nationally operated factories. Before the first stage was fully developed, a shift to the second stage took place. Scrapping of use of the mule was easy because it happened before it had fully developed—or, rather, there were many mills that failed and went under. In its place the ring, which was the second stage of machinery, was immediately adopted. Thus, new mills came to the forefront in industry. The foremost was Osakabo (the Osaka Textile), which subsequently became Toyobo. New machinery and methods of labor use excluding male skilled workers were the foundation of world domination by the Japanese textile industry. If a country can dominate the world by low wages, developing nations should always win. The transition to the second stage is easier for late-developing countries.

If necessary, machines and equipments can be discarded. However, it is not the same way regarding personnel matters. In other words, the greater the weight of the human element compared with the material element, the greater the transition cost. The core of the human factor is skills. Their formation is a kind of social institution, and, we argue that, although they are obviously influenced to a degree by environmental conditions such as technology and the economy, once they are formed they continue to exist somewhat independent of environmental conditions. Skills exist only within the person who possesses them, and they take the form of the person's career. It involves an excessive cost to discard a skill that has been attained and to switch to new ones. The time expended in the formation of skills would not be recovered. Furthermore, this is not limited to one generation. The formation of skills takes place only when there are persons who teach and persons who learn. It is implemented within a social organization such as the firm, apprenticeship, and labor union. The social organization that has been established has a tendency to endure even when environmental conditions change. In general, the institution of skills formation, which involves the human element, is associated with a high cost of transition and also time consumed in carrying out the transition.

With these thoughts as the premise, we can explain the differences in the institution of skill formation among advanced countries in the following manner. In each of the two development stages, there must be a suitable economy, a method of technology and a method of labor use—in other words, the types of skills and the method of their formation—and labor management relations. If we are to focus on the method of labor use, a suitable approach in the first stage is associated with the craftsman type of skilled workers, apprenticeship system, and craft unions. The second stage is associated with the internal promotion system and the labor management relations based at the firm level. Where the first stage has prospered for a long period of time, the suitable social system is deeply rooted. In such a case, even when the second stage is realized, the spread of the labor use method of the second stage is delayed because of the high cost of transition that occurs because the system of the previous stage is too entrenched. In this process, Japan made the characteristics of the second process more intensively widespread than in other advanced countries. In this sense, it was a half step ahead of other countries in the world. It is a kind of late-developing effect.

Incidentally, if it were simply a late-developing effect, any late-developing nation would be at an advantage. In reality, this is not so. Luckily, in the case of Japan, internal development happened to coincide with a period of transition. As we touched upon earlier, the industrialization of Japan had already started toward the end of the first stage. Many other late-developing countries began industrialization after the second stage was well on its way. For them, the chance of moving ahead would probably have had to wait until the arrival of the third stage.

Within the confine of this broad framework, if we are to examine the process of white collarization of blue-collar workers in Japan in somewhat greater detail, it seems perhaps more appropriate to separate two substages: the interwar period and the post–World War II period. The approach of high-level skill formation in the process of the worker's advancement within the firm appears to have emerged with the World War I era as the benchmark. Before that time, even at a typical large corporation, the annual separation of skilled workers exceeded 100 percent.[6] It is reasonable to think that the situation of labor use was entirely of the "craft" type. After World War I, the mobility rate fell and the periodic raise system began to spread among blue-collar workers. One piece of supporting evidence is the wage curve by age. The earliest government statistics of wages by age, with detailed age breakdowns, was for 1927, and the wage curve by age for that year was no different from that for the 1950s.[7] However, the gap between white-collar and blue-collar workers remained in many ways including in wage levels. For example, the system of the year-end bonus applied mainly to white-collar workers,[8] and the system of qualifications was based on entirely different classifications between white-collar and blue-collar workers.

The defeat in World War II demolished these gaps completely. They were referred to derisively as the "interclass gap," and the society strove to destroy it as a symbol of *ancien régime* and eventually succeeded in its abolishment. As a consequence, the gap in wage levels between white-collar workers and blue-collar workers narrowed considerably. The system of qualifications (*shikaku seido*) brought the two together under one system. In addition, with respect to the year-end bonus, the gap between the two groups of workers was eliminated by making it an amount that is a multiple of monthly wages. We speculate that, probably preceded by such equalization in terms of pay, the growth of intellectual proficiencies in skills began during the 1950s and advanced rapidly during the 1960s and the 1970s. Empirical study on this point must await future efforts.[9]

Notes

1. This idea was already noted in Koike (1988); thus, we develop it here accompanied by data, only with respect to white-collar workers in the United States.
2. Perhaps because of it in large corporations, labor unions exist. According to a survey by a private research organization of blue-collar workers in Britain, whereas only two percent of firms had performance evaluations in 1977, the proportion rose to twenty-four percent in 1986 (Wickens 1987, p. 123).
3. This point is discussed in Kazuo Koike, "The Long-run Competition and Intellectual Proficiencies—An Explanation of the Japanese Business," *Business Review*, Vol. 35, No. 1; and later in Ryutaro Komiya and Ken-ichi Imai, eds., *Nihon No Kigyo* (Business in Japan), Tokyo University Press, 1989.
4. A representative reference is Williamson (1975), in particular, Chapter 4.
5. This point has already been developed by Kazuo Koike (1980), pp. 29–33.
6. The most detailed empirical study was done by Odaka (1984). At the time, of course, there were no government statistics; the only available materials were internal data of typical large corporations such as Mitsubishi Heavy Industries. This was a study that made use of those data.
7. Among the wage statistics by age before the war that are the most broad in coverage is the On-site Survey of Labor Statistics, of which the 1927 version was the first instance of a detailed age breakdown. However, there is no cross tabulation by years of continuous service and firm size.
8. According to the Home Affairs Ministry survey of 1935, whereas the bonus for blue-collar workers at plants with over thirty employees was about one to two weeks of wages, that of white-collar workers was two to four months of wages. In addition, this figure for white-collar workers excludes high-salaried ones. (Showa Dojin Kai, *Waga Kuni Chingin Kozo no Shiteki Kosatsu* [A Historical Analysis of the Wage Structure in Japan], Shiseido, 1960, p. 168).
9. Section 6, which is omitted in this translation, discusses policy recommendations based on observations presented thus far. First, it recommends the adoption of "a much broader field type," especially for the non-express group, with transfers within a given field every three years and the preparation of work schedules that tabulate workers' experiences within the given field as a basis for promotion. Second, problems with the slow promotion approach are noted: how to maintain the slow promotion approach of large Japanese firms when it comes into contact with the fast promotion approach of overseas firms, either in foreign countries where Japanese firms advance or in Japan, where foreign firms come; and whether the slow promotion approach can be maintained in Japan, where small firms compete with large ones, with the former having a fast promotion approach.

References

Doeringer, Peter B., and Michael Piore. *Internal Labor Markets and Manpower Analysis.* Heath, 1971.
Knight, Frank H. *Risk, Uncertainty, and Profit.* University of Chicago Press, 1971. Originally published in 1921.
Koike, Kazuo. 1961. "Chingin Rodo Joken Kanri no Jittai Bunseki" (Empirical Analysis of Management of Wages and Labor Conditions). In Ujihara, Shojiro, and Shin'ichi Tatsumi, eds. *Romu Kanri* (Management of Labor Affairs). Kobundo.
———. 1980. *Nihon no Jukuren* (Skills in Japan). Yuhikara.

————. 1988. *Understanding Industrial Relations in Modern Japan.* Macmillan.

————. 1991a. "Introduction." In K. Koike, ed. *Daisotsu White Collar no Jinzai Kaihatsu* (Human Resource Development of College-Graduate White-Collar Workers). Toyo Keizai Shimposha.

————. 1991b. "Eigyo Bunya no Jinzai Kaihatsu" (Human Resource Development in the Operations Field). In K. Koike, ed., *op. cit.*

Nakamura, Megumu. "Seizogyo Jimukei no Career Keisei" (The Career Formation of Clerical Workers in Manufacturing Firms). In K. Koike, ed., *op. cit.,* 1991.

Odaka, Konosuke. *Rodo Shijo Bunseki* (Analysis of the Labor Market). Iwanami Shoten, 1984.

Wickens, Peter. *The Road to Nissan: Flexibility, Quality, Teamwork.* Macmillan, 1987.

Williamson, Oliver E. *Markets and Hierarchy.* Free Press, 1975.

Kazuo Koike is professor of labor economics, Hosei University, Tokyo.

*Source/Permission:*Kazuo Koike, *Amerika no White Collar—Nichibei no Dochiraga yori Jitsuryoku.* Tokyo: Toyo Keizai Shimpo Sha, 1993. This translation of Chapter 8, "Shorai no Seisaku" [The Future Policy], omits Section 6, "Policy Recommendations." (Translation originally appeared in *Japanese Economic Studies* 22, No. 1 [January–February 1994].) Translated with permission by Mamoru Ishikawa.

7

Japanese-Style Employment Practices and Male-Female Wage Differentials

Machiko Osawa

In the previous chapter, we considered how women coped with economic change and how that influenced male-female wage differentials.* Women's employment patterns have changed dramatically depending on their decisions about childbirth. During the prewar generation it was common practice for women to marry and become homemakers. Employment patterns changed for the wartime and postwar generations when women worked as regular workers before marriage and childbirth and then sought reentry into the labor force as nonregular workers. Now a new generation is emerging in which women are delaying marriage and childbirth as they attempt to combine career and matrimony. In this chapter, we consider how firms have dealt with the economic change and the male-female wage differentials from the labor–demand side.

1. What Produces Wage Differentials?

In the previous chapter, we considered the major determinant of male-female wage differentials to be the difference in human capital accumulation—interpreted as the formation of skills—between men's and women's career patterns. We then considered how human capital accumulation, represented by variables of education level and years of continuous service, changed through economic development and how those factors influenced wage differentials. From that analysis, we concluded that the major determinant of male-female wage differentials was the difference in job tenure. However, it was not clear why job tenure for women was so short.

If we follow the human capital theory (which formed the premise of the previous chapter's analysis), women who quit work to marry and raise a family have less capital accumulation than men during their younger years because of the differential in male-female career plans. However, if a firm implements

---

*See source note on p. 235.

differential on-the-job training and job rotation for men and women based on the premise that women will terminate employment when they marry, the explanation then lies with the firm's hiring system. We will explore the reasons why firms engage in discriminatory hiring practices in our discussion of discrimination theories below.

Discrimination Theories

1. Becker's Model of Discrimination

Becker (1957) hypothesized that paying different wages to workers of comparable skill and productivity is due to biases held by employers toward some workers. To compensate for the manager's psychological attitude, those being discriminated against think they have no alternative but to accept low wages. The stronger the manager's preference for discrimination, the more pronounced the wage differential between the regular workers (men) and the discriminated-against workers (women). Employers with strong tendencies for discrimination who cannot accept wage differentials in the market will only hire male workers.

In competitive product markets, firms with a strong tendency toward discrimination will incur higher labor costs because they hire more male workers compared to firms that do not. This means that over the long term they will lose out to their competitors. In other words, firms that practice discrimination must bear the burden of such costs. In a competitive situation, if a new business enters the markets, it must be a firm with less discrimination if it is to survive in the long run. The problem with using Becker's theory to explain male-female wage differentials is its inability to explain why such substantial wage differentials continue to exist in the long term.

2. Madden's Theory of Monopsony

In contrast to Becker's theory, which is based on a competitive market, Madden (1975) demonstrated that the market is monopsonistic (a small number of firms have monopoly power over the hiring of workers). Moreover, the labor market is segmented between regular workers (men) and workers who are discriminated against (women). The underlying assumption of this theory is that the supply of discriminated-against workers has a lower correspondence to wages than that of regular workers—that is, their labor supply does not respond much to variations in wages. Thus, a firm maximizes its profits by paying lower wages to women.

However, this theory does not hold up in the real-world situation for women workers. As shown in the estimated results in Chapter 2, wage elasticity is higher for women than for men, and it is higher for nonregular employees than for regular employees.

3. Bergmann's Crowding Hypothesis

Bergmann's (1971) crowding hypothesis did not specifically address the issue of wage discrimination against women but related wage differentials to occupational discrimination. As we saw in Chapter 3, women in all countries tend to be concentrated in a smaller number of occupations than men. Bergmann called this the crowding phenomenon which occurs because women are excluded from many fields and are thus concentrated in specific occupations.

In other words, the male-female labor market is structurally segmented. Wages are lower in predominantly female occupations which are fewer in number because women concentrate in fewer occupations. On the other hand, women's exclusion from male occupations leads to a relatively small labor supply to satisfy labor demand. Compared to cases in which women are not structurally restricted in the labor market, wage levels in male-dominated occupations rise and generate male-female wage differentials. Therefore, according to this theory, male-female wage differentials generate occupational discrimination against women in the market.

Empirical research results from the United States show that the greater the division between the occupations, the smaller the male-female wage differential. We can determine from the results that the male-female wage differentials are generated by women who typically concentrate in low-wage occupations or jobs rather than being generated within similar occupations or jobs. However, this hypothesis fails to explain why women are concentrated in specific occupations and, moreover, why male-female differentials exist within similar occupations.

On the other hand, according to the human capital theory, female occupations are specialized with minimal skill loss associated with the interruption of employment. Following this theory, women voluntarily base their occupational selection on this anticipated interruption in employment. In reality, women are more enthusiastic than men about learning the necessary skills that lead to specialized qualifications and practical ability. Moreover, these qualifications are very useful in finding employment. A "qualification boom" is currently being carried out for women in Japan.

4. The Dual Labor Market Theory

Bergmann's crowding hypothesis contended that a male-female differential exists in occupational distribution, and that structurally restricted movement between these two occupational groups is the primary determinant of male-female wage differentials. In contrast, Doeringer and Piore (1971) advocated the dual labor market theory, which holds that the structural division of the labor market into two segments, rather than occupations, determines wage differentials. The two labor markets they describe are distinguished by on-the-job opportunities for workers and differences in skill formation.

Within internal labor markets, skills are formed through formal, on-the-job opportunities or informal training provided by senior staff members coupled with repeated job rotations, promotions, and job upgradings. This type of skill formation can only be realized through stable employment and long-term, continuous service. Moreover, the costs of losing an employee are high and the skills a worker attains through on-the-job training are not useful in other firms. Therefore, firms and workers alike are motivated to establish internal promotion and pay-raise systems and to organize unions to maintain routine labor practices.[2]

In external labor markets, on the other hand, most work is simple and repetitive and incurs no worker-training costs. In addition, management incentives to establish long-term, stable employment relationships are minimal. Workers fear layoffs caused by economic recession; for the most part, wage increases corresponding to educational background and years of service are rare. Moreover, these two labor markets are segmented, and movements from external labor markets to internal labor markets are fundamentally restricted.

Then, what produces this kind of labor market segmentation? According to this theory, the external labor market must compensate for the established employment and wage systems in internal markets which cannot flexibly handle external economic shock. In the United States, unions within internal labor markets are also said to facilitate the development of external labor markets. Minorities and women constitute the largest majority of workers in external markets. If entry into internal labor markets is structurally restricted and women are forced to work in external labor markets, then the wage differentials generated here are caused by structural restrictions in the labor market and entrance barriers.

The problem with the dual labor market theory lies in the difficulty of providing empirical evidence. First, classifying data using comprehensive employment experience and wage information to explain the existence of dual labor markets is problematic. The criteria for classification are necessarily arbitrary. Second, if we classify an industry or an occupation as being within an external market because of low wages, it is natural for the effect of education and continuous service to be low as reflected in worker wages. In other words, because the range of explanatory variables has been restricted a priori, the resultant bias tends to make the hypothesis easy to prove.

Recently, however, a new econometric method of switch regression analysis has been used in studies. Instead of researchers classifying industries and occupations, it is now possible to judge classification effectiveness on the data itself (Dickens and Lang 1985). Using this method, the development of new research confirms the existence of dual labor markets and clarifies wage differentials by firm size in both markets.

5. *Theory of Statistical Discrimination*

To explain the persistence of wage differentials, some theories focus on exogenous factors: structural discrimination in the labor market (the dual labor market theory and Bergmann's crowding hypothesis) or employer preference

(Becker's theory). Another theory contends that discrimination results from imperfect information received about the ability and productivity of workers, even if structural discrimination does not exist in the labor market. This is referred to as the "theory of statistical discrimination" and has been theorized by Phelps (1972), Arrow (1972), and others.

It is impossible for firms to accurately judge the ability and future productivity of workers when they are hired because of the high cost of collecting information. Therefore, employers judge workers by substituting indicators such as sex, race, age, and societal assessments such as the university from which an applicant graduated. Statistically speaking, women have fewer years of job tenure than men and have higher resignation rates. Because firms do not want to jeopardize their chances to recoup on-the-job training costs, they provide more educational training for men than they do for women. As compared to men, there is a drop in productivity for women, which results in their receiving lower wages.

The theory of dual labor markets explains the wage differentials that cannot be captured in human capital variables, such as educational attainment or job tenure. However, in contrast, this theory argues that discrimination exists in male-female differentials in educational training and length of continuous service. Compared to Becker's theory, which asserts that employer discrimination results in lower profits, this theory claims that firms engage in rational behavior to maximize profits but that such behavior also results in discriminatory treatment.

2. Research on Male-Female Wage Differentials

What kind of research on male-female wage differentials has been conducted in Japan, and what do we understand from the results? Two major arguments have been proposed from this research. The statistical discrimination theory is one argument; it contends that the lack of perfect information about individual workers produces discrimination between men and women in on-the-job training and promotion. The other argument is the "dual labor market" theory; it holds that the labor market's employment system itself is the main reason discriminatory treatment occurs. Let us look at the respective arguments below.

Wage Differentials Created by
Differences in On-the-Job Training

Yashiro's research (1980), which is representative of the statistical discrimination theory, holds that the high resignation rate for female workers is the reason for statistical discrimination in the Japanese workplace. The resignation rate for women rises when they are in their late twenties, that is during their marriage and childbirth years. According to Yashiro, statistical discrimination occurs because firms invest large sums of money in on-the-job training and in the cultivation of a capable workforce.

To support these claims, Yashiro indicates that the faster an industry advances technologically and the more importance it places on on-the-job training, the larger the male-female wage differential will be due to age and job tenure. In workplaces in which on-the-job training is of utmost importance (internal labor markets), there is a high degree of dependence on long-term workers. This forces female workers into small- to mid-sized firms or into light industries. Yashiro points out that a crowding phenomenon occurs in these sectors, and there is a trend toward lower starting salaries (Yashiro 1980, pp. 185–9).

Part of this argument is that a more important determinant of women's exclusion from desirable work is the high female resignation rate. To rectify wage differentials, it is important to make homemaking and outside employment compatible. This means reducing the rate at which females resign from their jobs as well as implementing policies that give reemployment opportunities to women who have interrupted work for family and childrearing.

Structural Discrimination Inherent in Labor Markets

The statistical discrimination theory questions the high female resignation rate and the low female rate of staying with the same employer. In contrast, there is a theory that contends that the high female resignation rate stems from discriminatory employment practices within firms.

Horne-Kawashima (1985) divides Japan's labor market into the concentrated sector and the competitive sector and analyzes the primary causes of male-female wage differentials in these two labor markets. The concentrated sector, in which the internal labor markets are formed, consists of firms with a strong, oligopolistic influence on the market. Worker wages are institutionally determined by long-term service, not competitively determined by labor market demand and supply. The competitive sector consists of firms with low levels of capital concentration, low productivity, and high worker resignation rates.

In the distribution of workers in these two sectors, there is a higher ratio of women than men working in the competitive industrial sector. Even within that sector, the smaller the firm size, the higher the percentage of women. Moreover, the primary economic determinants of male-female wage differentials in this sector (by controlling for both male and female job tenure for workers in the competitive sector) is reduced by as much as 75 percent. On the other hand, the respective number in the concentrated sector represents a reduction of only 26 percent (Horne-Kawashima 1985, p. 122). In other words, women working in the concentrated sector are assigned to clerical occupations or to occupations with specific but simple tasks, which carry limited or no promotional possibilities from the outset. Because men receive differential treatment, for example, the reduction of wage differentials by controlling for years of education across gender is minimal.

According to Nishimura (1977), when labor markets are segmented into internal and external components, women in internal markets receive differential treatment from the outset. That is women are treated as short-term workers and men as long-term workers. Nishimura's theory indicated that it is possible to perceive both discriminatory employment practices and persistent male-female wage differentials over time as long as the given conditions do not change. According to him, differential treatment leads to minimization of costs, and male-female discrimination in labor markets stems from the rational behavior of firms to maximize profits.

Nishimura's theory is that in internal labor markets, it is assumed that skills are acquired through on-the-job experience obtained, in turn, by remaining with a firm for a period of time. This necessitates paying workers a wage premium for long-term service. However, firms do not make long-term employment contracts with the entire work force. All workers are unskilled when hired and then are divided into two groups. One group is "future skilled workers" who become skilled through long-term service; the other is a group of "unskilled workers" who perform short-term support work. If workers know from the beginning which group they will join, firms can produce long-term workers while spending less on wage premiums paid to short-term workers.

Since information about workers is scarce at the time of hire, firms divide workers into long-term and short-term employment groups by using indicators such as sex, education, and race. If sufficient numbers are not assured with men only, female college graduates are the next to be included in the long-term employment group. Thus, if there is an acute labor shortage, women will be given an opportunity.

The policy implications for the assertions made by Horne-Kawashima and Nishimura differ from those of statistical discrimination, which argues that the high female resignation rate produces a male-female differential in on-the-job training, which, in turn, creates male-female wage differentials. Here, it is necessary to turn the focus to the discriminatory personnel policies of firms which play a significant role in obstructing women's internal promotion.

Japanese Personnel Management:
An International Comparison

What do we understand from international comparative research conducted in Japan and other countries? Mary Saso (1990, p. 189) did comparative research on women workers in Japanese firms which conduct business in both Japan and the Great Britain. She contrasts the Japanese workplace in which young, single women comprise the majority to the significant number of married women with long-term service in Great Britain. Saso surmises that once Japanese women marry and resign from their jobs, they have little chance of returning to large firms. The open entry to internal labor markets which exists for women in Great

Britain is closed to women in Japan, wherein lies the fundamental difference between female workers in Japan and Great Britain. This research is significant because it shows the differences between Japanese employment patterns and those of the same firms in foreign countries because of the different social environments and hiring practices.

Brinton (1992) compares the distribution of women workers in different sized firms in Japan and the United States. A higher rate of women working in small-scale firms is the same in both countries. However, Brinton points to a phenomenon, not seen in the United States, in which the larger the size of the Japanese firm, the younger the average age of its women workers.

Figure 1 compares the average age of male and female workers in Japan and the United States by the size of the firm. Except for Japanese women workers, there is no clear correlation between firm size and the average age of workers. For Japanese women workers, however, there is a clear difference in the average age in firms with 30 to 99 employees and firms with over 1,000 employees. The average age lowers proportionally as the size of the firm increases. *The Basic Survey of Employment Structure* (1987) shows the average age of women in firms with over 1,000 employees was 32 years, while the average age in firms with 1 to 4 employees was 40.4 years. On the other hand, the difference was minimal for men with an average age of 38.4 years in large firms and 42.5 years in small firms.

Does this reflect, as Saso indicated, the double standard of Japanese hiring practices which limits employment for young women to short-term job opportunities in large-sized firms and for married women to small- to mid-sized firms? Why does this characteristic of female workers exist in Japan when it is not seen in other industrialized countries? As Yashiro indicates, does this stem from large firms not offering women the same on-the-job training opportunities provided for men, using the high female resignation rate as justification?

However, the comparatively high female resignation rate is not a phenomenon found only in Japan so it cannot be used to explain the dual nature of the labor market for women in Japan. If women are excluded from the concentrated sector, as Horne-Kawashima argues, then what are the reasons for this exclusion? Does the reason lie in the way wage premiums are paid to workers, as Nishimura theorized? Supposing this theory is true, why did industrial management change their policies in the 1980s? In order to answer these questions, let us first analyze the primary determinants of male-female wage differentials by firm size.

3. Male-Female Wage Differentials by Firm Size

The previous discussion of research examining the male-female wage differentials indicated a tendency existed to exclude Japanese women from internal labor markets. In Japan, the internal labor market becomes more extensive as a firm

Figure 1

**Comparison of the Average Age of Employees
by Firm Size in the United States and Japan**

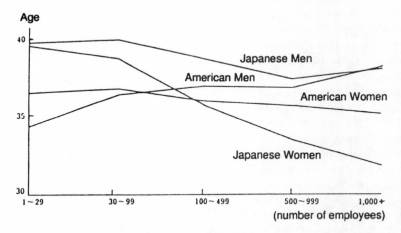

Source: Brinton, 1992, which was based on figures from the *Current Population Survey,* U.S. Census Bureau, 1979, and Japan, *Basic Survey of Employment Structure*, Ministry of Labor, 1982.

expands. To see if there is a correlation between firm size and male-female wage differentials, let us now examine these characteristics.

Characteristics of Wage Differentials by Firm Size

Table 1 compares the wages of women relative to the wages of men in large firms (with male wages set at 100 percent). In this table, large-sized firms contain over 1,000 employees and small- to mid-sized firms have 10 to 99 employees. First, comparing hourly wages (including bonuses) in 1975, small- to mid-sized firms had larger male-female wage differentials than did large-sized firms. However, between 1975 and 1980, those differentials tended to decrease in small- to mid-sized firms. In contrast, wage differentials expanded in large-sized firms during the same period; by 1980 the differential was greater in large firms. Subsequently, however, differentials decreased in both categories, and by 1990 those differentials could no longer be observed.

Next, in Table 2, comparing years of continuous service by size of a firm, there is a tendency toward long-term service for men as firm size increases; however, the size differential is comparatively small for women. As a result, the male-female differential for job tenure becomes larger as firm size increases. In 1990, in contrast to a male-female differential of 8.0 years in large-sized firms,

Table 1

Male-Female Wage Differentials by Firm Size and Educational Level

	Large firms (over 1,000 employees)			Small to Mid-sized Firms (10–99 employees)		
	High School Graduates	College Graduates	Total	High School Graduates	College Graduates	Total
1975	68.1	67.1	64.9	61.9	74.8	59.2
1980	62.9	55.8	58.7	63.7	75.6	60.3
1985	63.9	59.7	60.8	63.9	75.5	61.7
1990	67.5	57.1	62.3	64.1	74.1	62.5

Note: Hourly wage equals yearly earnings (including bonus) divided by total hours worked during the year.

the corresponding figure was a mere 2.7 years in small- to mid-sized firms. Because years of continuous service can be considered as an index of capital accumulation, this male-female differential can be said to increase in proportion to firm size. Moreover, if we look at the transition between 1975 and 1990, job tenure expanded for both men and women, with the expansion being somewhat greater for men. As a result, the male-female differential tended to widen regardless of firm size.

Moreover, Table 1 also shows male-female wage differentials in terms of educational level. In small- to mid-sized firms, there is little wage differential between workers who are college graduates and those who are high school graduates. In contrast, in large-sized firms employing over 1,000 employees, there is a significant difference between college graduates and high school graduates. Wage differentials due to differences in the size of a firm are the largest among college graduates for men, whereas they are small for women. For example, in 1990, wages in small- to mid-sized firms were 68.8 percent of wages for male college graduates of large firms; but for women, the difference was small at 89.2 percent.

As just stated, what emerges from the characteristics of male-female wage differentials in different sized firms is considerable differential treatment for men and women as they become core workers in the firm (represented by college graduates in large firms). Thus, the larger the company, the more differences appear in job tenure between men and women, and wage differentials are the largest for college graduates in large firms. This suggests that differences in the size of a firm should be considered when examining the primary factors involved in male-female wage differentials. Let us examine the theoretical explanations below of why wage differentials vary by firm size.

Table 2

Changes in Average Years of Job Tenure by Firm Size and Sex (in Years)

	Large firms (over 1,000 employees)			Small to Mid-sized Firms (10–99 employees)		
	Men	Women	Difference	Men	Women	Difference
1975	13.2	5.8	7.4	7.5	5.3	2.2
1980	13.9	6.3	7.6	8.5	6.2	2.3
1985	15.2	7.4	7.8	9.3	6.8	2.5
1990	15.8	7.8	8.0	10.0	7.3	2.7

Source: Ministry of Labor, *Wage Census*, 1975, 1980, 1985, 1990.

Reasons for Wage Differentials by Firm Size

Why do large firms pay higher wages than small- to mid-sized firms? Brown and Medoff (1989) organized their research findings into the following five-point theoretical explanation.

First, worker remuneration rises in proportion to increasing firm size, which is due to high worker quality and high productivity. The reason for this lies in the complementary relationship between physical capital and human capital. As production equipment is modernized (along with physical capital accumulation), workers who have accumulated a high level of human capital become essential for equipment management. The larger the firm, the higher the human capital level accumulated by workers, which confirms the high economic effects of worker investment (on-the-job training). Thus, wage differentials by firm size can be explained by differences in worker capital accumulation.

Second, another explanation for wage differentials by firm size explores different working conditions and workplace environments. As an organization grows, individual work is divided into smaller components. This makes it difficult to see the entirety of the work. Human relationships become more complex, rules and regulations are abundant, and individual work becomes less satisfying. In order to compensate for this work-related deficiency, it is necessary to attract workers by paying them higher wages (compensating differentials hypothesis).

Third, as a strategy to avoid unionization of workers, there is a tendency for larger firms to pay high compensation and fringe benefits to unorganized labor.

Fourth, wages in large firms are high because the degree of capital concentration (monopoly power) is high and capital costs are low. The larger firms not only have higher productivity, but they have stronger monopolistic power and higher rates of profit which is shared among the workers. Because the capital market is not perfect, capital costs are lower for large firms, making them capable of paying higher wages. This sort of market imperfection leads to wage differentials.

Fifth, as organizations grow, it becomes increasingly difficult to assess the attitudes and productivity of workers. That is, as a firm expands, the cost for management to evaluate workers increases. To reduce these monitoring costs by personnel and enhance work efforts, firms pay wage premiums. This assures a pool of high-quality workers with the ability to learn and also raises lifetime wages. As a result, the wages paid by large-sized firms are higher than those paid by small- to mid-sized firms.

Of the five explanations, the second and third are not considered applicable to Japan. As far as this author knows, there are no research findings that indicate a deterioration of the workplace environment or lowering of work satisfaction levels as companies expand. Moreover, there are union shops (in which union affiliation is obligatory on hiring) in larger Japanese companies and the rate of unionization is high. Thus, the contention that wage differentials occur as a means of avoiding unions is a limited explanation.

Previous research explains Japan's wage differentials by firm size according to differences in worker ability (productivity) acquired through both education and on-the-job training.[3] In other words, because large firms employ many workers with higher learning abilities, they incur lower training costs. The effectiveness of the training investment is reflected in higher wages. This is noted in the first explanation above.

In this case, if the market is competitive, the lifetime earnings of workers with similar abilities remain the same whether the worker is employed in a large-sized firm or in a small- to mid-sized firm, even though the rate for wage increases may differ (slopes of wage-age profiles) due to varying amounts of on-the-job training (Ishikawa 1991, pp. 286–7). However, wage differentials actually generated in different sized firms are due to large firms employing higher quality workers. Even if we consider the firm size differential in relation to worker quality, the existence of the remaining size differentials is problematic. Ishikawa refers to this as the "true wage differential."

Economic Analysis of Wage Differentials Related to Scale

In Japan, to what extent does the true wage differential exist in wage differentials across different sized firms? Table 3 shows regression estimates of the wage function for male workers 20 to 40 years old based on compiled data from the 1989 *Wage Census*. In the table, the first column represents wage differentials by firm size when differentials in worker ability are not taken into account. The second column indicates the estimates of wage differentials after controlling for differences in industry wage levels, education, job tenure, and age, as well as differences in the rate of wage increases based on these variables (quality differences).

The first column indicates that when productivity differentials are not taken into account, the wage level in firms with over 1,000 employees is higher by 44

Table 3

Wage Estimates by Weighted Regression Analysis
(Male Workers, 20 to 49 Years of Age)

	Column 1	Column 2
Intercept	7.3167* (0.00905)	5.5045 (0.052)
Mid-size = 1	0.16806* (0.01264)	0.039 (0.0052)
Large-size = 1	0.4416* (0.01275)	0.164* (0.00636)
Years of Education		0.057* (0.000961)
Years of Job Tenure		0.0536* (0.0022)
Years of Job Tenure^2		−0.000627* (0.000065)
Age		0.0325* (0.0034)
Age^2		−0.00034 (0.00044)
Construction		0.0157** (0.00738)
Electric, Gas, Water		0.1189* (0.0176)
Transportation		−0.0454* (0.00695)
Sales		0.00939 (0.0049)
Finance		0.3027* (0.00973)
Service		0.089*
Adjusted R^2	0.231	0.9014

Notes:
Standard deviations (in parentheses):
   * is significant at a 1% level
   ** is significant at 5% level
Number of cells equals 4,068.
Dependent variable = 1n (per hour compensation).
The superscript for job tenure and age refers to squared numbers.
Mid-sized = 100–999 employees, large-sized = over 1,000 employees.

percent than in firms with 10 to 99 employees. However, after controlling for variations in human capital accumulation, this difference drops to 16 percent. In other words, after considering worker quality and productivity differentials concerning education, years of continuous service, and human capital accumulation, there exists a true wage differential of 16 percent.[4]

Within this 16 percent, it is possible that worker quality differences—which cannot be measured in years of education or job tenure—are being reflected. Moreover, it is possible that the effects of job tenure are overestimated, and the remaining wage differential due to the size of the firm is underestimated because the distribution of job tenure in large-sized firms is skewed more to the right than in small- to mid-sized firms.[5]

Why, then, does the true wage differential continue to exist? Ishikawa (1991) contends that two conditions are necessary to generate true wage differentials over the long term: (1) large firms monopolize learning opportunities (skill formation opportunities) and (2) competition that revolves around entry fees is restricted. This entry fee refers to the deposit a worker pays a firm when hired. If the worker's work is satisfactory, employment is continued, and the deposit is returned to the worker in the form of salary increases. However, if the worker is discharged, the deposit is collected by the firm in the form of layoffs. Of course, although the actual collection of money for an entry fee is not practiced in reality, it is possible to think that the seniority-based wage system developed in Japan has a similar effect.

If the small- and mid-sized firms imitated the methods of the large-sized firms and offered similar learning opportunities, competition would be generated at the firm level, and, in the long run, wage differentials by firm size would be eliminated. As previously noted, to prevent this, it is necessary to have conditions that restrict learning opportunities in small- to mid-sized firms and that makes deposit contracts function imperfectly.

According to Ishikawa, if the entry-fee deposit mechanism is carried out in the form of lower starting salaries, management's power will increase as the economy worsens, starting salaries will drop because of the expanded collection of entry deposits, and the age-wage curve will become steeper, (that is, the slopes of age-wage profiles will be inversely correlated to the state of the economy). However, empirical research results do not show this relationship during any period for workers with college degrees, and the inverse correlation is not observed after the mid-1970s in high school graduates. That is, entry fees in the form of lower starting salaries has not functioned in Japan, particularly since the mid-1970s.

Furthermore, even if small- to mid-sized firms tried to implement training similar to that of large firms, such action would probably be restricted by borrowing constraints. In addition, after taking into account the different forms of training across firm sizes, wage differentials would probably persist in the long run. This produces wage inflexibility and an excess supply of labor in the internal labor market, generating involuntary unemployment and employment rationing.

One additional explanation for the creation of the true wage differential due to firm size concerns labor management, which is included in the fifth point above. It questions the assumption of neoclassical economic theory that "wages are equal to the marginal productivity of the workers." It is difficult to separate and measure individual effects (marginal productivity) because work is primarily accomplished in teams in the actual workplace.

There are high costs associated with hiring and layoffs, so management is motivated to enter into implicit, long-term employment contracts with workers to forestall them from changing companies. Ishikawa (1991) contends that when workers expect long-term employment, they (within a certain range) will manage their own work. Thus, it becomes important for firms to establish promotion and pay-raise systems including rewards and punishments which promote worker morale and worker efforts.

As noted in the fifth explanation above, as organizations expand, monitoring individuals and evaluating their work effort becomes costly and difficult. Therefore, workers might tend to cheat and shirk on the job. If a firm pays higher wages than other firms, then the cost to workers who are fired for shirking rises, and the firm can prevent them from neglecting their responsibilities. The lower the possibility of a worker finding another job and the lower the current wages are compared to future wages (the sharper the wage curve slope), the more worker productivity rises. This is referred to as the monitoring cost hypothesis.

There are other reasons why large firms pay higher than market wages to increase work effort. Collectively, they are usually referred to as the "efficiency wage hypothesis,"[6] which says:

1. The worker turnover model shows job turnover decreasing as paid wages increase. In addition, training and hiring costs are economized.

2. The adverse selection model illustrates firms trying to keep highly skilled workers by paying high wages. This is based on the premise that firms have less than perfect information about worker quality at the time of hiring.

3. The exchange gift model exemplifies the importance for workers to feel they are being treated fairly in the workplace to encourage work effort. If firms pay higher than average wages as a gift to workers, workers will return the gift by striving to work hard.

Rebick (1990) analyzed data by prefecture given in the *Wage Census* over four census dates—1970, 1975, 1980, and 1985. He shows that a statistically significant negative correlation between wage levels and unemployment rates in small- to mid-sized firms (after controlling for worker attributes) exists, whereas there is no correlation in large firms. He argues that this result corroborates the existence of dual labor markets. This duality consists of an internal labor market (which is not affected by short-term economic fluctuations and can hire and train workers based on a long-term perspective) and the external labor market (in which wages are affected by short-term economic variations caused by changes in supply and demand).

In sum, this section shows that dual labor markets are likely to exist in Japan, and that wage differentials are explained according to the systematic differences of employment management in the respective markets. What kind of influence does such a system have on the hiring and treatment of female workers? Let us examine the utilization of women in internal labor markets.

4. The System of Mandatory Retirement
After Marriage in Internal Labor Markets

As previously discussed, internal labor markets in Japan mainly develop in large firms. The term "internal labor market" used here is premised on long-term service, in which firms enter into implicit, long-term employment contracts with workers, and in which a talented work force is fostered through internal promotions. Since salaries and wages are structurally determined by certain rules, wages are seldom influenced by external shocks.

How has this been applied to female workers in the internal markets? Of interest here, the more internal labor markets develop, the younger the age of its female workers. This suggests the possibility that a system of marriage and early, mandatory retirement for women exists in internal labor markets. Let us consider the economic implications of this system.

Policy of Mandatory Retirement for Married Women

Much of the earlier research points to the old practice in various countries of women being obliged to resign from their jobs when they marry. In 1946, a British government survey recognized the existence of mandatory retirement in many firms when women married (Cohn 1985, pp. 97–98). This policy was not restricted to Great Britain but also existed in a wide range of countries including Australia, Canada, New Zealand, some Scandinavian countries, and the United States.

According to research conducted in the United States, many major financial and insurance companies, publishers, and advertising agencies had such a policy in place; a similar policy also applied to schoolteachers. A survey was conducted in 1931 and 1940 which studied 328 major financial and insurance companies, publishers, and advertising agencies in Chicago, Philadelphia, Los Angeles, and New York. The results show that, until 1940, 20 to 30 percent of all firms in the United States had a policy requiring female clerical workers to resign from their jobs after marriage. This figure rose to 30 to 40 percent when the practice was included in work rules and general procedures, although not always included in the actual regulations.

Between 1930 and 1940, the percentage of firms with such regulations or routine practices increased. On the other hand, 40 to 60 percent of firms chose not to hire married women, which was higher than the ratio of firms with a policy of mandatory retirement after marriage. Goldin (1990) indicated that the ratio of firms with this policy or routine practice rose in proportion to firm size. In addition, in 1928, 50 percent of urban schools established a system that called for female teachers to resign from their jobs when they married, and 60 percent also had regulations against the hiring of married women teachers.[7]

It is common knowledge that policies which require women to withdraw from the labor market following marriage or routine procedures that restrict the hiring of married women also exist in Japan. The 1974 "Survey of Conditions of the Employment Management of Women," (which is conducted annually by the Ministry of Labor) shows that 27.1 percent of the firms studied replied that they employed different mandatory retirement systems for men and women. In 1986, this number dropped to 14.3 percent.[8] However, even if such policies were not written down, many women still believed that they were practiced routinely.

In the 1990 "Basic Survey of Women's Employment Management," 46 percent of all women replied that "women routinely resign from their jobs before mandatory retirement." Viewing this across different industries, the percentage rises to 60 percent of women in financial and insurance companies and 58.3 percent of women in wholesale and retail businesses. With headlines that read "The Unwritten Law of Marriage and Retirement," the *Nihon Keizai Shinbun* (1991) indicated that, in major financial and insurance companies which practiced Japanese-style hiring, there was a deeply entrenched routine of women marrying and then resigning from their jobs in these organizations.

Of course, when mandatory retirement after marriage is a routine practice and not a formal regulation, it can be eliminated. However, if this is done, a supervisor can be held responsible for his failure to persuade his subordinates to resign. If eliminating this practice hinders a smooth relationship among workers or between supervisors and workers, women may opt for retirement as the best policy. Yet, this does not mean that women cannot continue working even if they marry. Many women, however, will be obliged to change their status and work on a contract or part-time basis rather than as regular workers.

In Japan, even if there is an unwritten law or routine procedure that establishes a policy of mandatory retirement after marriage, this policy does not necessarily exist in all firms. Small- to mid-sized firms are concerned about labor shortages, and so many of them want women to continue working even after they marry. The routine practice of mandatory retirement is seen mostly in industries in which wage levels are high and in large firms, such as financial and insurance companies, in which traditional, internal promotion systems are established.

This mandatory retirement after marriage assumes a policy in which women resign from their jobs when they marry. In various Western countries, it is referred to as the "marriage bar" ("bar" in English means to ban or prohibit). In this case, it means to prohibit the continued employment of women following marriage and to ban the hiring of married women. According to Goldin (1990), the system of mandatory retirement following marriage disappeared quickly in the United States, but discriminatory employment practices against married women continued over a comparatively long period.

In Japan, it is common practice to establish age limits for mid-career hiring and to restrict the hiring of married women. According to the 1991 survey entitled "Trends in Female Labor Force Reentry and the State of Employment Management for Firms," 60 percent of the firms studied restrict mid-career hiring for regular female workers and 50 percent do so for part-time workers. Age-restricted ceilings are set at a younger age in large firms, which also applies to financial and insurance companies, real estate agencies, and wholesale and retail businesses. In financial and insurance companies, 40 percent of the firms designate the twenties as their age ceiling.

Restrictions on the hiring of married women are also broadly enforced in large firms. Therefore, it is common for firms employing female reentrants to be smaller than the firms available to women prior to leaving their jobs for marriage. The distribution in firm size immediately before and after the women interrupt their labor force participation indicates that 19.1 percent of the women are employed in large companies before the interruption, but that figure drops to 5.2 percent after the break in service. These results show that the practice of women forced into mandatory retirement following marriage and the hiring restrictions imposed on married women still function in present-day Japan.

In Chapter 2, we noted that the high probability of women resigning from their jobs after marriage is a characteristic of Japanese women workers. We found that the period of interrupted service is long and that subsequent reemployment is often associated with poor working conditions. This situation occurs because women lose hard-earned, accumulated knowledge during the long period of interrupted service. However, it is not clear whether women are obliged to work at small- to mid-sized firms with poor working conditions because of the long period of interrupted service or whether the interrupted period lengthens because desirable job opportunities at large firms (which would enable workers to utilize past accumulation) are restricted.

In Japan, if an actual policy or routine practice were established in internal labor markets requiring women to resign from their work after marriage—denying opportunities in large firms, hindering the continued employment of married women, and restricting the mid-career hiring of married women—the very existence of such policies would prolong the interrupted period in women's employment and would be responsible for firms foregoing the reemployment of able women. If this is occurring, the labor policy should change. Let us examine below why the marriage bar exists in internal labor markets.

Why a System of Mandatory Retirement and Restriction Exists

Goldin (1990) states that companies establish the marriage bar, which prohibits married women from continuing in their jobs and restricts the hiring of married women, because the wage system in internal labor markets does not necessarily reflect individual productivity. In other words, the seniority-based wage system pays lower wages for productivity when workers are young and higher wages for productivity after long-term continuous service. This system enhances work effort and promotes long-term service. That is, the companies withhold "deposit" money from workers while they are young, then repaying the workers later in the form of higher wages.

However, long-term job tenure is not always desirable for all firms. In the workplace, there is difficult work requiring skills, but also a great deal of simple, repetitive work. Cohn (1985) says that if wages rise along with job tenure, even for simple work, it is better to employ young, inexperienced workers with a high degree of education who can learn the job quickly for (relatively) low wages for shorter periods than to employ experienced workers at high wages for longer periods. Prewar data of two British firms, the Great Western Railway and the General Post Office, showed that the difference between the productivity of women workers and wages rose after a particular level of job tenure. This explains why these firms mandated female job separation and established a policy of forced resignation after marriage.

If mandatory retirement after marriage were a commonly accepted idea in society, it would be possible to force women's job separation by institutionalizing it and measuring the regeneration of the workplace. In this case, because marriage, not age, marks the time for women to leave their jobs, women are able to avoid this policy by postponing or foregoing marriage. Recent trends toward women's long-term job tenure and late marriages seem to indicate this kind of response from women.

To summarize the above discussion, the system of mandatory retirement after marriage appears: (1) in firms in which wages are structurally determined in the workplace, are not correlated to worker productivity, and are raised to a certain extent along with job tenure and age, and (2) in cases in which women are assigned to do simple, support work.

Goldin (1986) stated that when women's wages are paid by the piece rate, this policy of mandatory retirement after marriage does not exist. Moreover, firms incur costs associated with losing capable, talented women in whom they have invested when they employ this policy of mandatory retirement or when they refrain from hiring married women. However, as long as women perform supportive work from the outset and are assigned to simple tasks, these costs are minimal. Labor costs, which can be reduced by this mandatory retirement system, are of great importance to these firms.

Wage Differentials and the Mandatory Retirement Policy

It was previously noted that companies which pay high wages and utilize routine Japanese-style employment practices (usually large firms) are more likely to require women to leave their jobs after marriage and to restrict the hiring of married women. Does the inflexible wage system in internal labor markets generate systems related to the hiring of married women and mandatory retirement? Moreover, do these wage systems vary by firm size? Let us consider these issues while estimating the wage function for women workers by firm size.

The data used in this analysis is from the same 1989 *Wage Census* noted above. The sample consists of workers between the ages of 20 and 49, excluding part-time workers. Regression analysis is used. Since the average of each variable's cell is used as data, a weighted regression analysis is carried out with the sample number of each cell as a weight. Variables included in the estimation are average years of education, years of service, and age. Moreover, wage level differentials between industries are controlled by introducing dummy variables.

Looking at the average wage differential of women working in large-sized

Figure 2

Age-Wage Curve by Firm Size and Sex

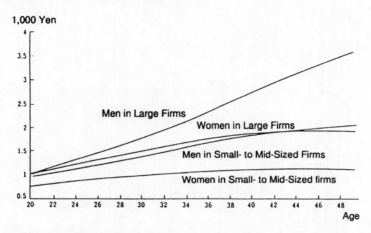

firms (over 1,000 employees) and in small- to mid-sized firms (10–99 employees), wages in large firms are 44.1 percent higher. When the differences in increased wages due to education, job tenure, and age in different sized firms are taken into account, this difference drops to 30.6 percent. However, this is merely a 13.5 point reduction in the wage differential; the significant wage differential for women due to the size of the firm remains unexplained by the skill formation differential represented in the above variables.[9]

Comparing this to men, if we consider the differences in skill formation, the wage differential drops 29.8 points from 44.2 to 16.4 percent, and the remaining unexplained difference drops to 30 percent. It shows a significant wage differential due to firm size differences that cannot be explained by differentials in women's productivity or skill formation.

Many Japanese workplaces use annual pay increases to assure long-term job tenure. Regular wage increases can be divided into two parts: those related to job tenure and those related to age. Annual pay increases accompanying job tenure are premised on increasing worker ability as job tenure lengthens. Wage increases associated with age reflect the extent of a worker's importance and contribution to the workplace. How are different wage increase rates related to job tenure and age by firm size? Figure 2 shows the wage changes related to age in different sized firms, using the results of the wage function estimates across different sized firms presented earlier. Note that in the relationship between wages and age indicated here, that the seniority factors in wages (wage-by-age system) and the wage increases by years of continuous service (service wages) are both included.

The figure shows that the larger the firm size, the higher the slope of the service-wage curve. This applies to both men and women. However, the slope

Figure 3

Wage Increases and Job Tenure of Women Workers by Firm Size

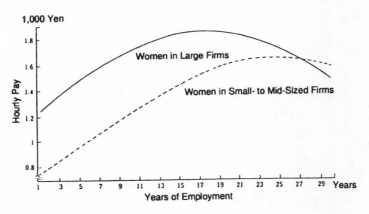

Note: Age and effect of education are held constant.

becomes flatter as the age for women rises. This is due to the male-female differential in service-wage increases. Women do not receive regular wage increases to the same extent that men do. Moreover, wages for men are higher than those for women at any age, except for women working in large-scale firms. The hourly wage (including bonuses) for women working in large-scale firms, as shown in this figure, is somewhat higher than men working in small-scale firms. However, this reverses for the first time when a worker reaches mid-forty.

Let us separate the effects of job tenure from the relationship between age and wage increases and examine wage changes. In labor economics, this is considered a change in productivity accompanied by job tenure. Although a significant male wage differential exists in different firm sizes, the job tenure-wage curve has a similar shape. (Due to space limitations, the information for men is not shown in the figure.) In both cases, wages rise with job tenure, but wages start to drop in large-sized firms after 25.3 years of service and 31.3 years of service in small- to mid-sized firms. The rise in productivity rate that accompanies job tenure is 7.5 percent in large-sized firms but is somewhat lower for small- to mid-sized firms at 6.2 percent.[10]

Looking at women in Figure 3, the relationship between job tenure and wage curve is an arc in both sized firms, and the reduction in productivity after a certain number of years of job tenure is remarkable. The rise in the productivity rate is higher and peaks earlier in large firms; it occurs after 17.3 years of job tenure in large-sized firms and 24.3 years in small- to mid-sized firms.[11]

In other words, human capital investment occurs through on-the-job training, and productivity is higher than in small- to mid-sized firms, although women's job tenure is shorter. However, after a certain number of years, on-the-job training is interrupted and productivity drops. On the other hand, the amount of on-the-job training in small- to mid-sized firms is smaller than that provided by large-sized firms. However, because smaller firms provide training for a longer period, productivity increases gradually along with job tenure, and the peak occurs later. After 25 years of continuous service, the productivity of women working in small- to mid-sized firms is higher than in large-sized firms.

Calculations which estimate the rate of increased productivity due to job tenure is 5.16 percent for women in large-sized firms in contrast to 6.9 percent in small- to mid-sized firms; average productivity of women workers in small- to mid-sized firms is high. That is, in contrast to men whose job performance ability and rate of wage increase along with job tenure are higher as firm size increases, the converse is true for women across different sized firms. In particular, the rise in women's job performance ability (productivity) in proportion to long-term job tenure stops in large firms, and the subsequent reversal and drop in productivity is significant.

The following is derived from the above analysis. For men and women, the larger the firm, the steeper the slope of seniority-based wages (age wages plus service wages). However, the change in productivity shows that the rise in women's productivity due to job tenure stops after a certain number of years and then turns downward. This peak occurs earlier in large-sized firms than in small- to mid-sized firms. We can see from this that there is a large gap between worker productivity (job ability) and actual wages in proportion to the size of the firm and the age of the women. It is necessary for firms to force women into early retirement before the difference between total wages paid and total output becomes too large. Here, economic grounds exist for establishing a system of early retirement for women.

If the concept of a suitable age for marriage existed in society along with strong pressure toward marriage, the system of mandatory retirement after marriage for women, which uses both of those elements, might be the perfect retirement method. Societal pressure toward marriage, which has restricted the behavior of women in their twenties, is an unquestioned reality in Japan.

If that is the case, it is more realistic to consider management systems and wage systems as determinants of male-female wage differentials in large firms than to accept the argument of statistical discrimination, which focuses on unequal on-the-job training opportunities due to women's shorter job tenure. According to the Labor Ministry's 1984 "Survey of Conditions of Women's Employment Management," 43.7 percent of firms studied do not have promotional opportunities for women. However, even if such opportunities were available, a ceiling is placed on women at the level of section chief. If department head and above are included, the rate drops to 20.6 percent. Providing such opportunities is considered impossible by 48.4 percent of firms because the nature of women's work is supportive, that is, women are thought from the very beginning to be support workers by many firms.

The Reason for Women's Short Job Tenure

The most important determinant of male-female wage differentials is the difference in job tenure. The previous section focused on Japan's personnel management as the reason for this.

When firms are asked why women are not being utilized more thoroughly, the majority reply that women tend to leave their jobs early. However, a firm cannot determine when a woman is hired if she intends to work for a long period. Even though there are some talented and capable women who want to work long term, firms cannot gather accurate information on each individual. As previously noted, the theory of statistical discrimination contends that firms treat women differently from men using sex as one representative indicator and place all women in the short-term employment group. Following this hypothesis, industries which show higher female voluntary resignation rate averages have greater male-female differentials in hiring. Tomita's article (1988) examined this hypothesis.

Using data from the "Survey of Employment Trends" and the "Survey of the Employment Management of Women Workers," Tomita chooses the proportion of firms which practice differential treatment for men and women in five employment categories as an endogenous variable. The categories consist of hiring discrimination, assignment discrimination, interfirm transfer, intrafirm transfer, and promotional opportunities.

After controlling for firm size and ratios of white-collar workers and women, Tomita (1988) used regression analysis to examine the correlation between these variables and the ratios for the voluntary resignation rate of men and women. If statistical discrimination exists, the larger the male-female differential resignation rate in industry, the higher the expected ratio of firms establishing male-female differentials in employment. However, the estimated result does not show a statistically significant correlation between these two variables.

Conclusions from the Higuchi study (1991), which uses the *Wage Census* and the "Survey of the Employment Management of Women Workers" to investigate management's influence on a woman's propensity to stay with the same employer, are introduced below:

1. The propensity for employment stability is high for women in industries with high wage levels.

2. The propensity is low in firms that utilize women only in support work.

3. The propensity is high in industries that implement on-the-job training for women as well as men and work toward the improvement of knowledge and skills essential for today's work.

4. The propensity rises in firms that enforce job rotation equally between men and women.

5. The propensity rises for female college graduates in firms that utilize women in special professional fields.

6. The propensity rises in firms that already have female managers and have opened promotional paths to women.

This indicates that the tendency for women to stay with the same employer can change depending on employment management. Nakamura (1988) concluded from a study of women managers of major supermarkets, the manner in which firms assign work elicits women's work efforts. Nakamura clarified this by stating "work changes people"—a statement that applies equally to men and women.

5. Changes in the Personnel Management System

In the latter half of the 1980s, indications of change appeared in methods of hiring and personnel management. Let us examine those changes below.

Changes in the Personnel Management of Women Workers

The first change seen in the 1980s was preparation for career-track occupations promising the same promotional route as men —which was added to the short promotion route of general clerical work as the career course of women in large firms. Large firms were more likely to introduce this differential course in personnel management. For example, in the 1989 "Survey of Women's Employment Management," 42.3 percent of firms with over 5,000 employees replied that they had introduced this policy, in contrast to 25.3 percent in firms with 1,000 to 4,999 employees, and 0.9 percent in firms with 30 to 99 employees. When asked about their policy objectives and turning points, about 70 percent of the firms replied that they were "responding to changes in the management environment" and were conscious of responding to economic changes such as internationalization, information, and structural change in industry.

The second change in the latter half of the 1980s concerned the increased hiring of female college graduates. After the second oil shock of the late 1970s, major firms tended to refrain from hiring female college graduates. Between 1975 and 1985, the ratio for female college graduates in large firms dropped 2.2 points from 6.1 to 4.9 percent, but between 1985 and 1990, the ratio took a 3.1-point upturn and went from 4.9 to 8.0 percent. In this regard, as shown in Chapter 3, wage differentials of female junior college graduates and college graduates aged 20 to 24 years expanded rapidly after 1980. It was clear that employment opportunities for women with high educational backgrounds expanded as the economy became more service oriented.

Why did firms change their personnel strategy toward women employees and allowed them to become part of the core work force? Let us look below at changes in the United States and contrast them with changes that occurred in Japan.

Economic Factors Causing Changes
in Personnel Management

In 1950, married women in the United States made a succession of social inroads. Except for airline stewardesses, firms no longer utilized the policy of mandatory retirement after marriage for women; instead, the number of short-term, part-time employees increased.

Goldin (1990), in the previously noted study, attributes these changes in personnel policies primarily to the rise in the education level of the U.S. population, the lowering of the age of first marriage, and the rising birth rate. In the U.S. labor market, Goldin states that the work force of young, single women simply declined because of these demographic changes. Measuring the population in the United States between 16 years and 64 years of age, the proportion of people between 16 years and 24 years dropped from 30.9 percent in 1900 to 20.3 percent in 1960. Behind the social advancement of married women, there was a feminization of clerical occupations. This was a phenomenon seen in the United States from the 1920s to 1930s, when women who had clerical work experience utilized their former work backgrounds and returned to the labor market. In the United States, necessary skills for office work could be retained without much loss even after job interruption, and such skills facilitated reemployment.

In the United States, the shortage of single workers brought about the elimination of mandatory retirement for women after marriage. In Japan, however, while there is a shortage of younger workers, young women are marrying later each year, enabling them to extend their labor force participation. This attests to the fact that the same factors are not necessarily involved.

In Japan, the primary factors behind firms changing their personnel policies regarding women workers are broadly divided into three categories. The first category deals with changes in women's labor supply patterns because of the rise in women's wages in large firms. The strong positive correlation between wages and the supply of women's labor is documented in Chapter 2.

The wage system of the internal labor market promotes long-term job tenure not only for men but for women as well. As seen earlier, particularly in the 1980s, job tenure for both men and women lengthened. By postponing marriage or not marrying at all, women were able to avoid the policy that required mandatory retirement after marriage. The rise in women's market wages weakened the effect of this unwritten law. Chapter 7 analyzes the relationship between women's employment, marriage, and childbirth.

The second category covers changes in the demand side of the labor market. Manpower needs changed within companies. The Keidanran [Federation of Economic Organizations] survey stated that in the 1970s the most desirable workers by management standards were fit, hard-working employees. In the 1980s that standard had changed to workers who possessed individuality and originality. Moreover, the demand for workers with high educational backgrounds was increasing.

While such changes provided the backdrop for the transition to a service-oriented economy, the introduction of advanced technology in workplaces also played a significant role. Differentials in education and ability rather than sex became increasingly significant in the workplace. These were the circumstances in the 1980s which compelled large companies to increase the number of female college graduates hired. The path leading to long-term employment was opened to women, which could be seen by the introduction of the separate career course implemented by personnel management. The following chapter discusses the relationship between the introduction of high technology into the workplace and the labor demand for workers with a high level of education.

The third category is the shortage of young workers over the long run. In the same way that dwindling numbers of young workers brought about the decline of the mandatory retirement for women following marriage in the United States, such shortages also gave rise to similar changes in Japan. (The supply of young workers will plunge dramatically in the next four to five years because of the drop in the birth rate beginning in 1974.) The next problem is how to create an environment in which women can continue to work even if they marry. If the practice of mandatory retirement after marriage for women does continue, firms must pay the cost of losing employees in whom they have invested a great deal of time and money.

6. Concluding Remarks

In this chapter, we focused on the employment management of firms and analyzed the major determinants of male-female wage differentials. As a result, we find that obliging women to pursue support work as short-term workers caused women's short-term job tenure. The wage differential was not due to the lack of progress in women's skill development related to their high resignation rates (the usual conclusion in the discussion of large firms). Firms which forced women's job separation and mandatory retirement after marriage did so because of the seniority-based salary system in which wages automatically rise with age and generate a differential between wages and women's productivity. Thus, the larger the firm (in which internal labor markets and the seniority-based wage systems were well developed), the younger the average age of women workers.

However, the situation is very different for small- to mid-sized firms in which the internal labor market does not develop to the same degree. In this market, women's short-term job tenure generates male-female wage differentials. If women's job tenure is the same as men's, the male-female wage differential in small- to mid-sized firms would be reduced by 8 percent; however, in large firms, the same effect would only be 3 percent.

Looking toward the twenty-first century, economic changes must occur that will force large firms to change their discriminatory personnel management practices that, on the whole, treat women as support workers. Those changes include: (1) increasing the importance of skill development for highly qualified workers because of the shift to a computer-based, information economy, (2) lengthening the job tenure for women which was created by the seniority-based wage system, and (3) supplying workers for the critical shortage of available young people in twenty-first century. Because of these changes, the utilization of women as core workers will become an important issue for the personnel management strategy of firms as they go into the next century.

In this chapter, we discussed the wage system as the primary factor hindering the utilization of women (in large firms). Characteristics of Japan's wage system are such that wages are determined by worker attributes such as sex, age, and education. In contrast, in countries such as the United States, wages linked to work and skill are said to be the norm. In other words, in Japan, a worker is hired by a company that determines the type of work assignment after the worker is hired. A worker in Western countries, on the other hand, chooses the type of work first and then chooses an appropriate company. This difference is reflected in wage systems.

Using Japan's wage system based on attributes of the worker, promotions are determined and wage increases are given according to sex, education, job tenure, and age, instead of individual ability. In contrast to other job-type wage systems, this system is advantageous because worker rotation can be accomplished easily, since wages do not change even if there are job transfers. On the other hand, this system is disadvantageous because it hinders the utilization of workers whose long-term service cannot be assured and because the short-term worker contribution (productivity) does not necessarily conform to wages.

However, some recent economic changes suggest that individual knowledge and ability, rather than sex or age, control work productivity—given economic changes such as the introduction of computers or internationalization and globalization of economies. A significant change in the wage system accompanies this. According to the 1992 "Labor White Paper," there is a general trend in Japan for the wage system to move toward a system based on ability and away from a system based on seniority in which wages rise in proportion to age and job tenure. It should be noted that over 50 percent of Japanese firms changed their wage system within the last five years, and within that figure, 80 percent changed with a consideration toward ability.

Moreover, if we look at the base wages of white-collar, college graduates, the proportion of those wages based on ability is greater for new employees. Such changes increasingly accelerate in proportion to the severity of the current shortage of young workers. The transition toward a wage system that emphasizes work and ability will have a positive effect on the utilization of a talented female work force. In either case, the utilization of future female employee capability calls for a reconsideration of female work assignments and, above all, a reconsideration of the wage system.

Notes

1. The book *Keizai Henka to Joshi Rodo, Nichibei no Hikaku Kenkyu* [Economic Change and Female Labor: A U.S.–Japan Comparison] consists of the following nine chapters:

(1) Economic Changes Which Facilitated Women's Social Advances: Economic Development and Female Labor

(2) The Analysis of Married Women's Labor Supply

(3) Male-Female Wage Differentials and Women's Employment Behavior

(4) Japanese-Style Employment Practices and Male-Female Wage Differentials: An Approach from the Labor Demand Side

(5) The Effect of Technical Change on Employment

(6) The Widening of Wage Differentials Between Regular and Nonregular Employees: The Limitation of the Wage Adjustment Mechanism of Internal Labor Markets

(7) Changes in Marriages and Births on Economic Changes

(8) Public Policy on Female Labor: Problems of Public Policy Based on Traditional Families

(9) Policy Proposals for the Twenty-First Century

2. Piore (1975) indicates the existence of high-ranking and low-ranking work in this internal labor market. High-ranking work refers to professional, technical, and management work, and there is frequent job switching motivated by a desire for improved employment opportunities and higher wages. This class of people is emerging even in Japan.

3. For example, there is detailed research concerning Japan's skill formation in Koike (1977) and Odaka (1984). Mincer and Higuchi (1988) detail empirical research comparing Japan and the United States.

4. Rebick's (1990) results from a similar estimate approximated that in 1977 the scale difference without the variable of human capital was 30 percent, and the actual wage differential with the variable was 17 percent. In 1988, respective figures were 31 percent and 16 percent.

5. See Ishikawa (1991), p. 299.

6. This theoretical argument is based on Akerlof and Yellen (1986) and Furugōri (1992). The "Hypothesis of Efficiency Wage" was also introduced in Ohashi et al. (1989), pp. 149–56.

7. This survey is discussed in detail in Chapter 6 of Goldin (1990).

8. For example, among cases of postwar female labor litigation concerning retirement and the age-limit system, there were six cases involving mandatory retirement for women following marriage. Among the 16 cases regarding separate male and female age-limit systems, there were three cases involving women-only early retirement and one case in which retirement was encouraged. Of the 23 cases of retirement, women's marital status was cited as the reason; 10 cases were concerned with part-time workers (drawn from *The State of Female Labor* compiled by the Ministry of Labor).

9. It is possible that the disparity of quality in workers not measured in years of education is reflected here as the primary factor generating wage differentials. Differences in learning ability, depending on the school from which they graduated, are often indicated by the alma mater of students graduating from the same four-year college system. The higher the student's learning ability, the higher the rate of employment in large firms, and that cannot be determined strictly by the number of years of education. Maybe this difference in learning ability is reflected in this differential.

10. The slope of the estimated relationship between job tenure and wage curve is 0.07 − 0.031 multiplied by the years of job tenure in large-sized firms, and 0.064 − 0.002

multiplied by the years of job tenure in small- to mid-sized firms. We can see that the peak of this gradient occurs in 25.16 years in large-sized firms and 30.7 years in small- to mid-sized firms.

11. In the case of women, the hypothesized relationship between job tenure and wage curve gradient is $0.052 - 0.003$ multiplied by the years of job tenure in large-sized firms, and $0.07 - 0.003$ multiplied by the years of job tenure in small- to mid-sized firms. We can see that the peak is 17.3 years in large-sized firms and 24.3 years in small- to mid-sized firms.

References

Akerlof, George, and Janet L. Yellen. 1986. *Efficiency Wage Models of the Labor Market.* Cambridge: Cambridge University Press.

Arrow, Kenneth. 1972. "Some Mathematical Models of Race Discrimination in the Labor Market." In *Racial Discrimination in Economic Life*, edited by Anthony Pascal. Lexington, MA: Lexington Books.

Becker, Gary. 1957. *The Economics of Discrimination.* Chicago: University of Chicago Press.

Bergmann, Barbara. 1971. "The Effect on White Incomes of Discrimination in Employment." *Journal of Political Economy* 79 (March/April).

Brinton, Mary C. 1992. *Women and the Economic Miracle: Gender and Work in Postwar Japan.* Berkeley: University of California Press.

Brown, William P., and Michael P. J. Medoff. 1989. "The Employer Size-Wage Effect." *Journal of Political Economy* 97 (October).

Cohn, Samuel. 1985. *The Feminization of Clerical Labor in Great Britain.* Philadelphia: Temple University Press.

Dickens, William T., and Kevin Lang. 1985. "A Test of the Dual Labor Market Theory." *American Economic Review* 75 (September).

Doeringer, Peter B., and Michael J. Piore. 1971. *Internal Labor Markets and Manpower Analysis.* Lexington, MA: D. C. Heath.

Furugōri, Tomoko. 1992. "Koritsu Chingin to Hiseiki Rodosha no Koyo Zoka" [Efficiency Wages and Increases in Nonregular Workers]. In *Rodoryoku no Kyokyu Seiyaku to Jukyu Chosei no Sotaiteki Mechanism* [Supply Constraint of Labor Force and the Relative Mechanism of Wage Adjustment]. Tokyo: Tokei Kenkyukai [The Institute of Statistics].

Goldin, Claudia. 1986. "Monitoring Costs and Occupation Segregation by Sex: A Historical Analysis." *Journal of Labor Economics* 4 (January).

———. 1990. *Understanding the Gender Gap.* Oxford: Oxford University Press.

Higuchi, Yoshio. 1991. Nihon Keizai to Shugyo Kodo [The Japanese Economy and Employment Behavior]. Tokyo: Toyo Keizai Shimposha.

Horne-Kawashima, Yoko. 1985. *Joshi Rodo to Rodoshijo Kozo no Bunseki* [Female Labor and the Analysis of the Labor Market Structure]. Tokyo: Nihon Keizai Hyoronsha.

Ishikawa, Tsuneo. 1991. *Shotoku to Tomi* [Income and Wealth]. Tokyo: Iwanami Shoten.

Koike, Kazuo. 1977. *Shokuba no Rodo Kumiai to Sanka: Roshi Kankei no Nichibei Hikaku* [Labor Unions in the Work Place and Participation: A U.S.–Japan Comparison of Labor–Management Relations]. Tokyo: Toyo Keizai Shimposha.

Madden, Janice. 1975. "Discrimination: A Manifestation of Male Market Power." In *Sex, Discrimination, and the Division of Labor*, edited by C. Lloyd. New York: Columbia University Press.

Mincer, Jacob, and Yoshio Higuchi. 1988. "Wage Structure and Labor Turnover in the

United States and Japan." *Journal of the Japanese and International Economies* 2 (June).
Nakamura, Megumu. 1988. "Ote Super niokeru Joshi Kanrishokusha Semmon-shokusha" [Female Managers and Specialists in Mamor Supermarkets]. In *Shokuba no Career Woman* [Career Women in Workplaces], edited by Kazuo Koike and Yasunobu Tomita. Tokyo: Toyo Keizai Shimposha.
Nihon Keizai Shinbun. December 5, 1991. "The Unwritten Law of Marriage and Retirement." Evening Edition.
Nishimura, Keiko. 1977. "Kigyo no Rodoryoku Bumpai to Chingin Kakusa" [Labor-Force Allocation and Wage Differentials in Firms]. *Economic Studies Quarterly* 38 (December).
Odaka, Konosuke. 1984. *Rodoshijo Bunseki* [The Analysis of Labor Markets]. Tokyo: Iwanami Shoten.
Ohashi, Isao, Arai Kazuhiro, and Chuma Hiroyuki, and Masutaka Nishijima. 1989. *Rodo Keizaigaku* [Labor Economics]. Tokyo: Yuhikaku.
Phelps, Edward S. 1972. "The Statistical Theory of Racism and Women." *American Economic Review* 62 (December).
Piore, Michael J. 1975. "Note for a Theory of Labor Market Stratification." In *Labor-Market Segmentation*, edited by Richard C. Edwards, Michael Reich, and David M. Gordon. Lexington: MA: D. C. Heath.
Rebick, Marcus. 1990. "Widening Employment Size Differentials in Japan: Higher Returns to Skill in the Japanese Economy." Mimeo (December).
Saso, Mary. 1990. *Women in the Japanese Workplace.* London: Hilary Shipman.
Tomita, Yasunobu. 1988. "Joshi no Koyo Kanri to Danjokan Chingin Kakusa" [Women's Employment Management and Male-Female Wage Differentials]. In *Shokuba no Career Woman* [Career Women in Workplaces], edited by Kazuo Koike and Yasunobu Tomita. Tokyo: Toyo Keizai Shimposha.
Yashiro, Naohiro. 1980. *Gendai Nihon no Byori Kaimei* [The Pathology of Contemporary Japan]. Tokyo: Toyo Keizai Shimposha.

Machiko Osawa is on the economics faculty of Asia University, Tokyo.

Source/Permission: "Nihon-teki Koyo Kanko to Danjokan Chingin Kakusa: Rodo Juyo Side kara no Approach." Chapter 4 of Machiko Osawa, *Keizai Henka to Joshi Rodo, Nichibei no Hikaku Kenkyu.* Tokyo: Nihon Keizai Hyonron Sha, 1993. (Translation originally appeared in *Japanese Economic Studies* 22, Nos. 5 and 6 [September/October-November-December 1994].) Translated with permission by Jane Kurokawa.

Part V

The Financial System

8

Economic Development and Financial Deepening: The Case of Japan

Kazuo Sato

The financial mess in which Japan finds itself in the mid-1990s has attracted much popular attention. After a sustained boom in the late 1980s, Japan went into a recession in the early 1990s. Though the recession ended in late 1993, Japan's growth rate has remained below one percent (1992–95). By 1995, the large number of nonperforming loans made the serious difficulties in Japan's financial system apparent.

How has the once-mighty nation fallen into this sorry state? To answer this question, one must first see how Japan's financial economy has progressed over time. This paper reviews the process of Japan's financial "deepening" that has accompanied its economic development over the past four decades. This review reveals how important a role the banking system and monetary policy have played in determining the pace of financial deepening.

When an economy develops from the stage of underdevelopment into that of maturity, it is said to go through the process of financial deepening—repression, liberalization and maturity.[1] Japan has performed remarkably well in this area and is by now far ahead of the United States, as far as macroeconomic figures can tell us. Japan's experience in this regard can give both positive and negative lessons to late-developing countries—positive, in showing how a country can achieve rapid financial growth in support of real growth; but negative, in showing that runaway financial deepening may lead to a serious systemic risk endangering real growth.

In this article, Section 1 gives an historical overview of Japan's financial deepening over the past four decades. Section 2 quantifies it on the basis of the national balance sheet. It indicates the dominant position of money in Japan's financial system. Section 3 examines salient features of Japan's financial system. Section 4 examines the role of monetary policy in setting the pace of financial deepening. Section 5 considers the experience of the last ten years. Section 6 considers household savings as the basic cause of financial deepening. Section 7 asks if financial deepening is to continue. Section 8 concludes the paper.[2]

1. Historical Record

On the real side, the Japanese economy has gone through several distinct phases since the end of World War II (August 1945):

1. *1945–51 (Occupation)*. Japan was occupied by the Allied Forces (actually, the United States). The war-devastated economy had to be rebuilt. Aggregate supply was low and aggregate demand high. The resultant inflation continued through this period.

2. *1952–59 (Pre-rapid Growth)*. With the end of the Occupation, the economy returned to normal conditions. Growth was high and inflation was brought under control.

3. *1960–69 (Rapid Growth)*. The economy achieved growth of more than 10 percent. Industry expanded, exports grew and the balance of trade went into a surplus.

4. *1970–74 (Transition)*. Growth was falling, but capital deepening propped up growth as it absorbed increasing saving. The first oil shock (1973–74) ended this phase.

5. *1975–90 (Slow Growth)*. The economy began its slow growth. The growth rate averaged around 5 percent. Though the early 1980s were a little more depressed, the late 1980s saw another long boom.

6. *1991–*. This new phase was started with the Heisei Recession (February 1991–October 1993). Although the economy emerged from the recession, economic growth has been abysmal. During the four years from 1992 to 1995, there was no growth in per capita real income.

The financial side matched the real side. The first phase (1) was a period of financial dislocation. During the war, people had been forced to save to pay for the war effort; but postwar hyperinflation (CPI, 1952/1945 = 36.5) reduced the real value of their accumulated financial assets to practically nothing.[3] Urban land prices were equally depressed because people had fled to the countryside. The recovery process in phase 2 started with very low values of assets and debt. Phases 2 and 3 were the period of financial repression. As growth was stepped up, the demand for investment was strong. But the supply of saving was low to begin with. The government enforced the low-interest policy, keeping interest rates at a rigidly low level. Funds had to be allocated by banks to business firms.[4] Credit rationing was in force.[5] This period of financial repression continued until the end of the 1960s. In phase 4, growth started to fall and investment demand was no longer as strong as before. On the other hand, saving continued to increase. Credit rationing was no longer needed, and interest rates started to fluctuate, in order to equalize fund supply and fund demand. This was the period of financial liberalization. In phase 5, liberalization continued and the financial markets moved toward maturity. In the late 1980s, asset prices soared,[6] in correspondence with the economic boom on the real side. The stock market collapsed in December 1989,[7] and the land market did likewise shortly afterward.[8] The real economy went into a recession in February 1991.[9] In phase 6, with the continued drop in stock and land prices, the financial economy has been much depressed. The financial mess of 1995 was the end result of this period of financial instability.

Japan's financial development has been fraught with violent upheavals—so-called bubbles. In the period under study, there were four "bubbles" identified with peak years of stock-price growth: 1954, 1961, 1973, and 1989. In each bubble, stock prices start to rise rapidly, reach a peak, and collapse with a bang. This sequence can take several years. Land prices follow suit after a time lag of one year or so. Bubbles are an important subject of study (Sato 1995a; 1995b).

2. Quantitative Review

Asset Balances

We examine the national balance sheet prepared as a part of Japan's national accounting system at the end of each year. Broadly classified, we have

$$
(1) \qquad \begin{aligned} NW &= T - DB \\ T &= L + K + F \end{aligned}
$$

where NW is net worth, T is total assets, L is land, K is reproducible tangible assets (inventories, business fixed capital stock and dwellings), F is financial assets and DB is debt. For subcategories, we emphasize money (M), which is the sum of currency (C) and deposits (D) (both demand and time).[10]

In Figure 1, we show T, L, K, F, and M in multiples of nominal GDP (Y) for 1954–94.[11] A few features already are apparent in this diagram. K has been relatively stationary except for the one-time jump in the early 1970s, when capital deepening took place.[12] L was relatively stable for most of the 1960s, but started to rise from 1970 on, with two big bulges at 1970–74 and 1985–92. Thus, there are two aspects of financial deepening that we need to study: "trends" and "bubbles."

Capital Gains and Net Accumulation

Asset values increase as more assets are accumulated through investment and saving, and as asset prices increase. For the former, gross accumulation must be

Figure 1

Asset Balances as Multiples of GDP, 1954–94

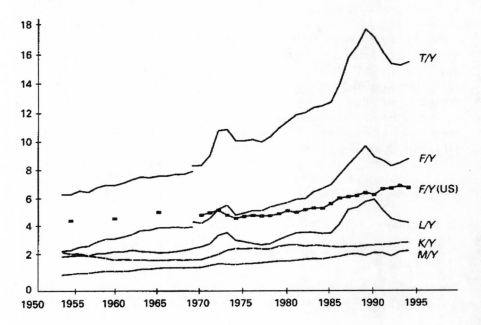

Sources: Japan: EPA, *ARNA*; United States: *SABUS* 1995, Table 786 and earlier issues.

adjusted for depreciation. For the latter, other adjustments include creation and improvement of land, and destruction of assets. We call these factors net accumulation (*NA*) and value adjustment (*VA*), respectively. The asset balance identity over a time period (0, 1) is

(2) $$A_1 = A_0 + NA + VA$$

where A is the asset balance. In ratio form, equation (2) is rewritten as

(3) $$\frac{A_1}{Y_1} = \frac{A_0}{Y_1} + \frac{NA}{Y_1} + \frac{VA}{Y_1}$$

where $Y1$ is the nominal GDP for year 1.

Based on Figure 1, we divide the entire period into six sub-periods: (i) 1954–69; (ii) 1969–73; (iii) 1973–77; (iv) 1977–85; (v) 1985–89; and (vi) 1989–94.

Sub-periods (ii) and (iii) correspond to Bubble I, and sub-periods (v) and (vi) to Bubble II. We apply equation (3) to these six periods. We consider four assets: land (L); corporate equity (E); money (M); and bank loans (BL); and all other financial assets ($F - E - [M + BL]$). Each category is considered sufficiently homogeneous for our purpose (see Table 1).

For land, we find that the major part of its value change was due to valuation adjustments. Needless to say, the land supply is fixed and its value change comes mainly from conversion of farm land to urban land.[13] In annual terms, VA was high in 1969–73 and 1985–89, and low in 1973–77 and 1989–94. The bubble effect is apparent.

As for financial assets, Table 1 shows that corporate equities (E) changed more because of value adjustment than net accumulation. By contrast, money plus loans grew almost exclusively because of net accumulation, as did the rest of financial assets.

In short, bubbles showed up in the form of asset inflation and deflation in the stock market and the land market, and in the form of rises and falls in net accumulation in the money and credit markets.

Trends of Financial Deepening

With bubbles deleted, the curves in Figure 1 all exhibit strong upward trends, except for K/Y. Dividing the entire period into three broad subperiods, we compare the growth rates of L/Y, F/Y, and M/Y in Table 2. Upward trends in these ratios are remarkable.

For a measure of financial deepening, we may take $F / (K + L)$, the ratio of financial assets to real assets. As shown in Figure 2, this ratio rose significantly in 1954–65, was more or less stable in 1965–83, and has risen somewhat since then. According to this measure, financial deepening in a narrow sense may have been most prominent in the early part of rapid growth.

An important feature of financial growth rates in Table 2 is the near parallel growth of F/Y and M/Y. This feature is verified in Figure 2, which shows changes in F/M and L/M. F/M seems to settle down at a long-run level of 4.0 or so, and L/M likewise to a long-run level of about 2.0, indicating the operation of some macroeconomic mechanism. (At the moment, I have not fully substantiated this mechanism.) This feature means that, in the final analysis, F/Y and L/Y depend on how M/Y grows over time. We consider this point in section 5, below.

Comparing Japan with the United States,[14] as shown in Figure 1, Japan's F/Y crossed that of the United States in the early 1970s, and the gap continued to widen. F/Y grew very slowly in the United States before 1980. As far as this comparison is concerned, Japan's financial deepening must have exceeded that of the United States by nearly 50 percent.

Table 1

Asset Balance: Net Accumulation (NA) and Valuation Adjustments (VA), 1954–1994

Subperiod	Years	A_1/Y_1	A_0/Y_1	D	NA/Y_1	Per annum	VA/Y_1	Per annum
				$A = L$				
1954–69	15	2.30	0.22	2.07	0.06	0.004	2.00	0.13
1969–73	4	3.35	1.27	2.08	0.04	0.010	2.04	0.51
1973–77	4	2.50	2.03	0.47	0.04	0.011	0.42	0.10
1977–85	8	3.27	1.45	1.83	0.07	0.009	1.76	0.22
1985–89	4	5.56	2.65	2.92	0.03	0.009	2.28	0.72
1989–94	5	3.95	4.57	−0.62	0.04	0.008	−0.66	−0.13
				$A = E$				
1954–69	15	0.16	0.02	0.14	0.13	0.009	0.01	0.001
1969–73	4	0.65	0.28	0.37	0.06	0.015	0.31	0.077
1973–77	4	0.43	0.40	0.03	0.24	0.060	−0.24	−0.053
1977–85	8	0.76	0.25	0.51	0.07	0.009	0.44	0.055
1985–89	4	2.23	0.61	1.62	0.20	0.051	1.42	0.354
1989–94	5	0.96	1.86	−0.90	0.01	0.002	−0.91	−0.183
				$A = M + BL$				
1954–69	15	2.26	0.17	2.09	2.09	0.14	0	0
1969–73	4	2.67	1.23	1.43	1.43	0.36	0	0
1973–77	4	2.81	1.64	1.16	1.16	0.29	0	0
1977–85	8	3.37	1.60	1.77	1.76	0.22	0.01	0
1985–89	4	3.99	2.70	1.29	1.28	0.32	0.01	0
1989–94	5	4.21	3.33	0.88	0.88	0.18	0	0
				$A = F - (M + BL) - E$				
1954–69	15	1.43	0.09	1.34	1.32	0.09	0.02	0
1969–73	4	1.65	0.78	0.86	0.92	0.23	−0.06	−0.02
1973–77	4	2.06	1.21	0.85	0.78	0.20	0.27	0.07
1977–85	8	2.53	0.98	1.55	1.48	0.19	0.06	0.01
1985–89	4	3.05	2.03	1.03	1.23	0.31	−0.20	−0.05
1989–94	5	3.21	2.55	0.66	0.69	0.14	−0.03	−0.01

Source: Computed from EPA, *ARNA.*

Notes: For each sub-period (0, 1), A_0, and A_1 are initial and end values of the asset balance, *NA* and *VA* are net accumulation and valuation adjustments during (0, 1) and Y_1 is nominal GDP at year 1. *L* is land, *F* is financial assets, *M* is money, *BL* is lendings of financial institutions, and *E* is corporate equities.

Table 2

Financial Deepening: Growth Rates, Percent

Period	L/Y	F/Y	M/Y	F/Y(U.S.)
1954–69	1.5	3.7	3.6	0.5
1969–80	2.7	2.5	2.8	0.5
1980–94	1.8	3.1	2.8	2.0

Source: See Figure 1.

The Importance of Money

Money plays a prominent role in Japan. This feature becomes clearer when Japan is compared with the United States. Table 3(a) compares the asset structures of the two countries in 1994. The large difference in F/Y between the two countries is mostly due to the difference in M/Y and its dual, BL/Y.[15] The net of $(M + BL)/Y$, the asset balance, is very close between the two countries.

The contrast is even sharper for the household sector. Japanese and American households do not differ much in F/Y, but money represents 60 percent of Japanese households' financial assets. For U.S. households, the money proportion is a mere 15 percent.

When we divide money into currency plus demand deposits and time deposits, as shown in Table 3(b), we find that time deposits are the most important financial assets for Japanese households. Even nonfinancial corporations carry more money in Japan than in the United States.

3. The Financial System: Salient Features

The Scarcity of Financial Institutions

Financial institutions (FIs) owe their existence to historical circumstances. In Japan, the banking system, originally implanted as an imitation of the U.S. system, at one time boasted a large number of small banks (2,385 at their peak, in 1901). To strengthen the banking system, the government encouraged the banks to merge. Finally, during World War II, the government enforced the one prefecture–one bank policy. Thus, the postwar period started with a total number of seventy banks. Their number stayed around ninety until 1989, when nearly seventy *sogo* (mutual) banks were elevated to the status of ordinary banks. The total number of domestically licensed banks (DLBs) was 171, as of December 1995.[16] Not only is the number of banks very small, but a few of them have the lion's

Figure 2

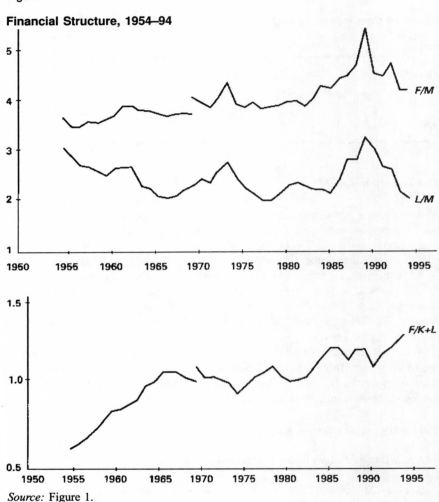

Financial Structure, 1954–94

Source: Figure 1.

share of the market. The eleven city banks account for 46 percent of the DLBs' total assets. Nine of the world's top ten banks are Japanese.[17] These city banks are associated with the *keiretsu* groups of big businesses. The contrast with the United States is very sharp. The United States, which does not allow interstate banking, has numerous tiny banks.[18] When banks are so different in size, the bank credit market must work quite differently.[19]

Insurance companies are another important group of financial institutions.

Table 3

The Importance of Money, 1994

(a) Asset balances / income

		$\frac{F}{Y}$	$\frac{M}{Y}$	$\frac{BL}{Y}$	$\frac{E}{Y}$	$\frac{(F-E-M-BL)}{Y}$
All economy	Japan	9.36	2.28	2.42	0.96	4.00
	U.S.	6.41	0.55	0.94	0.87	4.05
Households	Japan	3.37	2.03	(0.93)[a]	0.36	0.98[b]
	U.S.	3.58	0.55	(0.86)[a]	0.58	2.45[b]

Sources: Figure 1 and Table 1.
  a. Debt item
  b. $(F-E-M)/Y$
Note: Y is GDP for all economy and household disposable income for households.

(b) Money balances / income, 1994

		(Currency + Demand deposits) Income	Time deposits Income	Money Income
Households	Japan	0.32	1.71	2.03
	U.S	0.14	0.40	0.55
Nonfinancial corporations	Japan	0.17	0.41	0.58
	U.S.	0.08	0.05	0.14

Sources: See Figure 1.
Note: For Japan, households include individual proprietorships. Income for nonfinancial corporations is GDP of all industry, less agriculture, finance, and real estate, which overestimate the true value by approximately 10%.

For the United States, the money balance of nonfinancial corporations includes individual proprietorships.

They, too, are few in number and large in size, and also are important members of the *keiretsu* groups. The contrast with the United States is, once again, very sharp.[20]

There are other financial institutions than those considered above, but they are far less important.

The Importance of Public Financial Institutions

What is unique to Japan's financial system is its large postal savings.[21] The outstanding balance of postal savings rose from 11 percent of all deposits in 1954, to 21 percent in 1994. In addition, postal insurances also accounted for 29 percent of life insurance reserves, as of 1992. Japan's postal savings are thus the world's largest single bank–*cum*–life insurance company.[22] Funds collected by postal savings are entrusted with the Trust Fund Bureau of the Ministry of Finance, which invests and lends these monies.[23] It is important to remember that public FIs are outside the jurisdiction of the central bank.

Asset Ownership

Not only are financial institutions few in number, but they also are substantial owners of financial assets. The distribution of asset ownership, as of the end of fiscal year 1994, is given in Table 4.

Households own more than two-thirds of the land in the economy, but no more than one-quarter of tangible reproducible assets and financial assets. Of financial assets, they own very few bonds and are marginal holders of corporate equities. Exceptions are life insurance equities (89 percent), currency (89 percent), demand deposits (51 percent), and time deposits (76 percent), as a percentage of the total economy as of March 1995.[24]

Turning to individual assets, we find that government securities are owned by the Bank of Japan, private banks (including trust accounts), and public FIs (Trust Fund Bureau). New issues of government bonds are initially purchased by a consortium of financial institutions, including the Bank of Japan, and are mostly held by them. More than half of corporate securities are owned by FIs. One-third of corporate equities are owned by private FIs, another one-third by nonfinancial corporations, and only one-fourth by households. We consider corporate equity ownership in more detail below.

Corporate Equity Ownership

Corporate stock ownership has undergone the most dramatic turnaround during the half-century since World War II, and personifies the systemic change of Japan's corporate capitalism.

When Japan was defeated in World War II, the Americans believed that Japan's big business had been responsible for supporting Japan's military expansionism. The Occupation authorities pursued with reformers' zeal the deconcentration of economic power. Big *zaibatsu* firms were ordered to dissolve themselves into smaller units, and *zaibatsu* families to liquidate their equity holdings in *zaibatsu* firms. So, when the stock market was reopened in May 1949, individual shareholders held as much as 69 percent of the corporate equities of Japan's leading companies.

But as the Occupation ended in 1951 and the Japanese economy started its rapid growth, the disbanded *zaibatsu* firms were reunited into *keiretsu* firms, *sans* the *zaibatsu* families. Corporate shareholders rapidly increased their hold-

Table 4

Asset Ownership, March 1995 (Total = 100)

	K^a	L^a	F^b	D^c	M^d	GB	CB	E
Finance	1.7	3.0	42.8	42.8	0.4	87.5	57.2	35.1
Bank of Japan			1.4	1.4	0	12.2	0	0
Private FIs			31.6	31.6	0.4	45.3	44.1	35.0
Banks, etc.			20.9	20.9	0.4	22.8	19.3	12.6
Trust accounts			4.8	4.8	0	9.5	8.6	10.4
Insurance			5.5	5.5	0	9.3	7.6	11.6
Securities			0.4	0.4	0	2.7	0.6	1.0
Public FIs			10.9	10.9	0	30.0	22.0	0.1
Government	27.4	6.3	8.7	9.8	9.0	4.2	5.2	0.2
Nonfinancial corporations	46.3	26.9	17.1	30.7	21.9	(3.7)	(4.0)	34.4
Nonprofit organizations	2.7	0.9	0.9	0.7	2.7	0.3	1.3	0.1
Households	22.7	62.8	25.7	8.9	65.7	1.5	18.4	24.3
Foreign	0	0	4.3	6.1	0.2	(2.9)	(13.9)	5.9
Percent of total assets	17.4	26.4	56.1	56.1				
Percent of financial assets					23.8	6.4	6.5	10.1

Sources: EPA, *RNA* 1996.

   a. As of December 1994.

   b. Including foreign assets.

   c. Including foreign debt.

   d. Excluding vault cash held by FIs

Legend:
- K   Reproducible assets
- L   Land
- F   Financial assets
- D   Debt
- M   Money (currency, 4%; demand deposits, 13%; and time deposits, 83%)
- GB   Government securities (short-term securities, 9%; government bonds, 79%; and local government bonds, 12%)
- CB   Corporate securities (public corporation bonds, 21%; bank debentures, 29%; industrial bonds, 21%; investment trust securities, 17%; and external bonds, 11%)
- E   Corporate equities

Table 5

Ownership of Corporate Equities of Firms Listed in Stock Exchanges, in Number of Equities (Total = 100)

Year	Government	Financial institutions	Investment trust	Securities comp.	Nonfinancial corps.	Foreigners	Individuals
1949	5.6	10.0	—	12.6	5.6	—	69.1
1960	0.5	20.4	6.3	3.5	21.3	1.4	46.6
1970	0.3	29.3	1.4	1.2	23.1	2.4	39.9
1980	0.2	37.4	1.5	1.7	26.0	4.0	29.3
1990	0.5	41.6	3.6	1.7	25.2	4.2	23.1
1994	0.6	43.5	2.6	1.1	23.8	7.4	23.5

Source: BOJ, *ESA* 1995, Table 90 and earlier issues. Originally from the National Conference of Stock Exchanges.

ings, as shown in Table 5. Of particular note is the meteoric rise of private FIs (e.g., banks and insurance companies) as shareholders of other corporations.[25]

As we have noted, city banks and insurance companies are leading members of *keiretsu* groups. This means that *keiretsu* banks, insurance companies and nonfinancial businesses own each other (i.e, interlocking share ownership).

Interlocking share ownership is of particular importance to the control mechanism of *keiretsu* groups. Corporate shareholders who are members of the same *keiretsu* group serve as "stable shareholders," who remain as quasi-permanent shareholders. Thus, interlocking share ownership becomes an effective means of guaranteeing corporate control within the *keiretsu* group, eliminating any possibility of hostile takeovers by foreign investors. Individual shareholders have lost their status because corporations finance much of their equity increases through profit retention, rather than sales of new shares.[26]

4. Monetary Policy, Money Supply, and Financial Development

We have noted that F/M and L/M have tended to settle down to some long-term normal level, if "bubbles" are deleted. As a matter of fact, the close relationship between M and (F, L) also exists in the short run. We illustrate this for M and $F - M$ in Figure 3, which compares $g(M)$ and $g(F-M)$. The two curves have moved in parallel, not only in the long run, but also in the short run. But $g(F-M)$ is much more volatile than $g(M)$. In particular, Bubble I (early 1970s) and Bubble II (late 1980s) both involved a sharp rise and subsequent fall in $g(M)$, and a more magnified rise and fall in $g(F-M)$. This suggests that $g(M)$ must have been a prime cause of the bubbles.

The money supply we have considered so far is $M3 + CD$,[27] which is the sum

Figure 3

$g(M)$ (●) and $g(F-M)$ (■), 1955–1994

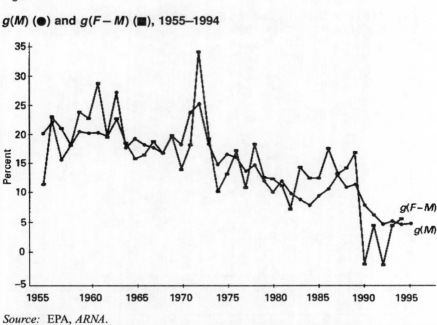

Source: EPA, *ARNA*.

of currency in circulation (C) and deposits (D) at all FIs. The money supply that the central bank controls is $M2 + CD$, which is the sum of currency outside of DMBs (deposit money banks) and deposits at DMBs.[28] Postal savings and deposits at private FIs other than DMBs are added to $M2 + CD$ to form $M3 + CD$.[29] Since $M3 + CD$ moves closely with $M2 + CD$, we can pretend that the Bank of Japan controls the whole money supply.[30] To control the money supply, the Bank of Japan determines the monetary base (MB), which is the sum of currency (C^{mb}) and bank reserves (R). R is equal to $rr \times D$, where rr is the required reserve ratio set by the Bank of Japan and D is deposits at DMBs. DMBs set aside vault cash, $V = vr \times D$. Currency outside DMBs is $C = C^{mb} - V$. Thus, the Bank of Japan influences the money supply $M2 + CD = C + D$ by setting C^{mb} and rr.

Changes in MB/Y and C/Y, where Y is nominal GDP, are shown in Figure 4 for 1959–95.[31] By comparing Figure 4 with Figure 3, we can readily observe that sharp rises and falls in $g(M)$ at the two bubbles were due to sharp rises and falls in MB/Y and C/Y at the same time.

Why are changes in $g(M)$ accompanied by more violent changes in $g(F-M)$? We give an heuristic explanation below.[32] The money supply must be equilibrated with the money demand. The money demand consists of two parts: the transaction demand, and the asset demand. The former is more or less in propor-

Figure 4

Currency Outside DMB (*C*) and the Monetary Base (*MB*), in Multiples of GDP (*Y*), 1959–1995

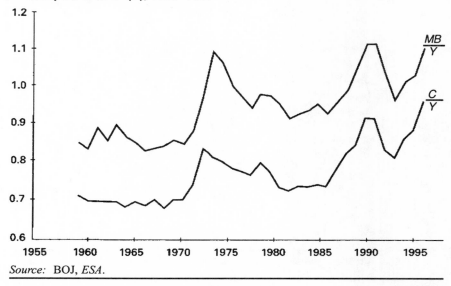

Source: BOJ, ESA.

tion to nominal income (*Y*), while the latter is more related to household wealth (*W*). When $g(M^s)$ is growing faster than $g(Y)$, the asset demand for money must be growing faster than the transactions demand. But this is possible if and only if wealth grows faster than income. Asset prices must increase. Asset inflation is stimulated further as the nominal interest rate falls—a direct consequence of money growth outpacing income growth. The nominal interest rate is conditioned by the discount rate (i_d), another instrument of monetary policy.[33] The central bank is likely to lower the discount rate as it expands the monetary base. In Japan, bank deposits and lending rates are linked to the discount rate.

Why, then, did the monetary base and currency in circulation increase so sharply at the two bubbles? To answer this question, we must look at the asset side of the monetary base. By increasing the supply of currency (C^{mb}), the monetary authorities match it with increasing assets, which consist of central bank credits to DMBs (loans and discounts) and to government (mainly purchases of government bonds), foreign reserve and other assets. Though all of them are important, here we pay particular attention to the bank's foreign reserve.

The monetary authorities believe that the main task of monetary policy is price stability. To achieve this objective, the central bank wishes to keep the country's exchange rate as stable as possible.[34] If the exchange rate threatens to fall (i.e., the real value of the yen rises), the central bank tries to increase its foreign reserve so as to prevent the ¥/$ rate from falling too much. When the central bank purchases foreign reserves, more currency is supplied. This has occurred twice—in 1971–72 and 1987–88. For the former, one must recall the Nixon Shock of August 1971, which resulted in an up-valuing of the yen. There was strong market pressure to adjust the yen's value even more. Japan's foreign reserve expanded sharply,[35] resulting in a sharp expansion of Japan's monetary base.[36] In the early 1980s, the U.S. dollar was expensive, worsening the imbalance in the U.S. balance of payments. The world's leading countries agreed, in the September 1985 Plaza Accord, to intervene in the foreign exchange market so as to lower the value of the dollar. The ¥/$ exchange rate consequently fell from a high of ¥260/$ in February 1985, to a low of ¥123/$ in November 1988. The sharp increase in Japan's foreign reserve in 1987–88[37] can be understood as a method of moderating the fall of the exchange rate. In either case, the monetary base sharply increased and was transmitted into a sharp rise in the money supply, contributing to asset inflation.[38]

5. Financial Instability, 1986–1995

The Japanese economy came out of a recession in November 1986. The cyclical upswing that followed turned out to be one of the longest in the last four decades. It lasted fifty-one months, until February 1991.[39] While real growth was not particularly remarkable (5.0 percent per annum), the boom was noteworthy because of the very strong bubble in the stock market and the land market. The stock market peaked in December 1989 and the urban land market began to go down in the fall of 1990 (based on the urban land price index for six metropolitan cities). The tailspin of stock prices had ended by 1995, and stocks were going up by mid-1996. Land prices had not stopped their descent as of early 1996. The depressed financial markets are matched by the equally depressed goods market. Real GDP was nearly at a standstill for four successive years (1992–95).[40] In this section, we see more details of monetary developments over the last decade.

Monetary Developments

See Table 6 for a few monetary indicators. For real GDP, the growth record was particularly dismal in 1992–95. The inflation rate was also quite low in the early 1990s (even negative in 1995). To appreciate how much the monetary factor contributed to the upswing and downswing of economic activities, one must compare $g(GDP)$ with $g(M2 + CD)$. $g(M2 + CD)$ was around 10 percent in the late 1980s. Subsequently, it declined and was even negative in 1992. Changes in $g(M2 + CD)$ were no doubt caused by changes in $g(MB)$. The discount rate (i_d) fell in the late 1980s, to a low of 2.50 percent that was maintained from March 1987

Table 6

Monetary Indicators, 1985–1996, Percent

Year	Growth Rates						Interest Rates	
	Nominal GDP	Real GDP	Deflator	MB	$M2+CD$	$M3+CD$	i_d	i_c
1985	6.6	4.9	1.6	3.8	8.7	8.6	5.00	6.44
1986	4.4	2.6	1.8	8.1	9.2	8.8	3.50	4.81
1987	4.1	4.1	0	8.4	10.8	10.0	2.50	3.31
1988	6.6	6.2	0.4	13.0	10.2	9.4	2.50	3.94
1989	6.6	4.7	1.8	12.9	12.0	11.1	3.25	5.34
1990	7.1	4.8	2.2	7.4	7.4	7.0	5.25	7.56
1991	6.3	4.2	2.0	−1.5	2.3	5.3	5.50	7.50
1992	2.6	1.1	1.5	−3.8	−0.2	3.4	3.75	4.09
1993	0.6	−0.2	0.8	5.9	2.2	4.0	2.50	3.31
1994	0.7	0.5	0.2	2.0	2.8	4.0	1.75	2.13
1995	0.5	0.6	−0.1	7.8	3.3	3.5	1.00	0.84
1996							0.50*	0.46*

Sources: GDP   EPA, *ARNA,* annual
         M BOJ, *ESA* 1995, Tables 3 and 5 (December to December)
         i_d Discount rate, July, BOJ, *ESA* 1995, Table 6
         i_c Call rate, noncollateral, overnight, July, BOJ, *ESA* 1995
  *March.

to May 1989. It then rose, finally reaching a peak of 6.00 percent in September 1990. Since then, the discount rate has been reduced successively, reaching an all-time low of 0.5 percent in September 1995. The market interest rate (here represented by the call rate (i_c)—the shortest-term interest rate) followed suit.[41]

In interpreting the indicators in Table 6, the chicken-or-egg question remains: Does money growth cause real growth, or is it the other way around? The Bank of Japan argues that the bank allowed the money supply to grow in the late 1980s in order to meet the then rising money demand. Subsequently, the bank cut the money supply because the money demand was falling. Our position is contrary. In particular, as we argued in the preceding section, it is money growth that triggered the two bubbles under study.[42]

Nonperforming Loans

A major after-effect of the latest bubble is the appearance of sizable "nonperforming" loans. An overexpansion of the money supply means an excessive increase of bank loans. When loans are increasing at a rate far higher than normal, more risky borrowers have to be accepted by lenders. In the late 1980s, as both stock prices and land prices were rising rapidly, investors were willing to borrow as much as possible to finance their investments in corporate equities and urban land. Banks were willing to make such loans to risky speculative investors in various ways. These investors in turn helped to raise asset prices further. But when asset markets collapsed, these risky loans went into default. Banks carried these loans on the books, under the name of "nonperforming" loans, although a large proportion of them was nonrecoverable. This subterfuge went on for some time. But finally, in 1995, the strain reached an intolerable level. Three small banks went bankrupt in succession in mid-1995.[43] In November 1995, the Ministry of Finance (MOF) finally released its estimate of nonperforming loans as of March 1995: ¥37.39 trillion, of which ¥18.29 trillion would be nonrecoverable. These amounts represent 7.5 percent and 3.7 percent of the total outstanding balance of loans and discounts, respectively, of DLBs (¥396.7 trillion).[44] The MOF expressed the optimistic view that banks would be able to take care of these nonperforming loans without much difficulty out of their business earnings, which had averaged ¥5 trillion per annum for the previous five years.[45]

But then, an equally huge amount of nonperforming loans (another ¥30 trillion) was reported by "nonbanks." Nonbanks include a wide array of money-lending institutions such as installment companies, credit card companies, consumer finance companies (*sarakin*), business finance companies, and housing loan companies. Narrowly defined, they are institutions that are engaged in "money lending without accepting deposits." Nonbanks came into being in the 1970s and expanded in the 1980s, when funds were in abundant supply. Banks created them to branch out into leasing and installment credit (which are legally outside of their business areas); they also set up housing loan companies to lend to real estate investors who were considered too risky, according to the banks' own criteria. Nonfinancial corporations also set up their own nonbanks to enable them to manage surplus funds for financial investments. Unlike financial institutions, nonbanks escape strict government regulations. They can go into business merely by registering with the MOF (there were 33,000 registered nonbanks as of January 1996). The Nonbank Law, a September 1991 revision of the Money Lender Law, requires a nonbank with an outstanding loan balance in excess of ¥50 billion to file an annual report on its loans to the MOF. As of March 1995, 278 nonbanks had filed this return. Their total loan balance was ¥55.8 trillion (including ¥20.4 trillion went to the real estate industry), of which ¥30 trillion was reported to be nonperforming (*Yomiuri Shimbun* 1996, 8 April).

Of the nonbanks, housing loan companies attracted public attention from late 1995 on, as the government tried to take over their nonperforming loans. Seven of these companies, which had been set up by city banks, went bankrupt. Of their total loan balance of ¥13 trillion, ¥6.27 trillion was identified as nonrecoverable (*Yomiuri Shimbun* 1996, 28 February). The government's 1996 budget, which passed the Diet on 10 May 1996, approved the spending of public funds in the amount of ¥0.685 trillion to liquidate them.

Monetary-Fiscal Policy, 1992–1995

Officially, the latest recession ended in October 1993. But the growth rate was dismal for four years, from 1992 to 1995. The government tried to pull the economy up by fiscal and monetary measures. Deficit spending was stepped up.[46] Monetary policy changed from contractionary to expansionary in 1993, and the discount rate continued to be cut (Table 6). Yet these active policy measures have not helped the economy to step up growth.

In this connection, the stance of monetary policy is of interest. As Figure 4 shows, MB/Y and C/Y were both rising from 1992 on. Like the two bubbles, their increases are associated with sharp increases in the monetary authorities' foreign reserve.[47] As in the two bubbles, this increase in the foreign reserve can be regarded as the bank's attempt to prevent the ¥/$ exchange rate from falling too far.[48] However, unlike the two bubbles, the asset market remained inactive (though the turnaround of the stock market in mid-1995 may be attributed to this factor).

6. Household Accumulation and Financial Deepening

MB/Y or C/Y had no trend except for a few discrete jumps (Figure 4). How then did M/Y increase with a strong upward trend? Obviously, because deposits (D) increased steadily. Deposits can be classified as primary or derived. The former are made by primary depositors, while the latter are created by banks based on the former, using the well-known money-multiplier mechanism. Households can be identified as primary depositors. Households are the principal owners of monetary assets—90 percent of currency, 51 percent of demand deposits, and 68 percent of time deposits.[49]

Figure 5 shows how household wealth increased from 1969 to 1994. Land is a major part of household wealth. As the price of land continued to rise, L/Y continued to rise. The effect of the two bubbles is apparent. F/Y is also influenced by the two bubbles to a lesser extent, apparently because Japanese households do not have much corporate equities in their portfolios.[50] M/Y increased much more steadily. The long-run stability of F/M is verified for the household sector as well. M is about 60 percent of F.[51]

Except for land value, household wealth is increased principally by net accumulation—that is, household net saving (S).[52] We then have the causal chain, S $\Rightarrow \Delta F, \Delta M$.

How, then, is S itself determined? Here, we apply the target wealth hypoth-

Figure 5

Household Wealth, in Multiples of Household Disposable Income, 1969–1994

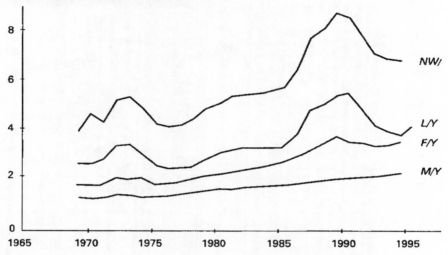

Source: EPA, *ARNA.*

esis (TWH) (Sato 1987; 1995c), which asserts that a household determines its current saving so as to achieve its wealth target (W^*) by the end of the plan period of T years. In a simplified case, we have

$$(4) \qquad S = \left(\frac{1}{T}\right)\left(W^* - W\right)$$

where W is the initial wealth balance.

An annual budget survey, conducted by the Bank of Japan in the week of 1 July since 1963,[53] asks Japanese households for the financial savings target (F^*) along with the financial asset balance (F). Thus, replacing W with F and deflating by household disposable income (Y), we have the household saving function based on the TWH:

$$(5) \qquad \frac{S}{Y} = \left(\frac{F^* - F}{TY}\right)$$

The same survey reports T to be around nine to ten years.[54]

Equation (5) is applied to a Japanese household saving (Sato 1995c). Figure 6(a) illustrates the financial savings gap based on the annual budget surveys for

Figure 6

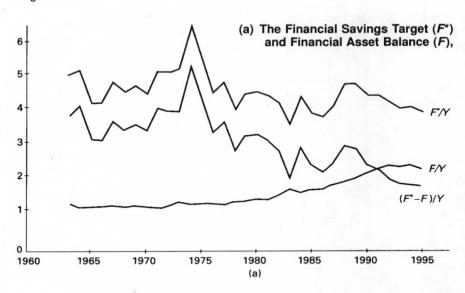

(a) **The Financial Savings Target (F^*) and Financial Asset Balance (F),**

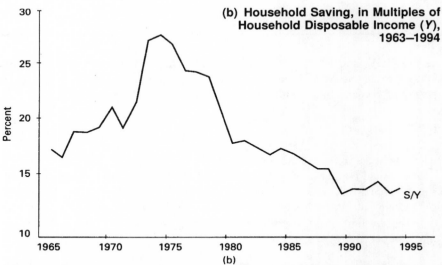

(b) **Household Saving, in Multiples of Household Disposable Income (Y), 1963–1994**

Sources: (a) BOJ, *ASSC*, as of 1 July of the year stated (Y is income after tax in the year preceding 1 July). (b) EPA, *ARNA*. S is for July of the year T to June of the year $T + 1$, and Y is for July of the year $T - 1$ to June of year T.

1963–95.[55] Figure 6(b) gives the household saving rate for the corresponding year, based on the *ARNA*.

Figure 6 reveals that rises and falls in S/Y are matched very well by rises and falls in $(F^* - F) / Y$. In particular, both peaked in 1974, the year of the first oil shock.[56] This observation makes an important point with respect to how Japanese households decide how much to save. F^* can be stated as f^*Y_T, where f^* is the target-wealth–income-ratio and Y_T is the nominal income expected T years hence. In year-to-year changes, Y_T dominates. When inflation is rampant as in the first oil shock, households believe that inflation will persist. Accordingly, they raise Y_T relative to Y. This change in expectations raises F^*/Y and, hence, S/Y. The same point can be made another way. Japanese households keep most of their financial assets in the form of fixed-price assets such as money. As inflation reduces the value of financial assets, households step up current saving to make up for the capital loss. From the mid-1970s on, both real growth and inflation remained low. Y_T/Y must have been low. F^*/Y fluctuated around a value of 4.0. Meanwhile, F/Y continued to rise. Thus, the wealth gap continued to close. The saving rate continued to fall in proportion to the shrinking wealth gap.

In the short run, f^* is likely to be stable, but is subject to change beyond the medium term. In the medium term, f^* may be influenced by the relative price of urban land. When urban land prices become higher, relative to income, households that wish to buy their dwellings must save more before hand.[57] Long-term factors are mostly demographic—in particular, population aging.[58] If one expects to live longer, one must save more while younger. However, when everybody gets older, they have to dissave. Thus, for households as a whole, population aging must cause saving to decrease over time.

For our present objective, what is important is the fact that households save much in monetary assets. With primary deposits rising, the total money supply continues to rise relative to GDP. Basically, the pace of financial deepening is set by the high level of household saving.

7. The Future of Financial Deepening

While rapid growth has been replaced by slow growth on the real side, financial deepening has continued unabated over the past four decades in Japan. Financial deepening is now more advanced in Japan than in the United States. Is this trend to continue?

The answer to this question can be found in the preceding section. F/Y tends to rise in parallel with M/Y. M/Y in turn is determined by household saving. The causal chain between the financial balance and saving is described below:

$$(6) \qquad \left(\frac{F^*}{Y} - \frac{F}{Y} \right) \rightarrow \frac{S}{Y} \rightarrow \frac{\Delta M}{Y} \rightarrow \frac{\Delta F}{Y}$$

If S/Y remains at its current high level, F/Y will continue to rise. Eventually, when the wealth gap is closed, F/Y will converge to a steady-state level. However, as the wealth gap narrows, the saving rate also falls. Hence, this convergence process will take a long time.[59]

A more promising venue for closing the wealth gap is the fall in F^*/Y. Assume that Y_T/Y will remain at the present low level. Then, will f^* be likely to fall? If f^* is to fall, it must be due to population aging. When there are more old people, both household and national saving must decline. This is tantamount to a fall in F^*. As we noted, however, population aging has more complex effects on saving. Young households must increase saving in anticipation of longer retirement living. As a result, total household saving will not decline too fast. Further, one must consider the labor supply behavior of older male workers, age 65 and over. Older males in Japan continue to work. Their labor force participation ratio (LFPR) had been on a downward trend, but this decline stopped in the mid-1980s at around 38 percent. Population aging means that, with the continued decline in younger working-age population, the demand for labor may remain strong for older male workers. Labor supply of older male workers may also remain strong because they must support themselves longer, as their lifespans increase. The budget survey of the Bank of Japan indicates that old-age working households save as much as younger households. Furthermore, the same survey shows that the bequest motive became stronger among affluent old-age households starting in the mid-1980s. Altogether, S/Y may not fall as fast as initially projected. If so, financial deepening may have still some distance to cover.

The continued rise in M/Y means that its dual, BL/Y also will continue to rise. Can the economy support more bank loans without raising the default risk? Long-term data on bankruptcies indicate that there has been no long-term trend in the rate of bankruptcies.[60]

However, if financial deepening continues and the stance of monetary policy remains unchanged, will there not be another bubble? As a Japanese proverb says, there is always a third time for anything that has already occurred twice. The third instance may be even more violent than the last two bubbles because, by then, financial deepening will be far more advanced. This means that the central bank must be extremely cautious in executing its monetary policy, especially in harmonizing the internal and external balances of the economy. So far, there is little evidence of such a change.

8. Conclusions

We have seen how financial deepening has proceeded in Japan over the past four decades, from 1954 to 1994. While the real economy moved from rapid growth to slow growth, the financial economy went through repression, liberalization and maturity. Financial deepening was particularly strong in the rapid growth period under financial repression. But even when Japan entered into slow growth, financial deepening continued. In fact, there were two violent bubbles, in the early 1970s and the late 1980s.

We have seen that money plays a particularly important role in Japan's financial economy, and that the pace of financial deepening is set by the speed of monetary expansion—which in turn is determined by household saving, as it continues to raise households' money balance. So long as the household saving rate remains high, financial deepening will continue.

The experience of the last two bubbles points to the systemic risk inherent in the excessive pace of financial deepening. While the monetary authorities may be criticized for the "too-liberal" monetary policy that gave rise to these bubbles, their root cause is found in household saving. Will household saving remain high, and will Japan's financial deepening continue? Already the Japanese economy is far more monetarized than the U.S. economy. Will not future systemic risks be too high, when financial deepening is at an unprecedented high level?

Unfortunately, the answer to this question lies in the realm of the unknown. One thing, however, is certain: Monetary policy must be set with extreme caution.

Notes

1. See Shaw (1973), McKinnon (1973) and Fry (1995). For Japan's experience, see Teranishi (1982, 1994).
2. Statistical sources are abbreviated as follows:

EPA, *ARNA*	Economic Planning Agency, *Annual Report on National Accounts*
BOJ, *ESA*	Bank of Japan, *Economic Statistics Annual*
USA, *SABUS*	Department of Commerce (U.S.), *Statistical Abstract of the United States*

3. The outstanding balance of national debt was 49 percent (1930), 204 percent (1944), and 13 percent (1952) of GDP.
4. Household savings were mostly deposited in banks and postal savings.
5. There were two tiers of credit rationing. At the first tier, the central bank assigned quotas on the volume of member banks' borrowings from the central bank. This "window guidance" was maintained until 1991 IIIQ, when it was finally discontinued. At the second tier, banks rationed credit to borrowing firms. This part of credit rationing came to an end by the early 1970s.
6. In the late 1980s, the so-called *zaitech* (financial technology) became a fad among Japanese businesses. Firms with excess funds decided to invest their funds in corporate equities and land for high returns. The *zaitech* fever was alleged to have been an important contributing factor to asset inflation in the late 1980s.
7. The Nikkei Stock Price Average rose from ¥7,042 in August 1982 to ¥38,130 in December 1989. It later bottomed out below ¥15,000 in June 1995, and was around ¥22,000 in June 1996.
8. The urban land price index (six metropolitan cities) rose from 55 in September 1985 to 105 in September 1990, but was 50 in September 1995. It was still falling in the early part of 1996.

9. The Business Cycle Dating Committee of the Economic Planning Agency shifted the peak forward from April to February 1991 (17 June 1996).

10. At the national level, $F = DB + NFA$ and $NW = L + K + NFA$, where NFA is the country's net foreign assets. In examining Japan's financial system, Sakakibara and Feldman (1983) focused on the debt side. We look more at the asset side in this paper.

11. In 1978, Japan's national accounting statistics was completely revised in conformity with the revised (1968) United Nations System of National Accounts. The revision was from 1970 onward. Later, the revision was extended back to 1955. However, there is a big break in the national balance sheet at 1969. The most important difference is that the valuation of corporate equities shifted from face value to market value. (This is why the bubble around 1961 is not apparent in Figure 1.)

12. During the rapid growth period, credit rationing depressed the level of investment to the available level of saving, thereby keeping the capital–output ratio at a low level and the profit rate at a high level. In the early 1970s, credit rationing ceased and capital deepening set in. Consequently, the capital–output ratio rose and the profit rate fell. When the profit rate reached a level compatible with the interest rate, capital deepening ceased.

13. For privately owned land, urban land was 4.9 percent in 1969 and 5.5 percent in 1992 (*Japan Statistical Yearbook* 1995, Table 1-9) of the total land area, and 72.5 percent and 82.4 percent of the total land value (*ARNA*). The urban land area grew at an average annual rate of 0.6 percent from 1969 to 1992. The underlying data indicate that the average unit price of urban land was 61 times that of farm land in 1992.

14. In the following analysis, we take the United States as a yardstick against which to compare Japan.

15. *BL* is roughly comparable in size to *M* in Japan. In the United States, *BL* is much larger than *M* on account of federally financed mortgages, which are not backed by deposits.

16. As of December 1995, DLBs are: city banks (11); regional banks I (64); regional banks II, formerly *sogo* banks (65); trust banks (28, up from 7 in 1992); and long-term credit banks (3) (BOJ, *ESA* 1995, Table 33).

17. At the top is Bank of Tokyo-Mitsubishi, which came into being in April 1996. The one non-Japanese bank in the top ten is a German bank, in seventh place.

18. In 1994, the United States had 10,450 insured commercial banks with total assets of $4,101 billion, or an average asset size of $0.38 billion (*SABUS* 1995, Table 794). In 1995, Japan, had 171 DLBs with total assets of ¥750.4 billion. At ¥107/$, total assets are $7,000 billion, or $41 billion per bank (BOJ, *ESA* 1995, Table 12).

19. Sakakibara and Feldman (1983), however, argue that competition must be more intense in Japanese banking than in American banking, for reasons that include larger numbers of bank branch offices and postal offices, which accept postal savings. Crum and Meerschwam (1986) argue that Japanese banking is more regulated than American banking.

20. In 1994, Japan had 27 life insurance companies and 25 non–life insurance companies with total assets of ¥175.7 trillion ($1.64 trillion) and ¥28.4 trillion ($0.27 trillion), respectively, for an average asset size of $61 billion and $11 billion (BOJ, *ESA* 1995, Tables 29 and 30). Seventeen of the life insurance companies, which account for 92 percent of the market share, are mutual companies—that is, insurance subscribers are company shareholders. In 1993, the United States had 1,840 life insurance companies with the total assets of $1,839 billion, for an average size of $1.0 billion. Property and casualty insurance firms had total assets of $0.651 trillion (*SABUS* 1995, Tables 841 and 845).

21. Japan's postal savings were created in 1875. The United States discontinued postal savings in the early 1960s. European countries have postal savings, but not to same the extent as in Japan.

22. Its deposit balance of ¥210 trillion in December 1995 is compared with the total assets of the largest bank, Tokyo-Mitsubishi, of ¥75 trillion as of April 1996.

23. The TFB finances a dozen government FIs, of which the largest, the Housing Loan Corporation, extends subsidized housing loans that accounted for 41 percent of total mortgages outstanding in 1994.

24. Of gross household wealth, the Japanese have land (47 percent), money (26 percent), reproducible assets (10 percent), life insurance (9 percent), and other financial assets (8 percent) (*ARNA* 1994, December).

25. Unlike banks in the United States and the United Kingdom, Japanese banks are legally allowed to own equities of other private corporations (subject to a 5 percent limit). Thus, corporate equity ownership is markedly different in Japan than, say, the United States. In 1994, U.S. corporate equity owners were households (48 percent), nonbank finance (46 percent), and foreigners (6 percent) (*SABUS* 1995, Table 786). Nonbank finance, such as pension funds and mutual funds, invest in corporate equities on behalf of their claimants who are households.

26. The propensity to retain profits (net of tax) is around 70 percent for Japanese firms, in contrast to around 50 percent for U.S. and European firms (MITI 1992, *White Paper on International Trade*).

27. M in *ARNA* (Figure 1) is slightly different from $M3 + CD$ in *ESA*.

28. DMBs are DLBs (excluding trust accounts and foreign trust banks), *shinkin* banks, the Norinchukin Bank and the Shokochukin Bank.

29. $M3 + CD/M2 + CD$ was 1.28 in 1955, and 1.73 in 1995. Postal savings, which are about one-half of $(M3 - M2)$, have grown faster than DMBs.

30. When deposit rates are changed in DMBs, they are usually (though not always) matched by similar changes in postal savings deposit rates.

31. The reserve requirement was formally adopted in 1959.

32. See Sato (1997) for a formal analysis of the monetary mechanism outlined here.

33. The discount rate is applied by the central bank in discounting commercial bills submitted by DMBs to the Bank's window.

34. See Yoshikawa et al. (1993, pp. 137–39).

35. It rose from ¥1.7 trillion in 1970 to ¥4.8 trillion in 1971 and ¥5.4 trillion in 1972, and then fell to ¥3.6 trillion in 1973 (as a percentage of the monetary base: 25 percent, 49 percent, 58 percent, and 23 percent, respectively) (Bank of Japan, *The Monetary Survey*).

36. For a critical review of Japan's monetary policy at the time of the 1973–74 inflation, see Komiya (1976).

37. The foreign reserve (in ¥ trillion) was 5.9 in 1985, 6.7 in 1986, 11.8 in 1987, 11.8 in 1988, and 8.9 in 1989 (as a percentage of the monetary base: 18 percent, 17 percent, 29 percent, 27 percent, and 20 percent, respectively) (BOJ, *op. cit.*).

38. In 1971 and 1972, goods inflation was still moderate (the GDP deflator rose by 5.4 percent and 5.6 percent, respectively). Serious inflation occurred in 1973 (12.7 percent) and 1974 (20.8 percent)—imported inflation due to the first oil shock. In the later 1980s, the inflation rate was very low (0.1 percent in 1987 and 0.7 percent in 1988).

39. The longest upswing lasted 57 months (October 1964–July 1970).

40. See Table 6. The population growth rate was 0.7 percent. The GDPO gap has been about 3.5 percent since 1993 IVQ (EPA 1996). The labor market has been depressed—the ratio of job openings to applications was about 0.66 (1994–95).

41. The call market is an interbank fund market in which very short-term loans are transacted. City banks are the main borrowers and trust banks are the main lenders. The call rate, uncollateraled and overnight, was introduced in July 1985. This rate is now considered the most sensitive reflection of the policy stance of the Bank of Japan, which intervenes in the call market to let its stance be known.

42. For pros and cons on the Bank of Japan's policy, see the exchange between Iwata (1993a) (cons) and Okina (1993) (pros). Criticizing the bank's policy, Iwata (1993b, pp. 223ff.) attributes the Bank's easy money policy in the late 1980s to its conviction that the money expansion was safe because it would not raise the rate of goods inflation.

In his November 1994 pre-retirement speech, Chancellor Mieno of the Bank of Japan (who retired in December 1994) observed that the Bank of Japan adopted the low-interest policy in response to the September 1985 Plaza Accord. Mieno acknowledged the Bank's responsibility for letting the low-interest policy unwittingly give rise to the bubble in the late 1980s.

To blame monetary policy wholly for the two bubbles may be too harsh. Asset inflation was a worldwide phenomenon in both the early 1970s and the late 1980s, although Japan's was the most severe. (See Chart 3, *The Economist* [1996], for a comparison of asset inflation for five leading countries.)

43. Two *shinkin* banks (Cosmo and Kizu) and a regional bank (Hyogo).

44. *Yomiuri Shimbun,* 15 November 1995. As a percentage of GDP in fiscal 1994 (¥466.8 trillion), 8.0 percent and 3.9 percent. This amount does not include debts of the three bankrupt banks mentioned above (¥2.88 trillion).

45. As banks decided to write off some of the bad loans, most banks reported losses in their March 1996 settlements.

46. The government budget went into a surplus from 1987 to 1991, was nearly in balance in 1992, and then turned increasingly into a deficit. In fiscal 1995, government deficits were 7.6 percent of GDP. National debt rose to 89 percent of GDP. In the United States, the corresponding figures were 2.8 percent and 69 percent in 1995. European countries showed similar figures (*Yomiuri Shimbun* 1996, 5 April).

47. The foreign reserve fell from ¥11.7 trillion in 1988 to ¥3.4 trillion in 1992 (December figures). After that, it continued to rise: to ¥5.2 trillion in 1993, ¥7.3 trillion in 1994, ¥11.5 trillion in 1995, and ¥21.9 trillion in May 1996 (respectively, 8, 11, 15, and 22 percent of the monetary base, 1992–95).

48. The ¥/$ rate began to fall sharply in 1995, from ¥100/$ in December 1994 to ¥80.4 in June 1995. The Bank of Japan's intervention helped to reverse the direction of change (the foreign reserve rose from ¥8.1 trillion in July 1995 to ¥10.3 trillion in August 1995, and to ¥12.5 trillion in September 1995).

49. Values in 1994 for *M*3 + *CD.* For *M*2 + *CD,* 49 percent of demand deposits and 63 percent of time deposits (BOJ, *ESA* 1995, Table 3).

50. As a percentage of *F*: 20 percent in 1969; 12 percent in 1975, 1980, and 1985; 25 percent in 1989; and 11 percent in 1994.

51. *F/M* was 1.57 in 1969, 1.64 in 1972, 1.46 in 1975, 1.53 in 1980, 1.57 in 1985, 2.06 in 1989, and 1.66 in 1994. *L/M* was somewhat more changeable.

52. According to *ARNA,* about 80 percent of household saving goes into net accumulation (*DF – DDB*).

53. *Public Opinion Survey of Savings and Consumption* (abbreviated below as *ASSC*), conducted by the Central Council of Savings Information, an outside organization of the Bank of Japan.

54. *T* varies with household age, from 14 years for age 20–29, to 7 years for age 70–79.

55. It must be noted that *F/Y* is about 50 percent as large in *ASSC* as in *ARNA.* The same is true with the *Family Saving Survey,* another official annual survey of household assets, in which *F/Y* is about 60 percent as large as in *ARNA.*

56. The first oil shock started in November 1973 and continued through 1974. The import price index (1975 = 100) rose from 59 in October 1973 to 96 in July 1974, while the CPI rose from 75 to 90.

57. Despite the high land prices, home ownership has been a little over 60 percent (comparable to the United States). For new houses, down payments have fallen from 50 percent (late 1980s) to 40 percent (late 1990s) of the house price (including land).

58. According to the population projection of the Ministry of Welfare (September 1992), the old-age dependency ratio (population 65 and over/total population) will increase from 25.1 percent in 1990 to 43.2 percent in 2020.

59. The gap fell from 3.18 in 1980 to 1.67 in 1995. If linearly extrapolated, the gap will close in 16 years. By that time, F/Y will be 75 percent higher than the 1995 level. But that assumes that S/Y will remain at the current level, which is unlikely.

60. As a percentage of the outstanding balance of loans of DLBs, the amounts of debt involved in banks' suspension-of-business transactions and bankruptcies show no long-term trends (1 percent and 2 percent, respectively) (*Japan Statistical Yearbook* 1995, Table 5-15). The total debt of bankruptcies of firms with more than ¥10 million changed as a percentage of the outstanding balance of loans of DLBs, as follows: 1978–83, 2.0 percent; 1984–86, 1.7 percent; 1987–90, 0.7 percent; and 1991–95, 1.7 percent (Tokyo Shoko Research, as reported in *Yomiuri Shimbun* 1996, 9 June).

References

Crum, Colyer, and David M. Meerschwam. 1986. "From Relationship to Price Banking: The Loss of Regulatory Control." In T.K. McCraw, ed., *America Versus Japan*, pp. 261–98. Boston: Harvard Business School Press.

Economic Planning Agency. 1996. *The Japanese Economy: Recent Trends and Outlook, 1996* (February). Tokyo: Economic Planning Agency.

Economist. 1996. "A Survey of International Banking: The Domino Effect" (17 April).

Fry, Maxwell J. 1995. *Money, Interest, and Banking in Economic Development*, 2d ed. Baltimore, MD: Johns Hopkins University Press.

Iwata, Kikuo. 1993a. *Kin'yu seisaku no keizaigaku, Nichigin riron no kensho* [Economics of Monetary Policy, Testing Bank of Japan Theory]. Tokyo: Nihon Keizai Shimbunsha.

———. 1993b. *Kin'yu nyumon* [Introduction to Finance]. Tokyo: Iwanami Shoten.

Komiya, Ryutaro. 1976. "Showa 48–49 nen no inflation no gen'in'" [Causes of 1973–74 inflation]. University of Tokyo, *Keizaigaku ronshu* 42 (April). Reprinted in R. Komiya, *Gendai Nihon keizai* [Contemporary Japanese Economy], chap. 1, pp. 1–61. Tokyo: University of Tokyo Press, 1988.

McKinnon, Ronald I. 1973. *Kin'yu seisaku, Chuo ginko no shiten to sentaku* [Monetary Policy: Central Bank Viewpoint and Options]. Tokyo: Toyo Keizai Shimposha.

Patrick, Hugh T., and Yung Chul Park, eds. 1994. *The Financial Development of Japan, Korea, and Taiwan—Growth, Repression, and Liberalization*. New York: Oxford University Press.

Sakakibara, Eisuke, and Robert A. Feldman. 1983. "The Japanese Financial System in Comparative Perspective." *Journal of Comparative Economics* 7 (March): 1–24.

Sato, Kazuo. 1987. "Saving and Investment." In K. Yamamura and Y. Yasuba, eds., *The Domestic Transformation*, vol. 1 of *The Political Economy of Japan*, pp. 137–85. Stanford: Stanford University Press.

———. 1995a. "Bubbles in Japan's Urban Land Market: An Analysis." *Journal of Asian Economics* 6 (Summer): 153–76.

———. 1995b. "Bubbles in Japan's Stock Market: A Macroeconomic Analysis" (in Japanese). *Nihon keizai kenkyu* 30 (December): 25–50.

———. 1995c. "The Target Wealth Hypothesis and Japan's Household Saving" (in Japanese). *Nihon keizai kenkyu* 30 (December): 1–24.

————. 1997. "The Monetary System, Monetary Policy, and Macroeconomics of Japan." In preparation.

Shaw, Edward S. 1973. *Financial Deepening in Economic Development.* New York: Oxford University Press.

Teranishi, Juro. 1982. *Nihon no keizai hatten to kin'yu* [Japan's Economic Development and Finance]. Tokyo: Iwanami Shoten.

————. 1994. "Japan: Development and Structural Change of the Financial System." In Hugh T. Patrick and Yung Chul Park, *The Financial Development of Japan, Korea, and Taiwan—Growth, Repression, and Liberalization*, pp. 27–80. New York: Oxford University Press.

Yoshikawa, Hiroshi, Masahiro Hoshi, Nobuaki Hori, Hiroyuki Imura, Toshio Watanabe, and Yohsuke Takeda. 1993. "Kin'yu seisaku to Nihon keizei" [Monetary Policy and the Japanese Econopmy]. *Keizai bunseki* [Economic Planning Agency] 128 (December): 1–254.

This article originally appeared in *Journal of the Asia-Pacific Economy* 1, No. 1 (1997): 1–27. Reprinted by permission of Routledge.

9

Japanese Banks in Deregulation and the Economic Bubble

Kazuo Tsuda

Black Ship of the Showa Era

The major trend of Japanese banking in the 1970s is represented by the shift of "rights," or attractive portions, of financial business from commercial banks to trust and long-term financial institutions and securities companies. The city banks, however, became more and more frustrated as their power to control declined. Very strict regulations governed the city banks which did not allow them to join in this shift of "rights" or to function as main banks.

Some people characterized the city banks of this time as "mismatches of personnel resources and businesses the banks could conduct." They were referring to the fact that graduates from elite universities of Japan were concentrated in commercial banks such as city banks, for which employees needed only physical stamina, rather than substantial knowledge and experience, to do the typical job. This was in contrast to Europe and the United States where someone's alma mater was not a topic of conversation at dinners and luncheons with commercial bank executives, because these European and U.S. counterparts usually reached their positions without much higher education. In these countries, university graduates usually went to work at merchant banks and investment banks.

If you look at the deregulation issues in Japan, the deregulation of interest rates for money on deposit occurred very slowly, even after the introduction of certificates of deposit (CDs) in 1979. Similarly, serious deregulation did not occur in the international financial field in spite of numerous administrative measures and a fundamental revision in the Foreign Exchange Control Law in 1980.

The impetus for the serious deregulation, internationalization, and securitization occurred when the "U.S.–Japan Dollar–Yen Committee Report" was published in 1984. This report was then referred to as the Black Ship of the Showa era. This report has been referred to in later history as an important event in the "financial revolution" or "declaration of deregulation" in Japan.

I believe it is somewhat one-sided to surmise that this report occurred due to outside pressure; we should not forget that internal pressures or domestic factors, such as extensive issuance of government bonds in the late 1970s, also functioned as a catalyst. I am also told that the Ministry of Finance invited outside pressures after extensive, high-level discussions with its counterpart in the U.S. government, but I have no way of confirming if such events even occurred.

By reviewing the deregulation which did occur, what follows will examine the process in which the entire nation of Japan plunged into the economic bubble, including the roles played by giant banks.

The Framework of the Deregulation of the 1980s

The U.S.–Japan Dollar–Yen Committee was established when U.S. President Reagan visited Japan in November 1983. The committee's objective was to discuss various measures for the harmonious development of international society and economies, with mutual recognition of the current status of the dollar–yen exchange rate at that time. In more understandable terms, the United States wanted "Japan to reduce its trade surplus and open its market more."

The result of the committee's discussion was announced in May 1984 as a report, which then became the foundation for financial deregulation in Japan. It contained a wide range of items—not limited to exchange rate adjustments—including deregulation of interest rates, creation of a new financial capital market, internationalization of the yen, and deregulation to allow foreign financial institutions to enter the Japanese market.

The outline produced by the committee was somewhat complex and contained many technical issues. However, many of the items contained in the report would extensively influence the management of the banks. Therefore, the major points are summarized below because the report is key to understanding the changes which occurred in the Japanese financial world in the 1980s.

1. Deregulation of large-deposit interest rates, including the abolition of interest rate regulation on large-term deposit accounts, deregulation concerning money market certificates (deposits connected to market rate interests), and further deregulation on the issuance of CDs.
2. Creation of a bond futures market.
3. Rearrangement of the market in Japan for easier issuance of yen-denominated foreign bonds and foreign-currency-denominated foreign bonds.
4. Creation of a yen-denominated banker's acceptance market within the securities market.
5. Entrance of foreign banks into the trust business in Japan.

6. Opening up the membership of the Tokyo Stock Exchange for foreign participation.
7. Flexible issuance of Euro-yen bonds.
   These goals materialized as of 1993, although ironically, the trade imbalance has further widened during this period.

The Period of the High Yen and Low Interest Rates

The Plaza Accord in 1985 was another historically memorable event which had extensive effects on the economy and financial arena of Japan. This was the agreement reached at the Plaza Hotel in New York City in a meeting attended by ministers of finance and presidents of central banks of five industrialized nations. The agreement's objective was to induce depreciation of the dollar for the purpose of international cooperation, and more particularly, to reduce the trade deficit of the United States.

Ever since 1985, the United States has called for international cooperation in financial measures and for easing financial regulations in order to induce dollar depreciation. At that time, the United States requested Japan and West Germany to lower their interest rates in order to stimulate the domestic economy and to meet expanding domestic demands. This is sometimes referred to as cooperation for lowering interest rates.

However, this cooperation in lowering interest rates became uncoordinated after the Louvre Accord in February 1987. In the United States, the inflationary trends reoccurred, provoking more demands for higher interest rates. For the first time after the Plaza Accord, the official discount rate was raised to 6 percent in September 1987. Except for a short period immediately after Black Monday in October 1987, the subsequent trend remained in the direction of tightening the economy.

In parallel with U.S. action, European countries shifted toward raising their interest rates. For all practical purposes, this ended the international cooperation in lowering interest rates after a relatively short period of time of cooperation. In spite of this, only Japan maintained measures for keeping the interest rates low. Domestic prices remained relatively stable since inflation was kept at a low level.

The official discount rate of Japan was lowered from 9 percent to 8.25 percent in August 1980, with further decreases in the interest rates over the following years. The historically lowest interest rate was recorded in February 1987 at 2.5 percent. This lowest rate was maintained for a relatively long period—two years and three months—until May 1989.

In addition, as a result of extensive deregulation, particularly the abolition of the regulation concerning yen conversion in 1984, the free transfer of funds began between banks in Japan and foreign countries. As the limitation was removed on the conversion of foreign-currency-denominated funds into yen, deposits increased at Japanese banks. This was one of the factors which contributed to the increase in the domestic money supply in Japan.

The money supply continued to increase at high, double-digit levels until 1991. The reason why prices remained stable during this period is that these funds were not spent on capital investments and consumption; rather, they stayed in areas which did not affect price increase, such as land speculation and savings. These funds also were invested in financial products within the financial system itself, such as domestic and foreign stocks and bonds, or simply deposited in bank accounts, resulting in an extremely relaxed relationship between demand and supply. This relationship raised financial asset values and lowered interest rates. This is the very macro factor which produced the bubble.

Deregulation of Interest Rates for Money on Deposit

During the latter half of the 1970s, when a large number of government bonds were sold on secondary markets, a market developed for repo (repurchase agreements) transactions of bonds. People became aware of the difference in interest rates, and funds flowed in from bank deposits to the repo market as more people preferred, naturally, the higher rates. In addition, securities companies developed a product called a "medium-term government bond fund," which it sold to retail investors. The banks suddenly felt threatened by this trend. They pushed strongly for deregulation and flexible interest rates on bank deposits. I have already mentioned that CDs were introduced as part of this deregulation.

However, the subsequent five years saw no changes in the system until money market certificates (MMCs) with market-connected interest rates were introduced. This was the first product from the serious deregulation measures introduced as a result of the report of the U.S.–Japan Dollar–Yen Committee. Initially, in March 1985, mutual banks (currently regional banks II) were authorized to issue MMCs; later commercial banks were also allowed to issue them.

The minimum deposit was 50 million yen, the initial period was one to six months, and the interest rate was that of the CDs minus 0.75 percent. Individual investors were the primary targets. This product went through a fairly complicated process of deregulation as well. The minimum amount was reduced from 50 million to 10 million to 3 million yen. It was ultimately included in the category of term deposits with completely deregulated interest rates. At this point, the historical role of deregulation was completed for all practical purposes.

Another important deregulation product was the large-term deposit accounts with unrestricted interest rates introduced in 1985. The minimum amount was high initially, at 1 billion yen, but this was eased gradually, until June 1993 when all term deposits became deregulated.

In 1993, the minimum amount for this type of term deposit, similar to any other term deposit, was one yen or more, with the minimum term of one month or longer. The term deposit was set up with voluntary regulation by the banks themselves considering processing and other costs. I would expect that various minimum amounts, such as 3 million or 10 million yen, will be introduced for term deposits with different names such as Super Term, Super 300, or Large Account Term.

The remaining regulation concerned the maximum terms for deposits. In 1993, they were set at two years for general term deposits and three years for term-specified term deposits. It was the desire on the part of city banks (commercial banks) to lengthen these maximum terms. There was opposition, however, as these products then competed with those of long-term credit banks and trust banks. The products of the latter included bank debentures with a five-year term maturity, as well as products that were called "wide" (bank debentures with a five-year maturity and a one-time payment of interest), and "big" (loan credits with a five-year term and a payment of interest at maturity).

In addition, there was the postal term savings, a competitive product which city banks, long-term credit banks, and trust banks cooperated in opposing. These savings were for ten-year terms, but it was possible to dissolve them any time after the money had been on deposit for six months. The interest was paid when the money on deposit was withdrawn.

The postal term savings allowed depositors to enjoy many of the advantages of different products without any of the risks or disadvantages. There was freedom of liquidity, that is, any time after six months on deposit, the money could be withdrawn.

When interest rates increased, the postal term savings enjoyed the freedom of liquidity because any time after six months on deposit the money could be withdrawn and switched to a product with a better rate of interest. At the same time, if interest rates decreased, the ten-year fixed high interest rate was guaranteed. In addition, the interest was compounded and was taxed only when the money was withdrawn. This was a product in which advantages were best calculated for the consumer whose main interest was a choice of higher interest rates.

This type of product cannot be introduced by the private sector if private financial institutions are intent on avoiding interest rate risks and on maintaining a guarded attitude toward asset/liability management. However, the product design plan for the ten-year term postal savings will go through complicated and difficult processes of change in the future, as this is governed by the Ministry of Posts and Telecommunications, and not by the Finance Ministry.

What we can say, however, is that, as of June 1993, the interest rates of the fixed-term deposits were almost completely deregulated. Although there were certain issues of merchantability for individual products still remaining, the qualities of different products were more or less equal in their competitive viabilities. The only remaining deregulation issue concerned the interest rates of liquid deposits.

Table 1

**Ratio of Deregulated Interest Rates for
Money on Deposit at City Banks** (in Percent)

	With Completely Deregulated Interest Rates (Large Term, Super Term, CD, and Foreign Currency Deposits)	With Deregulated Interests Rates in Broad Sense (Items in Left Column Plus MMC and Small-Scale MMC)
March 1986	13.7 (20.1)	15.9 (23.3)
March 1988	28.6 (40.3)	34.7 (48.9)
March 1992	56.9 (78.6)	61.2 (84.6)

Note: Figures in parentheses indicate ratios of fixed term deposits.

Source: Annual Report, *Banking Bureau, Ministry of Finance, 1992.*

Deregulation of the Interest Rates for Loans

It is quite natural that the previous, heavily regulated method of determining interest rates for loans became inadequate when interest rates for money on deposit became deregulated. Thus, new methods of determining interest rates for loans, called "new short-term prime rate" and "new long-term prime rate,"—set voluntarily by the city banks and long-term credit banks—appeared on the basis of their desire to protect themselves and to manage their own assets and liabilities more aggressively.

Prime rates in Japan are divided into short-term (one year or less) and long-term. The "short-term prime rate" was decided by city banks, and traditionally it was connected to the official discount rate plus some percentage. With the deregulation of interest rates, however, the procurement cost of funds began to rise as the ratio of deposits with deregulated interest rates at the banks began to rise sharply (see Table 1).

The "new short-term prime rate" was the method utilized by the banks in order to raise the lending interest rates to cope with this new situation. This short-term prime rate was determined by adding a certain percentage to the funds procurement cost. Mitsubishi Bank used this new method for the first time in January 1989.

At that time, the short-term prime rate was 4.25 percent using the new method, while it was 3.375 percent using the conventional method—a fairly substantial increase. Other banks followed suit until there were not any banks using the method connected to the official rate. The name then was changed to remove the word "new," so that afterward it was simply referred to as "the short-term prime rate."

Table 2

Long-Term Loans as Percent of All Loans (in Percent)

	National Banks	City Banks	Regional Banks	Trust Banks	Long-Term Credit Banks
1983	39.3	32.5	36.7	29.5	78.5
1985	39.9	34.6	38.5	23.3	72.1
1989	48.0	47.5	43.4	35.5	69.0
1990	52.7	52.9	45.6	39.1	77.1
1991	56.4	57.2	48.4	41.4	79.7

Source: Economic Statistics Annual Report, *Research Statistics Bureau, Bank of Japan, 1991.*

The "long-term prime rate," on the other hand, was determined by the long-term credit banks. The method used was to add 0.9 percent to the interest rate paid on the financial coupons of the interest-bearing five-year bank debentures. This "0.9 percent" was considered to be the total of the profits and the cost incurred by the long-term credit banks.

In principle, the long-term prime rate changed every month as issuing conditions for interest-bearing bank debentures and government bonds fluctuated every month.

As shown in Table 2, in general—in the process of easing the money supply—city banks shifted their business emphasis from the short-term loans to the long-term loans which had higher profitability. As far as the procurement of funds was concerned, however, the ratio of short-term, market-oriented funds continued to grow.

Although the management method of matching the periods of assets to the periods of liabilities was considered conservative for the banks, they also played the role of creating long-term assets from short-term liabilities (and vice versa). This function of banking was referred to as the "conversion function."

The problem, however, was that an abnormal situation, in which the short-term interest rates were higher than long-term interest rates, lasted for a considerable length of time during this period. The result was the deterioration in profitability for the banks since the long-term loans accumulated more losses. This occurred because the banks were loaning out money at low-interest, long-term rates using funds acquired from high-interest, short-term deposits.

This led to the emergence of a new method for determining long-term interest rates which was tied to the fund procurement situation. According to Fuji Bank, which led the adoption of this new method among city banks, the formal name of this method is "long-term lending interest rates connected to short-term prime rates." It is divided into two stipulated periods: (1) over one year and (2) over three years. Other city banks followed suit with more or less similar conditions.

Customers of the bank criticized the adoption of this new method for setting long-term interest rates as an attempt to shift any failure for asset and liability management from the banks to the customers, if a management failure should occur.

The long-term credit banks responded calmly to this new move by the city banks, taking the position that they would not oppose it as long as the term "long-term prime rate" is not used. The Bank of Tokyo did not adopt this new long-term prime rate method, since it specifically issued three-year, interest-bearing, bank debentures. The attitude taken by long-term credit banks seemed to be to avoid the controversy altogether. They did not want the traditional and sacred "0.9 percent" surcharge they added to be criticized as unreasonable and thus be reduced.

Response of Customers

Customers were not so willing to accept these new methods as this represented a practical increase in the interest rates. When the banks explained the cost factor as a clear reason for their desire to introduce the "new short-term prime rate," customers pressed the bank to abolish the customary procedure of captive deposits (that is, deposits required by the bank from the customer in order to receive a loan), which increased the actual borrowing cost for a loan.

We do not know what actually happened, because the relationship between interest rates charged to customers and the amount of the deposit they had at the banks to obtain a loan is a confidential, mutually understood, individual agreement between each customer and his or her bank. We do know that the introduction of this new rate was extremely difficult. In the end this also turned out to be a labor pain in the process of deregulation—the new rate took place while the captive deposits were eased.

What we have to pay attention to here is that these loans, although referred to as "short-term," were frequently used as long-term, base-operating capital. Funds were not returned for a long period of time by using a method called rollover, that is, by writing another promissory note at maturity of a loan. Thus, in many cases customers were borrowing long-term funds at short-term interest rates.

The Deregulation of Long-Term Interest Rates, While Short-Term Rates Continued to Be Regulated

Short-term interest rates were the basis for calculating the short-term prime rate. It included: (1) regulated term interest rates connected to the official discount rate and regular deposits, (2) large-term accounts, which were completely deregulated, and MMCs, which were almost completely (but not entirely) deregulated, and (3) deregulated interest rates which were established between customers and their banks, such as between large investors and banks for CDs.

These deregulated interest rates of the banks were affected by interbank interest rates which were connected to the call market (the participation was limited to the Bank of Japan and other banks) and the commercial paper market. They fairly faithfully reflected the policy intentions of the Bank of Japan, and thus may be characterized as having some regulatory flavor.

As for long-term interest rates, the entire long-term interest rate structure was established on the basis of quotations among financial institutions by special references to transactions of ten-year government bonds (usually one popular issue considered appropriate for the transaction) and the quotations of government bond futures (established in 1985). This market was an open market in which not only banks, but business corporations and institutional investors as well as individuals, could participate.

The coupons of newly issued government bonds were partially (60 percent) determined through the method of bidding on the basis of this interest rate structure, which in turn was used as the basis for determining the rate for bank debenture coupons and the long-term prime rate. Thus, the long-term interest rate market had a higher level of freedom, allowing many different participants into the market. Attention should be paid to the fact that, not only long-term funds but also short-term funds (primarily from institutional investors) were managed by the market as well. In fact, there was a time when the secondary market interest rate of government bonds decreased to a level almost as low as the official discount rate itself.

The issues were made more complex by the presence of the strange phenomena: "short-term interest rates applied to long-term funds" and "long-term interest rates applied to short-term funds." At times, the long-term interest rate market, which was already highly deregulated, was higher than the short-term interest rate market, in which some regulations still remained. The fact that such a phenomenon occurred suggests that there were discrepancies in the actual market conditions and the fiscal policies of the Bank of Japan, including the official discount rate policy.

I hope the readers have a good understanding by now that the Japanese financial market needed considerably more time and patience to solve all the problems and to reconcile the principles of a free market, since its historical background was so complex and the problems involved are so complicated. As in the field of lending interest rates, considerations must be given to the fiscal policies, the different mechanisms of determining interest rates, the various interests involved depending on what types of business in which the banks were associated, and the dynamics that existed between business corporations and the banks.

The Road to the Bubble in the Latter Half of the 1980s

Issuance of bonds related to stocks, such as convertible bonds and bonds with equity warrants, became very popular with Japanese business corporations in the latter half of the 1980s. This occurred often in the European and Swiss markets. This was made possible by extensive deregulation of overseas transactions and was the very measure which created excessive funds. These bond issues played an important role in the bubble economy.

Equity finance was a method of raising funds for business corporations by issuing stock-related bonds such as convertible bonds and bonds with equity warrants. This could be done only by the underwriting divisions of securities companies and not by banks. This was because the Japanese legal system (prior to the implementation of revisions in April 1993) limited the four basic businesses of dealing, brokerage, underwriting, and selling stock-related bonds to the securities companies. In principle, banks were not allowed to participate (Article 65, Securities and Exchange Law).

Equity financing meant the securities companies were sailing with a full tail wind. They were allowed to tackle corporate financing squarely. This was the same as being the main bank for a business corporation. This also meant that the business corporations routinely believed that the only financial institution to be trusted and relied on was the securities company. The banks appeared to be an assembly of "incapable people" with the only purpose of collecting deposits.

On the other hand, the stock prices continued to rise in the latter half of the 1980s, supported by lenient money policies and extremely low interest rates. The deregulation of foreign exchange control and the introduction of more flexible administrative measures allowed business corporations to turn their sights outside Japan.

The conditions necessary to deregulate issuance of bonds with equity warrants were completely ripe when the Commercial Law was revised in 1981. The only thing left was the invitation by the securities companies for business corporations to issue such bonds. This was the time when giant securities companies became prominently featured.

No collateral was required for issuing foreign bonds. The only requirement was a bank guarantee or rating. The standards for an appropriate amount of money to be loaned in bonds—suggested by the Finance Ministry on the basis of the corporation's debt ratio—were also gradually eased. The local offices of the securities companies did all the necessary work for the overseas market. The procedure for floating a bond issue was simple. The only action required by the business corporation was to sign the contract at a first-rate hotel abroad. At the invitation of the securities companies, large corporations en masse began to raise funds which by far exceeded their actual needs (see Figure 1).

Figure 1

Japan's Foreign Bonds: Annual Issues by Type

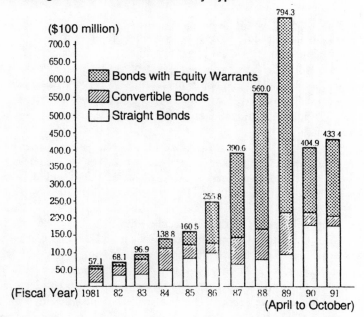

Note: Private foreign bonds, etc., means both private foreign bonds and government-guaranteed foreign bonds.

Source: Based on signed contracts and compiled by the International Finance Bureau. Adopted from *Zusetsu Kokusai Kinyu* [International Finance Illustrated], Ministry of Finance, ed.

Magical Attractions of Equity Finance

The involvement the banks were allowed to have in this business was to give guarantees. Even this was not required for issuing convertible bonds, since they were considered the same as issuing stocks at market price, which means the banks played no role at all.

As far as equity finance was concerned, the banks were not its promoters; if anything, they were its victims. Some people maintain that it was the banks which originated the bubble, but I must mention here that to say the banks were behind it is a complete misunderstanding of the facts of the matter.

With the backing of both issuers and investors, and with the sales activities of the securities companies rising with yen appreciation and high stock prices, equity financing allowed corporations to raise capital at extremely low interest rates, at times even zero percent.

It should be pointed out that it was legally possible for overseas local corporations of Japanese banks to underwrite equity financing on the overseas markets. To that end, the next section briefly discusses overseas local securities corporations owned by Japanese banks.

The establishment of securities companies as overseas local corporations of Japanese banks began in the 1970s. It originated as joint ventures with foreign securities companies (such as local merchant banks) with capital investment of 50 percent or less by the Japanese. By 1993, this initial capital ratio had gradually increased to nearly 100 percent in most cases. The overseas local corporations handled such businesses as underwriting and sales of foreign bonds (Eurobonds) on the Euromarkets (such as London, Luxembourg, Brussels, etc.) and the Swiss market.

Initially, the role played by the banks was limited to general participation at the level of local market survey and research activities. The syndicate was led by their European joint venture partners. However, subsequently, with the increased popularity of FRNs (floating rate notes), underwriting activities became more aggressive.

The FRN was extremely popular from around the end of the 1970s to the first half of the 1980s, particularly attracting the attention of the overseas local securities companies of Japanese banks. The product itself was a type of syndicated loan, and the interest rate for this type of bond was determined by adding a certain margin of profit to a short-term interest rate (e.g., six-month LIBOR).

Due to the nature of the product, this market consisted only of banks which acted as issuers, underwriters, and investors. Particularly active were the cases in which Japanese banks provided the funds (e.g., a foreign bank issues, a local corporation of a Japanese city bank underwrites, and a regional bank invests). However, the FRN's margin of profit was lowered to the bare minimum as a result of severe global competition for excess funds.

Various techniques were employed in order to secure some margins. The market changed, however. It continuously favored the issuers until, finally, it was perpetually dominated by subordinate bonds. When its unhealthy conditions were revealed, there was regulation by the Bank of England, which, in turn, ended the FRN boom.

The next products to appear on the market were the note issuance facility (NIF) and the revolving underwriting facility (RUF). Both raised short-term funds within the framework of issuing bonds. However, these played only complementary roles to the FRN.

Overseas local corporations owned by Japanese banks were anxious to play an active role in the financing activities of Japanese corporations. They considered these financing activities not quite essential to the banking business of the parent banks. However, they were in the shameful position of having to ask securities companies to let them be included in the syndication, even when the bonds to be issued were from the major business partners of the bank. Administrative regulations prevented the banks from taking the lead position over from the securities companies in the syndication. This certainly was not favorable material for the public relations department.

In addition, with respect to bond sales, the banks had to rely on help from the securities companies; the major obstacle was the fact that the banks were not allowed to participate in the Japanese secondary stock market. This was the very reason why the banks could not play central roles in equity financing. The secondary market of stocks was considered sacred by the securities companies.

There is no prospect for even domestic securities subsidiaries of banks to be able to enter in the foreseeable future, even though the establishment of such was made possible through the renovation of the financial system in fiscal 1993. We can be certain that there will be continuing battles between the securities companies and banks in the future.

The Special Technique of Banks: Swaps

What the banks could do overseas during this period of time was to develop new financial techniques for raising funds. They created foreign exchange swaps related to bonds with equity warrants. This removed the foreign exchange risks from the issuing corporations and gave funds to the banks in practical yen-denominated forms. This was appreciated by business corporations, because, domestically, issuance of bonds with equity warrants was limited by bond-issuing ceiling in accordance with the Commercial Law.

Swap transactions became specialties of the banks. The banks had the upper hand over securities companies because of their global information networks. Swap transactions became a major activity in the banks as part of their peripheral participation in the securities business.

Then, interest rate swaps (in which fixed rates were swapped with floating interest rates or vice versa) were introduced into the world of Eurobonds in the 1980s. This allowed for flexible combinations of investors and issuers regardless of the characteristics of a fund.

The benefit of this new technique was to allow subsidiary securities companies of banks to underwrite issues oriented to fixed interest rates, while being backed by investors (including their parent banks) which were more suited for floating interest rates. Their businesses expanded to a considerable degree and various types of combined financial products involving swaps appeared on the market.

Further, foreign exchange swaps began to appear as a highly sophisticated financial technique for avoiding foreign exchange risks in dealing with partners who had different currencies. Bonds with equity warrants and swaps (which were in a practical sense yen-denominated with lower interest rates) became extremely popular as they were very convenient for issuers.

Another area in which the banks became involved was the large-volume sales of bonds with equity warrants and swaps to domestic institutional investors, that is, investors who had available excess funds accumulated through their main businesses, such as life insurance companies and regional banks.

Overseas institutional investors in general, however, were far too cautious to become involved with such large bubblelike issues. This was the reason why no complaints were heard from overseas investors when stock prices crashed and bonds with equity warrants lost their value and became nothing but pieces of paper. This was similar to the sumo wrestling performances which were held abroad some time ago; only the Japanese were involved in the wrestling and the viewing in spite of the foreign locations.

Tokkin Trust Fund, Fund Trust, and Trust Banks

Excessive funds that were raised by business corporations through bonds with equity warrants and other means were first directed to capital investment, and then to research and development. Since the funds raised from overseas capital markets were more than necessary for these purposes, bank loans were repaid. If there were more funds available, the corporations used them for investing in stocks, bonds, and foreign securities.

There was very active use of Japanese money. The funds were also deposited in banks as large-term deposits and other financial products, but the key factors in understanding the stock bubble are the "Tokkin trust fund" (special money in cash trust accounts)" and the "fund trust" (designated nonmoney in cash trust accounts) of trust banks. These were the very accounts which were the main-stream of asset management technology (see Figure 2).

Let me say something technical related to accounting here. First, the notice of revision in the Corporation Tax Act by the National Tax Agency in 1980 introduced a method called "separation of book values." This means that the accounting department could consider the book values of securities (which take advantage of the trust fund) separately from the other securities owned by the company. This was helpful to the corporation in reducing tax liability.

In addition, another notice was sent out on January 4th, the first trading day on the stock exchanges in 1988, to allow flexible accounting of the "Tokkin trust fund and fund trust." The objective of this notice was to ease the closing accounts of institutional investors, such as life insurance companies, who had large unrealized losses due to Black Monday in the preceding year. This notice introduced a measure which gave corporations a choice of using the lower of the cost or the market value. In other words, companies could opt for the "cost method" if the stock prices fell so that any valuation loss would not show on the books.

Through the benefits of these measures, stock prices continued to rise sharply for the next two years, until the end of 1989, and the balances in the Tokkin trust fund and fund trust skyrocketed. Although the mass media did not seem to be paying much attention to this fact, I believe these changes in accounting method were another very important cause of the bubble.

Figure 2

Conceptual Diagram of the Trust Business

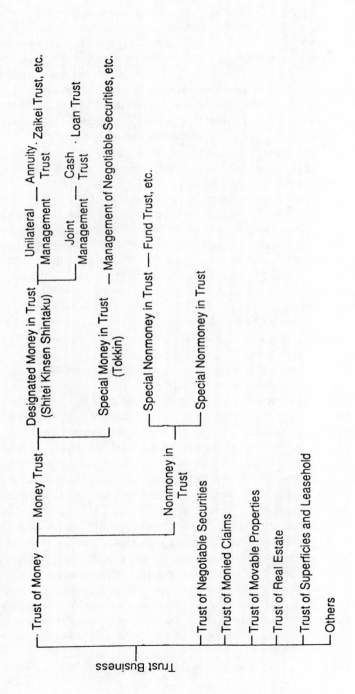

In other words, the attractiveness of these accounts lay in the two accounting procedures: (1) the separation of book value and (2) the choice of cost method if company's stock prices fell. Simply stated, financial assets, such as stocks, could be considered independently of any other securities investments the company owned.

In addition, profits due to an increase in the stock price could be taxed as income gains obtained in the form of interest and dividends, and not as capital gains. This created an advantage as an asset management technique, which was most desirable for corporations such as life insurance companies.

These accounting procedures gave trust banks unexpected commission income. I must introduce here some highly technical terms so that readers will be able to understand the following two points I am going to make.

In the Tokkin trust fund (special money in cash trust accounts), contractors or investors give specific instructions directly to the bank by placing orders for stocks by name of company and the amount of the transaction they wanted in the management of funds, for example, "Buy 100,000 shares of Nippon Steel at market price." On the other hand, in the fund trust (designated nonmoney in cash trust accounts), specific methods of management were left to the trust banks after certain high-level instructions are given by the account owner, for example, "Apply the money to stocks." In addition, the contract of the Tokkin trust fund was to entrust money to trust banks and to be paid back in money, while that of the fund trust was to entrust them with money and to be paid back in securities at the end of the trust period.

One important point was who was the person designated to give specific instructions for the management of funds.

The question could be very simply answered if the investor directly gave instructions. However, the "business Tokkin trust fund" was a common practice in which, although called a trust fund, the monies entrusted by the customers to the securities companies were used to buy and sell stocks completely at the discretion of the securities companies.

This was when the situation became complicated. Many difficulties occurred between customers and securities companies when stock prices crashed. Although in this type of fund the customer had the ultimate responsibility for the investment, many securities companies responded to the huge losses by committing the shameful action of compensating the customers.

What I still do not quite understand is the fact that loss compensation itself was deemed shameful when it was conducted in the moral execution of a "tacit guarantee of yield" by the securities companies. I wonder if what was shameful was the contract of the securities companies in which actions similar to "yield guarantees" were prescribed (suspiciously in violation of the Securities and Exchange Law). Comments such as "only for the benefit of large corporations, etc." are nothing but irrational.

Subsequently, the "business Tokkin trust fund" became prohibited, and loss compensation became clearly prohibited by the Securities and Exchange Law, but I really do not feel good about all this.

Fund trusts were entrusted to trust banks for their entire management. Although some of the problems they had were similar to the "business Tokkin trust fund" of the securities companies, their handling was not quite as transparent. The issue for fund trusts centered around how they dealt with individual contracts. Since the fund trusts tended to have huge monetary value, there were cases in which trust banks had to be responsible for the losses. This is an area of hidden jeopardy.

Since city banks and long-term credit banks could not carry out trust transactions, they were not involved in any of these situations, but they tried to enter the field using another method.

The Sudden Increase of Investment Consulting Firms

This "other method" was the use of investment consulting firms owned by banks. The consulting firm would carry out specific instructions for the management of money, that is, the selection of issues of stocks required in the Tokkin trust fund. This type of activity, called an "investment discretionary account," was a legitimate business activity of an investment consulting firm.

Investment consulting business has been long recognized in the United States and Europe as the fifth financial activity—following banking, securities, insurance, and trust—but they were introduced into Japan much later.

In the 1980s, with the expectation of the implementation of the law (passed in 1986), the number of investment consulting firms established by securities companies and banks suddenly increased. Initially, the banks expected to receive authorization for the management of customer funds in the form of discretionary accounts from bank-related investment firms. This would give opportunities to the bank to directly participate in the asset management of business corporations in the stock market, which would then open the road to their involvement to the secondary market of stocks. The expectation was that the banks would be allowed to participate in the secondary stock market in exactly the same way as the securities companies.

At that time, deposit interest rates had not been completely deregulated, and the banks wanted to use this new opportunity to recover their superior position, which had been lost because of their unattractive interest rates for money on deposit. They invited customers, who had taken their businesses elsewhere, back to the banks to let the bankers manage their assets, advertising the advantage of returning stock capital gains to customers as interest, and the safety of an investment which was backed by the banks.

Many people were recruited from the securities companies, with or without the consent of the latter, with the expectation that banks would acquire employees with know-how in stock transactions and also obtain internal information about the securities companies. There were also expectations on the part of the banks that orders for securities transactions from the banks to the securities companies would give the banks more say in what the latter was doing, involve them more intimately into their Keiretsu groups, or develop generally more intimate relations with them.

In order to invite corporate customer business to their investment consulting businesses, the banks did not simply wait for the business corporations to provide the excess funds. Some of the arrangements the banks were willing to offer involved "back" financing, that is, they were willing to lend money to corporations, which was then given back to the banks as investment funds for them to manage.

However, reasonable persons involved in these transactions were fully aware that this type of short-term asset management technique should not be considered a fundamental investment consulting activity. Nonetheless, in Japan, since the evaluation of investment consulting firms and the judgment standard used for authorization for management of annuities in the future were based not on the management results but on the amount of assets managed, there was no alternative for them but to try to expand their business. Thus, the banks were also promoting the stock bubble through their subsidiaries. The final station of the stock bubble was the "Tokkin trust fund" and the "fund trust."

They Did Not Kindle the Fire, But They Poured the Oil

As we have seen, the "Tokkin trust fund" and the "fund trust" represented an extremely convenient mechanism for asset management techniques. However, their problem was exposed in the stock price crash. This problem was the "shameful action" in the securities industry, that is, loss compensation.

It is a widely known fact in the securities industry that because the securities companies and investment consulting companies believed in the "myth of ever-rising stock prices," they were willing to engage in action called "*nigiri*" or consent, which almost guaranteed capital and interest rates to the investor, no matter what happened in the market. The crime—in which the entire industry was involved—was exposed: it was revealed that various measures had been taken in order to implement this "consent," and wholesale investors had been compensated for their losses. Although it was primarily securities companies that were criticized for doing this, investment consulting firms and trust banks should have shared the same responsibility in respect to management instructions.

The subsequent strengthening of legal regulations seemed to cause loss compensation to subside. The amount of money reported to be involved in loss compensation was only several hundred billion yen. However, a look at the balances of the "Tokkin fund trust" and the "trust fund," as well as the degree of stock price decrease, made it clear that at least several trillion yen of unrealized losses were involved.

This makes me think that the basic problem was not solved at all. There was a talk of new technique called "*tobashi*" or "shuttlecocking" whereby losses were transferred back and forth between different companies, which suggests there was still much "pus under the scab."

I recall when I was working at an investment consulting firm, I was reprimanded by the management of a large securities company that "one must never ever say something like stocks may come down." Whenever I remember this, I feel horrified anew, thinking that this has been the very nature of the Japanese securities companies, and is deeply ingrained in the revolving style of buying and selling stocks. Practices such as "loss compensation" and "shuttlecocking" were simply extensions of this same line of thinking.

Many of the business corporations (including large ones) received no loss compensation, and huge amounts of loss had to be accounted for as a result of cancellations in the Tokkin trust fund. The management, as well as much of their staff, in the departments involved in asset management technology lost their jobs. This kind of tragedy will continue until the balances of the Tokkin trust fund and the fund trust, which is still close to 30 trillion yen (in 1993), falls to zero.

Certainly, the corporations, which did not recognize that investment transactions were their own responsibility, should be seriously reproached; however, securities companies, investment consulting firms, and trust banks should receive more reproach; they were the ones who enticed business corporations to neglect their responsibilities, in spite of the fact that the former are professionals in this field.

It also suggests two possibilities to me. One is that the commercial banks were too limited in their knowledge and experience to enable them to explain to the business corporations that such asset management techniques were dangerous. The second is, if the banks knew such procedures were hazardous, then circumstances partly allowed this to happen because the business corporations did not pay much attention to what the banks were saying and what the banks were saying did not have much authority.

In addition, one cannot deny the fact that the banks did not fully study or research the basics of financing, which should have been the main business of the banks, as they had been separated and segregated away from the market mechanism too long. Just as ordinary business corporations were easily tempted by seductive asset management technology, the banks were impressed with the superficial, attention-getting behavior of the securities companies and mistook it to represent state-of-the-art technology.

I also recall being instructed that: "The know-how of an investment consultant is not sufficient if he cannot clearly tell important customers what the future yield will be. One should extend one's efforts in high-yield management by obtaining information from the securities companies earlier than others."

This remark contains a twofold violation of the law: "yield guarantee" and "transactions based on insider information." What this represents is that the sense of guilt for committing such crimes was attenuated for the old-timer bank management. They spent day and night on operations which were always on the borderline of regulations. In addition, they were anxious and pressed to recover the ground they lost in the competition.

Thus, although it is true that the banks did not start the fire on the stock bubble, it is equally true that, lacking caution, they poured a large amount of oil on it. In the fund trust, the contract was over when the stocks were returned to the customer. When the stock prices crashed, how could an employee of a trust bank return the stocks to a customer and look his customer in the eye? The mechanism was understood only by the trust banks.

Problems which arose were the same as those of the Tokkin trust fund. Are they keeping their mouths shut and simply waiting for the stock index to go back over 30 thousand yen? Here also lies the reason for expecting a minibubble in the future.

Banks Were Responsible for the Land Bubble

Giant banks were all involved in the land bubble. Statistics for real estate and construction loans of all banks in Japan showed a high level of increase (more than 10 percent) in the years from 1985 to 1990. The total amount of loans to these industries in 1992 was 74 trillion yen, or 15 percent of the total loan portfolio for the country.[1]

Further, statistics for mortgage loans for individual family homes show high levels of increase when 1991 is compared to 1986, 2.4 times for national banks and 3.0 times for city banks.[2] These figures include loans for purchasing land.

The average amount per loan showed a sharp increase from 5 million to 9 million yen, which seems to suggest that more than an increase in actual demand was reflected. Certainly, if the banks had not provided money for land and property loans, such a sharp increase in land prices would not have occurred (see Tables 3 and 4).

Around 1990 the increase in land prices began to subside, and from April 1990 to December 1991, regulations put a limit on the total amount of loans for the real estate industry.

The reverse trend became obvious, the land myth was gone, and problems suddenly surfaced. Pieces of land, which had been bought all over Japan with the sole belief in ever-increasing prices, and had been sold and resold among various land brokers, found no more buyers. Real estate, a fixed asset, became immovable in the true sense of the term. There were no bidders when attempts were made to auction the land.

When a loan for land is given at the full value or higher, and then the land price falls, the borrower cannot return all of the mortgage loan, even when the property is sold, let alone if the borrower cannot find a buyer at all. Even the interest on the loan cannot be paid unless a profitable business is operated by the

Table 3

Loan Balance of All Banks for Real Estate and Construction Industries
(in 100 Million Yen)

End of Month, Year	For Real Estate Industry	For Construction Industry	Total Loan Balance
1975	76,193 (5.1)	65,471 (10.7)	1,034,880 (11.2)
1980	110,857 (4.8)	96,701 (3.1)	1,660,548 (7.5)
1984	174,926 (15.2)	137,661 (11.9)	2,396,598 (10.3)
1985	200,917 (14.9)	154,667 (12.4)	2,678,546 (11.8)
1986	253,026 (25.9)	166,499 (7.6)	2,964,838 (10.7)
1987	335,650 (32.7)	177,548 (6.6)	3,304,775 (11.5)
1988	373,680 (11.3)	182,336 (2.7)	3,685,104 (11.5)
1989	423,242 (13.3)	193,108 (5.9)	4,064,098 (10.3)
1990	487,887 (15.3)	206,298 (6.8)	4,544,795 (11.8)
1991	489,280 (0.3)	214,309 (3.9)	4,801,349 (5.6)
1992	510,779 (4.4)	233,979 (9.2)	4,963,224 (3.4)

Note: Percent in parentheses is the rate of increase over the preceding year.

Source: Adopted from *Annual Report*, Banking Bureau, Ministry of Finance, 1992.

Table 4

Home Mortgage Loans of All Banks (in 100 Million Yen)

Year	New Loans (Annual)	Balance (Year End)
1986	53,654	172,566 (3,081)
1987	88,684	212,283 (3,242)
1988	78,650	250,164 (3,299)
1989	105,308	344,752 (4,155)
1990	87,825	381,509 (4,167)
1991	74,026	405,496 (4,182)

Note: The figure in parentheses is the number of cases (in 1,000).

Source: Economic Statistics Annual Report, Research Statistics Bureau, Bank of Japan, 1991.

borrower. There are many, many corporations and individuals who found themselves in this situation.

Almost all of the loans using real estate properties as collateral, including those owned by giant business corporations with acronyms like AIDS and FOKAS, became bad loans. These huge debts originated with the giant banks and their nonbank subsidiaries. It appeared that each of the giant banks had bad loans reaching hundreds of billions or several trillion yen. As mentioned earlier, the actual figures are not known to us.

I wish readers could have a chance to take a look at a registration book containing the title for a piece of real estate property which was handled by such bubble corporations. The reader would clearly see that the mortgaging and leasing rights attached to it were so extensive and so complex that even a very experienced lawyer would not be able to untangle the web.

It is almost impossible using ordinary procedures to clarify the relationship of rights for such real estate properties. If one examined the entire country of Japan, it was as though only the debts remained in the bubble prices while asset values crashed. It is a situation in which there was no light at the end of the tunnel. We do not know how effective the Cooperative Credit Purchase Company will be.

Even if half of the 74 trillion yen in real estate loans is collected, this means that 37 trillion yen has to be depreciated as a loss. In other words, with an annual depreciation of 2 trillion yen, it would take more than ten years to fully depreciate.

What would have happened if loans of this magnitude had not been made? One may say that deposits could have been reduced if the banks found it difficult to lend out the money. This might be so, but would this have been really possible in a situation in which the collection of deposits was the most central part of banking activity for half a century?

Assuming this would have been possible, where would excess funds of business corporations have been directed? They would have invested, after all, more money in the "Tokkin trust fund" and the "fund trust." Excess funds cause overheating somewhere. Another might say that this means it is better not to have excess funds. This is also true, but who could have stopped the raising of funds at low interest rates overseas?

Banks Were Deeply Immersed in Land Financing

I recall I was persistently asked by the bank management at that time if there were any risks and dangers in bonds with equity warrants and other overseas products, since the bank management found the attention-getting behavior of the securities companies rather offensive. I could only answer with the assumption that "if stock prices crash, etc." Nobody, however, even dreamed of a crash to the extent that prices fell to less than half. Consequently, the only thing I could say was that "such products will probably withstand some degree of fall."

The situation as described above, therefore, caused the banks to rush and immerse themselves in land financing. They considered that land financing was part of their basic field of business and that they were the center of the information network for real estate properties.

I mentioned earlier that harmony is emphasized inside a bank to the extent that employees find it difficult to voice their own opinions if they happen to have different views. Consequently, when an announcement was made that this was the time for real estate financing, no person stepped forward to stop it. Loan checkers, who wanted to adhere strictly to the internal rules—such as the maximum amount of loan based on the collateral (e.g., up to only 70 percent of the land value)—were characterized as inflexible, antiquated, and lacking in their understanding of the business policies of the bank, etc. These loan checkers eventually disappeared.

We cannot deny the fact that the bank management of yesteryear found the land-secured loans easier to understand and more comfortable than the "new games" such as dealings and swaps. Land-secured loans gave them more confidence and a feeling of being in control.

The banks, which had by then become insensitive to breaking rules, did not hesitate to ignore the 30 percent which exceeded the internal regulations. They continued to repeat the same rule-violating transactions, or they told related companies and intimate nonbank subsidiaries to take over.

At times the banks were willing to create land-value appraisal documents which contained inflated values for the land concerned. The nonbank subsidiaries responded to the requests for financing from the banks simply because such transactions were intermediated by giant banks.

It was possible to carry out real estate and housing site development activities with no capital at hand, since 100 percent of the required funds could be borrowed. Weak and small companies as well as lay people joined in one after another simply because they were attracted to the lucrative nature of this business. The banks themselves acted as intermediaries or real estate brokers by providing information, and financed projects based on their own information. The balance sheets of the banks thus became inflated. It was difficult for them to notice even if some of the borrowers were antisocial business corporations.

During the period when no one suspected the land myth, everybody was optimistic. People thought that no matter how complex the relations of rights and obligations connected with properties might be, everything would turn out all right as long as prices went up. No problems will be solved now by trying to find out who was responsible for the land bubble from a moral and ethical point of view. It does no good to point a finger and say the banks were at fault, the securities companies were the culprits, or the fiscal policies of the government were wrong. It will take a long time, but there is no other way to recover except to try to remove the scare of the land price crash and repair the situation.

I find it more useful to critically view this time as having been the result of our cultural influence or our national characteristic of collective action, ignoring all diversified value judgments, different opinions, and opposing views. This was the background for Japan's problems.

Some government officials say that regulations and guidance are therefore necessary. This idea is also dangerous since it would create a situation which existed in wartime Japan and the old Soviet Union, in which no criticism is allowed against the unitary value judgment of the authorities. On the basis of the historical trends, this type of regime is destined to self-destruct.

In either case, this was the process by which the giant banks of Japan turned themselves into "the giant bad loan banks" of Japan.

Notes

1. *Okurasho Ginkokyoku Kinyu Nenpo* [Annual Financial Report of the Banking Bureau], Ministry of Finance, 1992.
2. *Keizai Tokei Nenpo*, [Annual Report of Economic Statistics], Bank of Japan, Research and Statistics Bureau, 1992.

Kazuo Tsuda is auditor of Bussan Sepac Company, Tokyo, and adjunct professor at Aoyama Gakuin University and Saga University.

Source/Permission: "Ginko no Hanseiki 2—Jiyuka to Bubbleka" [A Half Century of Banks 2—Deregulation and the Economic Bubble]. Chapter 7 of Kazuo Tsuda, *Kyodai Ginko no Kozo* [The Structure of Giant Banks]. Tokyo: Kodansha, 1993. (Translation originally appeared in *Japanese Economic Studies* 22, Nos. 3 and 4 [May/June–July—August 1994].) Translated with permission by Yoko Yamamoto.

10

Bubbles in Japan's Stock Market: A Macroeconomic Analysis

Kazuo Sato

I. Introduction

Since the 1950s, Japan's stock market has gone into bubbles every ten years or so (early 1950s, early 1960s, and early 1970s). Then the 1980s saw a strong bubble that continued for several years (late 1982 to the end of 1989). What caused this bubble to be so strong? Our analysis of the fundamental equation reveals that the key factor was the nominal interest rate which continued to decline until the late 1980s owing to the extremely relaxed monetary policy pursued by the Bank of Japan. The forecasts for stock prices made by investors added to the effect of the low interest rates. We will show that investors tend to forecast fluctuations on the real side two- to three-quarters ahead of time. The bubble burst when the forecasts of the investors collapsed. Since then investors have remained bearish and the stock market has remained in the doldrums.

In Japan's remarkable growth process after the end of World War II, financial development was even more spectacular than real growth. Corporate stocks stand out among financial assets because their prices maintained double-digit growth, even in the slow growth periods that occurred since the mid-1970s.

Stock prices were exceptionally vigorous throughout the 1980s. The Nikkei Stock Price Average (Japan's equivalent of the Dow-Jones Industrial Average) started from a low of ¥7,042 in August 1982 and continued to rise almost without interruption to a high of ¥38,150 in December 1989—a more than five-fold increase.[1] Following the stock market crash, the Nikkei Average bottomed out at ¥15,790 in August 1992. The subsequent recovery has been sluggish, and the Nikkei Average hovered around ¥20,000 throughout 1994. Thus there was a very robust bubble throughout most of the 1980s and a subsequent collapse.

What was responsible for the stock market bubble and its demise? Was it, as is commonly alleged, the speculative zeal of investors? Or were there more mundane factors, such as a mismanaged monetary policy or business cycles in the corporate sector? This common allegation is apparently based on a first impression that is not necessarily correct. The problem requires a rigorous analysis of statistics. In this article, we shall show that the basic cause of the bubble was not the optimism of the investors, but was more objective factors.

In the second section, we shall review the ownership structure of Japan's corporate stocks. The third section presents a simple stock market model, from which we derive the familiar "fundamental equation." Our point of departure from the popular literature is to incorporate explicitly the formation of the forecasts. The fourth section explains the data we employ and the fifth section interprets the data in terms of the fundamental equation. The sixth section examines the causality governing our basic variables; the seventh section breaks the bubble into a few components; and the eighth section examines the properties of stock-price appreciation forecasts. The ninth section is the conclusion.[2]

II. The Structure of Japan's Corporate Finance

The way in which Japanese firms finance their financial needs has an important bearing on the functioning of Japan's stock market. Therefore, we will begin by reviewing the structure of Japan's corporate finance.

Funds originate in the household sector. In Japan, the largest part of the funds moves through financial intermediaries. Banks receive deposits from households and, based on those funds, supply loans to client firms. Although direct financing through the new equity and bond markets expanded in the late 1980s, it declined again in the latest recession. Bank loan rates and industrial bond yields move together. Bank deposit rates are linked to the central bank's discount rate, which is adjusted as the interest rate structure changes. Thus, the deposit rate moves with the loan rate and bond yield, but at a lower level.

Another route for obtaining corporate financing is the issuance of corporate stocks, which then enter into the stock circulation market. A significant feature is that only one-quarter of the stocks are owned by individuals.[3] In 1992, 23.1 percent of stocks were owned by individuals, 41.3 percent by financial institutions, and 24.4 percent by nonfinancial corporations.[4]

This means that, in Japan, businesses own one another. The proportion of cross-share ownership among firms is estimated to be about 40 percent between 1981 and 1991, with little fluctuation around the mean. Furthermore, Japanese firms have a high propensity to retain earnings. The dividend-earnings ratio averaged 32 percent between 1981 and 1991, much lower than the 50 percent ratio for U.S. firms.[5]

The low level of stock ownership by individuals and the low ratio between dividends and earnings implies that the corporate sector lives its own life, largely independently of the household sector as far as asset management and earnings distribution are concerned. It also means that the level of the stock prices are strongly influenced by corporations themselves.[6] To understand the performance of Japan's stock market, this feature must be kept in mind.

III. A Stock Market Model

A. Assumptions

Since we are interested in a macroeconomic analysis of the stock market, we will assume that all stocks are homogeneous.[7] Also, the stock market is treated as a spot market.[8] P_E is the market-determined price of the representative stock and R_E is its net earnings per unit of time (year). The price-earnings ratio is P_E/R_E. The closest alternative financial asset for stocks is assumed to be corporate bonds.

B. Stock-Price Appreciation Expectations by Investors

Let us assume, for the time being, that investors are principally interested in making short-term capital gains by buying or selling stocks. Those who believe that stock prices will rise increase their stockholdings. Those who believe that the stock prices will decline reduce their holdings. Let $g(P_E)^e$ be the expected rate of stock-price appreciation. Then each investor has his or her own demand schedule, rising from negative to positive with $g(P_E)^e$.

We assume that investors can sell to the level to which they initially hold shares and buy to the level of whatever financial resources they can mobilize.[9] The crossover point from negative to positive differs among investors.[10] For any given value of $g(P_E)^e$, add up the positive demands into $\tilde{D}(E)$ and the negative demand (in absolute value) into $\tilde{S}(E)$, where E is the number of stocks to be traded.[11] $\tilde{D}$ is the downward slope and $\tilde{S}$ is upward slope (see Figure 1). The equilibrium $(g(P_E)^e*, E*)$ is stable and holds at the point of intersection of these two slopes.

C. The Supply-and-Demand Equilibrium

We restate the equilibrium process in terms of the conventional supply-and-demand framework. Let $g(P_E)^e_D$ and $g(P_E)^e_S$ be the values of $g(P_E)^e$ held by a buyer and a seller, respectively.

A buyer compares the cost of buying the stock to the returns he or she expects to receive when the stock is resold at the end of the unit time. The former is the annual cost, covering both interest cost and "risk premium."[12] We denote their sum by i. The latter is the sum of net earnings—which are wholly distributed to the shareholder—and the expected capital gains. The investor decides to buy the stock if and only if:

$$P_E i < R_E + P_E g(P_E)^e_D.$$

The demand price of the stock is the price that makes this inequality an equality, that is:

Figure 1

Stock-Price Appreciation Forecast and Trading Volume

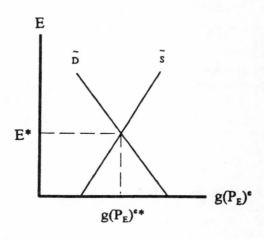

Equation 1
$$P_E^D = \frac{R_E}{i - g(P_E)_D^e}.$$

Note that $g(P_E)_D^e = \mathcal{D}(E)$, thus Equation 1 gives the downward-sloped demand function. Likewise, a seller decides to sell if and only if:

$$P_E i > R_E + P_E g(P_E)_S^e.$$

Then the supply price of the stock is given by:

Equation 2
$$P_E^S = \frac{R_E}{i - g(P_E)_S^e}.$$

We have $g(P_E)_S^e = \mathcal{S}(E)$, which is the upward-sloped supply curve.

Equations 1 and 2 yield the familiar supply-and-demand diagram between E and P_E (Figure 2). At equilibrium, we have:

Equation 3
$$P_E* = \frac{R_E}{i - g(P_E)^{e*}}.$$

Equation 3 is the "fundamental equation" of the stock market. There is an existence condition, that is, both $g(P_E)_D^e$ and $g(P_E)_S^e$ must be less than i. Therefore, $g(P_E)^{e*}$ must also be less than i.

Figure 2

The Supply-and-Demand System in the Stock Market

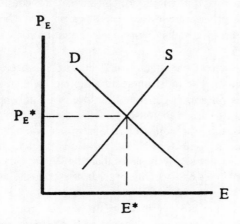

D. The Fundamental Equation

In the above model, we assumed that investors were interested in a quick resale of the stock. As an alternative model, assume that investors are interested in holding the stock for a long period of time as a permanent asset in their portfolio. In that case, P_E should be equal to the present discounted value of future income streams. Assume that R_E is expected to grow at a constant rate, represented by $g(R_E)^e$, and that the discount variable i is expected to remain stationary.[13] Then we have:

Equation 4
$$P_E = \frac{R_E}{i - g(R_E)^e}.$$

Equation 4 is the earnings-discount model.[14] In this case, the forecasting variable is not $g(P_E)^e$ but $g(R_E)^e$.

In general, the present discounted value of the stock depends on three factors: $g(R_E)^e$, $g(P_E)^e$, and T (which is the date at which the stock is expected to be resold). Since T is an unknown factor, there is no unique formula for the fundamental equation (see explanation in Appendix Note). However, T becomes irrelevant when $g(P_E)^e = g(R_E)^e$. We assume that this condition is approximately satisfied.

In what follows, we denote the forecasting variable by $g(P_E)^e$ rather than using $g(R_E)^e$. Additionally, since the risk premium is statistically unobservable, i is limited to the market interest rate while the risk premium is subsumed into the variable $g(P_E)^e$.

E. Displacement of the Equilibrium

The fundamental equation, thus modified, shows that the equilibrium solution P_E*, $E*$ is subject to three separate influences: the earnings rate, shown in R_E, the interest rate, represented by i, and stock-price appreciation forecast, as shown in $g(P_E)^e*$.

As we shall show below, the fundamental equation is useful in dissecting bubbles into basic factors. The most interesting among them is $g(P_E)^e*$. Unlike the other two, how this variable is generated is not immediately apparent. As our model has indicated, this variable is based (behind the scene) on how the forecasts of individual investors (including the risk premium) are distributed. If most investors become bullish, their forecasting functions shift to the right. As a result, the demand curve shifts upward more than the supply curve and P_E* rises more than $E*$. If most investors become bearish, the opposite takes place, and P_E* falls more than $E*$.[15]

Since P_E*, R_E, and i are directly measurable, we can obtain $g(P_E)^e*$ as the residual of the fundamental equation. The rest of this article analyzes how this residual behaved in the case of Japanese stock prices.

IV. The Data

Japan's stock exchanges suspended normal operations at the end of World War II. They resumed operations on May 16, 1949. Initially, there were three stock exchanges (Tokyo, Osaka, and Nagoya). This later expanded to eight exchanges. However, the Tokyo Stock Exchange retained the lion's share of the stock being traded.[16]

The Tokyo Stock Exchange is composed of two sections. The First Section is by far the more important in terms of both market size and quality of firms listed.[17] The stock price index, called TOPIX, is prepared for stocks traded in the First Section. Our P_E is this index.[18] The price-earnings ratio given for the First Section is our P_E/R_E.[19] From this we derive R_E. It is important to remember when computing the price-earnings ratio that the Tokyo Stock Exchange takes earnings recorded for the preceding accounting period. Thus, there is a built-in time lag of approximately one quarter in the statistics of R_E.

There are several interest rates. The rate closest to corporate stocks is industrial or corporate bonds. Hence, we take industrial bond yields for our interest rate.[20]

Although these variables are available in monthly cycles, we will use their quarterly averages for our analysis. The interest rate, R_E, and $g(P_E)^e*$ are expressed in annual rates.

The sample period is the first quarter of 1981 through the first quarter of 1994. This is because the monthly cycles of the price-earnings ratio only began

Figure 3

The Average Stock Price Index, P_E

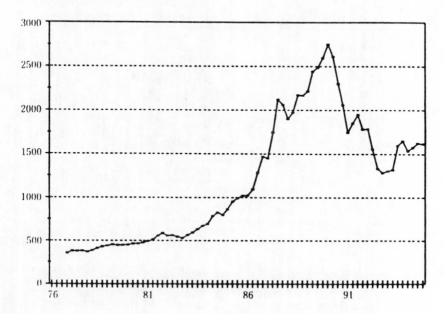

in 1981. Before that date, only annual cycles are available. In any case, Japan's financial system was strictly regulated and underdeveloped until around 1973. This underdevelopment is why the statistics on industrial bond yields started in 1974 and then were only reported annually. Though the financial markets were considerably deregulated by the late 1970s, the data reveal that the fundamental equation of the stock market did not perform well during the decade of the 1970s.

V. The Fundamental Equation: Basic Variables

A. The Stock-Price Index

Figure 3 shows the movement of the stock-price index P_E from the third quarter of 1976 to the third quarter of 1994. As $g(P_E)$ (shown in Figure 4) indicates, the curve contains considerable zigzags. However, trends are unmistakable. There was a mini-bubble around 1981. P_E then went on a sharp, upward path from late 1982 to mid-1987. After a dip corresponding to Black Monday, P_E resumed its upward path, albeit at a reduced speed, until the last quarter of 1989. Then the bubble collapsed, and P_E seems to bottom out by late 1992.

Figure 4

$g(P_E) = (P_E - P_{E, -1})/P_{E, -1}$ (in percent)

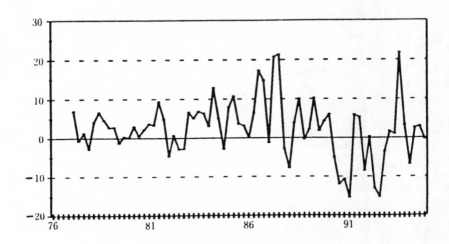

B. The Earnings Rate

Figure 6C shows the movement of the earnings rate R_E from the first quarter of 1979 to the first quarter of 1994. While the curve shows many zigzags, it can be divided into four phases: (1) a rise from the first quarter of 1979 to the third quarter of 1981; (2) a fall from the third quarter of 1981 to the fourth quarter of 1983; (3) a long upswing from the fourth quarter of 1983 to the fourth quarter of 1991; and (4) a sharp descent from the fourth quarter of 1991 to the first quarter of 1994. Note that the first and second phases correspond to the 1980–1983 minibubble. It is also interesting that R_E continued to rise in 1990–91 period while P_E started to fall.

C. The Interest Rate and the Price-Earnings Ratio

Figure 5 shows the interest rate i and the price-earnings ratio R_E/P_E. It is unmistakable that the two variables are interconnected. This is definitely what the fundamental equation tells us, provided that $g(P_E)^{e*}$ does not fully offset the interest rate.

D. Stock-Price Appreciation Expectations

In the fundamental equation, all variables are measurable except the stock-price appreciation forecasts $g(P_E)^{e*}$. It can be measured as the residual,[21] that is:

Figure 5

i and R_E/P_E, (in percent)

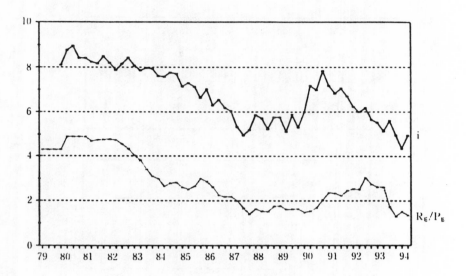

Equation 5 $$g(P_E)^{e*} = i - R_E/P_E.$$

When this derived statistic is inspected, the first feature that comes to our attention is that it is positively related to Δi. This is not a mere statistical aberration. There is a reason. In our model, when P_E is determined, investors may not respond fully to the current value of i because of imperfect information. Let $\hat{i}$ be their estimate of i. Then the fundamental equation must be modified to read:

Equation 6 $$\hat{i} = R_E/P_E + g(P_E)^{e*}.$$

Taking the simplest version of $\hat{i}$:

Equation 7 $$\hat{i} = ai + (1-a)\,i_{-1}, \quad 1 > a > 0.$$

Then we have:

Equation 8 $$i - R_E/P_E = (1-a)\Delta i + g(P_E)^{e*}.$$

We estimate a by regressing $(i - R_E/P_E)$ on Δi and a few other instrumental variables.[22] This exercise yields robust estimates of a which range between 0.50 and 0.55 (s.e. = 0.25).[23] Thus, we assume that:

Figure 6

Cyclical Correspondence

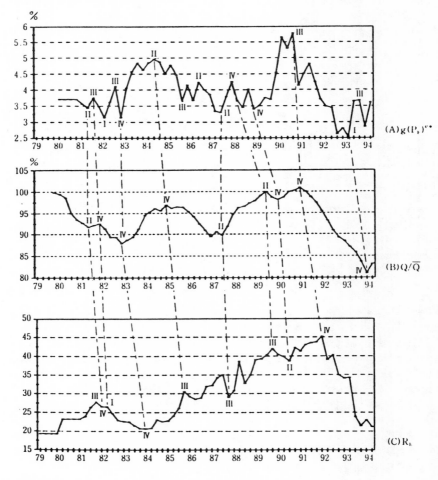

Equation 9 $\hat{\imath} = \frac{1}{2}(i + i_{-1})$.

An important related finding is that $(i - R_E/P_E)$ is not related to i_{t+1}. This supports our assumption that interest expectations are not forward-looking.

Given $\hat{\imath}$, we estimate $g(P_E)^e*$ by:

Equation 10 $g(P_E)^e* = \hat{\imath} - R_E/P_E$.

See Figure 6A.

Table 1

The Lead and Lag Times of $g(P_E)^{e*}$ and R_E, vis-à-vis $Q/\bar{Q}$, 1Q81–1Q94

Quarters	$g(P_E)^{e*}$ leads	R_E lags
0	3	0
1	0	3
2	1	2
3	3	1
4	1	2
5	0	0
6	1	0
Total	9	8

VI. Causality Governing Cyclical Variations

A. Cyclical Variations of Variables

1. The interest rate i. This is a procyclical, lagging economic indicator. In the early 1980s, however, i was on a strong downward path throughout two business cycles (Number 9, peaking in February 1980 and Number 10, peaking in July 1985). From mid-1985 on, i behaved more or less as conventionally expected.

2. Price-earnings ratio R_E/P_E. This variable moved very much in parallel with i until 1989. Then the two parted company, especially in 1990–91.

3. Stock-price appreciation forecast $g(P_E)^{e*}$. Figure 6A shows this variable remained positive throughout the period and fluctuated around the mean of 4.0 percent.

B. Causal Relationships with Outside Markets

The fundamental equation says that P_E is determined by three variables. Of these three, i is linked to the financial market in which the government's monetary policy plays an influential role. As for R_E, it depends on total corporate earnings and outstanding volume of corporate stock. Total corporate earnings depend on the growth and the fluctuations of business activities. The growth reflects changes in the business sector's aggregate production function. Fluctuations depend on changes in the aggregate demand. The best indicator of the latter is the degree of capacity utilization in manufacturing, stated as $Q/\bar{Q}$.[24]

Figure 6A compares stock-price appreciation forecast in $g(P_E)^{e*}$, Figure 6B compares the degree of capacity utilization in manufacturing as $Q/\bar{Q}$, and Figure 6C compares the net earnings of stock per unit of time as R_E. Identifying the turning points of the three curves (which seem to be interrelated), we see that in these points, $g(P_E)^{e*}$ generally leads R_E and lags $Q/\bar{Q}$. The lead and lag times are reported in Table 1.

The table shows that R_E tends to lag behind $Q/\overline{Q}$. The lag must be due to, among other factors, the accounting practice of taking earnings in earlier months. More interesting is the lead time of $g(P_E)^{e*}$. While lead time varies considerably, the most likely length of the lead is three of the quarters.

C. Regression Results

We make our impressionistic comparison more quantitative by estimating regression equations.

First, we regress R_E on $Q/\overline{Q}$. However, R_E must be taken out of the trend because its trend growth rate is estimated to be 4.0 percent per annum. $\tilde{R}_E$ is the detrended value according to:

$$\ln \tilde{R}_E = \ln R_E - 0.010(t - 3Q87).$$

The regression equation estimate is:

Equation R.1 $\ln \tilde{R}_E = 2.29 \ln (Q/\overline{Q})_{-1} + 3.057, R^2 = 0.393, D.W. = 0.21.$
$\phantom{Equation R.1   \ln \tilde{R}_E = }$ (0.41) $\phantom{\ln (Q/\overline{Q})_{-1} + }$ (0.0025)

As residuals are highly autocorrelated, we add $\ln \tilde{R}_{E,-1}$ as an explanatory variable. This yields:

Equation R.2

$\ln \tilde{R}_E = -1.13 \ln (Q/\overline{Q})_{-1} + 1.26 \ln \tilde{R}_{E,-1} - 0.791, R^2 = 0.830, D.W. = 1.75.$
$\phantom{\ln \tilde{R}_E = }$ (0.37) $\phantom{\ln (Q/\overline{Q})_{-1} + }$ (0.11) $\phantom{\ln \tilde{R}_{E,-1} }$ (0.0051)

In Equation R.2, the immediate effect of $(Q/\overline{Q})_{-1}$ is negative, but this is due to the overestimation of the autoregressive part. In a steady state, Equation R.2 yields:

$$\ln \tilde{R}_E = 4.41 \ln (Q/\overline{Q}) + 3.077.$$

We conjecture that the true short-run elasticity of R_E with respect to $(Q/\overline{Q})_{-1}$ is about 3.

The autoregressiveness of R_E seems to reflect the way business profits are generated. The trend part of R_E seems to be due to shifts in the aggregate production function.

We next turn to the relationship between $g(P_E)^{e*}$ and $Q/\overline{Q}$. Suppose that the lead time is, on average, three of the quarters. Then we compare $g(P_E)^{e*}$ with

$Q/\bar{Q}$ three quarters later. When this is done, it is found that the residuals follow very long cycles. To account for them, a dummy variable D is introduced. D takes the value of 1 from the third quarter of 1981 through the fourth quarter of 1986 and from the third quarter of 1990 through the first quarter of 1994; otherwise it takes the value of zero. The regression is performed over the period from the first quarter of 1981 through the second quarter of 1993. We have:

Equation R.3

$$\ln Q/\bar{Q}_{t+3} = 0.655\, g(P_E)^{e}* - 0.614D - 0.030, R^2 = 0.603, D.W. = 1.00$$
$$(0.097) \qquad\qquad (0.121) \quad (0.010)$$

As $D.W.$ is low and R^2 is relatively low, the regression may be improved by adding further explanatory variables. However, Equation R.3 suffices to indicate that $g(P_E)^{e}*$ is a leading cyclical indicator, turning some three quarters ahead of the cyclical turning points in the real sector. We note that, for $Q/\bar{Q} = 1$, $g(P_E)^e$ takes the value of 4.5 percent when $D = 0$ and 5.5 percent when $D = 1$. This means that the full capacity value of $g(P_E)^{e}*$ was lower than otherwise from the first quarter of 1987 through the second quarter of 1990, that is, at the height of the latest bubble and for a while after the collapse of the bubble.

VII. The Fundamental Equation: The Bubble Mechanism

A. Variations of the Three Elements

The fundamental equation tells how ΔP_E is broken down into the changes of the three basic variables, namely ΔR_E, $\Delta \hat{\imath}$, and $\Delta g(P_E)^{e}*$. Since each can be positive or negative, we have eight possible sign combinations for the three variables.

We classify the total of 53 quarters (from the first quarter of 1981 to the first quarter of 1994) into these eight cases (see Appendix Table). In addition, we divide the whole period into two subperiods—bubble and off-bubble. The $g(P_E)$ rose above 5 percent in the fourth quarter of 1982 and fell below that level in the fourth quarter of 1989. Thus, the 29 quarters between the fourth quarter of 1982 and the fourth quarter of 1989 are the bubble period,[25] and the remaining 24 quarters are the off-bubble period.

Table 2 shows the number of quarters according to the sign mix in the bubble and off-bubble periods (see the Appendix Table). If ΔR_E is held constant, the best mix for $\Delta P_E > 0$ is ($\Delta \hat{\imath} < 0$, $\Delta R_E > 0$). There are 14 quarters with this negative-positive mix, as shown in Cases 1 and 2 in Table 2. Case 1, in which $\Delta R_E > 0$, definitely makes ΔP_E positive. It occurred three times in the bubble and one time in the off-bubble. Case 2, in which $\Delta R_E < 0$, occurred six times in the bubble and four times in the off-bubble.

Table 2

Signs of ΔR_E, $\Delta \hat{\imath}$ and $\Delta g(P_E)^{e*}$ From 1Q81 Through 1Q94

Case	ΔR_E	$\Delta \hat{\imath}$	$\Delta g(P_E)^{e*}$	Bubble	Off-Bubble	Total	
1	+	−	+	3	1	4	
2	−	−	+	6	4	10	14
3	+	−	−	9	8	17	
4	−	−	−	3	3	6	23
5	+	+	+	3	1	4	
6	−	+	+	4	5	9	13
7	+	+	−	1	1	2	
8	−	+	−	0	1	1	3
Total				29	24	53	

Source: Appendix Table.

At the other extreme is the positive-negative mix, which makes for a negative ΔP_E, as in Cases 7 and 8. There were only three such quarters. The worst, Case 8, occurred in the fourth quarter of 1990. The negative-negative combination was most common, occurring 23 times, equally divided between bubble and off-bubble. The positive-positive mix also occurred frequently and was also roughly divided between bubble and off-bubble.

This examination of the sign mix reveals that it is rather rare for all three variables to move simultaneously in the directions required for the strongest bubble condition. At the same time, it is also rare for all three to move concurrently in the directions required to bring about a worst-case scenario. In the majority of quarters, the three tend to offset one another. This means that the relative contributions of these three variables must be carefully compared in evaluating changes in P_E.

B. The Decomposition of the Bubble

To make such a comparison in a proper fashion, we break down the stock-price change into the three elements by means of the fundamental equation. By taking the log changes of the fundamental equation, we have:

Equation 11 $\Delta P_E = \Delta \ln R_E - \Delta \ln (\hat{\imath} - g(P_E)^{e*})$

$= \ln R_E - P_E/R_E\, \hat{\imath} + P_E/R_E\, g(P_E)^{e*} + \text{approx. error.}$

Considering the directions of change in both P_E and $g(P_E)^{e*}$, the period under study is divided into several segments. See Table 3 for the seven subperiods. The bubble is divided into four phases plus one intermission.

Table 3 shows that none of the three effects assumed the same sign except in the post-bubble, indicating the severity of the collapse of the bubble. Over the bubble period as a whole, the interest effect was the strongest of the three, while the forecasting effect was the weakest. Looking at subperiods of the bubble, we find that the interest and the forecasting effects offset each other except in subperiod I. The forecasting effect was overwhelmed by the sum of the earnings and the interest effects except in subperiods I and IV. Overall, quantitatively speaking, the forecasting effect was not the prime mover of the stock market.

VIII. The Nature of Stock-Price Appreciation Forecasts

A. Stock-Price Appreciation Forecast as a Cyclical Predictor

When considered as a cyclical variable, stock-price appreciation $g(P_E)$ tends to peak soon after a trough. This property follows from the fundamental equation. Since R_E lags $Q/\bar{Q}$ while $g(P_E)^{e*}$ leads $Q/\bar{Q}$, the two together do not impart any clear impact on $g(P_E)$. Thus, the main variable which affects P_E cyclically is the interest rate, which is known to be a lagging, procyclical indicator. Obviously, P_E responds inversely to i. This means that P_E and/or $g(P_E)$ cannot be a leading cyclical indicator.[26]

However, that is not the case with the forecast, represented by $g(P_E)^{e*}$. As is clear from Figure 6, $g(P_E)^{e*}$ correctly predicted all of the turning points of $Q/\bar{Q}$, though there were a few false alarms. This means that, taken with due caution, $g(P_E)^{e*}$ is an excellent indicator of business cycles. The only serious problem is that the lead time is not uniform.

The superiority of $g(P_E)^{e*}$ as a business cycle predictor becomes apparent when its actual performance in that capacity is compared with that of other well-known business predictorss. There are a few varieties in these forecasts.

One group is the forecasts derived from macroeconometric models. Most forecasts prepared by government and private research institutes or by commercial organizations such as banks belong to this category. Japan has a legion of such forecasts.[27] However, as reviewed in my earlier study (Sato 1986), their performances are not very good.[28]

The second group is those based on economic indicators, that is, the diffusion index constructed from a set of leading, coincident, and lagging indicators. It is prepared by the Economic Planning Agency (EPA) and provides the statistical basis for defining business cycle dating (see Sato 1994).

The third group is the quarterly surveys of business firms. These surveys are not only quantitative but also qualitative, for example, asking whether business leaders expect the future economic climate to be better or worse.

Table 3

The Breakdown of the Bubble

	Bubble Phase:	Pre-Bubble	Whole Bubble	BUBBLE					Post-Bubble
				I	II	Intermission	III	IV	
From		3Q81	4Q82	4Q82	1Q84	2Q87	1Q88	4Q88	4Q89
To		4Q82	4Q89	1Q84	2Q87	1Q88	4Q88	4Q89	3Q92
Stock-Price Change	$\Delta \ln P_E$	0.020	1.585	0.327	0.998	−0.072	0.115	0.217	−0.768
Earnings Effect	$\Delta \ln R_E$	−0.162	0.579	−0.085	0.524	−0.160	0.394	−0.094	−0.146
	$\Delta \ln (\hat{\imath} - g(P_E)^{e}*)$	0.182	1.006	0.412	0.474	0.088	−0.279	0.311	−0.622
Interest Effect	Due to $-\Delta \hat{\imath}$	0.023	0.871	0.211	1.015	−0.444	0.216	−0.127	−0.119
Forecasting Effect	Due to $\Delta g(P_E)^{e}*$	0.096	0.218	0.269	−0.539	0.536	−0.359	0.311	−0.462
Error Term		0.063	−0.074	−0.068	−0.002	−0.004	−0.136	0.127	−0.041

The Bank of Japan (BOJ) has two such surveys—one for large firms and another for all firms.[29] The Economic Planning Agency conducts a similar survey called the *Business Survey Index*.[30]

To see the performance of $g(P_E)^{e*}$ as a business forecaster, we compare it with the two most authoritative surveys of the third group, namely the BOJ's *Principal Enterprise Survey* and the EPA's *Business Survey Index*. Among many items reported in these surveys, we find the items which come closest to the actual business cycles to be the forecasts by respondents on business conditions in general and within their own industries.[31] Since both surveys produce identical findings, we will refer to these results as the *Business Survey*. From the BOJ's *Principal Enterprise Survey*, we include as separate items for comparison both the outlook on sales (for all industries) and the outlook on operating profits (on a semiannual basis).

These surveys report percentage differences between better and worse responses. When the difference is positive, respondents as a whole believe that both the economy and their particular industry will improve over the next quarter. When the difference is negative, both the economy and the industry are believed to be deteriorating.

Figure 7 compares $g(P_E)^{e*}$ with the two surveys. Contraction phases in business cycles and in the $Q/\overline{Q}$ are shown for a basis of comparison. Declining phases of $g(P_E)^{e*}$ are marked,[32] as are negative differences for the two surveys.

From Figure 7, we see that $Q/\overline{Q}$ was more volatile than the business cycles. In addition, $g(P_E)^{e*}$ predicted all the turning points of $Q/\overline{Q}$ in the period under study. The EPA's *Business Survey Index* captured four of the five downswings in the $Q/\overline{Q}$, but only predicted one of the eight turning points of the $Q/\overline{Q}$ before the event. Of the two, $g(P_E)^{e*}$ is clearly the superior predictor. The BOJ's *Survey* is not much better as a predictor than the EPA's *Survey*. Hence, we conclude that $g(P_E)^{e*}$ is a business forecaster *par excellence*.

A forecast is effective only if it is timely. The data needed to construct $g(P_E)^{e*}$ is taken from readily available statistical information. Thus, $g(P_E)^{e*}$ is an accurate and useful forecasting indicator that can be constructed at little cost.

B. Risk Premium

The $g(P_E)^{e*}$ as measured here consists of two parts: price-change forecasts and the risk premium, that is:

Equation 12 $$g(P_E)^{e*} = E(g(P_E)) - \delta.$$

The $E(g(P_E))$ is some measure of the expected rate of growth of P_E; δ is the risk premium, which must be non-negative. The relative contributions of these components to the level and fluctuations of $g(P_E)^{e*}$ must be determined. For the level, take the means of Equation 12:

Figure 7

Cyclical Indicators (Contraction Phases), 1Q90–2Q94

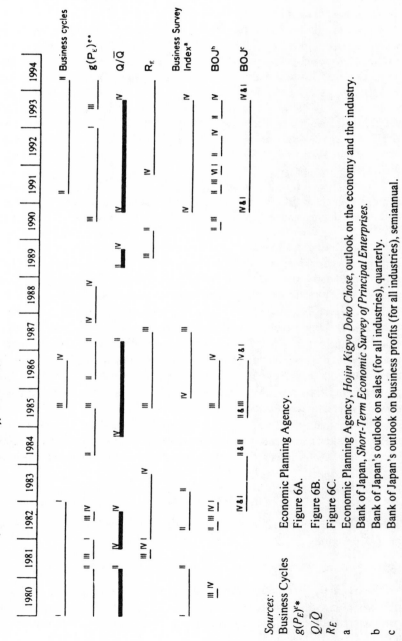

Sources:

Business Cycles Economic Planning Agency.
$g(P_E)^c*$ Figure 6A.
$Q/\bar{Q}$ Figure 6B.
R_E Figure 6C.
a Economic Planning Agency, *Hojin Kigyo Doko Chose*, outlook on the economy and the industry.
   Bank of Japan, *Short-Term Economic Survey of Principal Enterprises.*
b Bank of Japan's outlook on sales (for all industries), quarterly.
c Bank of Japan's outlook on business profits (for all industries), semiannual.

Table 4

Estimates of Risk Premium, 4Q82–4Q89 (in percent)

Estimator	Mean $E(g(P_E))$[1]	Mean δ
$g(P_E)$[2]	25.4	21.4
$g(R_E)$[2]	8.7	4.7
$g(PY/TE)$[3]	1.2	−2.8
$g(PY/TE)$[4]	2.1	−1.9

Notes:
1. Mean $g(P_E)^{e}* = 4.0$ percent; $g(TE) = 4.55$ percent.
2. $g(P_E)$ and $g(R_E)$ are the trend growth rates over the period.
3. PY = Nominal GDP, 1Q82–4Q89.
4. PY = Gross value added of nonfinancial corporation, 1982–89 (Ministry of Finance, *Corporate Enterprise Statistics*).

Equation 13 $\qquad mean\ g(P_E)^{e}* = mean\ E(g(P_E)) - mean\ \delta.$

We consider the entire bubble period as being from the fourth quarter of 1982 through the fourth quarter of 1989. Over that period, the mean $g(P_E)^{e}*$ was 4.0 percent. We expect that the mean $E(g(P_E))$ to be some sort of weighted average of the trend values of $g(P_E)$ and $g(R_E)$. We also consider the possibility that the mean $E(g(P_E))$ is $g(PY/TE)$, taking PY as either the nominal GDP or the gross value added, and TE as the total number of stocks outstanding in the Tokyo Stock Exchange First Section (see Table 4).

Since $g(P_E)$ leads to too high a risk premium and $g(PY/TE)$ leads to a negative risk premium, we reject both as estimators for the mean $E(g(P_E))$ in favor of the more plausible mean $g(R_E)$.[33]

However, $g(R_E)$ is approximately ten times as volatile as $g(P_E)^{e}*$; fluctuations in the latter are much more subdued. Nonetheless, they are persistent, rising or falling over several quarters, apparently reflecting the general bullish or bearish mood of the investors. Risk premium presumably remains constant.

C. Why Were Japan's Stock Prices High?

It is well known that Japan's stock prices were too high. In the period between 1982 and 1989, the price-earnings ratio was low and stable in other countries. The mean price-earnings ratio was 12.0 in the United States, 12.3 in the United Kingdom, 13.6 in Germany, and 12.0 in France. In Japan, the price-earnings ratio rose steadily from 23 in 1982 to 62 in 1989 (Omura and Kawakita 1992, Table 4-1).

Table 5

Comparison of Rates in Japan and the United States (in percent)

	Japan	United States	
	4Q82 – 4Q89	1982 – 1989	U.S.–Japan
mean R_E/P_E	2.4	8.1	5.7
mean i	6.4	10.9	4.5
mean $-g(P_E)^e*$	– 4.0	– 2.8	1.2
if $-E(g(P_E)) =$			
mean $-g(P_E)$	– 25.4	– 15.2	10.2
mean δ	21.4	12.5	– 9.0
if $-E(g(P_E)) =$			
mean $-g(R_E)$	– 8.7	– 8.7	0.0
mean δ	4.7	5.9	1.2
mean $g(P_C)$	1.3	4.2	2.9
mean $(i - g(P_C))$	5.1	6.7	1.6

Source: United States, *Economic Report of the President*, 1994, Statistical Appendix.

Notes:
R_E/P_E Price-earnings ratio, S&P Composite Index.
P_E S&P Composite Stock Price Index.
i Corporate bond yields, AAA.
P_C Consumer expenditure deflator.

Why were Japan's stock prices so high?[34] Omura and Kawakita (1992, 103) cite four reasons: (1) low interest rates, (2) differences in accounting practices (e.g., in depreciation methods), (3) higher growth potential, and (4) cross-share holdings. We have rejected the fourth reason because it is not valid. What about the others? To answer this question, we apply the fundamental equation to Japan and to the United States, which we take as a representative country.

In the United States, the $g(P_E)^e*$ was negative for most of the years in the 1970s, but forecasts were revived and the $g(P_E)^e*$ turned positive beginning in 1982. This revival owes much to the long boom of the 1980s, which lasted 108 months from November 1982 to July 1990. For the United States, we take the annual data from 1982 to 1989. Table 5 reports relevant rates.

We note that, according to R_E/P_E, the mean Japanese stock prices were three times higher than the mean American stock prices, with the difference widening through the period under study. It is seen that nearly 80 percent of the difference between the United States and Japan is attributable to the difference in the interest rate, and only 20 percent is attributable to the difference in the $g(P_E)^e*$.

We have seen that $E(g(P_E))$ is poorly approximated by the mean $g(P_E)$. If we suppose that the $E(g(P_E))$ is approximated by the mean $g(R_E)$, then we find that the mean $g(R_E)$ was identical between the two countries. This means that the differences in accounting practices is not reflected in the mean $g(R_E)$. Then, the difference in the mean $-g(P_E)^{e*}$ must be solely attributable to the difference in the risk premium. The risk premium turns out to be slightly higher in the United States than in Japan. Presumably, this difference is due to the higher growth potential, and the more rapid growth in Japan lowered its risk premium.

The nominal interest rate may be broken down into the rate of inflation and the real interest rate. Measuring the former in terms of the consumption expenditure deflator, we observe that inflation was far more moderate in Japan than in the United States.

All in all, the most important single factor for raising Japan's stock prices was Japan's low interest rate. It should be noted that the loose monetary policy allowed the money supply to grow at a double-digit rate in Japan through most of the 1980s. Since the expanding money supply was absorbed into asset portfolios of households, it did not exacerbate inflation. However, this expanding money balance was coupled with the land-market bubble that occurred in the later 1980s. Thus, while goods inflation was averted, asset inflation occurred (see Sato 1994).

In short, the behavior of the nominal interest rate during the decade of the 1980s owed much to Japan's mismanaged monetary policy. We can say that the stock-market and land-market bubbles in the 1980s were the products of this monetary policy rather than being the speculative activities of the investors as such.

IX. Concluding Remarks

In this article, we have examined stock-price formation in Japan in the 1980s and the early 1990s. We have applied the fundamental equation to break down the stock-price fluctuations into changes in the earnings rate, the interest rate, and stock-price appreciation forecasts.

We have empirically shown that—contrary to the common belief—the forecasting factor contributed less to the bubble than the interest factor. In fact, we have shown that, under ordinary circumstances, the forecasting factor and the interest factor offset each other. Forecasts seem to have played the leading role only in the beginning and the end of the bubble period, as well as in the post-bubble period. During the bubble period, most of the blame must be placed on the interest factor.

The loose monetary policy was pursued during most of the 1980s, causing the continual decline in the interest rate. We have, therefore, attributed the stock market bubble of the 1980s to this monetary policy.[35] We have also argued that the interest rate, much lower in Japan than in the United States and Europe, caused Japan's stock prices to be too high. The high rate of the land-price inflation in the late 1980s was also attributed to the high rate of money growth (Sato 1994).

In the 1980s, the Japanese economy faced a macroeconomic contradiction—a low rate of goods inflation and a high rate of asset inflation. Our analysis has resolved this apparent contradiction. The double-digit rate of money growth did not lend itself to goods inflation. Instead, it gave rise to asset inflation, both in stock prices and in land prices.

Notes

1. The rise continued except for a major drop toward the end of 1987. On Black Monday (October 19, 1987), the Nikkei Average fell by 14.9 percent in one day. Other stock markets all over the world fell by similar amounts.

2. Asset inflation in the late 1980s and asset deflation in the early 1990s led to an outpouring of analyses and policy debates on stock pricing. For analyses, see, for example, Asako et al. 1992; Iwata 1992, chapter 5; Miwa 1990; Tachi et al. 1993; and Ueda (1990). For the role of economic policies, see, for example, Iwata 1993, chapter 8; and Noguchi 1994.

3. The share was 69 percent in 1949, 47 percent in 1960, 40 percent in 1970, 29 percent in 1980, and 23 percent in 1990–92.

4. Other owners in 1992 were: government, 0.6 percent; investment trusts, 3.2 percent; securities firms, 1.2 percent; and foreigners, 5.5 percent. See Bank of Japan, *Economic Statistics Annual*, 1993, Table 90.

5. See Asako et al. 1994, Table 3.

6. In terms of stock trading, the share of individuals declined from a little over 40 percent at the beginning of 1980 to 23 percent in 1990. The share of securities firms, acting on behalf of their clients, remained around 25 percent through the 1980s. The share of banks increased from about 3 percent in 1980 to 20 percent or so by the end of the 1980s. See Omura and Kawakita 1992, Table 3–3.

7. Stocks not qualified to be traded on the stock exchanges are excluded.

8. The futures and option markets came into being in Japan in 1988.

9. When investors are allowed margin trading, these minimum and maximum limits are affected.

10. The microdemand schedule need not be continuous. It may be a step-wise function, being negative or positive only at low or high values of $g(P_E)^e$. In between, the schedule may be at the zero level. This zero stretch becomes longer when the stock market is depressed, as it was in the early 1990s.

11. New stock issues can be included in the $\mathfrak{z}$ curve.

12. The cost of transactions cost, including the capital gains tax, are not figured into the calculation.

13. This means that the elasticity of the forecasts is 1 as far as i is concerned. The empirical validity of this assumption will be seen later in this article.

14. The dividend-discount model uses P_E as the present discounted value of future dividends. If the dividend D_E is expected to grow at a constant rate $g(D_E)^e$, we have:

Equation 4′
$$P_E = \frac{D_E}{i - g(D_E)^e}.$$

If the dividend-earnings ratio is to be constant, we have $g(D_E)^e = g(R_E)^e$. Then, apparently, Equation 4′ yields a lower value than Equation 4. Since Equation 4 and Equation 4′

refer to the same firm, Equation 4' must be incorrect, because it obviously excludes the contribution of retained earnings to the stock price. Amazingly, Equation 4' is very frequently employed in the investment literature.

15. Stock market bubbles appear in both P_E* and $E*$. The movement of $E*$ is analyzed but not reported here to save space.

16. In 1989, the year stock trading peaked, the market shares handled by various exchanges were: Tokyo, 86.1 percent; Osaka, 10.8 percent; Nagoya, 2.7 percent; Kyoto, 0.1 percent; and the other four (Sapporo, Niigata, Hiroshima, and Fukuoka), 0.3 percent. See Bank of Japan, *Economic Statistics Annual*, 1991, Table 104.

17. In 1990, the First Section covered 1,197 brands (1,091 firms) and the Second Section covered 437 brands (436 firms). In terms of the market value of the corporations listed, the First Section accounted for 96.7 percent (December 1989).

18. The base date of the TOPIX is January 4, 1968. The weights used are the market values of brands on that date. Before that date, the Tokyo Stock Exchange stock-price index was the unweighted arithmetic average of the stock prices of 225 brands. The latter index was carried into the more well-known Nikkei Stock-Price Average. The Nikkei Average and the TOPIX move in close parallel.

19. The price-earnings ratio is also available for the Second Section.

One statistical problem with the price-earnings ratio is that R_E tends to be overstated because of dividends paid to stockholder firms. Let s equal the cross-firm share ownership and d equal the dividend-earnings ratio. Then the true measure of earnings is $R_E(1-sd)$. As noted earlier, $s = 0.41$ and $d = 0.32$, so R_E must be reduced by 13 percent.

The commonly accepted procedure then adjusts P_E for cross-share holdings. Thus, the modified price-earnings ratio is $(P_E/R_E)(1-s)/(1-sd)$, or 68 percent of the reported price-earnings ratio in the Japanese case (Omura and Kawakita 1992, 105; Asako et al. 1994, Figure 3). This formula, however, is incorrect because it does not consider the fact that real assets (which are represented by the stock holdings) remain unchanged even after cross-held stocks are eliminated. When a merger of the involved firms eliminates cross-share holdings, the stock price will rise. Therefore, the price-earnings ratio ought to be raised by 13 percent, not reduced by 32 percent.

As long as s and d are stable over time, revisions will affect the absolute level but not the relative changes in the price-earnings ratio.

20. The monthly cycles of industrial bond yields (prepared by the Japan Securities Association) started in May of 1975. Most studies of the fundamental equation use the government bond yields.

21. The investment literature calls this residual the "spread."

22. These include the degree of manufacturing capacity utilization $Q/\bar{Q}$, the GNP gap $\ln Y/\bar{Y}$, and $(i - R_E/P_E)_{-1}$.

23. Since i appears on both sides of the regression equation, the estimate of a is biased upward. Small differences in a do not affect our subsequent empirical analysis.

24. Manufacturing is the major activity of corporations listed on the Tokyo Stock Exchange, applicable to about two-thirds of the companies listed. Also, in the early 1980s, the GNP gap did not fluctuate as much as $Q/\bar{Q}$.

25. In some quarters in the bubble period, $g(P_E)$ was below 5 percent, and sometimes even became negative.

26. Until its revision in the mid-1970s, the TOPIX was one of the leading indicators for the diffusion index.

27. At the last count, 59 such forecasts are listed (Toyo Keizai, *Keizai Tokei*, 1994, 16–21).

28. However, the best among them, prepared by the Nomura Institute, had a batting average of 0.800. Professor Lawrence Klein states this is a highly satisfactory record.

29. They are called the *Short-Term Economic Survey of Principal Enterprises* and the *Short-Term Economic Survey of Enterprises*. Both are conducted during February, May, August, and November, and they both cover the current and subsequent quarters. The former survey covers about 500 major firms, which accounts for 80 percent of all nonfinancial corporations in aggregate size. The latter covers some 5,500 corporations.

30. The official name is *Hojin Kigyo Doko Chosa* [Business Operators' Outlook]. It is conducted four times a year, also in February, May, August, and November and covers about 1,900 firms.

31. In announcing the end of the latest recession on September 6, 1994, the Bank of Japan based its judgment on the movement of this indicator (called *DI*) from May to August. The Economic Planning Agency later dated the end of the recession as November 1993.

32. There is the possibility of a political business cycle. Of the seven peaks in $g(P_E)^{e*}$, five fell in years in which there were House of Representative elections (June 1980, December 1983, July 1986, February 1990, and July 1993). A general election may help to revive people's confidence, thereby giving a stimulus to the economy. Recall that the mass media predicted that the general election of July 1993 would revive the Japanese economy. However, this prediction turned out to be false for 1993.

33. Asako et al. (1994) assume that $E(g(P_E))$ is equivalent to the five-year, centered, moving average of $g(PY)$, where PY is the nominal GDP. Taking the average for 1977–86, they derived the mean of $\delta = 3.86$ percent. By assuming that δ remained at the same level throughout, they computed the "theoretical" value of P_E for January 1981–December 1993 according to:

$$\tilde{P}_E = \frac{R_E}{i - \overline{\delta} - g(PY)}$$

where i is the government bond yields.

They found that $(P_E - \tilde{P}_E)$ was positive throughout the entire period except in 1987. They then concluded that the bubble lasted throughout the entire period, including during the latest recession. This conclusion is completely contrary to intuition. Since there is no theoretical justification that $E(g(P_E))$ can be approximated by the formula $g(PY)$, we reject this finding.

Ueda (1990), in a more elaborate model, derived the following formula for the "theoretical" value of the price-earnings ratio:

$$P_E/R_E = 1/((i_C - g(P_Y) + \delta) - g(P_K) + sg(Y))$$

where i_C is the call rate, $g(P_Y)$ and $g(Y)$ are the growth rates of the implicit GNP deflator and the real GNP respectively, $g(P_K)$ is the rate of inflation for real assets, and s is the cross-share ownership. $(i_C - g(P_Y) + \delta)$ is the required rate of return, which is the sum of the real interest rate and the risk premium.

Ueda derived the risk premium as the difference between the *ex post* rate of return on stocks (R_E/P_E) and the call rate (i_C) averaged for 1956–87. The former was 21.5 percent and the latter was 7.5 percent. Thus, he estimated δ to be 14.0 percent. The derived theoretical value of the price-earnings ratio was about 50 percent of the measured value in 1956–82 and 15 percent of the measured value in 1983–88. From this, he concluded that the Japanese stock prices were too high, especially in the 1980s.

We criticize Ueda's conclusion along the same lines as we did Asako et al.

34. Ueda 1990; French and Poterda 1991.

35. In late 1994, the outgoing Chancellor of the Bank of Japan admitted publicly that the Bank of Japan's failure in monetary policy was mostly responsible for the bubbles in the late 1980s.

Appendix Note: The Fundamental Equation

Suppose that the buyer of a stock intends to resell the stock after T years. Then the present value equation is:

$$P_E = \frac{R_E}{1 + i} + \frac{R_E(1 + g(R_E)^e)}{(1 + i)^2} + \ldots + \frac{R_E(1 + g(R_E)^e)^{T-1}}{(1 + i)^T} + \frac{P_E(1 + g(R_E)^e)^T}{(1 + i)^T}$$

$$= X \frac{R_E}{i - g(R_E)^e}$$

where:

$$X = \frac{1 - \left(\dfrac{1 + g(R_E)^e}{1 + i}\right)^T}{1 - \left(\dfrac{1 + g(P_E)^e}{1 + i}\right)^T} \cdot$$

We note that:

$$\frac{1}{i - g(P_E)^e} \gtreqless X \gtreqless \frac{1}{i - g(R_E)^e} \text{ according to } g(P_E)^e \gtreqless g(R_E)^e.$$

We immediately find that:

$$P_E = \frac{R_E}{i - g(P_E)^e}$$

holds over if $T = 1$, or if $T > 1$ and $g(P_E)^e = g(R_E)^e$.

X is approximated by:

$$X = 1 - \frac{g(R_E)^e - g(P_E)^e}{i - g(P_E)^e}.$$

This equation holds exactly for $T = 1$.

Hence, as $g(R_E)^e$ approaches $g(P_E)^e$, X approaches 1.

Appendix Table

Signs of ΔR_E, $\Delta \hat{\imath}$, $\Delta g(P_E)^e$, and ΔP_E, 1Q81–1Q94

Year	Quarter	ΔR_E	$\Delta \hat{\imath}$	$\Delta g(P_E)^e$	ΔP_E
1981	1	+	−	−	+
	2	+	−	−	+
	3	+	+	+	+
	4	−	+	+	−
1982	1	−	−	−	+
	2	−	−	+	−
	3	−	+	+	−
	4	−	−	+	+
1983	1	−	−	−	+
	2	−	−	+	+
	3	−	+	+	+
	4	−	−	−	+
1984	1	+	−	+	+
	2	+	+	−	+
	3	−	+	+	−
	4	+	−	−	+
1985	1	+	−	−	+
	2	+	−(0)	−	+
	3	+	−	−	+
	4	−	−	+	+
1986	1	−	−	+	+
	2	+	−	+	+
	3	+	−	+	+
	4	+	−	−	+
1987	1	+	−	−	+
	2	+	−	−	+
	3	−	−	+	−
	4	+	+	+	−
1988	1	+	+	+	+
	2	−	−	−	+
	3	+	−	−	−
	4	+	−	−	+
1989	1	+	−	−	+
	2	+	+	+	+
	3	+	+	+	+
	4	−	+	+	+
1990	1	−	+	+	−
	2	−	+	+	−
	3	+	+	−	−
	4	−	+	−	−
1991	1	+	−	−	+
	2	+	−	+	+
	3	+	−	−	−
	4	+	−	−	+
1992	1	+	−	−	−
	2	+	−	−	−
	3	−	−	+	−
	4	−	−	−	+
1993	1	+	−	−	+
	2	−	+	+	+
	3	−	−	+	−
	4	+	−	−	−
1994	1	−	−	+	+
	2		+		+

References

Asako, K. 1992. "Shisan Kakaku no Mekanizumu" [The Mechanism of Asset Pricing]. Chapter 2 in *Bunseki Nihon Keizai no Sutokkuka* [Analysis: Japan Turning into a Stock Economy], edited by T. Ito and Y. Noguchi, 21–56. Tokyo: Nihon Keizai Shinbunsha.

Asako, K., et al. 1990. "Kabuka no Baburu" [Stock Prices and the Bubble]. In *Nihon no Chika Bukka: Kakaku Keisei no Medanizuma* [Japan's Stock Prices and Land Prices: The Price Formation Mechanism], edited by K. Nishimuro and Y. Miwa, 37–86. Tokyo: University of Tokyo Press.

Asako, K., et al. 1994. "Nihon no Kabuka: Note" [Japan's Stock Prices: Note]. *Financial Review* (Ministry of Finance) 32 (June): 187–97.

French, K., and J. Poterda. 1991. "Were Japanese Stock Prices Too High?" *Journal of Financial Economics* 29.

Iwata, K. 1992. *Sutokkuka Keizai no Kozo* [The Structure of a Stock Economy]. Tokyo: Iwanami Shoten.

———. 1993. *Kin'yu Seisaku no Keizaigaku* [Economy of Monetary Policy]. Tokyo: Nihon Keizai Shinbunsha.

Miwa, Y. 1990. "Kabuka 'Moderu' to Nihon no Kabuka" [Stock-Price Model and Japan's Stock Prices]. Chapter 1 in *Nihon no Chika Bukka: Kakaku Keisei no Medanizuma* [Japan's Stock Prices and Land Prices: The Price Formation Mechanism], edited by K. Nishimuro and Y. Miwa, 3–26. Tokyo: University of Tokyo Press.

Nishimura, K., and Y. Miwa, eds. 1990. *Nihon no Chika Bukka: Kakaku Keisei no Medanizuma* [Japan's Stock Prices and Land Prices: The Price Formation Mechanism]. Tokyo: University of Tokyo Press.

Noguchi, Y. 1994. "The 'Bubble' and Economic Policies in the 1980s." *Journal of Japanese Studies* 20 (Summer): 291–330.

Omura, K., and H. Kawakita. 1992. *Zeminaru Nihon no Kabushiki Shijo* [Japan's Stock Markets]. Tokyo: Toyo Keizai Shinposha.

Sato, K. 1986. "Evaluation of Forecasts" (in Japanese). *Nihon Keizai Kenkyu* 15 (November): 2–13.

Sato, K. 1994. "Bubbles in Japan's Urban Land Market: An Analysis." *Journal of Asian Economics* 6(2): 153–76.

Tachi, R., et al. 1993. "Shisan Kakaku Hendo no Mekanizumu to sono Keizai Koka" [The Mechanism of Asset Price Fluctuations and its Economic Effect]. *Finance Review* (Ministry of Finance) 30: 1–76.

Source/Permission: **Kazuo Sato**, "Nihon no Kabuka no Bubbles: Makuro Bunseki." *Nihon Keizai Kenkyu* [Journal of Japanese Economic Research] 30 (December 1995). (The English version originally appeared in *Japanese Economic Studies* 23, No. 4 [July–August 1995].)

Part VI

The International System

11

The Destruction of the Full-Set Industrial Structure— East Asia's Tripolar Structure

Mitsuhiro Seki

Since the days of the dollar shock and the oil crises, debates over Japan's industrial structure have taken several twists and turns. During boom times, Japan's industrial prowess was ascribed to structural factors. Now, during a recession that has seen the upward spiral that had continued since the close of World War II come to an end, serious discussion has ensued on such topics as shifts in the industrial structure and the need for structural adjustments. Published in the midst of this recession, *Beyond the Full-Set Industrial Structure** is therefore truly a product of its times.

If this book differs from others of its genre, it is in its examination of the issues of Japan's industrial structure within the context of Asia's overall industrial and technological restructuring and in its awareness of the deepening of Japan's relationship with the rest of East Asia in the 1980s and 1990s. Japan, which largely ignored its neighbors during its own industrial buildup, now finds itself having to seek a far different mode of economic development than in the past. Specifically, it finds itself having to develop within a larger context—that of East Asia, especially China, which is likely to become an economic dynamo in the twenty-first century.

Observers point out that as adjustments in industry proceed across East Asia as a whole, Japan's full-set industrial structure, in which all industrial and technological processes are contained within its borders—a situation that evolved during Japan's hundred years of industrialization—is falling apart. The coming era will instead be based on a new relationship of mutual interdependence among the nations of East Asia. Japan is being forced to make a speedy shift from a closed, self-sufficient industrial structure to a structure that is open and mutually interdependent on others. Now that the pattern of East Asia's development has

---

*See source note on page 339.

altered so radically, this trend will be central in the twenty-first century, regardless of whether the general economic situation is one of boom or bust.

Based on an awareness of the foregoing, I would like to examine the outlook for future changes in Japan's industrial structure in the new East Asian age. I will do so by utilizing the somewhat macro-economic concept of the full-set industrial structure and the rather microeconomic concept, as it relates to corporate behavior, of what can be referred to as a corporate in-house geographical division of labor.

The Formation of the Full-Set Industrial Structure

It has long been common, when pointing out the characteristics of Japan's industrial structure, to use the terms full set or one set. These expressions, somewhat pejorative in tone, gained their greatest currency in the mid-1970s, after the end of the years of high economic growth, when the nation was suffering the effects of the dollar shock and the oil shocks. The mass media of the day used the term full set in a negative way to characterize the nation's industrial structure. The media's interpretation was that in the future Japan would become a stable-growth or low-growth economy. The feeling, part prognostication and part expectation, was that Japanese industry, which in the past looked exclusively to the United States, would assume a European-style, mature, relaxed-growth pattern. Those in the media wrote with anticipation about a horizontal division of labor as seen in Europe.

The Significance of the Full-Set Industrial Structure

The meaning of "full-set" industrial structure was that Japan, alone among the developed countries, possessed within its borders all industrial sectors at a reasonably high level of development. The term was used neither in conceit nor in ridicule. Japan contained within its borders such well-developed industries as steel, shipbuilding, chemicals, automobiles, electrical machinery, and textiles.

In contrast, the European style of industrial structure of which the Japanese were enamored seemed to embody the benefits of the theory of comparative production costs popular since the time of David Ricardo. That is, each nation seemed to have its own fields of expertise within a system of mutual interdependence: Germany in steel, the United Kingdom in shipbuilding, France and Germany in chemicals, Switzerland in precision machinery, France and Italy in textiles, and so on. This European-style horizontal division of labor appeared to be ideal for Japan as its industry completed its development and headed toward maturity. To have all industrial sectors within one's own borders was considered natural in the Soviet Union, China, and other socialist powers. But as a member of the community of developed nations Japan found the thought of having to do everything itself increasingly oppressive. Moreover, the mid-1970s was a period in which textiles, formerly one of Japan's leading industries, was becoming a net importer, while such sectors as steel and shipbuilding were beginning to fall on hard times. The nation was becoming aware that some sorts of adjustments in the industrial structure were afoot.

The Story of Asia's Only Modern Industrial State

Among the developed countries, only Japan possessed a full-set industrial structure comprising all industries at a relatively high level of sophistication. The reason for that undoubtedly is deeply connected to Japan's history of modern industrial development. About 100 years ago, when Japan first clearly conceived of itself becoming a modern industrial nation, many parts of East Asia were colonies of other countries and lacked the conditions conducive to industrializing under their own steam. Japan, isolated geographically in the extreme eastern end of Asia from its neighbors and uncolonized, was both forced and able to set out to independently develop industries in multiple fields.

Japan's engagement in several wars, including the Sino-Japanese War (1894–1895), the Russo-Japanese War (1904–1905), and World War I, merely furthered the country's industrialization. Isolated from the rest of East Asia, its relations with its neighbors always tense, Japan was forced to provide for itself. It had, for example, to procure its own weaponry, such as guns, tanks, and warships. This situation applied also to military clothing, bags, and shoes, nowadays all items of common, everyday use. Indeed, such basic industries as special steel, machine tools, and industrial equipment got their start around the middle of the Meiji Era as military industries, as did the production of knits, shoes, bags, and the like.

Thus began Japan's belated process of industrial modernization. With none of its neighbors doing the same, and with relations with those neighbors always tense, Japan found it unavoidable, at least for the time being, to adopt the pattern for developing a full-set, in-country spectrum of industries.

From Prototype Creation to the Mass Production of Mature Commodities

It was under those historical circumstances that Japanese industry came to establish its full-set character. It is my belief, however, that inherent in the full-set industrial structure is a more important implication than the complete range of industries the structure encompasses, that being its functional aspects.

The Prototype Creation Function

Looking at industries and corporations—the trend being most evident at the corporate level—we see that, for example, at one end of the scale of corporate behavior is the function of creating something entirely new. I refer to that as the "prototype creation" function. It relates to the development of new products, to research and development, and to the creation of original technology.

At the other end of the scale is the function of mass producing mature prod-

Figure 1. **Full-set Structure of Japanese Industry (defined by function)**

Own technology

Established technologies. production facilities

Prototype creation function

Process of industrial modernization

Mass production of mature products

(Tokyo area)

Investment

(Provincial areas)

Start-up of own company

Export

Earning foreign currency

ucts using established technologies and production facilities. Between those two extremes lies a huge spectrum ranging from new products to mature goods. All products fall somewhere on that scale. For instance, to borrow two somewhat dissimilar concepts, items generally described as high in added value and those requiring small-lot production in multiple varieties would each have their respective places somewhere on that scale.

Look at automobiles as a means of understanding this concept. When the first auto made its appearance, it would truly have been a prototype. During the subsequent century, production technology vastly improved and the market expanded. Now, autos are the archetypical mass-produced, mature product. Likewise, when the word processor first appeared it, too, was a prototype. Yet, as a result of speedy technological progress it also is now a very mature, mass-produced product. In this way, all products follow a common path of transition, depicted as moving from the left side of the scale in Figure 1 to the right. That movement represents the product cycle. Viewing industries and corporations from that perspective, we see that they perform two functions: that of prototype creation and that of the mass production of mature goods using established technologies and facilities.

The Process of Japanese Industrial Modernization

When Japan got its belated start on the road to industrial modernization, it possessed no fund of modern industrial technology. It thus had no choice but to begin by importing well-established technologies and production facilities from the advanced Western countries.

Fortunately for Japan, in the late nineteenth century the basic industrial technologies of steel, shipbuilding, and chemicals had already been developed to some extent. Thus, rushing to create modern industry, Japan was able to obtain up-to-date technologies and production facilities. Japan imported the functions represented by the right side of Figure 1, then began its drive toward the functions represented by the figure's left side: the development of original technology and research and development capabilities. As a latecomer to industrial modernization, it has been Japan's fondest wish during the past century to find a way, having started on the right side of the figure, to gain the ability to perform the function of prototype creation and thereby make the transition to the figure's left side.

First, Japan imported existing technologies and production facilities and gave them domestic roots. Next, it employed massive numbers of skilled, low-wage workers and began turning out the lowest-cost, highest-quality goods in the world. Taking advantage of a foreign exchange system in which the yen was relatively cheap, Japan then exported those goods for foreign currency. In this way, Japan established its pattern of export-based industrialization. The valuable foreign currency the nation earned through its massive exports was then invested for the purpose of prototype creation to attain industrial self-sufficiency.

As this process reached approximately the 100-year mark, the period of rapid economic growth ended, brought to a close by the tribulations of the dollar shock, the oil shocks, and the rising yen. Japan, though, finds itself having acquired the ability to create prototypes in many, although not all, industries, thereby generally realizing the dream it held during its century-long process of industrial modernization. There are many differing perspectives on the history of Japan's industrialization, but most observers would probably agree that there has been a recognizable evolution away from the mere introduction of established technologies and production facilities to prototype creation, with Japan formulating its own technologies.

The Functional Meaning of the Full-Set Industrial Structure

Japan began industrializing by importing established technologies and production facilities and over a 100-year span gained the capability for prototype creation. Yet although Japanese industry has reached the level where it can build prototypes it still mass produces mature products using established technologies and facilities. Japan has therefore taken on a full-set industrial structure capable of all functions, from the mass production of mature goods to prototype creation. The process of advancing from one function to the other did not entail abandoning one for the other. Rather, it involved the maintenance of one function and the assumption of the other, and it is in that light that we must judge the fundamental characteristics of Japanese industry and companies.

We can say that the defining characteristic of Japanese industry is the fact that, in addition to having a full-set structure in the sense of possessing all industrial sectors, it also had a full-set structure in terms of the functions its companies perform. Indeed, it is because Japanese industry retains the functional characteristic of its full-set structure that some challenging problems relating to the recent industrialization of East Asia remain.

The Tokyo Area versus Provincial Areas

If we view the spectrum of Japan's industrial development—from the introduction of established technologies and production facilities to the mass production of mature goods, on the one hand, to prototype creation, on the other—through the filter of geography, we become aware of yet another dimension to the country's industrialization.

Many of the technologies and production facilities imported by Japan in the initial stages of its industrialization were already fairly well perfected in the middle of the nineteenth century. It is well known that Japan made the adoption of those technologies and facilities a national priority and aggressively promoted their establishment in the form of factories operated by the government. The nation imported what were at the time state-of-the-art technologies and production facilities in the basic industries of steel, chemicals, shipbuilding, and others.

The Birth of Single-Industry Towns

The bulk of the large, advanced facilities were set up in the countryside of Japan. This was done, as might be expected, partly out of strategic military considerations. It also seems fair to conclude that Japan, believing itself fated to import foreign ore and other resources and to create an industrial and trade structure based on the processing of those resources, made specific site selection based on the following criteria: first, the availability of vast tracts of land to accommodate the huge facilities; second, access to good ports; and, third, an abundance of labor.

In addition, prior activity at a site, such as the mining of iron or coal, would provide all the more encouragement for selecting that site. In any event, the best conditions for site selection were considered to be wide-open spaces, good ports, and the availability of large numbers of low-wage workers. Examining some specific areas that met those criteria, we find that most are what might now be termed single-industry towns. Muroran, Hokkaido, a steel town, has a port and coal deposits; Kamaishi, Iwate Prefecture, also a steel town, has a port and an iron ore mine that has been in operation since the early days; Omuta, Fukuoka Prefecture, a coal and chemical town, has a coal mine; and Aioi, Tamano, and Innoshima, in the Seto Island, Sea of Japan area, are shipbuilding cities with outstanding ports. There is also the case of the company towns that formed around the export-driven and highly labor-intensive auto plants that are located in the suburbs of large urban areas that featured good ports. This development occurred against a backdrop of a massive exodus of people from the agricultural villages into the large urban areas after World War II. Regardless of industry, most of the major technologies and production facilities imported from overseas during Japan's industrial modernization were brought to the countryside, forming industrial or company towns in the process.

One-Way Traffic from the Countryside to Tokyo

At the time of writing, Japan's foreign reserve balance is reported to be pushing US$100 billion. Yet until quite recently Japan was a country short of finances. To industrialize, it had to export and earn foreign currency. Moreover, being poor in minerals and natural resources, Japan invested huge amounts of funds in developing areas with good ports to turn those areas into earners of foreign exchange. Until the dollar shock, with world trade expanding and the value of the yen low under the fixed-rate foreign currency mechanism, Japan's industrial towns enjoyed boom times and shone as the star earners of foreign currency. Those days can accurately be called the golden age of the Japanese provinces.

Since the Edo Period, many so-called local industries, their existence dependent on the availability of nearby raw materials, have sprung up in the Japanese countryside. The number of those local industries is estimated variously at from 300 to 500, encompassing textiles, ceramics, woodworking, and others. Local industries with large output capacity took on an export orientation to earn foreign currency. Some examples are the Western-style tableware makers of Tsubame, Niigata Prefecture; the cloth makers of the Hokuriku region and of Kiryu, Gunma Prefecture; and the ceramics manufactures of Seto, Aichi Prefecture. These industries even undertook reorganizations to better facilitate the earning of foreign currency.

Thus, the industrial towns and areas with high-output local industries outside Tokyo followed their own unique course of development and served as key earners of the foreign currency that fueled Japan's industrial modernization.

Little of the foreign currency earned by the industrial towns and other country-side industries was reinvested locally, except for the expansion of production facilities. Most was probably invested for the purpose of attaining the capability of prototype creation that had been the dream since the advent of the Meiji Era. The basic industrial pattern of the day was to earn foreign currency through exports, mainly to the United States, based on up-to-date facilities and cheap, plentiful labor while taking advantage of favorable foreign exchange rates. Earned foreign currency was then invested with the aim of prototype creation in mind.

In many cases, it is likely that the foreign currency earned by outlying areas was invested in the Tokyo area, where the returns on investment were greatest. Thus, the pattern was to earn the money in the countryside and to invest it in Tokyo to nurture an indigenous prototype development capability. This one-way flow from the countryside into Tokyo was at the foundation of Japan's industrial modernization and remained so through the postwar period of high economic growth.

The Destruction of the Full-Set Structure and East Asia's Tripolar Structure

As I have described, we can think of the process of industrial modernization as one of first incorporating established technologies and production facilities and of then charging ahead to develop the capability of prototype creation. In Japan's case, money earned in the countryside by industries that had done the former was invested in Tokyo for the purpose of attaining the latter. Until the time of the dollar shock and the oil shocks, Japanese industry managed to function quite effectively, despite some peaks and troughs due to economic cycles.

Beginning around the mid-1970s, however, the fundamental conditions that had governed the pattern of Japan's industrial development began a radical transformation.

Industrial Modernization in East Asia

The alteration in the fundamental conditions of Japan's industrial development is varied and complex, involving such issues as the country's changing relationship with the United States. From the perspective of industrial modernization, the most crucial point is the emergence of the East Asian nations. As mentioned, ever since Japan embarked on industrial modernization in the Meiji Era to very recently, none of the countries and regions neighboring Japan evidenced a clear desire to pursue industrial modernization on their own initiative. Also as mentioned above, it was because that very situation prevailed in East Asia that Japan felt compelled to develop the full-set industrial structure that became the defining characteristic of its industrial modernization.

It was not until around 1970, some 20 to 30 years after the end of the war, that the countries of East Asia began to show a desire to develop and modernize their own industries. That change is attributable to several factors, such as postwar world economic development, independence from colonial economic systems, and the influences on East Asia of the Cold War. In addition, one cannot ignore the stimulative effects of the postwar resurgence of Japan and its subsequent rapid economic growth. So, during the past 10 to 20 years many of Japan's East Asian neighbors have trod the path toward rapid industrial modernization. The situation in East Asia, therefore, has changed from one in which only Japan was riding the wave of industrial modernization to one in which many of its neighbors now share the same dream.

The Upsurge of Neighboring States and Mutual Interdependence

At this point the question arises as to what course the industrial modernization of these neighboring states will take. In all likelihood, it will begin the same way as it did in Japan, with the adoption of established, world-class technologies and production facilities. Naturally, the hope of any country pursuing industrial modernization is to have, like Japan, its, own technology—the ability to create prototypes. And, in fact, that is the goal toward which many of Japan's neighbors, like Japan before them, are headed now that they have started industrializing.

For South Korea, Taiwan, Hong Kong, and Singapore, 20 years have elapsed since they opted for industrial modernization. Collectively, they are known as the Four Little Dragons, and each is on the verge of being accepted within the community of developed nations. Next in line are Thailand and Malaysia, followed by China. This pattern of East Asian development, which is often likened to a flock of wild geese flying across the sky in an inverted V formation, with Japan in the lead, is the focus of world attention. The East Asian region, rich in vitality, is sure to reach new heights of prosperity as the world enters the twenty-first century.

This implies that for the first time, Japan has in East Asia the possibility of both powerful rivals and partners. Numerous obstacles must be overcome before the situation matures to the point where a European-style horizontal division of labor evolves. One thing is for sure, however, and that is that, unlike in the past, no one country monopolizes all industrial and technological functions. It is hoped that the East Asian states will eventually come to share a multiplicity of industrial and technological functions to form a new, mutually interdependent industrial network.

Until that time, adjustments will be forced on Japan's full-set industrial structure. These adjustments will be painful. Yet, for the sake of a prosperous, stable Asia, Japan must lend a helping hand to its neighbors in their industrial modernization. The halcyon days of Japan's full-set industrial model are gone. Needed now is a program for achieving a balanced prosperity, at least within Asia as a whole, with the member nations building mutually interdependent relationships that complement one another's strengths and that leverage one another's growth.

East Asia's Tripolar Structure

The structure that must emerge, moreover, is not a relationship between East Asia and Japan. Rather, it is, on the one hand, a matter of East Asia and Japan and, on the other hand, a matter, within Japan, of the Tokyo area and the country's provincial areas. Together, this gives us a two-layered, tripolar structure. And what we find is that, of the three poles in this structure, the Japanese provincial areas are in the most difficult position.

Since the dollar shock and the oil shocks, the need for adjustments in Japan's industrial structure has often been cited. Insofar as its role in East Asia is concerned, Japan, well aware of the industrial modernization of the region, has concentrated on shifting into the region only its low-added-value and labor-intensive industrial sectors. This macroeconomic approach focuses almost solely on the mutual relationship between maturing Japanese industry and still-developing East Asian industry. It does not precisely address the structural adjustment issue. The key issue for Japan, as it adjusts its industrial structure vis-à-vis East Asia, revolves very much around the relationship between the East Asian countries and Japan's provincial areas.

In terms of the functions of mass producing mature products and creating prototypes, the focus of East Asian industrial modernization is likely to continue to be mass production. This is the role that the hinterlands play in Japanese industry's full-set structure, and it is the hinterlands that will bear the brunt of the fierce competition being posed by East Asia. In that sense, the crux of the issue is not in the relationship between the East Asian countries and Japan as a whole, but between East Asian countries and Japan's provincial areas. And it is on this relationship that the issue of Japanese industry's structural adjustments hinges.

The Invisible Border

Between Japan and the countries of East Asia is a very real border. Adjustments in the international economic environment, such as fluctuations in foreign exchange rates and the like, have direct cross-border impact. Each nation being sovereign, each has the ability to set its own customs and tariffs and to control its own finances to its utmost advantage.

In contrast, there is nothing like a national border between Tokyo and the outlying areas of Japan, all of whose autonomy, moreover, is quite limited. Nonetheless, in Japan the provincial areas handle the mass production of mature goods and the Tokyo area carries out the function of prototype creation. It is as if an invisible border lay between them, with the role of the hinterlands analogous to that of the developing countries and Tokyo's function analogous to that of a developed nation. Separated as they are from Japan by clearly defined national boundaries, however, the developing countries of East Asia are able to enjoy, for example, the advantage given them by the upward trend in the value of the yen that has occurred since the initiation of the system of floating exchange rates. For Japan's provincial areas, no such advantages accrue. Not only do they compete with Tokyo across an invisible border, they also increasingly find themselves losing competitiveness against the nations of East Asia.

Figure 1 reveals the striking similarity between the functions performed by Japan's provincial areas, which have underpinned Japan's industrial modernization, and those performed by the neighboring East Asian countries that have embarked on industrial modernization. As Japan formed its full-set industrial structure and made headway toward performing all industrial and technological functions itself, including the creation of prototypes, the countryside has in many cases continued to carry out the function of mass producing mature products by employing established technologies and production facilities. In that sense, the role of Japan's provincial areas is almost identical with that of the East Asian countries that have only recently commenced industrial modernization.

The function of electronic parts assembly was performed until recently by Japan's provincial areas. The transfer of this production to East Asian countries, however, has been accomplished quite smoothly. To be aware of the similarity in the industrial functions of Japan's provincial areas and the countries of East Asia is to understand how the electronic component assembly plants of the Japanese hinterlands could suddenly one day find themselves heading elsewhere in East Asia.

The Tribulations of the Provincial Areas

Thus, in the near term the focus of competition within East Asia will not be between Japan and its neighbors, but between Japan's hinterlands and the East Asian countries. Advantageous borders separate the East Asian countries from Japan, and the continued upward trend in the value of the yen is sure to add to the weight of the blow their growing industrial prowess will deal Japan's hinterlands.

The Tokyo area, meanwhile, has completed much of the structural adjustment thought to be needed to solve problems within Japanese industry in general. Tokyo has a virtual monopoly within Japan, and, indeed, East Asia, on the prototype creation function, one of the ultimate goals of modern industrialization and Japan's long-standing dream. Attaining that same capability will likely become the major objective of other East Asian nations as they rush toward industrial modernization. At present, however, Tokyo is far ahead of the pack in East Asia.

That implies that for now the Tokyo area has no competitors within East Asia. It also implies several other things: that within Japan, only the Tokyo area has been able to attain the long-held dream of prototype creation; that a wide gulf separates the Tokyo area from the hinterlands, which made the greatest contribution to Japan's industrial modernization; and that the invisible boundary between the Tokyo area and the countryside serves to alienate the two.

Given that situation, Japan's position within the tripolar structure of East Asia can be evaluated as follows.

The Tokyo area, which increasingly specializes in prototype creation, is faced with certain problems, including rising land prices and structural labor shortages in the industrial sectors that are based on fundamental technologies. Taken as a whole, though, the Tokyo area is approaching the culmination of modern industrialization.

In the opposite situation are Japan's provincial areas, which provided the foundation for Japan's industrial growth. They are in dire straits for structural reasons and will probably need to undertake major restructuring as they compete with East Asia. Although East Asia still has chronic needs to develop infrastructure, to train personnel, and to build a technological base, overall the region is reaping the rewards of industrial modernization. Within the tripolar industrial structure of East Asia, it is Japan's hinterlands whose problems are the most severe. Therein lies the key issue for Japan's local industry in the new age that will follow the dissolution of Japan's full-set industrial structure.

The Prototype Creation Function and the Corporate Geographical In-House Division of Labor

As Japanese industry, originally an importer of established technologies and production facilities, comes to realize its dream of prototype creation, the structural disparities between the Tokyo area and the hinterlands grow all the more evident. In recent years, attention has focused on the concentration of the nation's political, economic, cultural, and other power in the Tokyo area, but that situation also clearly exists in the fields of industry and lifestyles.

At this point, I would like to analyze that latter phenomenon in terms of the concept of a corporate in-house geographic (or international) division of labor that unfolds in a context of technological advances. I would then like to clarify the issues confronting Japan's industry after the dissolution of the full-set industrial structure.

In the foregoing discussion, I posited a scenario for the coming age by indicating that one of the directions for Japanese industry after the breakup of the full-set industrial structure would be the formation of a new network incorporating East Asia. But I would like to go further by asking what sort of new underlying industrial structure will arise as Japan in its entirety acquires the capability of prototype creation.

Advanced Technology and the Corporate In-House Geographical Division of Labor

Japan's traditional leading industries—steel, automobiles, electrical equipment, and others—face serious problems that are structural in nature. Yet, at the same time, the advanced technology sectors that were the darlings of the 1980s—new materials, biotechnology, and mechatronics, for instance—do not seem to have found a springboard for further development. The popularity of starting up new types of businesses, at its peak during the years of the bubble, has waned since the so-called compound recession set in beginning in 1991. Amid the recession, which itself is considered to be structural in nature, such phrases as "returning to the main lines of business" and "eliminating new business ventures" have become commonplace in the economic press.

Even if a pullback is justified in light of the recession, Japanese corporations clearly cannot expect to compete with growing East Asian industrial power merely by sticking to their traditional "main lines of business." Every company will inevitably have to restructure. In the future, that function of the full-set industrial structure whereby mature products are mass produced using established technologies and facilities—the right side of Figure 1—will continue to shift to the emerging East Asian countries. For Japanese industry, therefore, the primary task to ensure survival and prosperity entails fulfilling the promise of prototype creation, the function shown on the left side of Figure 1. Accordingly, Japanese industry and its corporations will have to go beyond the boundaries of their traditional businesses to tackle advanced technologies in a multiplicity of fields and must not allow themselves to be swayed by temporary swings in the economy.

The Importance of Research and Development

There are several approaches to take when analyzing a corporation. Insofar as our discussion relates to the function of prototype creation, I would like to posit four phases of that process: basic research, production research, trial mass production, and mass production. Based on those phases, I will examine the nature of the gap between the Tokyo area, the only region in East Asia that has succeeded in developing the capability of prototype creation, and Japan's provincial areas, which are facing structural difficulties (see Figure 2).

Basic research, defined broadly, is the investigation of first principles, looking ahead 10 or 20 years. In the past, Japan relied heavily on the United States for basic research. Now that the importance of leading investment for the development of advanced technologies has taken on greater significance, however, Japanese corporations are increasingly striking out on their own in search of business opportunities, even if those opportunities do not pan out in the short term. For this, basic research is indispensable and is clearly becoming a fundamental requirement for Japanese companies that must base their futures on the prototype creation function. Research institutes with names like Central Research Laboratory, Basic Research Laboratory, and so on are generally coming to fill this role for the large corporations that own them. The boom in the building of research institutes that became the subject of debate in the bubble economy was a response to a growing need for basic research capabilities.

Production research is applied research that delves into the question of whether it is possible to make a product by combining reasonably well-established elemental technologies. It is a specialty among Japanese companies. In recent years, especially since broad-based research encompassing new fields of technology in areas other than a firm's main lines of business have come to be considered an absolute must, the importance of this type of research has grown. As a result, a constant flow of various new products has begun to appear.

However, even when it is determined that a new product concept is possible during the process of production research, further investigation is required to ascertain the profitability of a business based on the product. A specific market study is conducted, and appropriate cost levels are set. Then further study is undertaken to determine whether production is feasible under those conditions.

Figure 2.   **Corporate In-house Geographic (International)
Division of Labor**

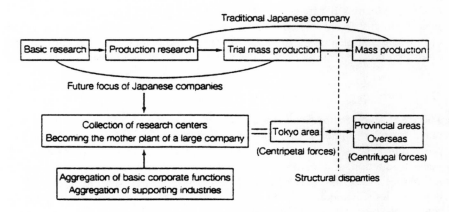

For example, even if it is possible to create a word processor by combining elemental technologies one cannot just jump into the market with it. To ensure a growing market for this word processor, the product must be an item that individuals can afford. To achieve entry into the overall word processor market, it would be best if a manufacturer could provide the product at a price where a businessperson could purchase one personally. For instance, if most businesspeople's discretionary income is ¥200,000, the technology and equipment for production and other factors necessary to supply the word processor at that price must be developed. This stage in the production process is called trial mass production and has been Japanese companies' strongest suit. It is safe to say that the production systems of Toyota and some other companies elevated this process to the height of perfection.

The Corporate In-House Geographical Division of Labor

The activities described so far are a company's basic functions. As technology advances, these functions take on added importance. When it comes time for actual (mass) production, the company selects the most suitable production facility from among its plants in Japan and elsewhere, taking into consideration the specifics, such as size and weight, of the product and the various factors involved in producing it and in production in general. Semiconductors, for example, which are high in added value relative to their size and weight, could be produced at a plant in a location near an airport in Kyushu. White goods, such as refrigerators and washing machines, however, would be better produced at plants no more than 200 to 300 kilometers from the Tokyo area, their largest market, since long-distance shipping of bulky, essentially empty items is inefficient.

To describe the growing sophistication of these basic corporate functions, bolstered as they are by advanced technology, and to give a name to the phenomenon of the diffusion of mass production over a network of plants covering wide geographical areas, the terms "corporate in-house international division of labor" or "corporate in-house international division of labor" are appropriate. The main plants in a corporate network are those that perform the basic functions described above. Insofar as they also work to enhance their technological capabilities, they function as a company's "mother plants." Plants in the network that handle mass production by taking in established technologies and production facilities rely upon the research and development conducted by the mother plants, giving rise to a multilayered structure within the corporate-wide network of plants.

Tokyo-Area Plants Converting to Mother Plant Status

From a geographical perspective, we are faced with the reality that Japanese corporate systems of production are bifurcated. Mother plants are located in the Tokyo area, concentrated especially in the western sections in the Tama River and Tsurumi River basins. Plants carrying out mass production are located in the hinterlands or overseas.

The plants of Japan's leading companies are situated in long arcs within the two river basins named above. In the Tama River basin, they start at the mouth of the river where the city of Kawasaki in Kanagawa Prefecture and Tokyo's Ota Ward are located. This is the heart of the Tokyo–Yokohama industrial district. The line of plants moves upriver through the districts of Inagi, Fuchu, Kokubunji, Hino, Hachioji, Tachikawa, Akishima, Hamura, and Ome. In the Tsurumi River basin, plants extend in the direction of Yokohama. Beginning in the 1980s, the plants in these river basins began a transformation that made them into the mother plants of their respective companies, had them performing the basic corporate functions described above, or turned them into research centers for applied R&D. In all cases, these plants upgraded their capabilities and their roles within their corporate contexts.

As an example, Toshiba's Horikawacho plant, in Kawasaki, has shifted from the production of fluorescent lightbulbs to the high-tech fields of microwave and electronic equipment. And Canon moved a camera plant to the city of Fukushima, turning its Ota Ward plant into a research facility. Japan Steel Works likewise turned its Fuchu plant, which had been producing injection molding equipment, into a research center, as did Toshiba its Hino plant, which used to produce telephones and similar items. In this way, most of the factories in the Tama and Tsurumi river basins are rapidly being turned into research centers or plants used for product development and prototyping. It is thus safe to conclude that, whether as mother plants conducting R&D and creating prototypes or as research facilities handling applied R&D, the plants of the large corporations that dot these river basins are elevating their capabilities. In contrast, the provincial factories and the overseas plants of those companies are provided with established production facilities and technologies and function as mass production centers. Typically, they operate without any independent development capabilities and are considered to be divisions of the mother plants, which have a distinct role within the corporate in-house geographical division of labor.

Mother Plants and Their Support Structures

With the trend toward the corporate in-house geographical division of labor, which makes possible the perfection of the function of prototype creation, large corporations' mother plants and applied R&D centers are becoming concentrated in the Tokyo area, specifically in the western sections in the Tama River and Tsurumi River basins. We must now discuss why those two areas have become the targets for plant sitings. Such upstream Tama River cities as Hachioji and Ome, for example, are about 50 kilometers from central Tokyo and have been increasingly devoted to high technology in recent years. There are reasons why the neighboring prefectures of Saitama and Chiba, which are about equally distant from central Tokyo as Hachioji and Ome and which feature low land prices, have not evolved in this manner.

Talent and Information

Basic corporate functions such as R&D tend to concentrate in Tokyo chiefly because outside Tokyo it is often hard to obtain high-level technical people or because of a need to attract the expertise available in Tokyo. Take for instance the case of Hitachi, Ltd. When Hitachi's headquarters was in the city of Hitachi, in Tochigi Prefecture, it was surrounded by research centers, but the company still found it very difficult to recruit researchers and engineers. The company responded by moving its headquarters to the Ochanomizu section of Tokyo. The company's Central Research Laboratory in the Tama area city of Kokubunji has no trouble recruiting technicians. And although Matsushita Electric Industrial Co., Ltd., headquartered in the city of Kadoma, Osaka Prefecture, is fully able to recruit college graduates in western Japan in the sciences and engineering, it is reported to have trouble recruiting Tokyo-area graduates. Students at leading Tokyo universities are reported to regard posting to the western parts of Japan with some disdain. This would pose no particular problem for Matsushita if the company were willing to stake its future on simple extensions of its traditional business. However, Matsushita is becoming increasingly conscious of the need for employees of diverse backgrounds in preparation for the day when the company diverges from its main lines of business and launches into various other fields. Accordingly, Matsushita some years ago opened a research center in Kawasaki as a means of recruiting Tokyo-area talent.

Another inducement to locate within Tokyo is the availability of information. Regional differences in the availability of information would seem to be shrinking with the rise of new media. Yet, primary information not yet available to the general public is best passed along and refined in face-to-face interaction among diverse researchers in a fairly concentrated setting. Tokyo, with its mammoth complex of politics, economics, and culture, offers not only a vast amount of information but also a massive network by which that information can be communicated and shared.

No Profits in the Main Business

Talent and information, therefore, are among the principal factors contributing to the concentration of R&D functions in the Tokyo area. But those factors alone do not explain why the mother plants and the applied R&D centers of the large companies are concentrated in the Tama and Tsurumi river basins in the western part of greater Tokyo.

For that, we need to look at one more critical factor: the rapid development of advanced technologies and the expansion into new areas of endeavor that go beyond companies' main lines of business. Companies intent on creating new businesses and technologies must maintain ongoing programs that encompass basic research, production research, and trial mass production. Lead times for development are rapidly shortening, and a wide variety of new products must be turned out. If companies were simply extending their core business, their plants and research organizations could make use of existing facilities—experimental research and testing facilities and other equipment—with a good idea of how long it would take to build prototypes and accomplish other tasks.

Companies, however, that try merely to build on their already existing activities can no longer make the grade. They must adopt a comprehensive outlook that encompasses fields with which they have no experience. The equipment required for experimenting and testing is unique and varied, and vast combinations of work processes are required to build prototypes. It is unrealistic to expect even the biggest firms to be able on their own to equip their mother plants or research institutes with all that is needed. They must rely on outside sources for much of the work processes required in the manufacture and prototyping of special equipment for experimentation and testing. If a company tried to handle everything in-house, the cost burden would be staggering. The further technology advances, the truer this becomes.

Supporting Foundations for Japanese Industry

Fortunately, there is an area of dense industrial concentration in Japan that is capable of taking on the multiplicity of sophisticated manufacturing tasks required to build specialized experimentation and testing equipment. That area is at the center of the Tokyo–Yokohama industrial district comprising Tokyo's two southernmost wards of Ota and Shinagawa on one bank of the Tama River and the cities of Kawasaki and Yokohama on the other bank. The area possesses all of the manufacturing capabilities and sophisticated technologies for machinery production.

After the years of high economic growth came to an end, the factories in this area were targeted for relocation to the countryside. With the encroachment of housing developments, the smaller plants that were primary sources of pollution also have been pushed out. As a result, many plants have left the area. Even so, approximately 20,000 plants remain within the vicinity of Ota, Shinagawa, Kawasaki, and Yokohama. Those operations suffer the burdens of increasingly rigorous pollution control, rising land prices, steep labor costs, restrictions on land utilization, and other obstacles. They nevertheless form a unique and sophisticated concentration of industries capable of meeting all the demands of the machinery and metals industries. It is said that any kind of industrial process can be undertaken in the Tokyo–Yokohama industrial district.

If, for example, a mother plant requires a special piece of equipment for experimentation or testing, all it needs to do is call on the small factories of Ota, Shinagawa, Kawasaki, or Yokohama and the need will be met in no time. If, moreover, a firm requires special processing to build a prototype of a new product, it will find among the approximately 20,000 factories some small shop that has the highest level of expertise available in that type of process. Indeed, many tenants of the rows of high-rise condominiums that have appeared in recent years around the Japan Railway's Kamata Station in the center of Ota Ward are small systems planning and design firms. Why they have situated in the area is explained in this humorous comment by a systems planner: "Within a radius of one and a half hours travel from here are located all of the development divisions of Japan's leading companies that make up our customer base. I can make a paper airplane with one of my blueprints, toss it out the window, and in a few days, the finished product will be ready."

In that sense, the massive concentration of highly skilled small shops in this area will serve as the foundation for next-generation Japanese industry. Without them, Japanese industry, buffeted by the winds of advancing technology and massive structural change, would be unable to survive. The small industrial plants of the area provide a base that is a sort of community property or public trust that works for the benefit of Japan's continued industrial development.

Most large companies' mother plants and applied research institutes are situated where they have the best access to this area in preference to other sites in the Tokyo–Yokohama industrial district. They are widely dispersed in the Tama River and Tsurumi River basins, which form the axes from which the small shops of Ota, Shinagawa, Kawasaki, and Yokohama radiate like the spokes of a tire. We can conclude, therefore, that the nexus represented by the Tama and Tsurumi river basins, home as it is are to the mother plants and applied research facilities of most of Japan's large companies and to the proliferation of small shops that have developed the very sophisticated technologies that are the foundation of those companies' future business lines, will play the pivotal role in the next generation of Japanese industry.

Concerns Over the Future of Supporting Technologies

Immense concentrations, meanwhile, of small factories responsible for the fundamental technologies that have supported Japan's industrial development are gradually disappearing. The casting, forging, plating, and machinery manufacturing sectors, for example, are thought of as typical three-K industries. Young people eschew working in them, and many shops have workforces averaging over 50 years of age. Indeed, many have already gone out of business, and there is concern that the output capacity of those industries will drop precipitously in the near future. The work done by those sectors cannot be completely mechanized, and they are still heavily dependent upon skilled workmanship. The work, in fact, done by the skilled people in these sectors is often precisely what meets the needs of the high-tech sector. The ages of the skilled workers in the small factories in Ota, Shinagawa, Kawasaki, and Yokohama are quite high, and those shops hold little hope of finding successors to these people. There is much concern that by the advent of the twenty-first century the store of industrial skill and know-how of Ota, Shinagawa, Kawasaki, Yokohama—the supporting foundation of Japanese industry and its community property—will have dissolved.

So, as the prototype creation capabilities of Japanese industry grow the crumbling of Japan's full-set industrial structure is under way. The future course of the nation's fundamental technologies will largely determine the future course of Japanese industry as a whole. We touched on the structural difficulties faced by the Japanese provinces within the tripolar structure of East Asian industrial technology. But even the Tokyo area, which already possesses the capability of prototype creation, faces some thorny issues of its own, revealing a dark side to its prosperity. Our premonition of the dissolution of the full-set industrial structure and the formation of an interdependent network in East Asia is gradually becoming a reality. Now foremost on everyone's mind is the question of what to do about the weakening structure of the fundamental technologies of Japanese industry.

Mitsuhiro Seki is on the faculty of the Department of Economic Information, Tokyo University of Information Sciences.

Source/Permission: "Full Set Gata Sangyo Kozo no Kaitai." Chapter 2 of Mitsuhiro Seki, *Full Set Gata Sangyo Kozo o Koete, Higashi Asia Shinjidai nonakno Nihon Sangyo* [Beyond the Full Set Industrial Structure—Japanese Industry in the Midst of the New East Asia Era]. Tokyo: Chuo Koransha, 1993. Reprinted with permission from the English translation, *Beyond the Full-Set Industrial Structure, Japanese Industry in the New Age of East Asia* (Tokyo: LTCB International Library Foundations, 1994), LTCB (Long-Term Credit Bank of Japan) International Library Selection No. 2, Chapter 2, "The Destruction of the Full-Set Industrial Structure—East Asia's Tripolar Structure," pp. 33–58. (Translation also appeared in *Japanese Economic Studies* 23, No. 1 [January–February 1995].)

12

Economic Growth, Foreign Trade, and Trade Policy in Japan

Kazuo Sato

1. Introduction

As an economy grows, its economic structure undergoes change. Correspondingly, its trade structure changes. The savings-investment balance also changes as the economy's developmental stage evolves. Trade policy intervenes in this process by influencing resource allocations within the economy and regulating capital flows with the rest of the world.

In the case of Japan, economic growth has been tremendous over the last four decades and its trade structure has correspondingly undergone considerable transformation. Reflecting its poor resource endowments, Japan specializes almost exclusively on exporting manufactured goods and importing resource goods. Its exports moved away from light-industry to heave-industry products and its imports tended to concentrate on food, crude materials, and mineral fuels. In the 1980s, imports of manufactured goods started to expand—from a little below 30 percent of total imports in the 1970s to about 50 percent by the end of the 1980s. Despite this recent increase, there still remains a large imbalance between exports and imports of manufactured goods; an imbalance which has been a principal source of Japan's recurrent and intense trade frictions.

Japan has been a net exporter of capital since the mid-1960s. Its net capital outflows increased considerably in the 1980s, reaching to a high of 4 percent of GDP in 1986. In the late 1980s, when the U.S. became the largest net debtor in the world, Japan became the world's largest net creditor. This new development adds to the intensity of international economic conflicts involving Japan.

This chapter reviews Japan's experiences in the areas of economic growth, foreign trade, and trade policy. Section 2 surveys the history of postwar growth and discusses how growth influenced foreign trade and capital flows. Section 3 examines major structural features of Japan's foreign trade and capital flows.

Section 4 focuses on the role that trade policy has played. Section 5 speculates on the future of Japan's growth and trade.[1]

2. Economic Growth and Foreign Trade: Historical Changes[2]

a. 1951–59

It took the entire Occupation period (August 1945 to April 1952) for Japan to overcome the wartime devastations. As the economy built back its productive capacity, the tenacious inflation (the CPI rose 100 times) was finally controlled by 1952. Per capita income recovered its prewar peak (1935–36) level. The economy started to grow at a high rate, average 7–8 percent in the late 1950s. Workers who had been forced to return to villages were coming back to cities.

High growth required investment to grow. Rising investment was made possible by rapidly expanding savings since people had to build up household wealth, most of which was dissipated in the course of the postwar inflation. The bottleneck was the balance of payments. While the need for imports of crude materials was strong and rising, Japan had very little to export. At that time Japan's exports were dominated by light manufactures (such as cotton textiles). The Korean War (June 1950 to July 1953) was a boon to the Japanese economy as the American military forces in Korea requisitioned goods and services from Japan. "Special procurements" by the UN forces added substantially to Japan's exports of goods and services through most of the 1950s.[3]

Business cycles at this time took a simple form. The national government was under the injunction of the balanced budget (the Public Finance Law of 1947). Thus, when the economy overheated, while investment tended to overrun savings, exports tended to exceed imports. As the foreign exchange reserves contracted, the Bank of Japan initiated a tight-money policy, which killed two birds with one stone: both the internal and external disequilibria were brought back into line simultaneously. This sort of macroeconomic adjustment was repeated until the mid-1960s; there were recessions in 1951, 1954, 1967–58, and 1965.

b. 1960–70

Though economic growth was high in the 1950s, it was mostly to recover the ground that had been lost by World War II. The real takeoff of the Japanese economy occurred in the 1960s. The economy grew at an average annual rate in excess of 10 percent. Industry grew even faster.[4] The rapid expansion of industry required an expansion of the industrial work force. As middle-aged farmers started to move from farms to factories, the agricultural labor force continued to contract in absolute number.[5]

Rapid growth did not cause inflation, since productivity was rising at a high rate. Thus, while money wages were rising rapidly, the general price level rose at only a moderate rate.[6] The rise in productivity made possible by the adoption of new technologies embedded in new investment. It owed a great deal to borrowings of foreign technologies from the U.S. and Western Europe. "Technology imports," i.e., payments of license fees and royalties to foreign patents, expanded rapidly.[7] Not only large firms but also small firms participated vigorously in this modernization of technology.

By the mid-1960s, heavy industries (e.g., steel, shipbuilding, automobiles, and electronics) grew out of the infant-industry stage and became internationally competitive. Japan's exports rapidly shifted from light to heavy manufactures. Since world trade had been moving toward capital goods as countries adopted ambitious development programs, Japan's exports, which met this worldwide shift in emphasis, grew faster than world trade. However, trade frictions were still minor because Japan was still economically a small country.

c. 1971–74

Rapid growth was finally nearing its end. However the labor market was getting very tight as the supply of labor to industry was being exhausted. As wages continued to rise, businesses were induced to substitute capital for labor. In the meantime, as economic growth slackened, the demand for investment was no longer as strong as the supply of savings which was still growing relative to GDP. The credit rationing which regulates bank loans to firms was no longer in force. Thus, businesses were able to borrow more so as to engage in capital deepening. The associated multiplier effect sustained aggregate demand.

In the meantime, the ¥/$ exchange rate which had been fixed at ¥360/$ since 1949 was finally revalued to ¥308/$ in the Smithsonian Agreement of December 1971. It had been feared that such a revaluation would depress the Japanese economy, but the actual outcome was a further expansion of the current account surplus. As Japan's foreign reserves soared,[8] the domestic money supply expanded. At the same time, there was worldwide inflation. Altogether, the Japanese economy became very inflationary. There was a land speculation boom in the early 1970s which collapsed in 1973.[9]

The first oil shock of October 1973 occurred at this juncture. Oil prices quadrupled (in $), and the Japanese COI rose by 23 percent in 1974. The economy went into a heavy recession. The real growth rate was negative (−0.8 percent) for the first time since the end of the war. The current account went into deficit.

d. 1975–90

The Japanese economy quickly recovered from the first oil shock, but the growth rate fell permanently to the level of 5 percent, which was maintained more or less through the next decade and a half. The slowdown of growth entailed a sizable reduction in investment. Savings also fell, but not as much as investment.

The resulting savings surplus was mostly absorbed by a rising government deficit which amounted to as much as 4 percent of GDP in the late 1970s. After running government deficits for several years, the national debt came to be some 40–50 percent of GDP. Balancing the budget became an imperative to the national government. It succeeded in belt-tightening by the late 1980s.

The early 1980s was a relatively depressed period for the Japanese economy. As the government was trying to restore the balanced budget, the rising savings surplus had to find a way into capital outflows. Thus, the current-account surplus continued to expand, reaching the highest position of 4 percent of GDP in 1986.

The Japanese economy then recovered and began its second longest boom in the late 1980s (November 1986 to March 1991). The private savings surplus decreased, and the current acount surplus fell, reaching its lowest at 0.7 percent of GDP in 1990.

In the early 1980s when Japan's net capital outflow expanded, the undervalued yen helped to expand Japan's exports of goods. Then, from 1986 to 1988, the dollar value of the yen halved and this strong yen contributed to depressing Japan's exports. But there was a reverse oil shock which made prices of petroleum and other primary goods very cheap. Hence, Japan's Japan's imports (in value) shrank more than its exports. This development enabled Japan to maintain a sizable current account surplus. By the late 1980s, Japan elevated itself into the position of the largest net creditor in the world economy.

e. 1991–

The boom in the late 1980s was accompanied by "bubbles" in the stock and land markets. The stock market crashed in early 1990 and the land market in late 1991.[10] A recession started in March 1991, and became the longest in the post-war decades; the previous longest recession period was 36 months, from February 1980 to February 1983. The GDP growth rate fell from 4.1 percent in 1991 to 1.5 percent in 1992 and 0.5 percent in 1993. In early 1993, when the economy seemed to show some signs of recovery, the yen became very strong (falling from ¥126/$ at the end of 1992 to reach almost ¥100/$ in August 1993). While the yen value hovered around ¥100/$ in late 1993, the quick fix through export expansion was not an option available to Japan's macroeconomic policy makers.

This short account of Japan's growth process over the last four decades is intended to indicate the macroeconomic interactions between economic growth and foreign trade. In the next section, attention will turn to the present state of Japan's foreign trade and capital flows.

3. The Structure of Foreign Trade and Capital Flows

In the international setting, Japan is a significant outlier as far as its structures of foreign trade and capital flows are concerned. Their major features are examined below.

a. The Structure of Foreign Trade

(i) Openness of the economy

To compare the openness of a national economy, consider the shares of exports and imports in GDP (Table 1). Among the G7 nations, the U.S. and Japan are the least open;[11] the others have far larger shares of exports and imports. This, however, does not mean that exports and imports are unimportant to Japan. On the contrary, foreign trade is of vital importance to the Japanese economy.

(ii) Commodity composition of trade

To begin with, we note that, on both the export and import sides, Japan differs significantly from the other G7 nations. As shown in Table 1, in the other countries, manufactured goods (SITC 5 to 8) account for about 75 percent of total exports and imports of goods. By contrast, Japan's exports are almost entirely in manufactured goods and Japan's imports are only one half in manufactured goods. Furthermore, while exports are mostly in capital goods (SITC 7), imports are only marginally in capital goods.

(iii) Exports of goods

Commodity composition. A salient feature of Japan's exports is that they concentrate on a few major commodities.[12] Those commodities are products of large manufacturing firms. In their total sales, exports make up a major portion.[13] When foreign economies go into a recession (as in 1993), export firms suffer economically. Since small firms supply parts and components to large firms as their subcontractors, the adverse effect of depressed exports spreads from large firms to small firms.

Geographical composition. Another major feature of Japan's exports is their geographical composition. A typical developed country exports about 75 percent of its exports to other developed countries and only 25 percent to developing countries. In contrast, Japan exports about 55 percent of exports to developed countries and 45 percent to developing countries. Among developed countries, the U.S. is the largest importer, accounting for 25 to 35 percent of Japan's total exports. Among developing countries, Asia accounts for some 20 percent of total exports.

(iv) Imports of goods

Foods and raw materials.[14] There were two requirements for rapid growth in the 1950s and 1960s. First, to sustain the rapid growth, the supply of crude industrial materials had to be guaranteed. Crude petroleum had to be wholly imported. Lumber, coal, iron ore, and other mineral ores had to depend increasingly more on imports (Table 2). Since these materials were incorporated into industrial goods directly or indirectly (like fuels), they were imported light of duty or with little import restrictions.[15]

Table 1

The Commodity Composition of Foreign Trade (X = exports and M = imports) and the Openness of Economy, 1990, Percent

Country		0 + 1	2 + 4	3	5 to 8	5	7	6 + 8	Goods (Fob)	Goods and Services
					SITC				Percent of GDP	
Japan	X	0.5	0.7	0.4	96.7	5.4	70.6	20.7	9.7	10.9
	M	13.4	12.5	24.5	46.8	6.4	15.3	25.1	7.3	10.1
U.S.	X	9.5	7.2	3.2	75.3	9.8	46.5	19.0	7.1	10.0
	M	5.6	3.1	13.3	74.5	4.5	41.2	28.8	9.0	11.3
Canada	X	7.8	13.8	9.8	62.0	5.1	37.2	19.7	22.1	25.2
	M	5.9	3.4	6.3	81.3	6.5	50.2	24.6	20.9	24.8
France	X	15.0	3.2	2.4	78.7	13.3	37.2	28.2	18.1	22.6
	M	9.7	4.4	14.6	79.9	10.9	35.7	33.3	18.9	21.6
Germany (West)	X	4.5	1.8	6.4	78.7	12.4	49.3	16.6	27.5	36.7
	M	9.4	5.6	8.3	74.3	8.8	32.4	33.1	22.5	29.8
Italy	X	6.0	1.4	2.0	85.4	6.2	37.5	45.7	15.5	19.1
	M	11.0	8.2	10.5	65.6	10.9	30.1	24.6	15.5	19.5
U.K.	X	6.8	2.1	7.6	81.4	12.5	40.5	28.4	18.9	24.4
	M	9.8	4.8	6.2	77.9	8.4	37.5	32.0	22.0	26.9

Notes: SITC (Standard International Trade Classification)
0 + 1 food, beverages, and tobacco,
2 + 4 crude materials and oils and fats,
3 mineral fuels,
5 chemical products,
7 machinery and transport equipment,
6 + 8 other manufactured goods,
9 miscellaneous.

Sources: UN, *Yearbook of International Trade Statistics*; IMF, *International Financial Yearbook*.

Table 2

Self-sufficiency Ratios[a] for Selected Primary Commodities, 1960–91
(Percentage)

Year	1960	1970	1980	1990	1991
Agriculture and fisheries	93	81	76	68	67
Rice	102	104	87	100	100
Wheat	39	9	10	15	12
Pulse	44	13	7	8	7
Vegetables	100	99	97	91	90
Fruits	100	84	81	63	60
Meat	93	89	81	70	67
Milk and dairy	89	89	86	78	77
Fish and shellfish	110	108	97	86	85
Sugar	13	15	29	33	36
Fats and oils	42	22	27	29	24
Lumber	91	97	32	26	38
Crude petroleum	1.9	0.4	0.2	0.3	0.4
Coal	80	46	21	7	7
Iron ore	7.9	0.8	0.8	0	0
Copper ore	16	19	6	1	
Lead ore	48	32	22	4	
Zinc ore	59	39	37	16	
Tungsten	22	16	35	14[b]	

Notes: [a] 1988. [b] (Domestic production/consumption × 100.

Second, rapid growth was achieved through relocating workers from agriculture to industry. The rising demand for food had to be met by a smaller work force in farms. Not only farming came to be the domain of old farmers and farmers' wives, but also full-time farmers were replaced increasingly by part-time farmers. Thus supplies of farm products were supplemented by increasing imports, as clearly evidenced by the fall in the self-sufficiency ratios of wheat, soy beans and sugar, etc.[16]

Manufactured goods. Until the late 1970s, about 75 percent of Japan's imports consisted of food and crude unprocessed materials. The situation changed dramatically in the 1980s when the share of manufactured goods rose to around 50 percent. Though this increase must be discounted somewhat for the reduction in payments for petroleum and other primary-good imports on account of the reverse oil shock in the late 1980s, still the increase is impressive.

Table 3 shows the commodity composition of Japan's imports in 1980 and 1990 and the expansion ratios between them. The increase is more pronounced in finished goods than in semi-fabricated industrial materials. Of finished goods, imports of durable consumer goods such as passenger cards and consumer electronics expanded most, followed by nondurable consumer goods (two-thirds of

Table 3

The Composition and Increase of Japan's Imports of Goods, 1980 and 1990
(in U.S. Dollars)

| | | | 1990 value |
| | | | --- |
	1980	1990	1980 value
(A) By type of goods			
Total	100.0	100.0	1.7
Food and other direct consumption goods	11.5	13.8	2.0
Industrial materials and supplies	77.1	54.3	1.2
Crude materials	15.4	11.4	1.2
Crude petroleum	49.8	24.4	0.8
Industrial chemicals	4.3	6.7	2.6
Metals	3.8	6.2	2.7
Textiles	1.0	1.5	2.6
Other	2.8	4.3	3.0
Capital goods	6.5	14.0	3.6
General machinery	2.7	6.0	3.7
Electric machinery	1.8	5.5	5.1
Transport equipment	1.3	2.2	2.8
Other	0.6	0.3	1.0
Durable consumer goods	1.7	8.6	8.5
Household equipment	0.1	0.3	4.5
Household electric appliances	0.1	0.5	8.9
Passenger cars	0.3	2.6	13.7
Toys and musical instruments	0.4	0.4	1.3
Other	0.8	4.8	10.4
Nondurable consumer goods	1.9	6.0	5.3
Textile products	1.3	4.0	5.1
Other	0.6	2.0	6.7
Manufactured goods	22.8	50.3	3.7
Finished	10.1	28.7	4.7
Other	12.7	21.6	2.8
Other	1.3	3.1	4.1
(B) By source (SITC 5 to 8)			
Total	100.0	100.0	3.9
Developed areas	66.5	62.5	3.7
U.S.	33.5	27.6	3.2
EEC	21.3	24.6	4.5
EFTA	5.2	5.4	3.9
Other	6.7	4.9	3.2
Developing areas	33.5	37.5	4.5
Asia	25.1	32.5	5.0
Other	8.4	5.0	2.5

Sources: (A) Ministry of Finance, *Foreign Trade Returns.* (B) UN, *Monthly Bulletin of Statistics,* February and May 1993.

Table 4

The Import (fob)/Export (fob) Ratio of Manufactured Goods

SITC	Description	1980 Japan	1990 Japan	USA	EEC	EFTA
(5 to 8)	All manufacturing	0.21	0.36	1.29	0.90	0.97
5	Chemicals	0.81	0.85	0.58	0.83	0.86
7	Machinery and transport equipment	0.10	0.18	1.22	0.88	1.06
(78)	Passenger cars	0.022	0.13	3.39	0.88	2.57
—	All others	0.12	0.19	1.02	0.89	0.95
(6 + 8)	Other manufactured goods	0.31	0.87	1.85	0.87	0.93
65	Textile yarns and fabrics	0.33	0.66	1.30	0.94	1.13
67	Iron and steel	0.052	0.32	3.12	0.87	0.81
68	Nonferrous metals	1.92	3.29	1.87	1.29	0.62
(69)	Other metal products	0.10	0.38	1.43	0.85	1.01
84	Clothing	2.89	14.20	9.80	1.22	3.47
—	All others	0.84	0.77	1.64	0.85	0.82

Source: UN, *Monthly Bulletin of Statistics,* February and May 1992, Spectial Table D.

which are textile products) and producer durables, especially electric machinery.[17] Looked at by source, imports of manufactured goods rose more from Western Europe and Asia and less from the U.S. and the non-Asian developing areas.

Despite this rapid increase in manufactured imports in terms of dollar figures, the increase turns out to be modest when compared with the manufacturing sector's GDP, because of the appreciation of the yen value. The ratio rose from 10.4 percent in 1980 to 13.9 percent in 1990.[18]

(v) Intra-industry vs. inter-industry trade

Nowadays, in the trade in manufactured goods between industrial countries, intra-industry trade is more common than inter-industry trade. Inter-industry trade is governed by the traditional principle of comparative advantage: a country exports goods at comparative advantage and imports goods at comparative disadvantage. By contrast, intra-industry trade is trade in goods subject to product differentiation. While the other advanced countries gravitated toward intra-industry trade in manufactured goods, Japan still clings to inter-industry trade (called "horizontal trade" in the Japanese literature). The fact that Japan's manufactured trade is heavily unbalanced between the export and import side (Table 1) is a ready-made piece of corroboration of this assertion.

To be more specific, one can look at Table 4 which compares the import–export ratios of sufficiently narrowly defined commodity groupings (SITC 1– and 2–digits) for the U.S., EU, and EFTA in 1990 with Japan in 1980 and 1990.[19]

For a commodity group for which the ratio is close to 1, intra-industry trade can be judged to be dominant, and while in the case of a commodity group for which the ratio is close to 0 or very large, inter-industry trade is likely to dominate. By this criterion, trade is mostly of intra-industry type in the U.S. and Western Europe. Significant exceptions are passenger cars (U.S. and EFTA), iron and steel (U.S.), nonferrous metals (U.S.), and clothing (U.S. and EFTA).

In the case of Japan, while there was a general increase in the import–export ratio from 1980 to 1990, the increase was not large enough to shift Japan's trade from the inter-industry to intra-industry type. However, the ratio increased substantially for textile yarns and fabrics and, especially, clothing and nonferrous metals. Japan lacks comparative advantage in the production of nonferrous metals. The loss of comparative advantage was aggravated in the case of finished textile products. Thus, while Japan's imports of manufactured goods expanded considerably in the 1980s, the increase was not enough to establish intra-industry trade as the main mode of trade.[20]

(vi) Export–import imbalance by region

The export–import imbalance by commodity also implies the export–import imbalance by region. Even if Japan exports and imports are globally balanced, they are distributed unevenly by region on the export and import sides. In bilateral trade balances, there would always be surpluses with the U.S., European countries, and East Asia and deficits with the Middle East from which Japan imports crude petroleum. This imbalance is an inevitable consequence of Japan's trade structure. When Japan's exports exceeded its imports by a substantial margin, Japan maintains trade surpluses with almost all countries. The imbalance is the largest with the U.S. Since the largest trade deficit the U.S. has is with Japan, it is natural that the U.S. administration is particularly concerned with this deficit.[21] It is the direct cause of the public sentiment in the U.S. against Japan, leading to its proposal of restricting Japan's exports to the U.S.[22] As noted, the U.S. shared less in Japan's expansion of imports of manufactured goods in the 1980s. Since Japan increased its imports from Western Europe and East Asia, this must mean that either U.S. goods are not sufficiently competitive, or fail to meet Japanese preferences, or are not promoted enough to penetrate the opening Japanese market. Whatever the underlying reason may be, trade frictions with the U.S. are likely to continue if the present condition persists.

(vii) The issue of market access

The Structural Impediment Initiative (SII), the latest round of U.S.-Japan trade negotiations beginning in 1989 (replaced in 1993 by the Comprehensive Action Program), broadened the coverage of trade issues from Japan's exports to Japan's imports. It is alleged that the bilateral trade deficit which the U.S. has with Japan is not only due to the excessive export promotion by Japan but also to the closedness of Japan's domestic market. The U.S. side argues that non-tariff barriers, especially various practices in domestic trade, prevent U.S. goods from penetrating Japanese markets. The Japanese side always rebuts by noting that the Japanese markets are as open to foreign goods as to domestic goods, claiming that the U.S. failure to penetrate Japanese markets is due to the lack of effort on the part of U.S. exporters.

Whatever the argument may be, it is true that the accessibility to Japanese markets is poor on account of Japan's complicated distribution system. Imported manufactured goods are usually sold by large-scale retail stores (department stores, large supermarkets, etc.), but the expansion of large-scale retail stores was strictly restricted by the Large-Scale Retail Store Law (Daitenho), an outgrowth of the Department Store Law, which has been in force since 1974.[23] The law required large retail stores (defined by floor space) to get prior approval for any change in their operations (including new entry, expansion of space, opening hours, etc.) from the government authorities. Since the authorizing commissions were strongly influenced by local merchants, the approval was stringent and slow to come. Thus, when American retailers wanted to advance into Japan, they met stiff resistance from the Japanese government. It became a serious issue in the U.S.-Japan trade negotiations. The Ministry of International Trade and Industry (MITI) finally agreed in 1992 to relax the law. Now the approval process is to be expedited. Also, large stores can now install sales floors for imported goods with no government approval within a certain limit. (The law is expected to be repealed in a few years.)

The relaxation of the Daitenho is supposed to increase imports of finished consumer goods. Note, however, the foreign consumer goods which are likely to be imported are those which compete with large-firm products which are largely standardized or expensive, luxury goods. Small-firm products are still successfully resisting the inroad of foreign goods. This point is clear from Table 3. Imports of nondurable consumer goods except textile products are still only a very small fraction of Japan's consumption. Thus prices of small-firm products have been affected very little by cheaper import goods.[24]

One contributing factor for poor market access in Japan is the dominant role of giant trading firms which handle the bulk of Japan's imports.[25] Vertical integration in the domestic markets running from manufacturers to retailers is also pronounced for keiretsu groups (Lawrence 1993).

b. The Structure of Capital Flows

(i) The current-account balance[26]

Japan's current account began to register a surplus since the mid-1960s except for the duration of the two oil shocks (1973–75 and 1979–80). The surplus was as much as 4 percent of GDP in 1986 (Table 5).

The persistent current-account surplus can be seen in the well-known investment-savings identity:

Table 5

Japan's Foreign-Trade Indicators, 1970–92. (A) exports and imports as percent of GDP; (B) nominal exchange rate and purchasing power parity (¥/$); (C) manufactured imports/total imports of goods percent

	(A)						(B)			(C)
	Exports		Imports		Balance					
Year	G&S	G	G&S	G	G&S	G	e	ep	e/ep	M_{mfg}/M
1970	10.8	9.5	9.5	7.7	1.3	1.8	360.00	241	149	29.8
1971	11.7	10.4	9.0	7.2	2.7	3.2	349.33	242	144	27.9
1972	10.6	9.5	8.3	6.6	2.3	2.9	303.17	245	124	28.9
1973	10.0	8.9	10.0	8.0	0	0.9	271.70	260	105	30.2
1974	13.6	12.1	14.4	11.9	-0.8	0.2	292.08	286	102	23.4
1975	12.8	11.2	12.8	10.2	0	1.0	296.79	280	106	20.7
1976	13.6	12.0	12.8	10.3	0.8	1.7	294.35	284	104	21.5
1977	13.1	11.7	11.5	9.3	1.6	2.4	268.51	283	95	21.5
1978	11.1	10.0	9.4	7.4	1.7	2.6	210.44	277	76	26.7
1979	11.6	10.2	10.5	9.9	1.1	0.3	219.14	261	84	26.0
1980	13.7	12.4	14.6	12.2	-0.9	0.2	226.74	250	91	22.8
1981	14.7	13.0	13.9	11.3	0.8	1.7	220.54	237	93	24.3
1982	14.6	12.7	13.8	11.2	0.8	1.5	249.08	226	110	26.0
1983	13.9	12.4	12.2	9.9	1.7	2.5	237.51	222	107	25.2
1984	15.0	13.4	12.3	10.0	2.7	3.4	237.52	219	108	29.8
1985	14.5	13.1	11.1	9.0	3.4	4.1	238.54	217	110	31.0
1986	11.4	10.5	7.4	5.9	4.0	4.6	168.52	216	78	41.8
1987	10.4	9.6	7.2	6.1	3.2	3.8	144.64	210	69	44.1
1988	10.1	9.1	7.8	5.9	2.3	3.2	128.15	204	63	49.0
1989	10.7	9.0	9.3	6.7	1.4	2.3	137.96	200	69	50.3
1990	10.8	9.8	10.1	7.3	0.7	2.5	144.79	196	74	54.9
1991	10.4	9.4	8.5	6.5	1.9	2.9	134.71	192	70	50.8
1992	10.2	9.3	7.8	5.9	2.4	3.4	126.65	190	67	50.2

Sources: (A) IMF, *International Financial Statistics Yearbook, 1993*, (G&S = goods and services, G = goods [fob]). (B) OECD, *National Accounts* (e = annual average of the exchange rate, ep = purchasing power parity). (C) Ministry of Finance, *Foreign Trade Statistics*.

$$(S-I) = (G-T) + (X-M)$$

where $(S-I)$ is the saving surplus in the private domestic economy, $(G-T)$ the government budget deficit, and $(X-M)$ the current-account surplus. In the rapid growth period, investment was constrained by savings, while the government operated under the injunction of the balanced budget. The current account began to register a surplus only from the mid-1960s. Then, in the late seventies, economic growth slowed down. Relative to GDP, investment fell more than savings. The resulting savings surplus was absorbed into the government deficit, which came to be some 4 percent of GDP. National debt soon rose from 6 percent of GDP (1972–74) to above 40 percent. It became imperative for the Treasury to balance the budget. The growth of government expenditure was tempered while the tax revenue continued to increase with economic growth. By the late 1980s, the national government succeeded in balancing the budget and began to maintain a surplus. While this went on, the Japanese economy was depressed in the early 1980s. As investment fell, the savings surplus expanded. It went into the capital account, and the capital account deficit (= the current-account surplus) continued to rise as a percent of GDP. The Japanese economy then went into a long boom (November 1986 to March 1991). As the domestic economy recovered, the savings surplus diminished and the current-account surplus fell to 0.7 percent of GDP in 1990. In the latest recession, it again rose (Table 5).

(ii) The real exchange rate

Changes in the balance-of-payments position which took place since the floating of the yen exchange rate in 1973 are associated with changes in the real exchange rate. The real exchange rate is conveniently expressed as the ratio of the nominal exchange rate (e) to purchasing power parity $(e\rho)$, both in ¥/$ terms. As shown in Table 5 (B), $e\rho$ has been on a downward trend since the mid-1970s, reflecting the fact that inflation has been more moderate in Japan than in the U.S. The nominal exchange rate has been on a sharper downward trend, owing to the fact that Japan's export goods, produced mainly by large firms, became increasingly cheaper relative to goods and services at large, on account of more rapid productivity growth in the export sector. Thus, the real exchange rate fell far below 1. The exception, however, was in the early 1980s (1979 to 1985) when the yen was very cheap.

One can assume that the real exchange rate is determined at the intersection of the net export curve and the net capital outflow curve, both as functions of the real exchange rate.[27] In the early 1980s when the domestic economy generated a rising savings surplus, the surplus was exported as capital outflows. As the net capital outflow curve shifted to the right, the real exchange rate rose. It made exports cheaper (in dollars) and imports dearer (in yen). Then, the current-account balance came into a surplus.

In the late 1980s, this mechanism worked in a reverse gear. As the domestic

Table 6

The Balances of Foreign Assets and Liabilities as Percent of GDP (Balances as of Year-end)

Year	Assets	Liabilities	Net Assets
1970	9.9	7.6	2.3
1975	12.1	10.7	1.4
1980	16.1	14.9	1.2
1985	34.7	24.4	10.3
1990	65.6	53.9	11.6

Source: Economic Planning Agency (Japan), *Annual Report on National Accounts,* various issues.

economy recovered, the savings surplus diminished and, consequently, the net capital outflow curve shifted to the left. The real exchange rate fell. After it bottomed out in 1988, it rose somewhat but again has been falling. While the dollar is undervalued relative to most OECD currencies, the under-valuation has been most pronounced with the yen.

The especially sharp increase in the real value of the yen since 1986 indicates the widening of price differentials between traded goods and nontraded goods in Japan. Services and nontradeables became increasingly more expensive in the late 1980s. The latter category apparently includes Japan's small-firm manufactured goods.

(iii) The structure of foreign assets and liabilities

Capital flows add up to the country's balance of foreign assets and liabilities. With the persistent surpluses in the current account, Japan became the largest net creditor to the rest of the world. By contrast, the U.S. turned itself into the largest net debtor in the late 1980s. Japan apparently has become the most important creditor to the U.S. This situation puts the U.S. in an awkward position in dealing with Japan. On the one hand, the U.S. deplores its large trade deficit with Japan but, on the other hand, it has to depend much on Japan for financing its own deficits.

Table 6 shows how Japan's balances of foreign assets and liabilities changed over time. They were relatively modest through the 1970s. The explosion occurred in the 1980s when Japan maintained chronic current account surpluses. The increases in assets, liabilities, and net assets in the first half of the eighties are impressive. The increases in assets in liabilities continued in the second half of the decade, though net assets remained more stable relative to GDP (on account of the fall in the ¥/S rate).

A salient feature of Japan's foreign balance through all these years is that Japan lends long and borrows short. As seen in Table 7, the net balance is

Table 7

Japan's Foreign Assets and Liabilities (as of March 1993 in U.S. $bn)

	Assets	Liabilities	Net Assets
Long-term	1,315.6	658.5	657.1
Private	1,132.2	578.8	553.4
Direct investment	248.1	15.5	232.6
Government	183.4	79.6	103.8
Short-term	719.7	863.2	−143.5
Private	646.9	807.2	−160.3
Financial accounts	600.0	684.7	−84.7
Government	72.8	55.9	16.9
Total	2,035.2	1,521.6	513.6

Source: Ministry of Finance (Japan), *Zaisei Kin'yu tokei Geppo.*

positive on the long-term account and negative on the short-term account. The latter is largely due to the financial account of private financial institutions. Financial institutions, if they find surplus funds after meeting the domestic demand for loanable funds, channel them into short-term overseas investment. Thus, the net short-term balance is seen to be relatively volatile over the course of a business cycle. It is apparent that this part of the foreign balance plays the role of a safety valve in macroeconomic adjustments.

Another important feature is the limited position of direct investment; almost nil on the liabilities side. This point is made clearer if one compares the relative structure of foreign assets and liabilities between the U.S. and Japan (Table 8). The U.S. is the biggest direct investor, but it receives nearly as much foreign direct investment from foreign investors. By contrast, Japan is not only a small direct investor[28] but has very little foreign direct investment in Japan. This is stark evidence that the Japanese economy is still closed in this area.

4. Trade Policy[29]

a. Trade Policy

Trade policy intervenes in the interactive process between economic growth and foreign trade, either by accelerating it or retarding it (positive or passive policies). It also regulates capital flows.

The positive policy was particularly emphasized in the 1950s in the form of infant-industry protection. A number of infant industries targeted for expansion was given strong protection through tariffs and quotas. The case in point is the automobile industry. In the 1950s, Japanese automobiles were poor in quality

Table 8

The Structure of Foreign Assets and Liabilities: U.S. vs. Japan (U.S., December 1991; Japan, March 1993)

	In bn $		Percent of GDP	
	U.S.	Japan	U.S.	Japan
Assets	2,107.0	2,035.2	37.1	54.6
Direct investment	800.0	148.1	14.1	4.0
Liabilities	2,488.9	1,521.6	43.8	40.8
Direct investment	654.1	15.5	11.5	0.4
Net assets	−381.9	513.6	−6.7	13.8
GDP	5,677.5	3,725.9	100.0	100.0

Note: GDP: U.S. (1991); Japan (1992, converted by the ¥/$ rate of 124.75).
Sources: U.S., *The Economic Report of the President,* 1993 (January 1993), Table B–99, Japan, Ministry of Finance, *Zaisei Kin'yu Tokei Geppo.*

and high in cost. Insulated from foreign competition by import restrictions, the industry was strengthened and became internationally competitive by the mid-1960s. In assisting the automobile industry, the government not only restricted imports of foreign cars but also gave preferential financing through the Japan Development Bank. Other export promotion measures include accelerated depreciation of equipment, export subsidies, export financing, and special tax provisions, etc. The "Buy Japanese" government procurement policy was also notable in computers. The "export-or-perish" mentality which permeated over Japan's trade policy at that time came to be increasingly under foreign criticism. Thus, export promotion measures were gradually removed as the Japanese economy became more mature.

It was noted earlier that import restrictions were heavier on manufactured goods and lighter on foods and crude materials.[30] On manufactured goods, these restrictions were largely removed and the tariff rates continued to be reduced. By now, in terms of the average tariff rate, Japan is quite comparable with other developed countries.[31] Some farm products, especially rice, beef, and citrus, were subject to quotas. Domestic producers' lobbying efforts were strong. However, toward the end of the 1980s, the quotas on beef and citrus were finally replaced by tariffs (though tariff rates remain very high—50 percent on beef in 1993).

The last bastion of import restrictions was rice, which has been officially controlled by the government since 1939. As the demand for rice has been steadily falling, the supply tended to overrun demand. However, the government continued to maintain official control over rice by annually setting official buying and selling rice prices as well as by limiting the rice acreage. While control still continues, a substantial amount of rice is now freely traded, with the official price setting the lower bound of free prices.[32] Since the government wanted to maintain income parity between farmers and industrial workers, the price of rice steadily rose and eventually became several (seven to eight) times as high as the international price. However, the importation of rice continued to be prohibited.

The U.S. is the second largest exporter of rice (next to Thailand), and from the mid-1980s American rice producers began to demand entry into the Japanese rice market. To appease American opinion, the Japanese government lowered the official rice price from 1987 onward.

U.S.-Japan negotiations on rice became very intense. Then, the bad weather of 1993 resulted in a rice crop failure, and the government had to lift the rice embargo temporarily through emergency imports to fill the 25 percent shortfall in rice supply. This event, along with the tariffication of rice imports by Korea shortly before, expedited the negotiations and a final agreement was concluded in December 1993 to allow a small amount of rice imports on a quota basis for the next several years before Japan switches to tariffs.[33] This is the beginning of the end of Japan's rice control, which has lived beyond its usefulness.[34]

b. Capital Control

Import restrictions cannot be effective unless movements of capital are also restricted. So, as an integral part of trade policy, the Japanese government enforced capital controls. Both capital outflows and inflows were controlled under the Foreign Exchange and Foreign Trade Control Law (enacted in 1949). For example, the Ministry of Finance used to turn down applications for joint ventures when foreign interests were to become the majority stockholder of such a firm. This restriction explains why there is only a very small amount of foreign direct investment in Japan. While liberalization of capital transactions was the condition of Japan's entry in the IMF and the OECD in 1964, full liberalization had to wait until 1980 when the law was finally revised. Prior government approvals were no longer required, and movements of capital were made "in principle" free. This coincided with the rapid expansion of Japan's capital outflows in the 1980s.

c. Trade Frictions

Another important task of trade policy is to cope with recurrent trade frictions. Various arrangements had to be agreed upon with trade partners. Frictions arise mainly because Japan's exports are concentrated in a few major industrial goods directed to a few regions (the U.S., Europe, and East Asia).

Trade frictions became increasingly serious since the late 1960s as Japan's industrial exports came to occupy a larger share of the world market. Goods under friction also changed in character, shifting from textiles in the last sixties to steel and TVs in the 1970s, and to automobiles and semi-conductors in the 1980s.[35] For example, Japan's automobile exports to the U.S. were placed on voluntary export restraints (VERs) in 1981 and the restriction is still in force.

As more Japanese capital goes abroad in foreign direct investment, another kind of conflict arises with the host country. Japanese subsidiary manufacturing firms often depend very much on parts and components imported from Japan ("knock-down" plant). They generate very little value added locally. Hence, a number of European countries now adopt a local content law whereby foreign-owned factories in their territory must incorporate a certain percentage of locally produced inputs in their finished products.[36]

5. The Future

a. Interpretation of the Present

The most significant macroeconomic feature of Japan has been its chronic current account surplus, and opinions are divided on how to look at this. At the one extreme, one can argue that the current account surplus is nothing but a reflection of the savings surplus and it is what should be expected from the operation of the macroeconomic mechanism (position most staunchily defended by Komiya).[37] Others, who are more concerned with the macroeconomic image of Japan or with promoting harmony in the world economy, recognize Japan's need to reduce the current account surplus through expanding imports (by making Japanese markets more open).[38]

I have already touched upon whether Japanese markets are really closed or not. The government position has always been that Japanese markets are as open as elsewhere and that the current account surplus cannot be attributed to the closedness of the Japanese markets.[39] Even so, it is an undeniable fact that Japan's imports of manufactured goods are very low relative to GDP, and as previously mentioned, the failure of more vigorous import expansion in recent years must be due to the strong market resistance of small domestic producers who cater much better for peculiar local preferences.[40] In fact, the 1987 Maekawa Commission Report which prepared a set of guidelines for restructuring the Panese economy recommended shifting aggregate demand toward domestic demand away from exports and stimulating imports of manufactured goods.[41]

b. The Future

Prying open Japan's market from the outside has proved to be rather futile. Hence, any major change must come from the inside. The most fundamental of internal factors is obviously the country's savings-investment balance. The current account position of Japan has undergone serious changes over time in the four decades under study, principally on account of basic changes in the domestic savings-investment balance. Thus, one must look at what will happen to the savings-investment balance in the future.

What is certain in this uncertain world is Japan's rapid population aging. With the continued decline in the birth rate, the working-age population (ages 15–64) is projected to begin to contract in the mid-1990s with the initial rate of minus 0.5 percent per annum. The total population will start declining around the year 2010. In between, the old-age dependency ratio (population aged 65 and above/working-age population) will increase from the present 17 percent (1990) to 34 percent (2010), and subsequently reach a peak of 43 percent (2020).[42]

Old people have to be supported publicly and privately. Since it is anticipated that public support will be reduced,[43] private support must be increased. The net effect is a further reduction in the national savings rate. While investment demand will also decrease (relative to GDP) because of slower growth, general circumstances seem to indicate that savings decrease more than investment. Then, the savings-investment balance may become even negative. Provided that the government maintains a balanced budget, the world-be savings deficit must be met by a current account deficit.[44]

How are Japan's exports and imports to perform while this is going on? Japan's exports grew faster than world trade until the mid-1990s. This was partly due to the favorable price effect (Table 9), and also the fact that Japan was growing faster than other countries. However, in the late 1980s, Japan's exports were growing at a rate comparable with world trade, while the price effect ceased to apply. It seems plausible that Japan's exports have now reached a plateau. One may therefore argue that, henceforth, Japan's exports will maintain their expansion *pari passu* with world trade. However, as the East Asian countries, which have been industrializing at a rapid rate since the mid-1980s, are to compete with Japan in the third-country market, Japan's exports can grow only if Japan upgrades its export products. This is no easy task.[45]

The slowdown in export expansion, however, is not inconsistent with the slowdown of economic growth. As noted above, the working-age population will begin falling at the rate of 0.5 percent per annum from 1995 onward.[46] Assume that the on-going reduction of working hours will be completed by the year 2000. One may take an optimistic view that hourly labor productivity will maintain its historical growth rate of 3.2 percent observed during 1975–90. Then, real GDP will grow at 2.7 percent.[47] The world GDP growth rate may be somewhat less than its historical rate of 3.1 percent (1975–90), say, 2.7–2.8 percent. Then, Japan's GDP growth rate will finally come down to be at par with the world growth rate. Likewise, Japan's export growth may keep in step with world-trade expansion.

More important is what will happen on the import side. If the savings deficit is to be met by current account deficit, imports must exceed exports. This in-

Table 9

Exports and Export Unit Value, Japan/World, Percent

	Exports	Export Unit Value (1985 = 100)
1970	6.6	129
1971	7.4	127
1972	7.5	131
1973	6.8	128
1974	6.8	114
1975	6.7	105
1976	7.1	105
1977	7.6	105
1978	7.4	102
1979	6.5	91
1980	6.8	97
1981	8.1	94
1982	8.0	94
1983	8.7	97
1984	9.4	99
1985	9.7	100
1986	10.5	110
1987	9.8	109
1988	9.8	114
1989	9.4	111
1990	8.6	101
1991	9.2	110
1992	9.3	

Source: IMF, *International Financial Statistics.*

crease in imports must come chiefly from manufactured goods, especially those goods which compete with small-firm products. In other words, this is the area where the restructuring of the Japanese economy should take place. When this barrier is broken, the widening gap between the exchange rate and purchasing power parity will be narrowed to some extent. It is only then that Japan's consumers can enjoy their rightful share of economic progress.

Notes

1. There has been a large outpouring of articles and books on Japan's trade and trade policy in recent years, reflecting the rise in international attention given to Japan's trade and capital flows. See Balassa and Noland (1989), Bergsten and Cline (1985), Bergsten and Noland (1993), Lincoln (1990), and Krugman (1992), to name just a few.

2. Sections 2 and 3 rely on Sato (1993). See Sugimoto and Fujiwara (1992) for a comprehensive survey and Japanese references.

3. As percent of foreign exchange earnings, special procurement amounted to as much as 38 percent in 1953 and was still 12 percent in 1959 (see Yamazawa and Yamamoto (1979), Table 2–7).

4. The 1974/1955 ratio of GDP produced (in current value) was 19 times for manufacturing and 14 times for non-manufacturing. (Their relative shares were 37:63 in 1974). The difference would be much greater in real terms since manufactured goods became relatively cheaper over time. (Data based on Economic Planning Agency, 1991).

5. The labor force in agriculture and forestry declined from 16.5 million (46 percent of the total labor force) in 1950, to 12.7 million (29 percent) in 1960, 8.4 million (17 percent) in 1970, 5.3 million (10 percent) in 1980, and 4.1 million (7 percent) in 1990. (See Management and Coordination Agency).

6. From 1960 to 1970, nominal wages increased by about 200 percent while the CPI rose by about 70 percent (see Ohkawa and Shinohara, 1979, Tables A-51 and A-52).

7. Technology imports rose from $2.6 million in 1950 to $95 million (1960), $433 million (1970), $1,439 million (1980), and $6,039 million (1990). Japan is still a net technology importer. In 1991, technology exports were 47 percent of technology imports (see Bank of Japan).

8. Japan's foreign reserve increased from 3.2 billion SDRs in 1970 to 12.7 in 1971 and 15.2 in 1972, then fell to 8.5 in 1973 (see IMF).

9. The urban land price index doubled from March 1970 to September 1974, then fell by about 5 percent. It began to climb back again in 1978. (See Japan Real Estate Institute).

10. The average stock price rose unbrokenly six times from early 1980 to early 1990, then more than halved by 1992. The average urban land price rose by 51 percent from September 1978 to September 1986 and by 54 percent from September 1986 to September 1991. Since then, it has been falling.

11. In the case of Japan, the exports/GDP ratio rose from a little over 10 percent before the 1973–74 oil shock to as high as 15 percent in 1985 and fell toward 10 percent since then. In the case of the U.S., the ratio rose from a little over 5 percent in the early 1970s, then increased toward 9–10 percent from 1974 on.

12. In 1990, some twenty commodities accounted for one half of Japan's merchandise exports. Exports as percent of total production range from VCRs (95 percent), Camera (82 percent), ships (80 percent), watches and clocks (80 percent), electronic calculators (49 percent), passenger cars (45 percent), TV receivers (39 percent), and down to iron and steel (17 percent) and washing machines (15 percent). For these commodities, the average share of exports in production was 35 percent in 1990. (See Sato 1993, Table 12).

13. For ten top manufacturing exporters, exports were 48 percent of sales in Japan and 17 percent in the U.S. (1984 figures as reported in *President,* 1985).

14. For details, see Sato (1991).

15. As the Japanese economy expanded faster than the rest of the world, its imports of primary goods continued to claim a larger share of world trade in primary goods. For example, in 1990, Japan was the top importer of iron ore (35.0 percent of world imports), coal (32.9 percent) and maize (28.5 percent) and the number 2 importer of crude petroleum (21.6 percent) and wheat (8.9 percent) (see UN).

16. Even those, of which the self-sufficiency ratio is still high, depend much on imported inputs (e.g., pork and chicken on imported feed grains and fish on petroleum required for ocean fishing).

17. Foreign luxury goods used to be sold at very high prices, owing to the high import duties and the "monopoly" profit exacted by the exclusive import agency agreements between foreign brand-good producers and Japanese importers (examples were Scotch

whisky, automobiles, high-class luggage, etc.). This practice broke down in the late 1980s when unauthorized importers began to import those goods and to undersell authorized importers (so-called parallel imports). Thus, for example, prices of Scotch whisky tumbled. On this issue, see Itoh (1992).

18. When the values of imports of finished manufactured goods are compared with corresponding GDP in 1980 and 1990, the ratio rose only slightly for durable goods (producer and consumer) from 9.2 to 10.2 percent. The ratio for nondurable goods rose from 1.0 to 6.8 percent and that for industrial supply and materials from 4.6 to 8.2 percent. (The corresponding U.S. figures for 1988 were 48.1, 14.8, and 8.4 percent respectively.) See Sato (1993), Table 13.

19. See, e.g., Saxonhouse (1993), Table 2 for an international comparison of intra-industry manufacturing trade indexes (1981 vs. 1991).

20. See Krugman (1983) for explaining that intra-industry trade expanded among developed countries on account of advantage in division of labor among these countries. Japan has apparently been an exception to the rule (more on this in Sato, 1990).

21. In 1991, U.S. imports from Japan (fob) amounted to $91.5 billion and exports to Japan $47.8 billion. The import surplus with Japan was $40.7 billion, while the U.S. maintained a trade surplus of $7.8 billion with all other industrial countries (*Economic Report of the President,* 1993).

22. The U.S. government, marshaling the reciprocity principle (when you export, you must import), called Japan and unfair trade country under its 1987 Omnibus Trade Act. Though the condemnation was latter lifted, the protectionist sentiment remains strong in the U.S. Congress.

23. On the Daitenho, see Kusano (1993).

24. In 1992 relative to 1982, the CPI was 1.028 for large-firm products and 1.152 for small-firm products (Bank of Japan). This disparity between them indicates that small firms so far have successfully insulated themselves from increased manufactured imports. (Compare the import price index of manufactured goods, which stood at 0.65.)

25. In 1990, the nine general trading firms handled 37 percent of Japan's exports and 58 percent of Japan's imports (Keizai Koho Center).

26. The current-account balance is the sum of the goods trade balance and the service trade balance. In Japan, the goods trade balance has been in surplus and the service trade balance has been in deficit, principally because trade in freight and insurance, tourism, etc., is in a deficit. The surplus in investment income has been increasing because Japan's net foreign assets balance has been on the rise.

27. See Sato and Lii (1994) for an econometric investigation of this mechanism with respect to Japan.

28. But Japan is the number three direct investor. As of the end of 1989, direct overseas investment outstanding was US$373 billion (30 percent of the world total), the U.K. $192 billion (15 percent), and Japan $154 billion (12 percent) (see JETRO, 1991).

29. On Japan's trade policy, see e.g., Komiya and Itoh (1988). The history of Japan's trade policy up to 1985 is reviewed in Sato (1992).

30. On Japan's import restrictions up to 1970, see Ozaki (1972).

31. For changes in the average tariff rate and restrictions on Japan's imports, see Komiya and Itoh (1988), Tables 4 and 5.

32. Of rice produced (net of farmers' own consumption), about one-third is now purchased by the government and the remaining two-thirds are sold on the free market at prices 30 percent or so higher than the official price.

33. The government will import rice at cheaper international prices and resell it at higher domestic prices. Unless domestic rice prices are lowered significantly, one cannot expect too much increase in rice demand.

Rice consumption is now a very small fraction of total personal consumption: 1.4 percent according to the 1991 Family Budget Survey. So, with the limited price effect, rice imports will not amount to too much even if all rice is imported. More important is its adverse effect on rice farmers who continued to enjoy a high-degree of government protection. Overcoming farmers' resistance was politically very hard to achieve.

34. The need for overhauling the antiquated Food Control Law (enacted in 1942) is very much recognized in Japan. But, strangely, consumer groups in Japan who should benefit from freer trade were very much lukewarm and did not give strong support for opening the rice market.

35. See Nagaoka (1993) on the history of Japan's trade frictions.

36. Another related problem is the trade between parent firms in Japan and their subsidiaries overseas. These subsidiaries both export to and import from Japan. What prices are employed in these intra-firm transactions becomes an important issue in corporate-income taxation.

37. Komiya is a leading authority on international economics and has been the Director-General of MITI's research institute.

38. One may argue that Japan's imports will increase substantially if all non-tariff barriers are removed (Gergsten and Noland, 1993).

39. Economic Planning Agency (1993, p. 289).

40. An opposite view is that, given population size, natural endowments, and human capital, Japan's imports are internationally no significant outlier (Saxonhouse, 1983). See also Sato (1986).

41. See the Maekawa Report as reported in EPA (1987). Commissioner Maekawa was ex-Chancellor of the Bank of Japan.

After Hosokawa became Prime Minister in August 1993, he organized a private study group in a similar vein to prepare a new set of guidelines for economic deregulations (including market access). This group is headed by Mr. Hiraiwa, president of the "Keidanren" (Employers' Organizations Federation).

42. These population projections are the latest prepared by the Ministry of Health and Welfare in 1992.

43. Social security benefits, which begin to be paid (at reduced rate) at age 60, are expected to be delayed to age 65 when the Public Pension Law is revised in 1995.

44. The latest long-term economic forecast prepared by the Japan Center for Economic Research, based on a detailed macroeconometric model, predicts a current account deficit in the target year 2000. See Murota and Kawamura (1993).

45. As noted, Japan's imports of manufactured goods increased from East Asia. Already, in 1993, Japan imported more color TVs than were exported.

46. It is assumed that the government holds on to the closed-door policy to shut out foreign workers. The number of illegal aliens who work in Japan rose sharply in the last few years (from 10,000 in 1986 to 300,000 in early 1993 according to the Ministry of Justice).

47. The latest five-year national plan (1992–96) calls for the better quality of life (*seikatsu taikoku* plan). While the target growth rate is 3.5 percent per annum, the plan is directed towards improvements in social welfare including a reduction of working hours from 2044 (1990) to 1800 hours.

Likewise, the JCER long-term forecast sets the growth rate at 3.3 percent for 1990–2000 and 2.7 percent for 2000–2010. Total manhours are to fall at −0.4 and −1.0 percent respectively. Thus, productivity growth rate is assumed to be 3.7 percent throughout. These rates are to be compared with the historical records of 1975–90: 4.3 percent (total growth), 1.1 percent (manhours), and 3.2 percent (productivity growth).

References

Balassa, B., and M. Noland (1988) *Japan in the World Economy* (Washington, DC: The Institute for International Economics).

Bank of Japan (various years), *Balance of Payments Monthly.*

Bank of Japan (various years), *Consumer Price Index.*

Bergsten, C.F., and W.R. Cline (1985), *The United States-Japan Economic Problem* (Washington, DC: The Institute for International Economics).

Economic Planning Agency (1991), *Report on National Accounts from 1955–1989* (Tokyo).

Economic Planning Agency (Japan) 1993), *Keizai Hakusho,* Economic White Paper of Japan (Tokyo: Government Printing Office).

IMF (1992), *International Financial Statistics Yearbook.*

Itoh, M. (1992). "Japan's Domestic-Foreign Price Gap, as viewed from the Firm's Price-Setting Behavior," *Japanese Economic Studies* 20 (Spring), 3–36.

Japan Real Estate Institute (various years), *Urban Land Price Index.*

JETRO (1991), *White Paper on Foreign Direct Investment.*

Keizai Koho Center (1992), *Japan 1992, An International Comparison* 45

Komiya, R., and M. Itoh (1988), "Japan's International Trade and Trade Policy," T. Inoguchi and D. Okimoto (eds.), *The Changing International Context,* vol. II of *The Political Economy of Japan* (Stanford, CA: Stanford University Press), 173–224.

Krugman, P. (1983), "New Theories of Trade Among Industrial Countries," *American Economic Review* 73 (May): 543–47.

———. (1992), *Trade with Japan, Has the Door Opened Wider?* (Chicago: University of Chicago Press).

Kusano, A. (1992), *Daitenho, Keizai Kisei no Kozo* (The Large-Scale Retail Store Law: The Structure of Economic Regulation) (Tokyo: Nihon Keizai Shimbunsha).

Lawrence, R.Z. (1993), "Japan's Different Trade Regime: An Analysis with Particular Reference to *Keiretsu,"* *Journal of Economic Perspectives* 7, 3–20.

Lincoln, E.J. (1990), *Japan's Unequal Trade* (Washington, DC: The Brookings Institution).

Management and Coordination Agency (various years), *Labor Force Survey.*

Murota, Y., and S. Kawamura (1993), "JCER Long-Term Economic Projections," *JCER Report* 5 (September).

Nagaoka, S. (1992), "An Economic Analysis of Trade Friction: Economic Effects of the Dumping Control and the Result-Oriented Trade Policy," *Japanese Economic Studies* 21 (Fall): 39–88.

Ohkawa, K., and M. Shinohara, eds. (1979), *Patterns of Japanese Economic Development, Quantitative Aspects* (New Haven: Yale University Press).

Ozaki, R. (1972), *The Control of Imports and Foreign Capital in Japan* (New York: Praeger). *President* (August 1985).

Sato, K. (1986), "The Externalization of Domestic Macroeconomic Performance: Export-led Growth or Growth-led Exports," M. Schmiegelow (ed.), *Japan's Response to Crisis and Change in the World Economy* (Armonk, NY: M.E. Sharpe), 181–209.

———. (1990) "Increasing Returns and International Trade: The Case of Japan," *Journal of Asian Economics* 1 (Spring): 87–114.

———. (1991), "Japan's Resource Imports," *Annals of the American Association of Political and Social Sciences,* no. 513 (January), 76–89.

———. (1992), "Trade Policies in Japan," D. Salvatore (ed.), *International Handbook of National Trade Policies* (Westport, CT: Greenwood Press), 109–30.

———. (1993), "Economic Growth and Foreign Trade in Japan," Y.Y.T. Kuark (ed.), *Comparative Asian Economics.*

Sato, K., and S.Y. Lii (1994), "Exchange-Rate Dynamics in Japan and Taiwan," *Journal of Asian Economics* 5 (Spring): 43–63.

Saxonhouse, G.R. (1993), "What Does Japanese Trade Structure Tell Us About Japanese Trade Policy?" *Journal of Economic Perspectives* 7 (Summer): 21–43.

Sugimoto, S., and S. Fujiwara, eds. (1992), *Nihon Boeki Tokuhon,* Reader on Japanese Trade (Tokyo: Toyo Keizai Shimposha).

UN (various years), *Yearbook of International Trade Statistics.*

Yamazawa, I., and Y. Yamamoto (1979), *Foreign Trade and Balance of Payments* (Tokyo: Toyo Keizai Shimposha).

Source/Permission: This article originally appeared in *The World Economy* 18, No. 2 (1995): 193–218. Reprinted by permission of Basil Blackwell, Ltd.

Part VII

The Government System

13

Recent Changes in Japanese Public Administration

Michio Muramatsu

Introduction

Japanese bureaucracy is in the process of transformation. This chapter will analyze the changes in Japanese public administration by way of presenting its underlying values. For a long time there has been a strong ideology of catch-up to the West that has regulated the implementation of all public policies in Japanese government. Among the various public policies, the policy that has been paid the most attention is economic and industrial policy.

There is no doubt that public administration has been regarded an important tool in promoting modernization and economic developments. However, the way in which Japanese public administration has contributed to economic development has not been directly granting aid or directing the industries by special industrial policies, but by keeping government small and saving resources for more direct economic investments and also by enhancing efficiency in the activities of public administration. Public administration with this idea of catch-up continued until the 1960s. In this period it has been said that Japan's public administration was oriented to producers rather than to consumers. Recently, however, there are signs of change in public administration. Japan has become a welfare state, expanding public finance. Furthermore, we now often hear that government is following a new logic of "consumers." I describe in this chapter the recent developments in Japanese public administration.

On the whole, I argue as follows. While given a goal of "catch-up to the West," Japanese government suffered from the scarcity of resources such as legal power or financial resources, while extending its business to building infrastructure in areas from education to health services as well as keeping peace and defending the country. Japan developed various ways and tools in order to overcome this problem and tried to fill the gap between ambition and resources.

Delegation of a large volume of government business to localities was one important way. Japanese local governments would be characterized by the size of their budgets and personnel. Central government introduced new technology and developed industries, typically textile, and then privatized them.

The purpose of this chapter is not to analyze the relation between government and industries in detail for the period of the past one hundred years, but to discuss the recent changes in public administration. I first examine what the ministry bureaucracies in central government have been doing in several policy areas and then show that they are trying to change themselves to adapt to new environments in the 1980s and later, after the Plaza Agreement in 1985 in particular.

Japanese Public Administration

Jurisdiction

It must be pointed out that the consideration of issues of administrative activities must be framed within jurisdictions. The substance of such jurisdiction is to permit and authorize various social activities, and sometimes to provide subsidies. Jurisdiction is also important in trials. The starting point for any litigation is determined by whether a court has jurisdiction for the case in question. The Meiji government was troubled when some of its domestic trial jurisdiction was usurped by foreign governments that had been granted with extraterritoriality through unequal treaties. Similarly, jurisdiction is a starting point in administration because it determines areas where authority can be exercised. Japan's public administration is characterized by the "extensive" jurisdiction. Modern governments have extensive jurisdictions over their people and their lands, whether it be policies governing rivers, education, or economic activities; however, the scope of the jurisdiction exercised by the Japanese government looks to be more extensive than any other advanced democratic country.

The principle of ultra vires restricts administrative activities in the United Kingdom and the United States. In the United Kingdom, the principle of ultra vires was weakened to some extent in the central government, but this principle strongly restricted local governments. When the welfare services provided by local governments expanded with the creation of the welfare state, restrictions on local governments as a whole were loosened. This stimulated Prime Minister Thatcher to advocate a new theory of local government that was more restrictive and preventive of expansion of its administrative activities. In Japan, the second article in the Local Government Act summarily defines the authority of local governments. There are many varieties of items listed in this article, and one might say that Japan's local governments have been given extensive roles to play. In addition, activities that are not clearly listed in this article may be legally and freely provided as long as they do not invade the rights of the citizens.

The central government interprets jurisdiction extensively so that any kind of activity may be carried out as long as it has relevance to the objectives of the law that establishes ministries and agencies. In other words, jurisdiction is defined not just by individual laws that give authority; it is based on Establishing Laws for Ministries and Agencies as well. Certainly, this does not necessarily mean that having jurisdiction grants the ability to influence or control (to use Samuels's word) a particular administrative agency. Having jurisdiction and having control are separate matters. As mentioned before, the Ministry of Finance controls budget procedures. However, the power to decide the contents of the budget lies largely with the government party (the Liberal Democratic Party; at least before the summer of 1993), and we must remember the aggressive activities of numerous pressure groups before we can talk about the government party. In a pluralistic political process, extensive jurisdiction means having many chips for bargaining negotiations. It appears that each of the ministries and agencies wants to have its own extensive jurisdiction for this purpose. In addition, Japanese administration is allowed to be interfering. Administrative guidance is an extensively used procedure. Japanese administration penetrates extensively into society.

Although I mentioned that Japanese public administration is interfering, this is separate from the issue of whether administrative agencies have the resources to do so. For example, if the execution of authority is resisted by some group or person, the administration overcomes such resistance by imposing sanctions. What is remarkable about Japan's public administration in this regard is the fact that sanctions are weak. For example, it frequently occurs that a law stipulates that a certain requirement has to be met, but the law does not specify sanctions to guarantee its execution. John Haley has pointed this out (Haley 1993). This weakness stems from the fact that the wording of laws is weak with respect to sanctions, but this weakness is also intimately connected with the fact that Japan's public administration has limited resources. The first question in this case is to what extent the will exists to execute an objective in the face of resistance, in other words, whether a supporting system exists for compulsory execution. The number of civil servants in Japan is about 47 per 1,000 working citizens. This is much fewer than the United States, where there are about 60 civil servants per 1,000 working citizens, or in France, where there are 50. It appears that the number of civil servants in Japan was not that large to start with, and since 1967 civil servants in the central ministries and agencies have been reduced in a real sense through the Law for the Fixed Number of Administrative Personnel. Positions such as nurses and police officers, however, were exempt from this reduction and were increased through various policies. Resources, such as authority, funds, and personnel, are scarce in Japan's public administration. The fact that it has "extensive jurisdiction but few resources" cannot help but determine the characteristics of Japan's public administration. Japanese ministry bureaucracies would compete for jurisdiction of a strong state in which state bureaucracy imposes its will upon private actions at every opportunity for the sake of increasing the resources in their territories, which would lead them to better positions for obtaining the *amakudai* jobs and their bargaining power vis-à-vis other political actors. However, "interfering" of Japanese ministries would not be that of a strong state in which state bureaucracy imposes its will upon those under regulation, but that of weak state in which state needs the consent of those under regulation to go farther.

Role of "Guarantor"

There are few developed analyses of the role of Japan's administration, although there is talk about the dominance of bureaucracy its size, and the presence of absence of the influence or dominance of political parties. This chapter, which discusses regulations and services, will be most appropriate to discuss this topic. The task here is to discover what general characteristics are common to all ministries and agencies, not to name the characteristics of individual areas such as the certification of textbooks by the Ministry of Education or financial and industrial policies of the Ministries of Finance (MOF) and International Trade and Industry (MITI). The most powerful and interesting thesis is Richard Samuels's concept of "guarantor" in describing the relationship. Using the energy industry as an example, he pointed out the following: The Japanese state does not manage the energy industry by monopolizing and managing it itself as France does; it does not create a monopolistic public enterprise that competes with the private sector. What it does is to act like a "guarantor" of the system by providing funds and networks so that the private sector can reach its maximum capability (Samuels 1987). Samuels attributes the system's success to this very role of the state. Indeed, there are many systems that attempt to support the efforts of the private sector to expand its capacities. These systems recognize maximally the autonomy of the private sector. By providing funds and information, MITI creates and supports consortiums that make cooperation between the private actors in the industrial sector concerned possible. Consortiums for which the Ministry of International Trade and Industry has mediated for the development of new technologies are numerous, including the Super LSI Technology Research Consortium and the Biochemical Development Center. In short, the state plays the role of mediator so that a mechanism is established through which enterprises in one industry can communicate with other industries. Organizing industrial associations is another typical activity. Furthermore, such organizations are not limited to economic administration alone; the National Social Welfare Council in welfare administration, and the Crime Prevention Association in police administration are two examples in other areas where the state may provide various services or solicit the cooperation of the citizens. Here again, the state does not take the responsibility of carrying out all associated work, be it day-care centers or community centers. It helps the activities of the private sector through its own special method, which may be referred to as playing the role of guarantor. That Samuels characterized Japanese-style administrative interference with the term "guarantor" is extremely to the point. A concrete example of the guarantor role is seen in the MOF's administration, where state is involved in the role of the escort to a convoy. Let us look at the administration of permits, licenses, and authorization to see how the guarantor concept is applied.

Regulation

Permits/Licenses and Authorizations

Permits and licenses refer to administrative activities in which, on the basis of certain activities that are generally prohibited in order to protect the public, an administrative agency lifts this prohibition in some cases and gives official approval to carry out such activities. Giving licenses to drivers and authorizing private railroads to charge fares are typical examples. In the more recent discussions of deregulation, the argument is for limiting the state's role of supervising permits/licenses or authorizations as much as possible because it is pointed out that this type of regulation has tended to create vested interests.

Although, legally speaking, permits/licenses or authorization should be granted as long as conditions that have been specified in the light of certain standards are met, the actual process is not an automatic application of clear-cut standards. Aggressive efforts are made to accomplish certain administrative objectives through such administrative means of giving permits/licenses or authorization. For example, the Ministry of International Trade and Industry would attempt to promote industry. Regardless of the success or failure of using such methods in promoting industry, it is clear that through this system of giving permits/licenses or authorizations the Japanese administration has placed a definite emphasis on production rather than using it for consumers' interests, at least up until the 1960s. Depending mainly on the bargaining power of the regulated, but at the same time depending on environmental factors such as internationalization, we see the different mixture of leadership on the side of administration and of the negotiating power on the side of private actors. In nurturing administration we see more the leadership of economic bureaucracy.

Nurturing Administration

The aggressive attitude of the Japanese public administration stems from its interest in nurturing industries. One extremely good example of this, all the more so because it was a shameful one, occurred in the banking securities industry between 1991 and 1993. It became publicly known that securities companies were compensating for their customers' losses in 1991. This issue of compensation created distrust among investors, resulting in their aversion to securities.

This in turn resulted in stock prices remaining very low for a prolonged period of time. Eventually, an auditing organization was established to eliminate the inappropriate practices of the securities companies. Let us look at this process.

The reason for the establishment of this auditing organization was the surging waves of criticism in the public opinion and calls for the creation of an organization independent of the Ministry of Finance so as to prevent the recurrence of similar incidents. At this point in time, the Second Administrative Reform Promotion Council [Daniji Gyosei Kaikaku Suishin Shingikai], which had been established in 1988 and had begun its activities, adopted this issue aggressively, proposing that a Japanese version of the SEC (Securities and Exchange Commission) be established. This was a criticism aimed at the Ministry of Finance, which was giving protection as well as regulation to the securities companies. This situation was like a baseball game in which the same person plays the role of coach as well as that of umpire.

The Ministry of Finance responded initially to this proposal with its own counterproposal for creating an auditing bureau or auditing department of the minister's secretariat by uniting the auditing sections for banking, securities, and international finance. As soon as the Ministry saw that its counterproposal would not be accepted, it proposed the establishment of the Financial Auditing Agency, which ultimately became the Supervisory Committee for Securities Exchanges [Shoken Torihiki Tou Kanshi Iinkai]. The initial ambitious attempt by the chairman of the Administrative Reform Promotion Council, Mr. Eiji Suzuki, was frustrated; the reform ultimately ended incompletely in that the committee has the authority to investigate but not to punish offenders. This was because of the desperate but successful efforts of the Ministry of Finance to prevent its jurisdiction from shrinking in any way. The background of this incident was Japan's economic administration's philosophy of playing the role of heading a "convoy" of industries.

Securities Administration

It is necessary to consider the beginning of the securities administration. In the past, a system of simple registration existed in the securities industry. It is said that there was a heated argument within the Ministry of Finance in 1975 as to whether a licensing system should be introduced. Some officials maintained that they were against a licensing system because that would make the ministry responsible for an unruly industry should a problem occur. Those who were in favor of the licensing system maintained that the very potential for such a risk meant that the licensing system should be introduced. The latter group is said to have voiced its opinion as follows: Administration of securities is not as solid as that of banking. Let us create a system where the securities industry can become responsible. It is the responsibility of the Ministry of Finance to create a solid securities market by shifting the role of the administration from one of policing to one of nurturing. Ultimately, the licensing system was introduced. Thus the nurturing of the securities industry became the purpose of the administration, and fees were fixed through an administrative guidance so that even if trading volume was small, profits could be made from the fees. This was an action in the so-called convoy escort style.

This convoy escort style was already practiced by the banking administration of the Banking Bureau of the Ministry of Finance. Since licenses were given to banks, it was unacceptable to the ministry to let financial institutions fall into financial difficulties. The solution to this was to make sure that in every measure taken, be it deciding on interest rates or planning for the schedule of deregulation, that the weakest financial institutions would be protected and keep up with others. In short, it is the same method of the convoy escort on the sea where the slowest ship sets the speed for the entire group. The Ministry of Finance would not recognize any new improved services, including better interest rates, of a bank that could go faster. The Ministry of Finance mediated in mergers if there was any financial institution whose finances deteriorated even in this protected environment. I cite the case of Sanwa Bank and Toyo Credit Bank in 1992 as an example of such a merger. This type of merger "administration" allows the rescue of the management of a weak bank, but this rescue administration operation is carried out at the expense of depositors of the bank whose finances are healthier. One of the problems of the nurturing administration is its neglect of consumers. This was clear in the loss compensation mechanism of securities companies when they compensated only for the losses of more powerful customers, and it has been exactly the same in banking.

Another problem of the nurturing administration is the fact that the relationship between the administration and industry becomes opaque as mutually dependent relations, or interdependent relations, develop between the administrative agency and a group that is the partner in this nurturing relationship (for example, the securities industry). Let me take an example from the securities administration again. Interdependence is related to the appointment of former government officials to positions of responsibility in private companies (a phenomenon known as *amakudari*, or "descent from heaven").

In order to rebuild the securities industry, which had been suffering from a business slump in 1965, Mr. Sadaichiro Morinaga, who was then the president of Japan Import Export Bank and one of the most prestigious vice-ministers of the Ministry of Finance, finally accepted the position of presidency of the Tokyo Stock Exchange after repeated invitations by the industry. Mr. Minoru Segawa, then the president of Nomura Securities, who was also acting as the chairman of the Tokyo Stock Exchange, played the central role in inviting him to the position. It was the talk at that time that "the don of the Finance Ministry" joined the world of stocks. Subsequently, many Finance Ministry officials took positions at companies in the securities industry.

Many "old boys" of the Finance Ministry took various positions in industry depending on the positions they held last: vice-minister level officials became the presidents of the Tokyo Stock Exchange; bureau chief level officials went to such associations as the Securities Association and the Credit Trust Association; and others went to various securities companies, their affiliated companies, research centers, and various other associations. It is said that there are currently about eighty career bureaucrats who are now working in the area of securities companies and other associations through this sort of "descent from heaven" and their numbers increase to well above one hundred if non-career bureaucrats are added.

The impression the general public gets from all this is that finance and securities administration are intimately connected to the old boys who take important positions in industry. However, the bureaucrats in the MOF dispute this interpretation. They assert that Japan's administration was successful because it was preventive. The Finance Ministry has to know before anybody else does what private businesses are doing and in what conditions they find themselves. Conversely, it is necessary for the private companies to know what the Finance Ministry is thinking so that smooth administration can be executed. Old boys are intermediaries in this exchange. It is extremely effective for the execution of administration and advantageous in collecting information to have old boys in the industry organizations and to have them control the industry. The number of retired officials taking important positions in areas like banking, securities, life insurance, and credit associations has thus increased year after year. It is said that it was not infrequent that some appointments were made at the very strong request of the Finance Ministry. City banks would take care of the retired officials in their economic research centers, overseas subsidiaries and affiliates, or as advisers, if not as their directors. The banks, which have accepted old boys, naturally expect some returns for their investments and began to demand them.

Securities and Exchange Law and Telecommunications Law

The jurisdiction for giving permits, licenses, and authorization is connected with the sectionalism of the ministries and agencies. Let me give you a famous example of sectionalism between two bureaus of the Ministry of Finance. In the winter of 1992, a financial system reform was in progress, planned to go into effect in 1993. The critical focus point was what to do with Article 65 of the Securities and Exchange Law, the issue of allowing banks and securities companies into their respective turfs. Article 65 prohibits banks and trust companies from carrying out securities business. This had the effect of protecting the securities industry.

In 1990, the Financial System Research Council [Kin'yu Seido Chosakai] (chaired by a former National Tax Agency director, Mr. Michio Kondo), which was under the Banking Bureau, and which functions as a spokesman for banks, as it were, put together an idea in its interim report, saying that it was necessary for respective financial institutions to enter into other business areas extensively.

The Banking Bureau, which was acting as the secretariat, maintained that Article 65 of the Securities and Exchange Law should be either revised or its application be changed, reflecting the desires of large banks to become universal banks where securities businesses are conducted in parallel.

Opposed to this group was the Securities Exchange Council [Shoken Torihiki Shingikai] (chaired by a former administrative vice-minister of the Finance Ministry, Mr. Hiroshi Tanimura), which is under the Securities Bureau and which is a cheer group for the securities industry. An interim report was also issued by the Securities Exchange Council, which was discussing issues surrounding financial deregulation, such as a bank entering into the securities businesses. What the council put together as its idea was, contrary to the Financial System Research Council, that there was no need for banks to enter the market of securities distribution. Personnel in the Securities Bureau went around lobbying committee members, explaining that if banks entered the stock selling and buying business, which was the profit source for small and medium-sized securities companies, their bottom line would become risky. This is because the banks would take away customers since they have stronger connections with business corporations. It was a confrontation of the two Finance Ministry bureaus, the Banking and the Securities, backed by the respective industries they are involved with. The position of the Securities Bureau within the Finance Ministry had been improved as the securities industry improved its position in society. Article 65 of the Securities and Exchange Law is referred to as the lifeline of the securities industry; it is the same for the Securities Bureau. It is possible for the Securities Bureau to deal with the Banking Bureau, which is a large bureau, on equal ground at times because this article exists. On the other hand, the Banking Bureau sought to satisfy the expectations of its industry by changing the application of Article 65 of the Securities and Exchange Law. The growth of the banking industry is connected to the increase in influence of the Banking Bureau. Coincidentally, it would lead to an expansion of the place where retired bureau officials can find employment.

At the stage when committees are putting forth their respective interim reports, it is enough to incorporate what is desired by their "clients"; at the stage of the final reports, however, when opinions have to be compromised, a serious confrontation can occur. Negotiating attempts are made at official meetings, and behind such meetings, the personnel of both the Banking and Securities Bureaus visit committee members, soliciting their support through *nemawashi*. This is how the so-called consensus of the three bureaus (Banking, Securities, and International Finance) is accomplished.

It is often said of the Ministry of Finance that "there are bureaus, but no ministry." This saying reflects the fact that each bureau is extremely anxious to expand the authority of its own field of involvement. Since each bureau already has extensive authority, if attempts are made to expand it further, confrontations will occur with other bureaus which have authority of their own. The desire of a bureau to expand its own authority leads to attempts to push away other bureaus, and ultimately might contradict the interests of the entire Ministry of Finance or the national interest. This desire to expand one's own authority has been the source of vitality for bureaucrats. This extra desire, however, creates an opaque system.

When a conflict occurs between two ministries, confrontations become more strident. One famous example of such is the telecommunication war. What initially induced this war was the advancement of telecommunication technologies. In the past, the Ministry of International Trade and Industry was in charge of administration on information equipment, while the Ministry of Posts and Telecommunications was in charge of communication networks.

Technological advancement, however, has allowed new entries into this business field of telecommunication (network and other Value-Added Network, or VAN, activities), which was previously considered naturally monopolistic on the one hand, and on the other, has made the borders between information equipment and communication networks unclear in their definitions. Internationalization, which was the requirement of the time, was another issue involved in this war. The conflicts between these two ministries have been multifaceted during the so-called VAN war. In spite of some fairly early agreements with respect to introduction of competition in communication network business, there still remained serious conflicts concerning definitions of the first (network) and second categories of business, and the degree of regulation for the second category of business. Depending on how categories are defined, and what degree of regulation would be imposed, the influence of the two ministries varied. With respect to regulation, although the appearance was that the Ministry of International Trade and Industry was complaining from the viewpoint of open markets about revisions in the telecommunications law proposed by the Ministry of Posts and Telecommunications, it would be more reasonable to believe that it was a conflict over jurisdictions (Muramatsu, "Privatization, Deregulation, and Reregulation"). The resolution of this interministerial conflict required the influence of powerful politicians of the Liberal Democratic Party. Interministerial conflicts can only be ended with the involvement of political parties. Since more and more important policies cut across ministry lines, that party involvement continues to grow.

Administrative Guidance

Administrative guidance is a means used in nurturing administration whose function is similar to giving permits, licenses, and authorizations. In addition, administrative guidance is an important conduit between the administrative agencies and concerned associations. Various administrative agencies attempt to carry out activities on behalf of social interests with this conduit as the background. We cannot simply say that administrative guidance is the "guidance" that the particular administrative agencies give to the associations concerned.

Administrative guidance is famous as a means of industrial policy execution by the Ministry of International Trade and Industry, and is often referred to as the catalyst of Japan's economic growth. But this is an overstatement. It is true that administrative guidance was extensively used and was quite influential from the 1950s to the first half of the 1960s. In the 1950s, in order to strengthen critical industries such as steel and machinery, the government gave priority to these industries by allotting foreign currency which these industries did not have in sufficient quantity. During the same period, in order to nurture the petrochemical and automobile industries, the government gave preferential treatment through fiscal, financial, and tax measures. Supply adjustments were made easier through suggestions for curtailing production and inhibiting capital investments during slack times. A typical example is the relationship with the textile industry. In the 1960s the government attempted to merge all automobile manufacturers into one company in order to compete successfully with the U.S. automobile industry, which was expected to enter the Japanese market. Even in the 1970s, it showed guidelines and created a system of cooperation so that the industrial structure of Japan would become knowledge-intensive and energy-saving.

Such activities that show guidelines for the future and those that encourage industries to move in a desired direction are not required by law, but Japan's administrative bureaucrats believed that such activities were within their role. The private sector, on the other hand, did not refuse such administrative guidance most of the time. Thus I believe that when administrative guidance was given, it was made certain that the substance of guidance was acceptable to the industries through prior negotiations.

Although it is believed that the influence of administrative guidance was considerable, there are disagreements as to the extent to which private enterprises complied with such guidance. More disputed is whether the involvement of the administration in the activities of the private enterprises was indeed effective in industrial development or not. Was the influence positive or negative? It is said that, in general, the prevention of new entries made it possible for industry to develop in a stable manner. Neoclassical economists, however, seriously question this view, which emphasizes the positive effect of administrative guidance. They believe as follows: Was it really beneficial to Japanese enterprises when a weak industry survived longer as a result of production cutbacks? Was it not better for the Japanese economy to make weak industries disappear from the market quickly during slack times so that industries with higher potential could grow faster? As a matter of fact, the automobile industry is so prosperous today because it refused to heed the administrative guidance that automobile manufacturers be merged together.

Negative Aspects of Administrative Guidance

The time has come to use the revisionist approach to evaluate the benefits of administrative guidance. Corresponding to this, the postwar economy itself has begun to be evaluated in a more balanced manner. It was not Japan's bureaucracy, but the entrepreneurial spirit of the private sector that aggressively promoted the postwar Japanese economy. It was Mr. Hisato Ichimada, then president of the Bank of Japan, believed to have been the most aggressive economist within the government, who is reputed to have objected to the plan of Kawasaki Steel when it wanted to secure a vast area of land in Chiba Prefecture at the beginning of the 1950s to build a new industrial complex. His objection went to the extent that he would not hesitate to destroy the company when it did not want to take his advice. Kawasaki executed its plan against government advice and succeeded in expanding the activities with much profit.

When the bureaucracy attempts to give "guidance" and establishes contacts with the "object" of the administration, it relies on the existence of industrial associations. I used the term "object," which is used in the administrative laws; the term used in the U.S. study of public administration is "customer." The role industrial associations play as a partner of the bureaucracy is extremely important in the execution of policies in Japan. Administration is executed by taking advantage of the unity of industry. Consequently, the bureaucracy easily tends to reflect the interests of industry. There is an intimate communication relationship established between the bureaucracy and the associations. Although policies that are formed on the basis of this relationship might be more easily executed, it sometimes happens that entities wishing to enter a particular industry anew may be treated unfairly, although the system allows fair treatment among all the existing members of the industrial association concerned. Competition that is generated within this framework is intraindustry, and is excessive thus precludes new entries. Intraindustry competition can be safely fought, even though it may be severe at times. Some take the view that this was the reason for Japan's success. Yasusuke Murakami referred to this as "compartmentalized competition" (Murakami 1984).

In Japan's economic administration, administrative guidance was used for the purpose of nurturing industry. Since administrative guidance tended to stabilize an industry while protecting less competitive companies, top companies in an industry were not necessarily satisfied with the administrative guidance. Therefore, it is not the case that all companies are happy to accept administrative guidance. It is necessary for the administrative bureaucrats to have intimate exchanges of information with an industry in order to execute industrial policies, thereby overcoming such dissatisfaction.

A positive aspect of administrative guidance is that it can be quite flexible. Through detailed instructions and agile flexibility in dealing with changing situations, bureaucrats of the Ministry of International Trade and Industry and the Ministry of Finance attempted to nurture the steel, petrochemical, and automobile industries in the 1950s, and the heavy chemical industry in the 1960s. The government accordingly developed guidelines in accordance to its plans, and gave preferential treatment to these industries by allotting controlled foreign currencies, and giving tax incentives and subsidies. As it turned out, administrative guidance was another means for nurturing industries, similar to giving permits, licenses, and authorizations, but able to accomplish the same objective more sensitively and subtly.

Even after permission, licenses, and authorizations are given, the bureaucracy as the supervising government agency tries to adjust the supply and demand of the entire industry. Supply and demand are adjusted, for example, by maintaining respective market shares of individual enterprises within the industry. Apparently supply and demand adjustment through administration, as mentioned before, tends to result in preventing new entries. Samuels called it "reciprocal consent" between those concerned, bureaucracy and industry in particular. What he was referring to is that a long-term trust relationship between the two has evolved into a cooperative relationship between the public and private sectors, smoothing the background for easy acceptance of administrative guidance.

Changes in Regulation Demanded

In this chapter, I would like to pay attention to the fact that, regardless of how it was in the past, the environment in which administrative guidance is evaluated has changed dramatically. First of all, the validity of interference which is not based on laws has come into question. It should be mentioned here that the Administrative Procedures Law, which has been recently introduced, has some rules about administrative guidance. Second, criticism that administrative guidance benefits only producers and does not take consumers into consideration has increased.

In the administration of banking, for example, the Ministry of Finance did not allow competitive financial institutions to offer more depositor services and raise interest rates on savings. Was this policy valid? Didn't the scandal of "loss compensation" occur among securities companies because such a framework of governmental interference existed? The process this incident went through showed that there were some problems in the manner in which traditional administrative guidance was carried out. Some legal scholars point out the problem that no legal relief can be attempted when interests of individual companies and industries are violated through administrative guidance that is not completely appropriate. When the bureaucracy imposes regulations without being liable, such regulations tend to be excessive and they are opaque. It is true that administrative guidance has contributed to the reduction of transaction costs (à la Ronald Coase) that private enterprises pay; the flexibility the administrative guidance has shown is a characteristic which is still valuable. Even today, ministries, agencies, and many industrial associations still consider administrative guidance to be necessary, even though it is widely criticized. In fact, the Administrative Procedures Law has "officially recognized" administrative guidance with certain conditions (such as documentation). However, the opinion of this author is that this adjustment of conflict of interest should be dealt with gradually in accordance with the rules of the justice system.

Changes in Service Provision

Reduced Resources

Also in the service-providing administration, the postwar administration began to change in the 1980s. The impetus for change came with the Second Extraordinary Administrative Reform Council [Dainiji Rinji Gyosei Chosa Kai]. Public corporations began to be privatized and cost-cutting was enthusiastically pursued. Even though the resources of Japan's public administration were scarce to start with, the decision was made to proceed further with still fewer resources. How did each ministry and agency respond? It is possible to discuss everything that occurred in the process of resource reduction, but I would like to analyze the minimum to see what has changed in the line ministries responsible for the implementation of public works in the ministries such as the Ministry of Construction.*

Depending on the responsibilities of a particular ministry or agency, the amount and characteristics of available resources varies. Some ministries emphasize their right to grant permits, licenses, and authorizations, while others find the budget important. Their influences are characterized by the nature of resources available to them. It can be said that line ministries and agencies were damaged by the zero-ceiling decision after the Second Extraordinary Council. Take the Ministry of Construction, for example. It had been said until then that, in spite of the fact that it handled projects of huge monetary value, it did not necessarily find the budget troublesome. That was because there was "the logic of necessity" for national construction projects which was supported by politicians. The Construction Ministry attempted to deal with the Second Extraordinary Council by tackling enthusiastically the issue of deregulation (such as the deregulation of housing site prospectus), rather than delaying public projects. It was also the Construction Ministry which tackled enthusiastically the issue of

Editor's note: There have been a series of Rincho [Extraordinary Administrative Reform Councils]. The second Rincho lasted from March 1981 to February 1983 under the chairmanship of Toshio Dokō (ex-president of Keidanren) and had nine committee members. It was succeeded by the first Gyokakushin [Administrative Reform Council] (June 1983–June 1986) under the chairmanship of Dokō, the second Gyokakushin (April 1983–April 1990) under the chairmanship of Bumpei Otsuki (ex-president of Nikkeiren), and the third Gyokakushin (October 1990–October 1993) under the chairmanship of Eiji Suzuki. These successive councils prepared recommendations on administrative reform for the central government. In 1982, the central government, in turn, began to announce administrative reform guidelines every year which outlined administrative reform measures to be pursued in that year.

activating the private sector under the Nakasone administration (November 1982–October 1987). After the Hosokawa administration (August 1993–March 1994), the Construction Ministry will have no choice but to show a more positive attitude toward dealing with the issue of deregulation in contracts of public works, since one of the reasons why a totally new administration was established was the revelation of tax evasion and bribery involving public projects by powerful Liberal Democratic Party politicians.

The work of the Construction Ministry may be divided into the three different categories: projects, development, and planning (Tetsuya Kitahara, Administrative Management Research Center, "Research Survey Report on Socio-Economic Changes and Changes in Administrative Styles," 1990). In the Second Extraordinary Council, it was maintained that decentralization and deregulation should occur in the third category. It appears that deregulation indeed took place to some extent. One example of deregulation is the expanded application of open biddings as doubts about politicians, governors, and mayors continued to emerge. However, as one can read into the revised Banking Law and the new Telecommunications Business Law [Denki Tsushin Jigyo Ho], some compensation for what is lost as a result of deregulation is often worked out in some other way. In urban planning, for example, it was possible for the Ministry of Agriculture, Forestry and Fishery to deal with the reduction of resources by combining subsidies and carrying out decentralization in such a way that rights are dispersed to the prefectures. In fact, as the total number of positions allowed for the ministries and agencies at the central government level has been reduced, the number of local public servants increased, indicating that some sort of decentralization has occurred. The Ministry of Home Affairs, on the other hand, has increased its influence in this policy environment as a general manager of the scope and scale of local finance. The Ministry of Home Affairs, with the help of the Second Extraordinary Council, intervened in the matter of quorums and salaries to an extent otherwise not possible. In addition, I observe that the changes in the value and reduction of resources actually expanded another role of the Ministry of Home Affairs. The Ministry of Home Affairs expanded its role as general manager of local administrative systems by activating the Local Systems Research Council [Chiho Seido Chosa Kai]. Reforms of local systems were first proposed by the administrative reform minded people of the Second Extraordinary Council and Administrative Reforms Council, not the Ministry of Home Affairs. Their proposal appears, however, to have stimulated the Home Affairs Ministry's latent desire for administrative system reforms at the local level. The only thing is, though, since the relationship between the central and local governments is complex and represents politicians' involvement, it is only possible when the Ministry of Home Affairs is determined to do so and politicians agree.

New Liberalism and Welfare State

The Ministry of Health and Welfare also experienced a severe reduction in resources due to the policy of the Second Extraordinary Council to reduce the cost of the welfare state in general. This ministry had experienced a sudden growth in the 1970s. It has been exploring the issue of long-term resource redistribution by making hitherto free Medicare partially chargeable to the elderly by revising the Elderly Health Insurance Act [Rojin Hoken Ho]. It has been working on the "Gold Plan" to deal with Japan's aging society. It is trying to deal with the general aging of the population by organizing and reorganizing case workers and health care volunteers. Reforms of welfare offices and public health centers are under way for the same purpose. It appears that a new system is being sought under these changing circumstances.

Espin-Andersen categorized the market-oriented countries of the world, analyzing their pension systems, employments, medical care, and assistance to the poor, into "thin welfare countries" (the United States), "middle-level welfare countries" (Japan, Italy, and Germany), and "high-level welfare countries" (Scandinavian countries). According to him, these nations are respectively politically liberal, corporatist, and social-democratic (for details, see Muramatsu 1994).

Espin-Andersen suggests that Japan belongs to the second category, which is also described characteristically as the system that pays most attention to the retention of statuses and social distinctions. In these countries the quality of welfare (particularly social insurance) and services provided varies depending on which layer of the social hierarchy one belongs to. Benefits vary depending on whether one has corporate insurance, mutual insurance, national railroad, or national health insurance. No priority was given to day care centers. It is believed that the state begins where the family ends. It makes it easier for us to understand why Japan lagged behind other countries in providing day care centers. Families have been viewed as important welfare service providers in Japan. As for Japan being in the second category, I would think it is difficult to say whether Japan fulfills the characteristics of the second category. In some respects, for example, through the merging into one of various mutual insurance organizations, Japan is closer to the third category. In addition, the quality of welfare has been enhanced by efforts to make the welfare services multi-faceted. Even though Japan might be viewed as belonging to the second category, the country has been going through changes.

Resource Reduction in Three Phases

Let us focus on the Ministry of Finance. The Ministry of Finance was the center of fiscal reform through the Second Extraordinary Council, being aware that its own resources might also be reduced. During this period it enthusiastically pursued revision of the budget compilation procedures (including the introduction of a ceiling) and privatization. According to Prime Minister Thatcher in the U.K., privatization was to some degree a means of systematic reform for the establishment of new liberal and popular capitalist principles. But for the Finance Ministry, it is a means of applying pressure on the budget by, on the one hand, cutting expenditures, and on the other, acquiring the proceeds from the sale of stocks for privatized companies. After the fiscal reform had gone forward to some extent, the MOF enthusiastically tackled the tax increase plan. Although it was ultimately decided upon by politicians and political parties through their policies, it is certain that the introduction of the current consumption tax reflects the strong backing and volition of the Finance Ministry. Altogether its resource reduction resulted in the reduction of its influence. Therefore, the Finance Ministry attempted a maneuver to regain its influence.

Fiscal reduction by the Second Extraordinary Council had unique characteristics. Ceilings were introduced with the same rate for all ministries; how this reduction was to be realized, however, was left up to each ministry. This method was referred to as decrementalism, while the budget compilation during the economic growth period was characterized as incrementalism. It became necessary to negotiate within each ministry.

When we look back at the process of responding to the reduction of resources in the postwar Japanese public administration, we know that it was the MITI that first experienced it; this reduction later became much more generalized to all government agencies in the 1980s. The reduction occurred primarily in the form of loss of rights to allot foreign currencies. After this reduction, MITI attempted to compensate for the regression of its leadership ability by introducing administrative guidances. This occurred in the first half of the 1960s. It is the belief of this author that MITI's network was developed and reinforced during this period. Is it not so that networking attempts were made in order to compensate for the meager resources available to it? Daniel Okimoto (1989) argues in the same vein about networking in his "Theory of Minimal State." Subsequently, MITI began to say that its competitive strength lay in its wisdom rather than in the power to grant licenses or exercise administrative guidance. In the 1970s every aspect of Japan's economic activities became a target for political debates and conflicts. MITI, as a forerunner and in order to confirm its jurisdiction, began to expand its say in areas where other ministries and agencies maintained their jurisdictions. This was a kind of resource (i.e., authority) expansion activity. In addition, since it has a lot of experience in negotiating with foreign countries, it knew how to interact with them. This may also be referred to as a kind of resource (i.e., know-how). What is interesting is that what MITI has insisted upon to other government agencies has gradually shifted from the perspective centering around producers to that centering around consumers; they justify their policies by saying that they are "in accordance with the citizens' economic benefits." Within MITI, more influential power has been given to the director of the International Trade and Industry Bureau in order to cope with the reduced resources. It was decided to prioritize budgets and those which had to be passed for sure were put under this bureau director. What is attempted here is to enhance the unity of the ministerial organization as much as possible, because it had a tendency to be split in multiple bureaus according to the industries involved. However, as far as the relationships with other government agencies are concerned, it is said that MITI became more aggressive.

The direction of resource reduction up to the administrative reform of the Second Extraordinary Council discussed so far in this section can be considered in three successive phases (Muramatsu 1994). The first phase is the period when authority was plentiful although fiscal resources were limited. This was from 1945 to about 1960. The second phase is the period when administrative guidance was used to compensate for the loss of legal power. A typical example of this period and the experience of the MITI in the 1960s was mentioned earlier. The third phase was the 1980s, when financial resources became a serious problem because of administrative reform. The response to the third phase started with the Second Extraordinary Council in 1981. Here, general responses to a reduction in financial resources included privatization, decentralization, subsidy recombination or reduction, and the setting or changing of priorities within the ministries. In terms of the administrative guidance characteristics, these three phases are depicted respectively as the period of bureaucracy and administration, the period of balance between bureaucracy and politicians, and the period of high expectations for top leadership. We can say that during the period when the administration and politics are balanced and in collusion, a union of the two was established, while sectionalism intensified. We are currently in the third phase, and the fact that cabinets, which are considered to be weak, such as Kaifu and Hosokawa Cabinets, have frequently made important decisions suggests that factors are functioning in such a way that the role of the top leadership is expanded regardless of whether it is desired or not.

It is necessary to enhance the functions of the Japanese government or the top leadership so that domestic and social, as well as international, requirements can be fulfilled.

The Period of Expansion in Public Administration

The bureaucracy, which attempted recovery from the ravages of war after World War II, was the continuation of the "classical bureaucracy." The "classical bureaucracy" had been modernizing the nation from above ever since the Meiji Reformation. Political power was stable under the rule of the Occupation Forces. The bureaucrats had many means of control such as foreign currency allotment up until the 1950s. However, in the 1960s, when market and capital were deregulated, the authority of the economic bureaucrats was extensively reduced. This is when they began to rack their brains to create "devices" so that they could maintain the level of authority they had become accustomed to.

Japan's bureaucracy invented various devices after this period so that their authority could be reinforced in the area of economic policies and other administrative areas. The most famous example of such devices is the case of the Special

Promotion Act [Tokushin Ho] with which MITI attempted to legislate the cooperation method of public and private sectors. This draft did not pass the Diet due to the opposition of banks, other government agencies, and politicians. MITI subsequently started to use administrative guidance frequently.

There is a case in which the Police Agency failed in its attempt to pass a revised version of the Performance of Police Functions Act [Keisatsukan Shokumu Shikko Ho] through the Diet. The Police Agency then secured the same level of influence by comprehensively utilizing the Minor Offenses Act and various other laws. Since the power of the state is weak in Japan, bureaucrats are always required to manage and make the best of their abilities.

Taking advantage of *zoku giin** might have been initially such a device as well, but the *zoku giin* have reversed the roles and gradually begun to take advantage of the bureaucracy. The third device was the utilization of foreign pressure. Let me take an example of the MOF. When partial financial deregulation was executed in the middle of the 1980s by the MOF, it was not simply because of the pressure the United States exerted on it. There were various factors in Japan that necessitated deregulation domestically as well. Examples of this include requests by competitive banks and demands to remove the barrier that separated banks and securities companies. It was convenient to remove interest rate controls and deregulate various financial markets so that huge amounts of government bonds could be refunded. It had become necessary to internationalize finances as Japan's industries had become increasingly internationalized. Corporations as well as individual citizens began to question the fact that only in bank interest rates, products and services were exactly the same for customers at any financial institution even though other areas had been deregulated. They were demanding deregulation so that customers could enjoy the benefits of free competition.

What would have happened if the MOF had proceeded with this logical deregulation by saying simply that deregulation of interest rates was necessary so that government bonds of substantial amounts could be smoothly refunded? What probably would have happened is that an all-out attempt of strong opposition by financial institutions would have developed. Financial institutions might have been damaged by this measure, particularly long-term credit banks with their concerns for a lowering in the popularity of bonds, and small and medium-sized financial institutions with concerns for their bottom line. Such opposition would certainly also have mobilized the politicians. However, it was presented as a strong demand from the United States, which had to be swallowed. The reason Japan frequently uses the concept of foreign pressures is that it is convenient and has low domestic political costs. However, inexpensive devices often have hidden costs.

---

*Editor's note: Zoku giin. LDP Diet members who exerted heavy influence on ministerial policy decisions through their memberships in various political affairs committees of the Liberal Democratic Party while the LDP held the majority in the Diet.

Impact of Internationalization

Internationalization is believed to have had the strongest impact on Japan's public administration. Let us consider this subject by searching for material and by expanding the above-mentioned example area a little more to see the impact of internationalization on the administrative system of Japan. When I use the term internationalization, I am referring to the impact on Japanese society made by foreign countries primarily in and after the 1960s, particularly in economic aspects. Internationalization in this sense started in the 1960s with deregulation in trade and capital necessary for Japan's public administration in the IMF as an Article 8 country and a member of the OECD. Recently, internationalization impact is felt more frequently being caused by severe economic conflicts between Japan and the United States.

A direct issue of internationalization is how to deal with foreign (primarily U.S.) pressures. At the root of this issue lies the problem of what to do with the existing "system of administrative interferences" and its various regulations. Guarantor networks have been an integral part of Japan's administration; environmental changes, however, now demand a reform of this guarantor network system.

MITI and Internationalization for the First Stage

MITI was the first agency to become aware of internationalization as an issue. This is a government agency whose original mandate was export promotion. The first stage of internationalization was to make foreign countries accept Japanese products. In the second stage, the problem became how to make the Japanese market accept foreign products. More specifically, the problem was the opening of its markets through the removal of customs and tariffs, and other means. Impetus was given when Japan became an IMF Article 8 country in 1964. However, MITI also felt it necessary to protect its markets at the same time. What system would allow Japan's economy to survive even when powerful U.S. enterprises entered the Japanese market? I believe it was MITI, more than the MOF, which seriously tackled this issue, even though its policies might have contained some errors. It is said that the initiative to execute industrial policies by taking extensive advantage of the framework of administrative guidance was born from its interests in this issue. In the first half of the 1970s, MITI executed an organizational reform in order to be prepared for the new situation by shifting from the principle of a vertically divided administration to that of more horizontally comprehensive administrator.

In the third stage of internationalization, demands were for truly open markets. MITI began its efforts for the internationalization of the third stage earlier than is generally believed. The principle of internationalization, where markets were to be truly opened, was already advocated in 1969 in MITI's "Trading

Policies of the 1970s." After this point in time, MITI stopped any administrative guidance activities for industries other than high-tech industries, which were recognized as strategically important for the nation. On the other hand, as far as the high-tech field is concerned, promotion of the information industry was still carried out as a major project even in 1983–84. However, these efforts are not so highly appraised.

Even though this strategy was highly limited, it was criticized during this period. Internationalization measures were promoted from 1985 to 1988 through the Maekawa Report and pressure by the United States for increased aid to developing nations, expansion of domestic demands, and technical cooperation. Further, the Hiraiwa Committee made proposals to the Hosokawa cabinet centering around deregulation. These two reports are similar in that the majority of the committee members represented business circles. It was after all the Ministry of Foreign Affairs that was quick in dealing with internationalization. The Ministry of Foreign Affairs, MITI, and part of the MOF (international finance people) negotiated with foreign countries. The Ministry of Foreign Affairs and MITI, were sensitive to the paradigm shift from the principle of producers to that of consumers, as this shift was observed in the politico-economic strategies of various countries in the world.

During my interview of representatives of the Ministry of Foreign Affairs in the spring of 1989 some representatives divided economic frictions into "the period of selling (representing the past)" and "the period of buying (representing the future)." Consequently, it is possible to arrange, from the point of view of the Ministry of Foreign Affairs, the responses of Japanese government agencies to economic frictions as a result of internationalization as in Table 1. In general, whenever economic issues arise vis-à-vis foreign countries, Group A government agencies are quick to respond as well as make internal decisions. On the other hand, it was maintained that Group B government agencies are slow in making internal decisions and in adapting to the standards that are considered necessary in international situations. For example, if a Group B government agency wants to take a strong stand and completely refuse the demands of a foreign country, officials responsible in that agency will attend an international negotiation with an interpreter. A good example of this is a case that occurred when a vice-minister of the Posts and Telecommunications attended negotiation with Motorola. The Ministry of Foreign Affairs watched.

This does not mean that the Ministry of Foreign Affairs finds it easier to side with Group A agencies, with which it shares similar ideas. Indeed, there is a stronger potential for an intensive conflict of interests to occur with respect to authority as well as procedures; all the more because the three parties in Group A are considering solutions in the same direction. Group C in this beginning "buying period" represents government agencies that are gradually adapting. The Ministry of Agriculture, Forestry and Fisheries took a big step toward internationalization when it made an international concession in the Uruguay Round

Table 1

Ministries' Attitudes Toward Internationalization

	Period of selling	Period of buying
Adaptive to foreign countries	(A) Foreign Ministry MITI MOF (partially)	
Resistive to foreign countries	(B) All other government agencies	⇧ Ministry of Agriculture (C) Ministry of Posts Ministry of Health and Welfare Others

negotiations at the end of 1993. Opening of the local network by the Ministry of Posts and Telecommunications is welcomed as a step in the right direction, and the Ministry of Health and Welfare is going forward with its internationalization as it tackles the issue of foreign workers. Japan's administrative system is going through changes.

Internally as well, new responses have become necessary because internationalization is creating interests that are more complex within each ministry and agency. For example, the Ministry of Foreign Affairs has created a position of Asia-Pacific ambassadorship. This was because of the recent increase in the number of conferences involving countries in the Asian-Pacific rim, and if there is an issue, four or five bureaus are involved. It was decided to ease the situation by establishing one new high post as regular coordinating procedures take too much time and trouble. Similarly in the Ministry of Foreign Affairs, I am informed that project teams are created more frequently now to deal with inter-bureau coordination problems. However, since it is still difficult to locate project team members in one place, project teams usually take the form of membership nomination and conferences by the people nominated.

Ministries and Agencies That Followed

It was the Construction Ministry, Ministry of Agriculture, Forestry and Fishery, and others who lagged behind in internationalization. I place the Ministry of Posts and Telecommunications in the middle group because it was affected somewhat in the issue of telecommunication parts purchases. Up until recently all the Construction Ministry had to say was that "it does not have much to do with internationalization." However, the feeling now is that this issue has reached even this ministry. That is, *dango*, or behind-the-scenes collaboration, has become a serious international issue. The United States made a strong point during the Strategic Imperative Initiative talks. Namely, when the United States strongly demanded a sworn statement that no *dango* would occur, the Construction Ministry compromised at first, issuing a notice stating that supervision would be provided to the extent that anti-monopoly law is not violated. But after a scandal broke open in 1993 the issue of *dango* has become a problem that simply cannot be ignored. Although various arguments are possible, the situation is such that the administration, centering around producers and in this case centering around construction companies, is being pressed to change. It is truly ironic that what the United States asserts is turning out to be for the benefit of Japanese consumers. Although it is not yet clear how the *dango* problem will ultimately be solved, it is certain that there is no alternative but to be responsive to reforms since in addition to the U.S. pressure, the formation of the Hosokawa administration is creating a strong impetus for change.

For the Ministry of Agriculture, Forestry and Fishery, internationalization means deregulation of import restrictions on agricultural products. The impact of internationalization is more serious than those stemming from prohibition of increase in rice prices and reduction in subsidies due to resource reductions. However, this ministry agreed to the U.S. assertion that the principle of importing no rice should be changed to allow imports of rice with the imposition of tariffs, permitting in 1993 and thereafter "minimum access" to the rice market "for the time being." It is expected that the next thing will be the tariffs, and then a demand for the lowering of tariffs imposed on rice. What this means is that it has become necessary to develop a true agricultural policy. Although some people refer to this as another example of the tactful use of foreign pressures by the Ministry of Agriculture, Forestry and Fishery, I myself do not believe that this ministry as a whole is capable of taking an initiative to that degree.

The United States used to pay much attention to the electorate supporting the Liberal Democratic Party for a considerable period of time. The Ministry of Agriculture, Forestry and Fishery used to have a powerful political resource for supporting the existing system. At some point in time, however, the United States stopped paying much attention completely from 1990 onward. In addition, the effect of the cold summer of 1993 on the rice issue was extensive, more so than that of structural reforms in the domestic politics of Japan. The fact that a decision was made to allow emergency rice imports has made it gradually easier to face and talk about this issue squarely. Even the Socialist Party, which used to say that not even one grain of rice would be imported to Japan, ultimately had to compromise under the coalition government, and the Liberal Democratic Party was recognizing the result, even though it was critical of the cabinet.

For the Ministry of Posts and Telecommunications, there was the major issue of the privatization of telecommunications. This may be viewed in some respects as a kind of deregulation, but as far as the substance of the 1984 Telecommunications Business Act [Denki Tsushin Jigyo Ho] is concerned, it was re-regulation. This was a typical example of deregulation and re-regulation occurring at the same time. This was also frequently seen in the conflict between Japan and the U.K. concerning the second KDD issue. There was a serious problem of how to adjust the intention of the Ministry of Posts and Telecommunications, which wanted, from the point of view of adjusting supply and demand, to limit access to international telecommunications business to one other company in addition to KDD. The ministry received applications from two companies, one of which had U.K. interests. Ultimately, authorization was given to both companies, but in this process it was confirmed that the Ministry of Posts and Telecommunications had some authority to impose a kind of re-regulation. In terms of the contents of the re-regulation, rules are set for conditions of entry by foreign capital and procedures for equipment certifications. This was an attempt by the Ministry of Posts and Telecommunications to maintain its authority by legislating what used to be done through administrative guidance. Similar to that case of the Banking Law, its significance probably lies in its objectives, (1) to enhance visibility, particularly with respect to foreigners, and (2) to secure minimal regulation (Mabuchi 1994).

I believe it is possible to categorize the impact of internationalization on the postwar regulatory administrations into three different periods—the period of regulation, the period of instructions and guidance, and the period of deregulations and re-regulations. These correspond roughly to the aforementioned subdivisions of the time of resource reduction. When Samuels talked about guarantors, he may have been describing successful incidents during the period of instructions and guidance. There were times when Japan's ministries and agencies attempted to give advice in certain areas, overstepping the role of guarantor. There were also times when they tried to get themselves involved in the substance of the subject, that is, private enterprise. However, in general, we can say that they have played the role of the minimal guarantor through regulations. It should be emphasized here that this guarantorship was exercised with the assumption that the subject, that is, the private sector, would be ultimately responsible; it was not that the state was moving the economy in order to replace the private sector.

Deregulation is a necessary condition for the private sector and individuals to exhibit their creativity. There are many areas in the past where administration was carried out with excessive concerns for the interests of the guarantor. Now is the time when strong demands to move toward consumer orientations and deregulations. The author would like readers to refer to manuals on economics to learn more about the benefits of deregulation; but even judging from common sense, it is very clear that deregulation will result in expanding business opportunities and diversify the kinds of products available to consumers. (Sony Walkman was successfully marketed because there happened to be no rules regulating this new product.) From the point of view of the administration, it will be useful in making the relationship between the administration and industries more clear, and it will be helpful to make clear the negotiation processes in the private sector when the administration gets involved in them. And these are matters of fundamental importance.

References

Haley, John. *Japan's Postwar Civil Service System: The Legal Framework* (Washington, DC: The World Bank, 1993).

Mabuchi, Masaru. *The Political Economy of the Ministry of Finance Regulation* [Okurasho Tosei no Seiji Keizaigaku] (Tokyo: Chuo Koron Sha, 1994).

Murakami, Yasusuke. *The Age of the New Middle Mass* [Shin Chukan Taishu no Jidai] (Tokyo: Chuo Koron Sha, 1984).

Muramatsu, Michio. *National Administration in the 1980s* [80–nendai Kokka no Gyosei] in (M. Nishio and M. Muramatsu, eds., *The Developments in Public Administration* [Gyosei no Hatten] (Tokyo: Yuhikaku, 1994).

Okimoto, Daniel. *Between MITI and Market* (Stanford, CA: Stanford University Press, 1989).

Samuels, Richard. *Business of Japanese State* (Ithaca, NY: Cornell University Press, 1987).

Source/Permission: **Michio Muramatsu**, "Gyosei Katsudo no Henyo." Chapter 5 of Michio Muramatsu, *Nihon no Gyosei, Katsudogata Kanryosei no Henbo* [Japan's Administration, Changes in Activist Bureaucracy], pp. 124–157. Translated by permission.

14

Leaving the "1940" System and Moving into a New System

Yukio Noguchi

For Japan, the year 1993 was a memorable year because it witnessed the demise of the 38-year hegemony of the Liberal Democratic Party (LDP). Japan's political system is now at an important turnaround. In what follows, we are concerned with what Japan's policy-making system should be.

The Iron Triangle

A nation's policy can be distinguished by the following three levels.

The first level is concerned with which system is to be chosen. It contains choices in ideology, such as socialism versus liberalism or whether the present Constitution should be maintained as is or amended. On the polar opposite are microlevel policies concerning specific items such as deciding on locations of public projects or issuing official approvals and permissions on individual items.

In between, there are strategic-level policies. They, under the system selected at the first level, give orientations to decisions to be made at the third level. More concretely, the orientations are on what tax system will be selected in the medium- and long-term perspectives, how to allocate government expenditures among competing fields, how to deregulate, or how to open up the country's domestic markets for foreign trade.

In Japan, until now, political parties have been characterized at the first level and their strategic-level positions are delineated accordingly. However, this is more appearance than reality. Policy decisions at the second and third levels have been governed by the "iron triangle" of special interest groups, the *zoku giin** or special-interest-dominated Diet members belonging to the Political Affairs Committee of the LDP, and bureaucracy.

Translator's note: Zoku giin for which *zoku* means a clique or a group. It also refers to LDP Diet members who belong to subcommittees of the LDP Political Affairs

This system was a highly exclusionary one in that masses of people such as urban residents who were not directly connected to the *zoku giin* were outside of this decision-making process. (Opinions are divided as to what makes up the special interest groups at the vertex of the triangle. They are generally thought to be big businesses, but it is farmers and small businesses that earnestly seek political protection.)

With the collapse of the one-party dominance by the LDP, this system is on the verge of change. Let us begin our discussion with an analysis of the system which is now being replaced.

The iron triangle is not peculiar to Japan but can be found in every country. In fact, the term was coined to describe the political situation in the United States. It is a ubiquitous phenomenon that businesses want to wrestle profits out of the political process and that politicians and bureaucrats interact with one another while they establish policies.

Also seen in many countries to various degrees is the phenomenon that the interests of producers are given priority and the interests of consumers are neglected. This phenomenon is as ancient as Adam Smith who, in his *Wealth of Nations* (1776), pointed out that producers always collude to have policies enacted on their own behalf. The problem is that Japan is distinct in this connection.

The Transformation of Zoku LDP Diet Members into De Facto Bureaucrats

Policy making under Japan's 1955 system was carried on jointly by zoku Diet members of the Political Affairs Committee of the LDP and central ministries, especially the Ministry of Finance which is in charge of national budget making and taxation.* The power balance between these two parties saw considerable changes from the rapid growth period to the 1980s. In the rapid growth period, policy making centered on the bureaucracy, while the LDP was content with putting some pressure on the bureaucracy. In the 1970s, however, this relationship underwent a change and the Political Affairs Committee of the LDP became more powerful in the policy-making process.

We may cite a few examples. In the field of agricultural administration, zoku Diet members of the LDP elevated themselves from an existence as a mere pressure group which set rice prices to a policy group of comprehensive farm

---

Committee. Through their intimate contacts with various ministries, they gain special expertise in ministerial policies. Their influence is said to exceed that of the minister. One becomes a subcommittee chairman after four to five terms in the Diet.

Translator's note: The 1955 system refers to the system formed by the LDP in November 1955 when the Liberal Party and the Democratic Party joined together. The 1995 system refers to the politico-economic system under LDP hegemony.

administration with a shift in focus from a rice-centered farm policy to a comprehensive, overall agricultural policy. In the field of public welfare administration determined by the Ministry of Health and Welfare, zoku Diet members (of the social and labor administration) began to play an important conciliatory role in reforming the medical insurance system, among other projects. In the field of taxation, the Tax System Committee of the LDP became more powerful than the Tax System Council of the national government. The basic reason for these changes is the emergence of policy experts in the LDP.

At the same time, the LDP became more bureaucratized. Zoku Diet members followed a well-ordered career path from the time they were elected to the Diet. After they served as political vice ministers, they were appointed to be division chiefs of the Political Affairs Committee. Then they served as chairs of the permanent committees of the House of Representatives, and finally as ministers.

This orderly step-by-step career advancement was possible only because the LDP perpetually remained the majority party. The general pattern in Japan's politics used to be that one worked as a bureaucrat until reaching the post of bureau director or administrative vice minister. Then the bureaucrat would turned himself into a politician. Later, however, the person had to leave the bureaucracy at a much earlier age because he had to become part of the seniority system within the LDP much earlier.

As the LDP became more adept in policy making and more bureaucratic, a policy-making system came into being in which the LDP and the national government were nearly united. Let me describe this by considering how the national budget is devised.

The Disappearance of the Boundary Between Politics and Administration

The relationship between politics and administration appears most clearly and symbolically in the budget-making process.

Under the 1955 system, Japan's national budget was prepared according to a very unusual procedure. The administration should have sole responsibility for the draft proposal of the national budget. However, in reality, the LDP was deeply involved at this early stage.

Requests made by individual ministries for budgets had to be approved beforehand by various subcommittees of the Political Affairs Committee of the LDP. Also zoku Diet members of the LDP used to interfere in the LDP's negotiations with the Ministry of Finance. It is natural that the minister concerned must be present at the last stage of budget negotiations regarding restorations of some disapproved items.

However, after that, in a very irregular procedure, three top executives of the LDP were, as a general rule, called in for the final round of negotiations. The strong intervention of the majority party with no clearly stated authority in a purely administrative process has been the actual state and salient characteristic of Japan's budget-making process.

The same is seen in other administrative fields as well. Approvals and permissions given by the administration regarding specific items were screened by LDP politicians. Though the iron triangle of the politics-bureaucracy-business collusion is a phenomenon seen in every country, political interventions are usually conducted through the country's parliament, as seen typically in the United States. Japan's case is unique in that LDP politicians intervened directly in administrative decision making instead of confining their participation to strategic orientations on policies in the political arena.

The 1940 System

The Foundation of the Japanese Economy

The iron triangle has a unique character in Japan because of the blurred distinction between politics and administration. To rephrase it, we may say that "politics is administerized." Behind this phenomenon, there is the fact that the participation of the administration in economic activities is wide-ranging and powerful taking the form of permissions, supervision, regulations, and so on. Let us call this the 1940 system.

The 1940 system is a term coined by myself to describe Japan's unique economic system which was formed around 1940 for the sake of national mobilization pursuant to the Pacific War. Its core was bureaucracy's extensive participation in economic activities. It is characterized by centralism and production superiority.

It may sound strange when I say that the prewar system has continued until today. However, we must note that many of the basic institutions of the contemporary Japanese economic system owe their existence to their introduction as parts of the 1940 system.

In the financial field, we see a shift from direct financing to indirect financing in the 1940s based mostly on lending done by banks in order to allocate resources and still give priority to munitions industries. In this connection, we note that the Bank of Japan Law was enacted in 1942 in order to reorient monetary policy to the national objective.

The tax collection which taxed wage income at its source was initiated in the tax reform of 1940. There was the income tax before that time, but the 1940 reform made it possible for the tax authorities to secure nearly complete control over wage income. This helped to reinforce the foundation of national finance. A system was also established whereby tax resources were centralized and then transferred to local governments in the form of special grants-in-aid.

In 1942, the Food Control Law was set up and the Land and House Lease Laws were strengthened. In the next few subsequent years, the focus of Japanese firms was shifted from stockholders to employees based on the National Mobilization Law of 1938. Numerous trade associations which are now the basis of administrative guidance by the government were rapidly organized in 1941–42.

In addition, public corporations and public financial institutions were formed around this time. They are subsequently reorganized and remain active today. Japan is said to be a homogeneous society, but its basis was configured at this time in the form of such policies as the standardization of education (National Elementary School System) as well as the standardization of manufactured products (Japan Industrial Standardization).

Significance and Problems

Various institutions, described above, were created to make better use of resources for the sake of supporting the total war efforts while regulating competition. There was no "end-of-war" as far as the 1940 system was concerned. In addition, this system survived the defeat in World War II and, in fact, greatly helped in achieving rapid growth.

For instance, the indirect financing system is believed to have functioned very efficiently in allocating scarce resources among priority industries. Also, trade associations played a very important role in the administrative guidance by various ministries. The centralized fiscal system which transferred tax revenue from wage income to local governments in the form of grants-in-aid also worked well.

We can also note the large influence which the 1940 system exerted on the basic social structure. Postwar Japan became an egalitarian society rarely found in the world, mainly because the landowner class was not extant—an effect of the strengthened Land Lease Law. This again was a result of the 1940 system. Landowners existed on paper but they were a class which had almost no social power. This was a very distinct difference from European society. We can give a high mark to the 1940 system on these points.

However, as economic conditions have changed, this system is now a handicap to the future development of the Japanese economy. As a matter of fact, many of Japan's contemporary problems are due to the difficulty of extracting itself from this system.

A typical example is the problem of opening the rice market to foreign rice. What the government should do with trade associations is another such problem. Regarding the financial system, the principle of not allowing even a single bank to declare bankruptcy is now at its limit. The greatest issue in the taxation field is how to reform the present tax system which is heavily biased toward wage income taxes collected at source. Equally serious is the task of how to shift from administrative centralism to decentralism.

Broadly stated, many points made by revisionists are closely tied into the 1940 system. Their criticisms are focused on Japan's economic structure which does not reflect consumer interests. These revisionists see an economic structure based on "corporatism" in which people's daily lives are centered around corporations. Viewed this way, the 1940 system is the starting point of government regulations, corporatism, and producer superiority. It is much more entrenched in shaping the fundamentals of Japanese society than the 1955 system. The 1940 system covers wide-ranging problems over the entire socioeconomic system of Japan.

Alternative Scenarios

The Scenarios of a Consumer-Centered Society and Political Instability

One can think of several different scenarios for the policy-making system which is to replace the 1955 system.

The first scenario states that the producer-centered society is to change to a consumer-centered society. Although many Americans seem to entertain this hope, such a hope seems to be forlorn. For example, in the 1993 general election, no political party committed itself to promoting liberalization of the rice market on behalf of consumers. Also slogans such as "deregulation" and "consumer priority" are very often mere lip services.

The second scenario views the political instability resulting from the emergence of many political parties as leading to the adoption of policies which cater to the interests of the electorate. For example, the income tax cut may be increasingly demanded. It is also conceivable that a single-issue party will appear in the midst of this political instability. If this party has a very strong influence, it may cast the deciding vote over a specific policy.

Not only that, but when diverse political demands are forthcoming, bureaucracy may, to some extent, lose its power. However, it is doubtful whether this scenario is realistic. For example, the income tax cut is likely to be ruled out because it means the accumulation of enormous public debt with a sharp drop in tax revenue. Politicians cannot confront the rationale of the Ministry of Finance which emphasizes the fiscal balance.

The Scenario of Bureaucratic Control

The third scenario is the relative increase in power held by the bureaucracy. As the power of zoku Diet members of the LDP definitely wanes, bureaucracy will gain in its freedom of choice. Needless to say, as it becomes more complex to control the proceedings of the Diet, it will become more difficult to enact policies which involve new laws. However, bureaucracy can step up its administrative guidance based on ministerial notifications.

For the tax system, what is important concerning the inheritance tax and the property tax system is how land value is assessed. At the moment, it is based on the discretion of the bureaucracy. The land value assessed for inheritance tax was raised from 70 percent to 80 percent of the officially posted land prices, but this decision was made as an administrative notification which required no change in law.

For the national budget, from the 1980s on, the budget allocations have been made by setting up special exemptions from the budget ceiling at the level of budget negotiations. Decisions on the ceiling itself are formed at the discretion of the administration. The operation of the monitoring system for land prices is also handled by the administration at its own discretion. The total credit control—which is alleged to have been instrumental in lowering land prices—was another administrative measure.

It is natural that judgments on approvals and permissions on specific items (third-level policies) are entrusted to the administration. However, the decisions enumerated above belong to the second level rather than to the third level. Similarly, many important decisions are carried out by the administration without the input of the legislature in the case of Japan.

Problems with the Scenario of Bureaucratic Control

Considering the ability and integrity of Japan's bureaucracy, an increase in bureaucracy's power is not necessarily bad. However, there is one important reservation. That is, no reform is possible under the present system regarding second-level policies (strategic-level policies). Japan's decision making has been weak at this level but it will be even weaker henceforth.

Regarding budget making, the rationale of the Ministry of Finance will become dominant. For the next few years, the budget will be restrictive because of the shortage of tax revenue. This is in contrast to the objective of domestic demand expansion. Also, along with the increased responsibility of Japan in the international community, the government must take many internal budgetary measures. The situation will be such that the government cannot respond to requests for such measures readily.

The most serious aspect in the increased difficulties of systemic reforms is what to do with the public pension system which is scheduled to be revised in the 1994 fiscal year. A number of political parties in the coalition government have expressed their vehement opposition to the reform of the public pension system and to the attendant tax reform which would cope with the expected increase in pension burdens. The pension reform will become increasingly more difficult the longer the reform is delayed. Not only the pension system but also the social security policy in general is faced with similar difficulties in the face of a continued population aging.

From the long-term point of view, what is important is not limited to the reform of public pensions and the consumption tax. Increased inequalities in household wealth will be a serious problem in the future as households continue to accumulate assets. To cope with this problem, what is necessary to plan how the inheritance tax will be strengthened. However, we can foresee how formidable it will be to obtain a consensus on this particular issue.

It will thus be difficult to change the status quo drastically. Maintaining the status quo means that vested interests will be protected. Excluded from these interests will be the new industries. Likewise, consumers will continue to be excluded from the policy-making process. An even greater problem is that one can only respond with structural adjustments to the Japanese economy so as to maintain the status quo. We will restate this problem at the end of the article.

Toward a New System

The Revival of the Political Process

How can we avoid this impasse?

First of all, it is important for us to recognize the possibility that the people can exert an influence on politics through the political process. As we noted earlier, politics tend to belittle consumer interests in general. However, this does not mean that the political process is completely inactive. It seems that people have lost any expectations in and have become disillusioned about politics because the one-party control has continued for so long. The first prerequisite is to alter this sort of recognition.

Secondly, political parties must make their stands clear regarding strategic-level policies. Until now, Japan's political parties, though they differ in ideology, have stayed on the strategic level with such policies in order to please everybody and so remain universally popular. With the end of the cold war, people's concern has shifted to the second level. Nonetheless, there has been no change in the situation. Each and every party merely proposes such abstract platforms as "reforms" and "livelihood priority."

In any field, there will be a group whose vested interests will be threatened. Thus, unless radical policies against such vested interests are forthcoming, politics cannot function at the strategic level. More specifically, new political parties must come into being to represent the interests of urban residents or they must propose concrete policies such as liberalization of rice imports or deregulation.

Correct Understanding of One's Own Interests

What is important in the final analysis is to have a correct understanding regarding the characteristics of the problem. As we stated earlier, individuals do not necessarily possess the correct understanding of policy issues and their structures.

It is sometimes pointed out that this situation arises because policy information is monopolized by the bureaucracy. This is true in a number of respects. For example, land value assessments for the property tax are not publicly available. Hence, we lack basic information for judging if such assessments are fairly made. Similarly, important information is not made public concerning public pensions. Not only for pensions but also for many policy issues, the information monopolized by the bureaucracy is not made public. Correct information ought to be made public.

However, even in the presence of correct information, people may still lack understanding regarding the policies. It then becomes important to let people educate themselves so they understand correctly where they stand.

It will probably be required that this task be carried out by opinion leaders, journalists, and labor union leaders rather than individual citizens. Leaders of labor unions and reformist parties should reflect on themselves. Economic conditions have changed in such ways that the conventional formulas for labor-management confrontation or the rich-versus-poor contest no longer enables one to grasp the core of the problem. However, many leaders still think only in the old terms.

Contemporary problems are far more complex. For example, there is the problem of intergenerational conflicts. Also, nowadays, even workers own assets. Seen from this perspective, many of the policy proposals made by labor unions or reformist parties sometimes sound as if a person is "choking oneself by one's own hands."

We can refer to the case of the consumption tax, which is a rare example of a strategic-level policy that was debated politically. With regard to this policy, interests were twisted. As the majority party, the LDP had to propose this tax. Labor unions and the Socialist Party (the minority party) opposed this tax merely because it was proposed by the government. Not only that, but also the opposition to the consumption tax even seemed to be the raison d'être of labor unions and the Socialist party.

However, for wage earners, the consumption tax is more equitable than the income tax which is heavily biased toward wage income. It is true that the consumption tax is much less progressive (sometimes regressive) than the income tax. However, this defect can be alleviated by increasing progressivity of direct taxes. Thus, for the tax system as a whole, there is no reason to reject the consumption tax.

A similar twist is seen also in public pensions. Interests in the public pension system vary widely across the generations. For young union members, active support should be given to the proposed delay of the starting age of pension benefits to age sixty-five in order to maintain the future pension system without sharp increases in contributions. However, because of the dominance of older union leaders, labor unions still think of the pension problem in the form of labor-management confrontation and, from this perspective, continue to oppose raising the pension starting age to sixty-five.

The inheritance tax is also understood imperfectly. The inheritance tax applies only to a small group of affluent households. Nonetheless, the relaxation of the inheritance tax continues to be demanded from the standpoint of common people. The mass media even report that someone committed suicide because he was not able to pay the inheritance tax. This is a gross distortion of fact. The same can be said of land taxes in general.

The Choice of a New System

We pointed out that people's concern has shifted to the second level as the cold war ended. This does not mean that the problem of what to choose on the first level has disappeared. It is true that there is no longer the problem of choice between socialism and capitalism. However, the choice regarding the basics of the economic system now appears in a new form. This new choice is concerned with the positioning of "competition." The 1940 system—which forms the foundation for Japan's current economic system—is based on restrictions of competition. Though the system is centered around the market mechanism, it is strongly governed by a negative attitude toward competition.

The denial of competition is basic to Japan's administration. Consider, for example, the problem of local decentralism. Local decentralism is usually emphasized in pursuing the decentralization of decision-making power with no consideration about fiscal resources. However, local decentralism in the true sense of the term is meaningless unless accompanied by fiscal decentralism.

However, local governments vary considerably among themselves with respect to fiscal power. Thus, unless adjustments are made to the fiscal resources, urban areas may become richer while other areas are left behind. This is an inevitable consequence of "interregional competition."

To promote local prosperity, it is necessary for each region to cultivate its own attraction without relying on assistance from the central government. One must not forget that the uniform improvement of the standard of living throughout the whole nation has been made possible by the resource reallocation via the central government.

As I emphasized before, Japan is now confronted by the need for a basic transformation in its economic structure. This will require surgery. Pain will be experienced. Therefore, there are strong forces to keep the present structure unchanged.

One may not go so far as to wish for another bubble as a painkiller but one may still wish to do without surgery by taking some painkiller pills. More concretely, such measures involve avoiding the strong yen, covering excess employment in the form of "in-firm unemployment," or giving various aids in return to firms in the form of special government spending, tax deductions, or barring new entries into the market.

Thus, the basic choice is between the following two scenarios: keeping the pain low by maintaining the system as it is, or instituting a basic structural reform which will shift to a new system with competition as its basic principle.

The latter means a departure from the Japanese-style system based on the 1940 system. In short, the choice depends on whether we can overcome the 1940 system or not. This is the new first-level problem.

Political control changed hands in 1993 but was not based on the fundamental policy debate. The demise of the LDP control was only a symbolic objective. No choice such as the one proposed here was presented. The task from now on is to take up this choice as a basic political issue.

Editor's Note: This article was written shortly after the July 1993 general election in which the Liberal Democratic Party (LDP) lost its majority control of the House of Representatives. As the LDP stepped down, a coalition government was formed by new political parties. However, this government was short-lived. In July 1994, it was replaced by a coalition of the LDP, the Japan Socialist Party (JSP), and the Sakigake party. Chairman Tomiichi Murayama of the JSP was appointed prime minister even though the JSP became an even smaller minority party. He resigned from the post in January 1966 and premiership passed to Ryutaro Hashimoto, newly elected president of the LDP.

Though the LDP has returned to political leadership, Japan's political system is no longer what it used to be. Hence, points that the author made in this article remain valid today.

Yukio Noguchi is a professor in the Department of Economics at Hitotsubashi University, Tokyo.

Source/Permission: " '1940–nen Taisei' no Chokoku to Arata na Taisei no Sentaku." Chapter 8 of Yukio Noguchi, *Nihon Keizai Kaikaku no Kozu* [The Design for Reforming the Japanese Economy]. Tokyo: Toyo Keizai Shimrosha, December 1993. (Translation originally appeared in *Japanese Economic Studies* 24: No. 3 [May–June 1996].) Translated with permission by Kazuo Sato.

Index

DEC 09 2001

DATE DUE

JUN 2 9 2000

NOV 3 0 2000

DEC 0 1 2000

JAN 2 3 2002

AUG 2 0 2002

OCT 3 0 2002

DEMCO, INC. 38-2931